TQM for
Computer Software

Other McGraw-Hill Books of Interest

ISBN	AUTHOR	TITLE
0-07-002560-6	Ayer	*Documenting the Software Development Process*
0-07-002603-3	Ayer	*Software Configuration Management*
0-07-006215-3	Boar	*Implementing Client / Server Computing*
0-07-016733-8	Dewire	*Application Development for Distributed Environments*
0-07-021219-8	Flecher	*Software Engineering and CASE*
0-07-032813-7	Jones	*Applied Software Measurement*
0-07-911366-4	Keyes	*Software Engineering Productivity Handbook*
0-07-040539-5	Marion	*Client / Server Strategies: Implementations in the IBM Environment*
0-07-044985-6	McClain	*OLTP Handbook*
0-07-050820-8	Pressman	*A Manager's Guide to Software Engineering*
0-07-054028-4	Rothstein	*Structured Analysis and Design for the CASE User*
0-07-061716-3	Stone	*Inside ADW and IEF*
0-07-064615-5	Tillman	*A Practical Guide to Logical Data Modeling*
0-07-072272-2	Yeh	*Software Process Quality*

To order or receive additional information on these or any other McGraw-Hill titles, in the United States please call 1-800-822-8158. In other countries, contact your local McGraw-Hill representative.   MH93

TQM for Computer Software

Robert H. Dunn

Richard S. Ullman

Second Edition

McGraw-Hill, Inc.

New York   San Francisco   Washington, D.C.   Auckland   Bogotá
Caracas   Lisbon   London   Madrid   Mexico City   Milan
Montreal   New Delhi   San Juan   Singapore
Sydney   Tokyo   Toronto

Library of Congress Cataloging-in-Publication Data

Dunn, Robert H.
    TQM for computer software / Robert H. Dunn, Richard S. Ullman.—
2nd ed.
        p.   cm.—(Systems design and implementation)
    Rev. ed. of: Quality assurance for computer software. c1982.
    Includes bibliographical references and index.
    ISBN 0-07-018314-7
    1. Computer software—Quality control. 2. Total quality
management. I. Ullman, Richard. II. Dunn, Robert H. Quality
assurance for computer software. III. Title. IV. Series: McGraw-
Hill systems design & implementation series.
QA76.76.Q35D88   1994
005.1′068′5—dc20   93-38089
                                                                  CIP

1 2 3 4 5 6 7 8 9 0 DOC/DOC 9 9 8 7 6 5 4 3

ISBN 0-07-018314-7

*The sponsoring editor for this book was Daniel A. Gonneau, the
editing supervisor was Fred Dahl, and the production supervisor was
Suzanne W. Babeuf. It was set in Century Schoolbook by
Inkwell Publishing Services.*

Printed and bound by R. R. Donnelley & Sons Company.

First Edition published as *Quality Assurance for Computer Software.*

Contents

Preface   xi
Trade Names   xiii

Part 1   Introduction

Chapter 1. How Did a Nice Discipline Like Quality Get Mixed Up
with Computer Software?   3

    1.1 A Historical Case for Software Quality Management   4
    1.2 More on Total Quality Management   7
    1.3 Software Quality Processes and Programs   9
        The Special Position of Embedded Software   11
    1.4 Hardware vs. Software: Similar but Different   12
    1.5 Built-In Quality — Getting There from Here   13
    1.6 Summary   14
        References   15

Part 2   Computer Software

Chapter 2. Fundamentals of Computer Software   19

    2.1 Computers: Things to Program   19
    2.2 Programs   22
    2.3 Third Generation Languages   25
    2.4 Third Generation Design and Code   31
    2.5 Fourth Generation Languages   34
    2.6 Object-Oriented Programming   37
    2.7 Systems Software   39
    2.8 Summary   43
        References   44

Chapter 3. The Life Cycle of Software   45

    3.1 Concept and Analysis   49
    3.2 Process Models   50

Top-Down Process Models   50
Process Models Incorporating Bottom-Up Activities   52
System Evolution   53
The Spiral Model   54
Other Process Models   54
3.3   Defining Requirements   55
Rapid Prototyping   57
Planning   59
3.4   Design   61
3.5   Code, Debug, and Test   68
Low-Level Tests   69
Integration and Top-Down Testing   71
How Much Testing?   74
Qualification   75
3.6   Installation and Evaluation   76
3.7   Operation and Maintenance   77
3.8   People Who Program   81
3.9   Summary   83
References   84

Chapter 4. The Problems   87

4.1   Defects   87
4.2   Usability   89
4.3   Maintenance   90
4.4   More on Obsolescence   92
4.5   Configuration Ambiguity   94
4.6   Department of Silver Linings   95
4.7   Summary   96

Part 3   The Quality Solution

Chapter 5. Prevention   99

5.1   The Discipline of Software Development   101
5.2   Specifying the Problem   104
Rapid Prototyping   106
Common Representations of Requirements Models   107
A Tip from Quality Function Deployment   113
5.3   Refinement of Estimates and Staffing Plans   114
5.4   Designing for Quality   117
Simplicity   117
Modularity   122
Robust Design and Fault Tolerance   130
5.5   Design Documentation   133
5.6   Coding for Quality   139
Data Typing   140
Information Hiding   141
Object-Oriented Programming   142
Compiler or Interpreter?   143
Expressiveness   144
Other Considerations   144
Some Concluding Observations   146

5.7   Order in Progress   146
5.8   Summary   148
      References   151

Chapter 6. Configuration Management   153

6.1   Baselines   154
6.2   Library Control   157
      Audits   158
      Code Control   159
      Build Control   160
      Edition Identification   161
6.3   Firmware   162
6.4   The Configuration Management Plan   163
      Catalog of Controlled Items   164
      Control Authority and Responsibility   166
      The Change Process   167
6.5   Distribution   170
6.6   Summary   171
      References   171

Chapter 7. Detection and Demonstration   173

7.1   Testability   174
7.2   Strategy   177
      Black Box, Glass Box   178
      Getting Back to Table 7.1   181
      Detection Effectiveness   183
7.3   Detection at the Module Level   185
      Static Analysis   185
      Design and Code Reviews   186
      Proving Correctness   192
      Unit Test   194
7.4   Team Development Testing   197
      Integration   197
      System Development Test   200
7.5   Qualification   206
      Controls   206
      Evaluation of Quality   207
      The Alpha and Beta of Testing   208
      Regression Testing   209
7.6   Independent V&V   209
7.7   Summary   210
      References   212

Chapter 8. Tools   213

8.1   Front-End Tools   216
8.2   Back-End Tools   218
      Basic Capabilities   218
      Source-Level Debugging   219
      Build Tools   220
      Coverage-Based Test Beds   221
      Regression Test Systems   222

		Test Case Generators	223
		Performance Measurement and Evaluation	224
	8.3	Management Tools	226
		Cost/Schedule/Fault Tracking and Prediction	226
		Project Planning and Accounting	226
		Configuration Management	231
		Audit	231
		Problem and Correction Logs	232
		Measurements	232
	8.4	Tool Integration	233
		Levels of Integration	234
		A User's View of Integration	235
		Common Interfaces	237
		Off-the-Shelf Systems	237
	8.5	Summary	239
		References	239

Chapter 9. The Quality Process — 241

	9.1	Management by Fact	244
		Data Collection	245
		Data Storage	248
		Analysis	248
		Dissemination of Data and Analysis Results	250
		On Counting Beans	251
	9.2	Staff Involvement	251
	9.3	Project Control	253
		Rites of Passage	253
		Trend Analysis	255
	9.4	Keeping the Books	257
	9.5	Supplier Relations	260
	9.6	Continuous Improvement	262
		Improvement Processes	262
		Effective Analysis	267
		Risk Reduction	271
		Changing Software Processes	274
	9.7	SQA Organizations	276
		Analyst	277
		Surrogate	278
		Collector	278
		Peacekeeper	279
		Planner	280
	9.8	Cost of Quality	280
	9.9	Summary	282
		References	284

Part 4   Implementation

Chapter 10. Assessment and Planning — 287

	10.1	Self-Assessment	288
		The SEI Capability Maturity Model	288
		The Malcolm Baldrige National Quality Award	299
	10.2	Developing a Strategy	304

Plotting the Course   304
Measurements   305
Emerging Technology   306
Help from the Staff   307
Benchmarking Redux   308
10.3   Standard Processes   308
Process Definition   308
Planning for Change   309
Generality   310
10.4   Summary   312
References   313

Chapter 11. Policies, Standards, and Quality Plans   315

11.1   A Software Quality Policy   315
11.2   Published Standards   318
Quality Planning   319
Measurements   322
11.3   Software Quality Project Plans   325
11.4   Reference Quality Documentation   327
11.5   Summary   330
References   331

Part 5   Measures of Goodness

Chapter 12. Predicting and Estimating Reliability   335

12.1   Modeling with Knowledge of the Code   336
Cyclomatic Complexity Model   336
Halstead's Software Science   337
Estimating Faults from Structure   338
12.2   Modeling with Seeded Faults   340
12.3   Modeling the Reliability of the Software Black Box   341
Jelinski-Moranda Model   343
Goel-Okumoto Nonhomogeneous Poisson Process Model (NHPP)   345
Littlewood Model   347
A Hatful of Other Models   348
12.4   The Musa and Musa-Okumoto Models   349
Execution Time Component   350
Calendar Time Component   351
12.5   A Bit of Perspective   352
12.6   Summary   354
References   355

Index   357

Preface to Second Edition

Over a decade has passed since, in *Quality Assurance for Computer Software*, we undertook to present a nonbureaucratic, constructive, booklength view of software quality improvement. Those years have witnessed many changes—the rise and fall of cabbage patch dolls, the dissolution of the Soviet Union, a soft fall of the U.S. economy that left many of us with dislocated jaws, a thousand-fold increase in computer power with a concomitant increase in the complexity of computer applications, and (on a personal note) more hair loss.[1,2] Perhaps less noticeably, but no less markedly, the two disciplines that parented our concept of software quality assurance also underwent change. We might have expected major advances in software engineering—indeed, in the 1982 book we prophesied many that have since occurred—but we did not expect that the more mature discipline of quality management would also have a new face in the early 1990s.

While software engineering and quality management were taking new shapes, we were learning that *Quality Assurance for Computer Software* was becoming a classic of sorts. You do not change certain classics—a Haydn string quartet or *Moby Dick*, for examples. Yet other classics do need updating. Most certainly, *Quality Assurance for Computer Software* no longer reflected current programming paradigms, tools, and measurement techniques. Most certainly, it needed to address explicitly process ownership, strategic quality planning, customer focus, and the other facets of total quality management (TQM) that have come to dominate the world view of quality assurance. Thus, *TQM for Computer Software*, the successor to *Quality Assurance for Computer Software*.

---

[1]Actually, Ullman was bald when we started—R.D.
[2]What Dunn lost on his head he unfortunately gained on his chin—R.U.

We have made major changes to nearly all the chapters of *Quality Assurance for Computer Software*. Much of the treatment of software engineering in the 1982 book is now old hat, the stuff of standard operating procedures and barely worth mentioning. (We *do* mention it, though, only to set the stage for a discussion of a larger set of productive techniques for improving the quality of software.) We have not only incorporated a number of changes in software engineering technology, we have regrouped software engineering topics to provide a more coherent picture. As in the 1982 book, we discuss software engineering practices within the context of quality management. However, the quality management we now write of is dominated by changes brought about by the increased acceptance of TQM. The astute reader, who in 1982 knew of TQM, probably noticed its influence then. TQM is more than an influence in the current book. TQM underscores our entire treatment of software quality management.

Toward the end of Chap. 1 the reader will find a "road map" to the balance of the book. For the most part, the topics covered in each chapter will look familiar to the reader still using the 1982 book. But make no mistake, this is a new book.

As in *Software Quality for Computer Software*, we have been careful to avoid becoming theoretical at the expense of practicality and careful to distinguish between technology still in development and that which has industrial strength. An audience of senior management, quality management, technical management, and quality and technical "wannabe" managers looked to the 1982 book for practical solutions to difficult problems. We have directed this book to the same audience.

While our presentation of software TQM is largely homegrown in concept, the references at the end of each chapter hint at the number of people who, directly or indirectly, have shaped our views and to whom we are grateful. We are in even greater debt to those who reviewed sections of the manuscript—Kurt Fischer, Fred Sayward, Don Reifer, and John Musa—and to perennial first reader Steve Dunn, all of whom were generous in their constructive suggestions.

Robert H. Dunn
Richard S. Ullman

Trade Names

Ada	DoD (Ada Joint Program Office)
Application Development Workbench	KnowledgeWare, Inc.
APS	Intersolv
Automated Testing System	Control Data Corp.
CCC	SofTool
CMS	Digital Equipment Corp.
COCOMO	NASA-Johnson Space Center
Cradle	Yourdon, Inc.
dBase	Borland International
DEC/Test Manager	Digital Equipment Corporation
Eiffel	Interactive Software Engineering, Inc.
Excelerator	Index Technologies
Focus	Information Builders, Inc.
FUSE	Digital Equipment Corporation
FConsole	Novell
Ingres	Ask/Ingres Division
Inspector	KnowledgeWare, Inc.
LDRA Test Bed	Liverpool Data Research Associates, Inc.
Logiscope	Verilog USA
MacIntosh	Apple Computer, Inc.

MathCad	MathSoft, Inc.
MS-DOS	Microsoft Corp.
MVS	IBM
Natural	Software A.G.
ObjectMaker	Mark 4 Systems
Oracle	Oracle Corp.
OS/2	IBM
PDL	Caine, Farber, and Gordon, Inc.
PIE	Carnegie Mellon Univ.
PolyMake	Sage Software
Project Workbench	Applied Business Technology Corp.
Promod	Meridian Software Systems
SLIM	Quantitative Software Measurement
Smalltalk-80	ParcPlace Systems, Inc.
SMARTS	Software Research, Inc.
SoftBench	Hewlett-Packard
SoftCost	Reifer Consultants
Software Backplane	Atherton Technologies
Software Through Pictures	Interactive Development Environments
SPQR	Software Productivity Research, Inc.
T and T++	Programming Environments, Inc.
TCAT	Software Research
Team*work*	Cadre Technologies
UNIX	AT&T
VAX	Digital Equipment Corporation
VMS	Digital Equipment Corporation
Xray/DX	Microtec Research

About the Authors

ROBERT H. DUNN is head of Systems for Quality Software (107 Buck Hill Road, Easton, CT 06612 U.S.A.), an international computer consulting firm specializing in quality improvement, software engineering, and systems management. He has more than 25 years of experience as a computer professional, working most recently with ITT Advanced Technology Center before founding his own company in 1986. Mr. Dunn is also the author of *Software Defect Removal* and *Software Quality: Concepts and Plans*.

RICHARD S. ULLMAN is Vice President of Product Assurance and Manufacturing for ITT Defense and Electronics. He has also held positions at ITT Avionics, Kollsman Instrument Corporation, and Ford Instrument Company. Mr. Ullman has been an examiner for the Malcolm Baldrige National Quality Award and is a contributor to the *Better Business Practices Handbook of Quality Management*.

TQM for
Computer Software

Introduction

How Did a Nice Discipline Like Quality Get Mixed Up with Computer Software?

Business is driven by competition; not only business but also public service organizations and even government agencies. Competition is a good thing. We flush with excitement when we play tennis or golf and we yell our heads off from our seats in the ballpark. In business, competition for the market, borrowing power, and equity dollars has often resulted in short-range planning and inappropriate cost cutting. This is not a good thing. In the long term, the strategy self-destructs for several reasons, not the least of which is the legion of dissatisfied customers left behind.

Recently, we have come to recognize the importance of customer satisfaction, and even more recently figured out how to achieve it: the customer wants quality. The customer wants finished goods to look like finished goods, machines and soft goods that last beyond the warranty, letters delivered in two days, responsive hotel staff, and cup holders in automobiles. We also figured out that it was not just consumers who want quality, but business itself. Business wants supplier deliveries on time and to specifications, payments posted the day of receipt, accurate and timely marketplace demographics, and software projects completed on time, within budget, and with a useable outcome. Indeed, we demand not only that software work properly when fresh out of the box, but continue working through the generations of modifications that consume the greater part of software costs.

We demand, but we do not always get. As consumers or business people, we are all witness to woeful software quality, and ever more so as the proliferation of computers affects our financial structures, the control of our manufacturing processes, the equipment vital to national defense, our everyday life (appliances, automobiles, home entertainment, home computers), and even the manner in which we make management decisions. As swamped as we now are by computers, we can expect the use of computers to continue expanding at ever-increasing rates as the cost per unit of computation continues to drop dramatically. More to the point, expanding computer use implies a concomitant expansion of software.

As customers, we are concerned with the quality of today's software. As producers using software in our businesses, selling software, producing software-intensive products, or buying software, we have even greater concern to fashion effective methods of managing software development, maintenance, and acquisition. This book addresses the contribution that can be made by quality processes, especially when focused on the front end of software development and maintenance. The software quality process, when interpreted within the larger scheme of total quality management (TQM), is directed squarely at the needs of both software customers and software producers.

1.1   A Historical Case for Software Quality Management

Before a closer examination of software quality processes, we shall take a look at the larger field of quality management, starting with its early beginnings and continuing on to its modern practice. By tracing quality's evolution from primitive origins to its present reflection of today's technological society, this survey will lay a foundation for the development of parallels to software.

Table 1.1 depicts the evolution of quality control. Before the era of mass production, quality control was strictly an inspection function. Even today, there are people who think of quality as an inspection function.

Nothing could be further from the truth. Back in the early days, the responsibility for inspection of a product was that of the artisan who made it. The inspection was not consciously performed as a formal and separate action; it was made simply to be sure that the item met the artisan's personal high standard of workmanship and that it was precisely what the customer had ordered. Curiously, one of the precepts of TQM places ultimate responsibility for quality back on the worker; so, in one sense, we may see the wheel come full circle. In any case, we can draw an analogy between the early artisan and the early software designer: the accuracy and effectiveness of software was at one time dependent solely on the designer's diligence, ability, and personal standards of quality.

TABLE 1.1 Evolution of Quality Control

	Quality control implementation	Remarks
Pre-20th century	Inspection by the producer	Pride in workmanship
1916	Introduction of quality control by Bell Labs	First formal programs
1920-1940	Standardization and inspection	Made necessary by mass production
1940-1950	Introduction of statistical quality control	To economically control more complex and higher output manufacturing processes
1950-1970	Formal programs encompassing all facets of design and development	Most prevalent in defense-type organizations
1970-1978	Product liability and product safety, management recognition	Expansion of quality control into all industries
1978-1985	Introduction of computers into products evolves into software quality assurance for all software	Welcome aboard
1985	Navy uses term Total Quality Management, importing Japanese adaptation of quality systems based on work by U.S. quality experts	Emphasis on process ownership and customer satisfaction influences formal quality programs, including those for software

As the industrial revolution took hold and the mass production of products became common, management recognized the need for standardization of production and inspection methods. These methods were coupled with formal programs necessary to the planning and management of these efforts. As operations became more complex, so did the need for increased controls to provide uniformity of the product. Acceptance and rejection criteria had to be established. The need for economical methods for applying these controls and criteria led to the adoption of statistical concepts in the control of the manufacturing processes. In the late 1930s, Walter Shewhart of Western Electric and AT&T Laboratories joined the diverse disciplines of statistics, engineering, and economics to found statistical quality control.

However sophisticated quality control techniques were getting, they remained directed at the results of manufacturing processes. Analyzing the data from a golf ball assembly line may permit one to tweak the machinery as needed to avoid production of sub-par balls, but this technique scarcely suffices for the complex products and systems (not to mention services) which engage much of our society. Enter total quality control. Quoting Armand Feigenbaum, "Total quality control is an effective system for integrating the quality-development, quality-maintenance, and quality-improvement efforts of the various groups in an organization so as to enable marketing, engineering, production, and service at the most economical levels which allow for full customer satisfaction."[1]

We see total quality control underlie the quality systems developed by Japanese industry. The Japanese model (really, a family of related models), when introduced into the United States gave the total quality control wheel another spin. In the mid-1980s we started hearing the term *total quality management*. In 1985, the Naval Air Systems Command used it to describe its adaptation of the Japanese model. Like many catchwords, TQM is reinterpreted by each new adherent. The American Society for Quality Control (ASQC) provides a definition that, if not concise, at least embraces the aspirations behind TQM:

> Simply put, TQM is a management approach to long-term success through customer satisfaction. TQM is based on the participation of all members of an organization to improving processes, products, services, and the culture they work in. TQM benefits all organization members and society. The methods for implementing this approach are found in the teachings of such quality leaders as Philip B. Crosby, W. Edwards Deming, Armand V. Feigenbaum, Kaoru Ishikawa, and J. M. Juran.[2]

Even before TQM received the acceptance it now has, quality was gaining prominence in large corporations. As an example, the ITT Corporation established the position of Vice President and Director of Quality, staffing the position with Philip Crosby. Crosby issued a quality policy to ensure that a quality management function was established in each ITT system unit with the following objectives:

- Meeting acceptance and performance requirements of products and services
- Meeting cost of quality goals for each ITT unit
- Implementing and properly directing consumer affairs, product safety, and environmental quality programs
- Providing quality personnel with required communications and training

To update Crosby's objectives to conform to the precepts of TQM, you need do little more than extend the last item to include *all* personnel. Implementing the objectives within the context of TQM involves a great deal more than the establishment of quality departments. Indeed, TQM does not demand the existence of quality departments, although most companies that have started to implement TQM have them. At the time, however, to apply and realize Crosby's policy, ITT established a quality function within each unit organization. To avoid an inevitable emasculation and to ensure a customer orientation, the functions were made independent of manufacturing, engineering, or service organizations.

During the historical development of quality control and quality management, "quality" itself took on diverse shades of meaning. In defending the quality of the car one drives, one driver might speak of the absence of defects on delivery and the subsequent reliability of the machine, while another thinks to praise the comfort of leather seats and slide-out cup holders. So too, in industry. Philip Crosby defined the objective of quality in terms of a black box: "Perform exactly like the requirement—or cause the requirement to be officially changed to what we and our customers really need."[3]

J. M. Juran, attempting to define the characteristics of quality, implicitly defined quality somewhat differently from Crosby: "Any feature (property, attribute, etc.) of the products, materials, or processes which is needed to achieve fitness for use is a quality characteristic."[4] This is a white box definition of quality.

Curiously, the Award Criteria (formerly Application Guidelines) for the Baldrige Award manage to avoid wading in the murky waters of quality semantics. Compensating for their pusillanimity, however, the authors of the criteria provide this powerful statement: "Quality is judged by the customer."[5]

We shall need to use all three views of quality—Crosby's, Juran's, and that implied by the Baldrige Award statement—in outlining a program of software quality assurance. And we shall want to define such programs within the context of TQM.

1.2 More on Total Quality Magement

The person operating the machine that dimples a golf ball "owns" the dimpling process. The engineers who designed the machine "owned" the design process. The reservations clerk at your hotel temporarily "owns" the process of making certain that you will have a room when you arrive. The computer programmers who developed the software for the reservation system "owned" the process of software development and still "own" the process of software maintenance. Processes of all kinds enter into commercial and noncommercial businesses, and all processes have "owners." At its core, TQM places responsibility for the quality of a process primarily with the owners of the process.

This differs from older notions of quality control in which quality control specialists were responsible for making sure that work was performed in conformance with established standards of quality. A given percentage of golf balls are still inspected before they are packed in shipping boxes. In large hotels, checkers still look over every breakfast order as it leaves the kitchen to ensure that the order has been completed and not burnt. Computer programs are still subjected to qualification checking—usually by a software quality assurance (SQA) team or an independent test team—before delivery. *But under a TQM regimen, we do not depend on checking and testing to get quality. We expect the process owners to build quality into their work.* (Indeed, increasingly we see a diminished role for checkers and inspectors in industry, although the complexity of software will never permit relaxing the standards of qualification.)

While the idea of placing responsibility for process quality with the process owners sounds simple enough, making it happen is quite another thing. Process owners need an understanding of what quality is all about. They need tools, measures of performance, education or training, and much more. Simply put, we need formal quality programs.

Today, we design formal quality processes within the context of TQM. At the most elemental level, the ingredients for a TQM system can be found in the seven categories of criteria for the Baldrige Award: leadership, information and analysis, strategic quality planning, human resource development and management, management of process quality, quality and operational results, and customer focus and satisfaction. With respect to the quality of computer software, let us rephrase the categories somewhat:

1. Leadership, starting from the top
2. Software measurements, analysis of measurements, and dissemination of the results of analyses
3. Planning for continuous quality improvement
4. Continuous upgrading of the skills of the programming staff, and involvement of the staff in quality improvement
5. Continuous upgrading of software engineering practices and tools
6. Assessing the results of software quality improvement processes (and comparing the results with those of others)
7. Working closely with customers (or internal software users) in defining requirements and evaluating products

Plainly, a total software quality process must encompass management practices at all levels, the technology and methods of software engineering, programming education and training, data and the use of data, and intensive customer or user involvement.

1.3   Software Quality Processes and Programs

We have used the term *software quality process* with little more than the context in which it was used to lend meaning to the term. Let's find a more explicit definition, starting with a return to the business of defining quality, only this time focusing on software quality.

Software must please those who use it, especially software such as operating systems for which we cannot formulate exact customer-oriented technical specifications.

Whatever the technical specifications, software must conform to the specifications. This is not simply a matter of producing the correct output for a given set of input data. We must also consider correct compliance with error-handling, user interface, resource allocation, and other specifications.

Software must be suitable for the intended application. That is, we must place a premium on the accuracy and fault tolerance of software for medical instrumentation, be alert to the user interfaces and the maintainability of software for hotel reservation systems, design the use of word-processing options to be as intuitive as possible, prepare easily understandable user manuals for the cases where intuition fails, and take pains to design efficient and robust algorithms for processing radar data.

> In short, quality software is fit to use, meets the explicit requirements set forth for it, and satisfies its users.

Now that we can speak about the quality of software, we can define software quality processes. Software quality processes are directed:

1. To producing software with the characteristics of quality software, and

2. To improving the quality of the processes that are used to produce quality software products.

When we don't carelessly use it as a synonym for software quality process, the term *software quality program* refers to the application of the process to a specific project. Returning to the definition of software quality processes, we have both products and processes to consider. Given a development (or maintenance) process of reasonable quality (notwithstanding the goal of making it even better), our concern with individual products is a matter of correctly applying the development process, measuring the product, and qualifying it for release.

It is one thing to say that we shall have a software quality program and another to make it happen. Measurements must be made and data analyzed, matters requiring correction need to be tracked, results need to be analyzed, training programs must be set up, adjustments to processes must be introduced, and so on. In the simplest of terms, software quality programs must be managed. The management of software quality programs is what we call *software quality assurance*. Put differently, SQA is a management tool to ensure that software quality programs are in place and operating. Recursively, SQA is, itself, a "formal program" as the term is used in Table 1.1.

SQA can happen with or without separate SQA functions or departments. However, we have a precedent for wanting to establish SQA functions staffed by software quality engineers. Even as a quality discipline developed to attend the growth of industry from an origin dominated by individual artisans, a quality discipline has developed to attend the growth of software development from the casual preparation of small programs to the massive efforts of large-scale programming. Like quality engineering directed to hardware production, SQA has its own techniques, tools, and methods directed specifically towards quality. To take a simple example, software quality engineers use Pareto analysis, a widely used quality technique, to identify those process or product elements that should get the most attention.

Note that we are not suggesting that one needs or wants to entrust all matters having to do with software quality to software quality engineers. To take another simple example, programmers, not software quality engineers, have the responsibility to find and fix bugs. Quality remains with the process owners. Moreover, as delineated in Chap. 9, software quality engineers staffing an SQA function have plenty to do without getting into an inspection mode of operation.

We have precedent for wanting to establish SQA organizations, and we have precedent for preferring to establish them within quality directorates. An obvious reason is to take advantage of the professional quality techniques that have been developed. Software quality engineers must have some programming background, but few programmers have much knowledge of the quality discipline. However, quality techniques will rub off on them if they work as software quality engineers within a quality discipline.

The less obvious advantage of placing SQA within a larger quality function is that of conflict of interest. Even within an established TQM environment, the interests of developers and users can at times be inimical. The customers say that service is terrible and that it takes too long to get the right people to respond. The software support manager says the support people are already overworked and the real problem is that customers expect the telephone crew to hold their hands in solving problems. What is the truth here? How can an objective finding be made? By a third party, that's who. And what better third party than an SQA function placed in the quality directorate?

Among quality directors, we have seen two divergent views of responsibility for managing software quality programs. Most say, "Great! My job just got more important." The other camp says "With all my other headaches, this I need like a sailor needs hurricanes." To the curmudgeons, we say that failure to rise to challenges is not why they have the positions they now hold. However, it is the aggressive group that most concerns us, partly because they are in the majority, and partly because we feel that not all understand that essential differences between software and hardware will affect their administration of quality policies and practices.

The special position of embedded software

We will get to the essential differences between software and hardware shortly, but as an aside, we wish to point out the singularity of embedded software within the history and current practice of SQA. When forming an integral part of an instrumentation system (e.g., aircraft autopilot, oil refinery control system, department store point-of-sale system, microwave oven), computers—whether microprocessors or larger machines—are said to be "embedded" within the system. Such computers connect directly with sensors, control devices, unique keyboards, or unique display devices. The software that drives these computers is also said to be "embedded." Unlike most computer applications, where the computer controls the input of data, *embedded software* often has to process data in *real time,* that is, at rates determined externally to the computer.

Many of the earliest SQA functions found within quality directorates were formed when quality directors recognized that the quality of the software embedded in a system bore upon the quality of the entire system. No system is of greater quality than the quality of its parts, and if one of the parts is a computer, then the quality of the program controlling that computer will affect the quality of the entire system. Computer programs, whether embedded or not, can, and nearly always do, have latent defects. These defects can cause the performance of a system to degrade, as in forcing overly long response times in an on-line reservation system, or they can cause a system to fail utterly, as when erroneously enabling a missile self-destruct mechanism during the launch phase. We can trace the origins of SQA to enlightened quality directors of the late 1970s whose departments had previously been concerned only with hardware.

Today, with the power of VLSI chips, we are witness to an ever-increasing number of embedded software applications, from video games to military systems and telephone switches of millions of lines of programmed code. Moreover, we see the software embedded within these systems exerting an influence on performance equal to or greater than that of the hardware. We can easily draw the corollary that the quality of the product is as much vested in the software as in the hardware. Parenthetically, we may infer from this that the value of the quality community, at least within the electronic and aerospace industries, will be maintained at its present level only if that community continues to cope with the quality aspects of tomorrow's embedded software.

1.4   Hardware vs. Software: Similar but Different

As promised, we return to the essential differences between hardware and software that require some rethinking, specifically in the manner in which the precepts of quality systems can be applied to software.

Quality assurance efforts are based on the certain knowledge that hardware degrades with use. Software, on the other hand, can be expected to improve. Once a program bug is found and corrected, it remains corrected. On the other hand, this software advantage disappears with poor software maintenance practices. Lack of attention to quality when software is fixed, adapted to new operating conditions, or modified in functionality can cause software to degrade as certainly as hardware.

Although diminished by TQM, perhaps the most visible quality assurance role has been in the inspection of hardware, where the expended effort is to ensure that the original design is being correctly copied in production units. There is no such need in SQA. After a program has been judged acceptable, there need be no further concern about the capability to copy it precisely.

Hardware can warn that a failure is likely to occur soon. In the electronics world, for example, one can, as part of quality assurance throughout the life cycle, periodically measure pulse shapes, power supply ripples, and other characteristics for evidence of an impending malfunction. Software will give no such warnings. But software can be designed to warn that the system in which it is installed may fail (e.g., network software may warn that server file space is nearly fully consumed). But that is quite another thing.

Hardware can be built of standardized components, from devices to complete assemblies, the reliability of which are known. On the other hand, software contains few program elements with which there has been any prior experience. As we learn to increasingly reuse software parts (see Chap. 3), this difference will diminish.

To repair hardware is to restore its original condition. The repair of software results in a new baseline (i.e., product definition), with the consequence that component edition records and program documentation must be updated if the success of future repairs is not to be jeopardized.

In general, equipment can be tested over the entire spectrum of operational conditions in which it will perform. (We say "in general" because VLSI circuits are often exceptions to this rule.) Thus, the performance aspects of equipment may be completely verified by test. The number of discrete states that software can assume is so great that exhaustive testing is impossible.

For quality directors and quality engineers, the sum of these differences between hardware and software means that while traditional quality assurance disciplines may apply, the practices will have to differ. More specifically, the practices will have to emphasize the concept of built-in quality, of "doing it right the first time"—but isn't that a precept of TQM?

1.5 Built-In Quality—
Getting There from Here

TQM almost seems to have been invented for building quality into computer software. However, even before we started consciously to apply TQM to software we understood that built-in software quality results from a number of interdependent technical and managerial techniques, tools, and procedures largely derived from the discipline of *software engineering*. This is the substance of Part 3, beginning with Chaps. 5, 6, 7, and 8. (Part 3 follows the introductory material of Part 2, which consists of Chaps. 2, 3, and 4. Software professionals will want to skim through Chaps. 2, 3, and 4.) Chapter 9 rounds out Part 3 with the synthesis of techniques, tools, and procedures into a comprehensive quality process. This chapter deals also with the role played by SQA functions within the framework of TQM.

Part 4 is about implementing a software quality process in one's business.* Chapter 9 treats the tactical operational aspects of TQM, and Chap. 10 deals with strategic matters needed to put TQM in place. Specifically, Chap. 10 is concerned with quality planning, helping to upgrade staff abilities, establishing standard processes, and assessing the success of one's quality process. Chapter 11 concludes the topic of implementation by addressing the application of software quality programs to specific projects, often with reference to project plan templates in common use.

---

*Unless noted, whenever we refer to a business we refer equally to a government office, university, hospital, or any other organization involved in using or producing software.

Finally, Part 5, an epilogue of sorts, deals with attempts to measure the goodness of software. Containing but one chapter, Chap. 12, it discusses models for predicting and estimating the reliability of software. Though but one attribute of software quality, reliability is both the most prominent and the one whose quantification has received the greatest effort.

1.6 Summary

1. The importance of computer software in our society will continue its unparalleled growth with the potential for unparalleled mischief and customer dissatisfaction traceable to poor quality processes.

2. Quality controls were introduced initially to industry as a response to manufacturing operations problems as production evolved from that of the individual artisan to that of the modern factory. Quality controls later evolved into formal systems encompassing industrial processes beyond those of production.

3. Software, too, is a product produced by complex operations and beset with problems analogous to the early problems of large-scale production.

4. Recently, we have come to view quality control as a part of a larger concept, namely, total quality management (TQM). TQM's process ownership precepts have particular significance to software.

5. Software quality processes and programs use formal approaches to improve the quality of software processes and products produced by these processes.

6. Without conflicting with the precept that ultimate responsibility for software quality rests with computer programmers, independent software quality assurance functions employ software quality engineers to implement certain aspects of software quality programs.

7. Although the disciplines of formal hardware quality programs can be applied to software, many practices need to be different to address a different set of conditions:

   - Hardware degrades with time, while software has the potential to improve.
   - Unlike hardware, software failures are never preceded by warnings.
   - Hardware components can be standard; software rarely.
   - Hardware repairs restore the original condition; software repairs establish a new configuration state.
   - Hardware can usually be tested exhaustively; not so software.

8. Productive software quality processes can be planned and implemented using the tools and techniques of software engineering, the analytical tools and procedures of quality assurance, and the management philosophy of TQM.

References

1. Feigenbaum, Armand V. *Total Quality Control,* 3rd ed., McGraw-Hill Book Company, New York, NY, 1983, p. 6.
2. Bemowski, Karen (Editor). "The Quality Glossary," *Quality Progress,* February 1992, p. 28.
3. Crosby, Philip B. *Quality Is Free,* McGraw-Hill, New York, NY, 1979, p. 67.
4. Juran, J. M. "Basic Concepts," *Quality Control Handbook,* 3rd ed. (edited by J. M. Juran, et al.), McGraw-Hill, New York, NY, 1979, p. 4.
5. 1992 Award Criteria, Malcolm Baldrige National Quality Award, National Institute of Standards and Technology, Gaithersburg, MD, 1992, p. 2.

Computer Software

2

Fundamentals of Computer Software

Thus far, we have said a great deal about the importance of computer software and how it affects society. It is time to define exactly what it is we're talking about when we say *computer software.* Computer professionals may find this to be ground previously trod too well, and may want to merely scan this chapter in the hope of finding something new. Those who have no background in computers will take a quick tour through programming languages, including a glimpse here and there of what programs look like, and will receive a brief exposition on systems software, the programs that improve the productivity of programmers and computer users and the quality of their work.

2.1 Computers: Things to Program

Since computer software is mostly a matter of computer programs, the stuff which computers are filled with, we shall start by defining the programmer's view of a naked computer. For our purposes, we may ignore the many elaborate definitions and simply, if somewhat pedantically, say the following:

> A computer is an adaptive device capable of performing certain logical operations based on the state of bistable electronic devices.

Our simple definition embodies two key concepts. One is found in the word *adaptive.* This is little more than a ruse to avoid being accused of using the word *programmable* before defining it. Actually, we can mount a reasonable defense of adaptive—the word implies a boundless range of application for computers. The other concept is the stark simplicity of hardware allowed by the definition: digital manipulation of the voltages or currents—bits, if you will, presented by electronic circuits. No more than that. The electronic hardware of a computer contains circuits to move bits from one place to another, to determine if two bits are identical, to sum two strings of bits, to test a bit to see in which of two states it is, to count bits, and so on. These are all primitive operations. There is little a computer can do in response to a single command that is beyond the ability of a grade school student. It is what a computer can do if given a sequence of commands that makes it the ubiquitous tool it has become. That sequence of commands or instructions, is, of course, what we mean by the word *program.*

But what is a computer? *Information processor* is a marketing term. *Electronic brain,* notwithstanding advances in artificial intelligence, belongs to the world of pulp and science fiction. Devoid of native intelligence, an inanimate collection of interconnected electronic parts, the computer sits, awaiting the touch of its muse, the computer programmer. It is, indeed, so lacking in innate capability that it cannot even perform arithmetic calculations in ordinary decimal numbers, as can decent folk. Rather, it computes in binary numbers.

Binary numbers are those having but two numerals, 1 and 0. A binary digit is a "bit," which we just defined somewhat differently. If it is true that humans learned to favor the decimal system because we have 10 fingers (digits), we can easily understand why computer designers favor binary numbers for their machines. Electronic devices have two discrete states: transistors can assume the stable states of conducting electricity, or of not conducting; ferrous elements can be polarized with clockwise magnetic flux, or counterclockwise; light-sensitive devices can be saturated with light, or not.

None of this is intended to be an apology for binary numbers. The binary number 01010001 and the decimal integer 81 can both express the same number of pumpkins in a patch. As an integer, a binary number can be operated upon by computer hardware for the purposes of addition, subtraction, multiplication, or division. Moreover, allowing the bits that represent an integer to be used in an entirely different, nonarithmetic, sense, the binary number can be used to represent a character—a letter, a typographic symbol, or a number. In the ASCII character code, the binary number 01010001 is used to represent the letter "Q." Similarly, 00111001 represents the number "9," and 00001101 means carriage control (as on a printer), but only if one intends to use the numbers that way. In brief, binary numbers can be integers, which in the nonabstract world we consider measures of something (distance, weight, numbers of pumpkins), or they can represent textual or control characters. The difference is simply in the way they are used by computer programs, and the interpretation is at the discretion of the computer programmer. To round out this presentation of binary numbers, we note that they can be used also to represent fractional and other kinds of numbers, again, at the choosing of the programmer.

It may appear that computer programmers have to deal with each number or character on a bit-by-bit basis. Primitive as the intellectual power of a computer may be, programmers are spared this level of detail. Generally, they can operate on whole numbers or characters. That is, they can instruct the computer to add two integers together, or they can move a string of characters to the end of a string of characters previously assembled. When performing the latter operations, programmers are aware that each character is represented by eight bits, or one *byte*, but when using modern programming languages they may be indifferent to the representation if they care to be. For the purposes of arithmetic, programmers like to call integers, especially if they are greater than eight bits in length, *words*. At one time, when programming arithmetic applications, programmers referred to the maximum number of bits that can be operated upon by the simplest class of instruction they deal with as the computer's *word length*. Today, word length is more likely determined by a programming language than by computer hardware, but we don't want to get ahead of ourselves.

We usually think of the guts of a computer as its *central processing unit* or CPU. The CPU performs arithmetic and logical operations, fetches data and instructions from memory, and manages the flow of information and programs to and from external storage devices (disk or tape). Any attempt to depict a typical computer system in terms of CPU, memory, and peripheral devices is simplistic. Computer systems, even those in personal computers, have become too complex and too varied for a common model except at the most abstract level. For example, it is now common to see control partly housed in a special memory containing *microcode,* which is used to interpret the commands generally considered to constitute the computer's repertoire of instructions. That the instructions used by programmers are actually operated upon by a lower, more primitive, level of instructions is invisible to them. They may know they're there (they often don't), but so far as they are concerned, the instructions are interpreted by "hard-wired" logic to control the operations within the arithmetic and logical unit.

Architectures of today's computers vary in other ways as well. A coprocessor may join the primary computer chip in shouldering the computing workload. The load may be shared by several processing units in a *parallel processor* configuration. In massively parallel architectures, sometimes called *fifth generation computers*, operating systems (there we go, getting ahead of ourselves again) divide the work among hundreds of identical microprocessors. For some time now, we have also had *array processing* architectures, wherein many data items are operated upon simultaneously, often by sets of microinstructions far more powerful (e.g., trigonometric functions) than ordinary arithmetic functions. And thus it goes: where once you could visualize the microdesign of a computer without unbolting its protective panels, advancements in hardware technology and computer science have created a variety of devices all bearing the same name, *computer.*

Even the packaging is marked by a wide range of concepts. Cartoonists still represent a computer by a set of side-by-side cabinets punctuated by an occasional set of lights or tape reels. In fact, while the tape units, disk drives, and printers of large computers do require considerable real estate, even the most powerful of modern computers are rarely larger than a pair of file cabinets. At the other end of the spectrum, we have notebook computers based on microprocessors the size of a thumbnail. The notebook computer may not be able to produce the same kind of output or process a given amount of input in the same time as the large mainframe, as it is often called, but in name it is no less a computer.

Between the mainframes and the class comprising personal computers of all kinds, we have the middle ground populated by minicomputers. The domain of minicomputers is being stretched thinner and thinner as more powerful ones offer much the same capability of many mainframes. At the bottom end, the minis are getting as small as desktop machines.* As one might expect, the borders between the three categories are often in dispute, and one person's minicomputer is another's microcomputer. As an example, half the community regards workstations as elaborate desktops, while the other half considers the workstation engines to be minicomputers.

2.2   Programs

Whatever the shape or design of a computer, it performs no useful work until it is told what to do. More precisely, how to do it. Since the computer is a binary device, we might expect that a single instruction to transfer the contents of a specific memory location to a register might appear as a binary number, say

---

*It's curious that we still call them desktop computers even though many are housed in a tower case sitting on the floor.

```
1100110000111010
```

This instruction contains an operation code to fetch from memory, the address of the memory location, and the specific register into which the contents are to be copied.

A set of instructions to solve the problem of finding the smallest of five positive numbers might take the following awesome form, which for practical purposes, is undecipherable save for the computer that will execute it:

```
1001110110011011
0111000111100011
1100110001010101
1001110001011010011101011
1110001110101011
0010011010001101110001011
10011010000111010 0011000
0110001110100011
0010011001100000 11100001
0010010000011110
0111111111111111
0000000000000110
0000000000000000
```

This looks like a clear case of overkill for solving a problem that we normally attack by sight, but remember that as many times as your automobile has turned from the street into your driveway, it still doesn't know when to start the turn until you instruct it. So computers: the simplest problems may require considerable instruction.

As is painfully evident, while these binary instructions are within the communications capability of a computer, indeed are the only language it can interpret, they are scarcely convenient for the people who must communicate with the computer. Even looking at each of the constituent parts of each instruction separately doesn't help matters much. How many seven-digit telephone numbers can the typical person remember? How many 8-, 12-, or 16-bit binary addresses for unique data items can we expect to remember?

It was recognized early in the age of computers that something had to be done to help programmers improve their productivity, as well as to maintain their equanimity. *Assembler languages* were invented. An assembler (also called *assembly*) language permits the various operation codes to be given simple mnemonic codes, allows programmers to christen the locations in memory where their data are stored with names, and even allows other instructions to be referred to by names assigned by the programmers. In assembler language, the same problem of finding the smallest of five positive numbers might be coded as follows:

```
         LD         BIG
         STO        LEAST
REPEAT   LDX    1   LEFT
         LD   L 1   VALUE
         S          LEAST
         MDX  L     CHECK
         LD   L 1   VALUE
         STO        LEAST
CHECK    MDX  L     LEFT, -1
         MDX        REPEAT
BIG DC              32767
LEFT     DC         6
VALUE    BSS        6
```

If somewhat arcane,* at least assembler language makes no unreasonable demands on the memory of the programmer. However, a computer is at a loss to decipher a program written in assembler language. What we need is something that will translate the program into the computer's native binary language. We need a computer program called, not surprisingly, an *assembler*. Figure 2.1 illustrates the assembly process. Both the assembler, in binary code, and the program written in assembler language are loaded into the computer. The assembler operates upon each of the assembler language instructions, and in short order outputs the equivalent binary code language.

At this point, we introduce two new terms, both of which will be used frequently in the next few chapters. The assembler language program is, by definition, the *source program*. The binary program output by the assembler is called the *object program*. Frequently, for reasons that will become apparent, the object program is called the *target program*.

We can now view the role of the assembler as that of transforming a source program into an object program. We can say the same thing slightly differently: the data domain upon which the assembler operates is the set of source statements, and the output data produced by the assembler is the equivalent string of object code.

The foregoing does more than add to the reader's vocabulary of software argot, it also implies the fundamental systems view of programming:

---

*For those who insist upon some explanation, the first column contains the names (labels) of program statements, constants, and data allocations referred to elsewhere. The second column has the symbols identifying machine operation codes or definitions of the forms of constants or data. The central columns modify the operation codes or provide supplementary information required for operations. The last column contains either constants or the operands (data, instruction labels, etc.) subject to the instruction.

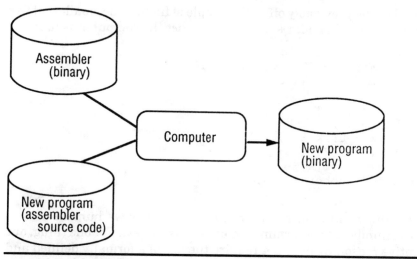

Figure 2.1 Process of assembly.

Input—Process (or Transform)—Output

That the input and output in this case are themselves programs is immaterial. From the software point of view, we have a program performing a transformation of data, whatever the set of data may represent, notwithstanding the physical fact that it is the computer that has processed the data and has processed the assembler program as well. Software people, unless reminded otherwise, see it only as the assembler processing the source program, much as bookkeepers see the general ledger program, not the computer, processing the week's accounts receivable. So too, personal computer users when they try to interpret a diagnostic from their spreadsheet or word-processing program.

If we think of our computer systems in terms of the software we are using, we are only recognizing the fact that the extent to which a computer appears to imitate human reasoning is no more than that endowed by the program being executed. In any event, as we introduce programs of greater complexity, it will become apparent that it is the software, not the hardware, that seems to be in charge of things.

2.3 Third Generation Languages

Assembler language may be more compatible with human thought processes than binary code, but it is still far removed from the way we think. For the previously offered example of finding the smallest of five numbers, it would be far simpler to instruct the computer as follows:

```
#include <studio.h>
int numb[5] = {12, 6, 3, 5, 10};
main ()
{
int s, k;
s = numb[0];
  for (k = 0; k < 5; ++k)
    if (numb[k] < s)
      s = numb[k];
printf ("number = %d\n",s);
}
```

Now this is still not representative of the way we humans view a table of numbers to determine which is the smallest. For one thing, our cognitive reasoning does not require the use of a formally defined and incremented index (k), nor do we approach so trivial a problem in such a formal manner. However, it is certainly more intelligible than the previous solution given in assembler language. Even those who have never seen a computer program before will agree that this example might well have something to do with the relative size of numbers. Programs written in such a language can be written much faster, can be debugged (made to work) more quickly, and can be understood more easily when reexamined months or years later for the purpose of modification.

A language such as the last is called a *compiler language*. The actual language of the example, *C*, is typical of a large class of compiler languages. Like natural languages, compiler languages are both large in number and diverse in their attributes. They have one thing in common: they all communicate the programmer's intentions. They communicate, that is, if the programmer has a *compiler* to translate a program written in compiler language to the binary language required by computers.

Figure 2.2 depicts the compilation process. The analogy between this and Fig. 2.1 is obvious. In both cases, a transforming process (compilation or assembly) is performed on a source program, and object code is output. For this reason, all language processors (i.e., compilers, assemblers, and others yet to be described) are frequently referred to simply as *processors*. This is an unfortunate term, since computers are often called processors as well. It is, however, not atypical. For a field as exacting as computation is, requiring the highest standards of precision in all matters, the practitioners have embraced a level of ambiguity in their speech and writing that has not been seen since the last general election. We shall see further examples of this as we go along.

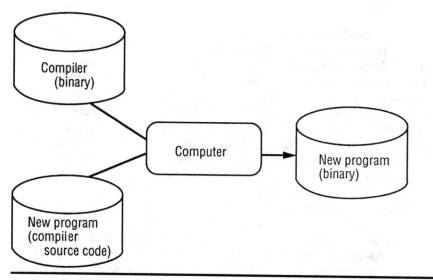

Figure 2.2   Process of compilation.

From appearance, one cannot tell if a language is a compiler language or an *interpreter* language. The difference between compilers and interpreters is that the latter only partly compiles the source code, leaving the balance of translation to be performed during execution, with the interpreter remaining in the computer and completing the language processing as the program is run. Obviously, this exacts a significant penalty on the time it takes a program to be executed. It would be most inefficient for a program that will be called upon to perform thousands of times during its lifetime. However, by leaving the processing of individual executable statements for *run time*, or the period of productive execution of a program, it is possible to present the programmer with diagnostic messages relating to program errors that are much more pertinent to the debugging process than otherwise would be obtainable. In the most ideal compromise, both an interpreter and a compiler are available to the programmer for the same language—one to be used during program development and the other for production.

In retrospect, we view assembler languages as second generation programming languages. (This implies the arguable assertion that binary code is a programming language.) The third generation is that of compiler and interpreter languages.

The first third generation languages (3GL) became available to programmers in the late 1950s. The improvement in programming efficiency was the major factor in their immediate acceptance. They also rapidly gained favor because they relieved the more creative, problem-oriented programmer from the tedium of having to contend with the detailed coding of efficient addressing schemes and with various hardware-oriented minutiae of assembler language programming. Few thought to greet 3GL as a means of reducing programming errors or making programs more easily maintained. While most programmers were eager to write in the new programming languages, a surprising number resisted the invasion of the more problem-oriented approach to programming. Some took special pride in their ability to master the intricacies of computers, while others felt that their quasi-professional status was threatened by languages that could be used by the general population. It is significant that, in those early days, computer programming was almost synonymous with coding. Today's emphasis on analysis and design techniques was still in the future.

Theoretically, programs in assembler languages can be more efficient, even with compiler optimization techniques, but only if well written. Assembler language programming is almost nonexistent today, having been driven out of circulation by concerns for programmer productivity and program maintainability. The last surviving assembler language programming is found (but rarely) in the development of systems software (which we have yet to define) and real-time software, especially for programming communications with external devices. Well, there is one more surviving sphere of assembler language programming: Incredibly, people are still maintaining assembler language systems developed decades ago.

Earlier, we alluded to the number and diversity of third generation languages. Each language offers linguistic and syntactical features tailored either to a class of applications (examples of classes are scientific programming, manipulation of strings of symbols, and information systems programming) or to the inventor's stylistic prejudices. Many of the available languages have become well known to those outside the field of programming, such has the world of computation invaded our consciousness, not to mention high-school and college programming courses. We list here a few of the languages that have proliferated since the 1950s.

ALGOL	Very early scientific language. ALGOL-60 has spawned many other languages and is still used.
COBOL	One of the earliest. The lingua franca for business applications.
LISP	Also early. Designed for list processing. Popular also with researchers in artificial intelligence.
FORTRAN	The first 3GL. Still the most popular for scientific and engineering applications.
JOVIAL	ALGOL-based. U.S Air Force standard for many years.
PASCAL	Descended from ALGOL. Popular in universities.

C	ALGOL-based. Current standard for systems programming, but used for almost all types of software.
APL	Succinct, but uses unconventional keyboard symbols.
CMS-2	U.S. Navy owns millions of lines of code in this one-of-a-kind language.
BASIC	Easy to learn, popular in schools and colleges, installed on most PCs.
PL/1	After a hundred or so languages had gained currency, IBM decided the world was ready for its own form of Esperanto, namely PL/1.
Ada	Based on PASCAL, the Department of Defense's standard for military software. Has gained currency elsewhere.

With the notable exception of COBOL, CMS-2, and Ada, the names of these and many other languages are generic descriptors of languages, to one extent or another. For example, under the name FORTRAN, we have the original FORTRAN (and its dialects), FORTRAN II (and its dialects), FORTRAN IV (and its dialects), and FORTRAN '77 (extended within a year after its introduction).[1] Dialects, we might note, are usually in the form of extensions or added capabilities. They may include linguistic modifications of the standard language forms as well. If these modifications are great enough, another dialect or new language can take form. Thus, some consider JOVIAL to be a dialect of one of the dialects of ALGOL, and some of the dialects of JOVIAL have been given separate names (e.g., J73). In the world of computer languages, only a quarter-century was required to produce the equivalent of the evolution of Proto-Indo-European language to English and French.

Much more information on the history of the earlier languages and on their characteristics is available in Jean Sammet's book, *Programming Languages.*[2] In the years since the publication of her book, the "tower of computational babel" has continued to rise, and several of the languages that will from time to time be referred to within these pages are not covered by Sammet.

That there exists a wide variety of compiler languages is not to suggest that all are available to a programmer for the coding of the problem at hand. For one thing, most software is written by programming teams, the members of which all use the same language selected for the project.

There is another obvious constraint on the choice of language. A programmer may be fluent in ALGOL, but if no ALGOL compiler is available in the programming shop, the programmer will be unable to use the language. In the most general case, the programmers in a shop will use one or, at most, two different languages. For example, in an Information Systems (IS) installation, we might see both COBOL and PL/1. Even here, we might guess that COBOL is being used only for modifications of old programs; that new data processing systems are being written in PL/1. The use of a single language is conducive to simpler programming standards, reduces the amount of maintenance on utility routines (standard software components for performing common operations) and, with all programmers proficient in the shop's standard language, provides greater freedom in assigning staff to new work and maintenance.

Given the plethora of languages, how does one decide which language to use for a new project or to standardize on for all projects? We should like to think the choice is objectively arrived at by weighing the attributes of various languages against the problem or class of problems at hand. All too often, languages are determined by precedent.

In his *Recollections of Socrates*, Xenophon attributes to Apollo the remark that "Everyone's true worship was that which he found in use in the place where he chanced to be." From a historical point of view, this is how most programmers and nonprogrammers who occasionally program their own problems choose languages. The language or languages used by their employers are those that they will use. As a result, few programmers who have stayed on one job for many years are truly multilingual. Programmers may study "foreign" languages on their own, but not until they have an opportunity to put a language to use (they have at their disposal a compiler or interpreter) can they gain fluency. Similarly, it is the rare French language student who feels entirely comfortable with the language until given the opportunity to use it in a French language environment.

Carrying the analogy a bit further, programmers often exhibit an overly fond attitude toward their first programming language. Until they acquire considerable experience with a new language, some programmers have even been known to first code a program in the "mother tongue" and then translate it to the new language. And indeed, programming languages can be as dissimilar as English and Basque. A few pages back we printed a routine in the language C to find the smallest of five numbers. C is an example of the class of "block-type" languages which includes ALGOL-60 and all its derivatives. Ignoring the declaration of the five integers, here is the same problem coded in Microsoft's version of Lisp:

```
(DEFUN LEAST (LAMBDA (NUMB SMALLEST)
    ((NULL NUMB) SMALLEST)
    ((LESSP (CAR NUMB) SMALLEST)
            (LEAST (CDR NUMB) (CAR NUMB)) )
    (LEAST (CDR NUMB) SMALLEST) ))
```

Compare the two program listings. It is scarcely surprising that software managers want to standardize on languages as much as possible.

Of the list of languages given above, all have been implemented by compilers. BASIC and APL were initially implemented by interpreters, and it is likely that most of the code written in these languages has been run in an interpreter environment. The most widely used versions of LISP are also used in an interpreted mode.

2.4 Third Generation Design and Code

Languages are the medium in which programs are coded. It is possible, given a problem, to directly write code. Usually, however, at least some thought has to be given to what it is that will be coded. As we shall see in the next chapter, for all but the most simple problems, this thinking process is far more significant to software quality than is coding. For now, we shall discuss the process of design (at the most detailed level) and code, by taking a very simple problem in order to see what thinking might be required.

For our problem we shall take the solution of the quadratic equation

$$AX^2 + BX + C = 0$$

As every eighth-grade student knows, there are two roots, and they may be found from

$$X = \frac{-B \pm \sqrt{B^2 - 4AC}}{2A}$$

We immediately recognize that the solution can take several forms. If $A = 0$, we shall not want to use the above equation, since we do not want to require the computer to divide by zero. Moreover, there will be but one root to the equation $X = -C/B$. However, if B, too, is zero, we shall want to avoid performing this operation. By inspection, we see that if $4AC > B^2$, the roots will be complex.

All of this implies that we cannot simply write out an equation for the solution, but that we shall have to employ *program branches* to permit alternative processing paths. The problem is still simple enough for experienced programmers, having gone through the above thinking process, to code without further intermediate steps. Less experienced programmers will want to document their thinking. Figure 2.3 depicts a common, but no longer universal, method of documentation, called a *flow chart*.

The most popular current method for documenting design decisions is a *programming design language* or *pdl*. Some pdls (e.g., the PDL of Caine, Farber, and Gordon, Inc.) have formal semantic and syntactical rules to enable quality checks, while at the other extreme pdl means no more than structured text. For more complex problems, pdls are usually supported by state diagrams, data flow diagrams, and other aids that we shall leave for later chapters. The next page shows the same design in structured text:

```
if A and B zero, return no solution
if A zero then return real root -C/B
form D = B² - 4AC
form X = -B/2A
form Y = SQRT(D)/2A
if D < 0
        then output complex roots (X + iY) and (X - iY)
        else output real roots (X + Y) and (X - Y)
return
```

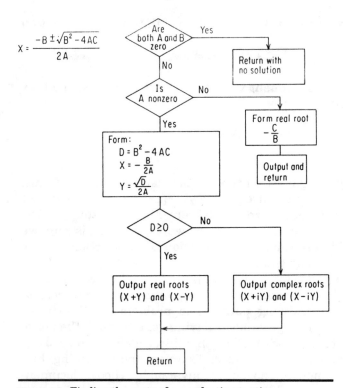

Figure 2.3 Finding the roots of a quadratic equation.

With the pdl (or perhaps the flowchart) in front of them, the programmers now write code. If they were using FORTRAN IV, the above flowchart or pdl might result in this:

```
  PROGRAM QUADRATIC
  IOUT = 5
  IN = 2
  READ (IN,1) A,B,C
1 FORMAT (3E20.7)
  IF (A.NE.0.OR.B.NE.0) GO TO 3
  WRITE (IOUT,2)
2 FORMAT ('NO SOLUTION)
  STOP
3 IF (A.NE.0) GO TO 5
  R = -C/B
  WRITE (IOUT,4) R
4 FORMAT ('SINGLE ROOT'E20.7)
5 D = B**2-4*A*C
  X = -B/(2*A)
  Y = SQRT(ABS(D))/(2*A)
  IF (D.LT.0) GO TO 7
  R1 = X+Y
  R2 = X-Y
  WRITE (IOUT,6) R1,R2
6 FORMAT ('REAL ROOTS'E20.7' AND 'E20.7)
  STOP
7 WRITE (IOUT,8) X,Y,X,Y
8 FORMAT ('ROOTS'E20.7'+ I'E20.7'AND'E20.7'+ I'E20.7)
  STOP
  END
```

Note that we had said "might code the following." There are other ways the program could be coded which would be consistent with the documented design. It has been said many times that there are many ways to code a program correctly. Unfortunately, there are even more ways to code a program incorrectly, but that is another matter. There are also many ways to design a program correctly. Programmers usually develop their own styles, representative of their analytic approaches to problems. It is often possible, by reading the code, to determine who of the staff of programmers wrote the program.

We cannot see all that goes into design with the two toy problems that have been presented in this chapter (finding the smallest of five values and solving the quadratic equation). Among the design tasks typical for real programs, we see programmers

- Determining appropriate algorithms
- Designing data structures

- Determining data transformations
- Apportioning much of the processing to subprograms

One of the characteristics of 3GL is that they are inherently procedural. They require the programmer to provide the logical sequence of tasks they want the computer to perform. In this sense, we might want to include among 3GL step-by-step applications languages. The following are examples of this group:

ATLAS   Programming of automatic test equipment

APT   Programming of automatic machine tools

GPSS   Simulation of systems of discrete events

3GL are certainly more problem-oriented than assembler languages, but they still require the programmer to think in terms of *how* the computer should operate. Would it not be lovely to have programming languages where the programmer simply tells the computer *what* should be done? This would be so lovely that we should want to attribute such languages to another generation.

2.5   Fourth Generation Languages

The fourth generation of programming languages allows the programmer to concentrate on *whats* rather than *hows*. In fact, many 4GL programs have been written by end-users, not professional programmers. Focus, for example, allows users to move a cursor through a set of menus to select operations (such an interface is appropriately referred to as *point-and-shoot*), and to specify reports through *query-by-example* (or fill in the blanks). While doing so, users see the 4GL code generated by their actions displayed at the bottom of the screen. While end-users now fashion many queries, we find that the queries are mostly of the data of large scale programs, coded in either 3GL or 4GL and developed by professional programmers.

Like Focus, most 4GL has to do with information systems. We tend to use the term 4GL for inquiry languages (examples are Natural and SQL), for the language of applications generators, and for data base management systems (DBMS) that allow the programmer to program his/her own application without regard to step-by-step algorithms. In addition to Focus, some other representative 4GL DBMS are Oracle, dBase (I through IV), Ingres, and Ramis II.

Application generators process problem-oriented 4GL code to produce a 3GL (usually COBOL) equivalent. While the output may not be as efficient as a programmer might write—indeed, is often manually "tightened up" by the programmer—it gets the job done. Application generators can be found at the "back end" of more complete development toolsets such as those provided by Intersolv (which supports the application language APS) and KnowledgeWare (whose back end tool produces both COBOL and a SQL specific to an IBM).

We need not think of the fourth generation languages as languages applied solely to information systems. Translator writing systems, or compiler-compilers, permit a programmer to specify the semantics and syntax of a compiler language of the programmer's own design and then automatically generate output that can be processed by a code generator specific to the target computer.* Able to avoid most of the tedium of compiler writing, programmers are more likely to invent new languages directed to narrow classes of problems.

We consider MathCad, a product of MathSoft, Inc., as a 4GL. Some might argue that it is an applications program (or system) in the model of the computer-aided design (CAD) systems used by architects and electronics engineers. Perhaps, but it is also a 4GL in that one can specify highly elaborate computational tasks for processing unbounded sets of input. To demonstrate the essential difference between 3GL and 4GL, Figure 2.4a shows a program written in MathCad to solve the same toy problem earlier shown in Fortran; namely, the solution to the quadratic equation.

In the first line of Fig. 2.4a we defined the specific coefficients for which we want a solution. We did this for clarity. We could also have written a statement that would input the coefficients from a data file. Below the first line we defined the forms for the solution. MathCad did the rest. The only output produced by the computer are the two results on the lower right, both produced in response to the queries $x1=$ and $x2=$. When we input a value of zero for the coefficient a, we got the result of Fig. 2.4b where MathCad told us not to be wiseguys by giving it a singularity to work with. That is the essence of the fourth generation: Tell the computer what you want and it will do it. Observe, however, that we had to tell the computer what we wanted within the constraints of formal linguistic rules. Although we think of 4GL as nonprocedural, most have certain procedural requirements. We had to define D before we could use it. Then there are the semantics: The definition of a variable or constant is denoted in the MathCad language by the symbol := with the symbol = reserved for a request to compute results. Similarly, a 4GL program to extract reports from a data base might contain a statement something like

```
Join {problem reports} and {customer X31} on_key {severe)
```

---

*Many compiler-compilers have been written. One of the most popular is YACC, Yet Another Compiler-Compiler.

Coefficients as follows:
$a := 3$ $b := 4$ $c := 2$
$d := b^2 - 4 \cdot a \cdot c$
$d := -8$

If discriminant is positive, both roots are real.
If negative, complex. If discriminant is zero, double the root.

Compute roots:

$$x1 := \frac{-b + \sqrt{d}}{2.a}$$

$$x2 := \frac{-b - \sqrt{d}}{2.a}$$

Below is the computer's output:
$x1 = 0.667 + 0.471i$
$x2 = 0.667 - 0.471i$

Figure 2.4a Finding the roots of a quadratic equation.

to create a new set of data for all the failures reported by a specific customer. The phrases in brackets are programmer-defined. The other words are part of the 4GL's semantics.

Program statements written in an artificial language, however problem-oriented it may be, suggest that such programs are more likely to be written by professional programmers than end-users. Programs written by professional programmers are the ones whose quality concerns us. Moreover, the more direct approach to programming the problem does not mean that 4GL languages can obviate the

Coefficients as follows:
$a := 0$ $b := -4$ $c := 2$
$d := b^2 - 4 \cdot a \cdot c$
$d := 16$

If discriminant is positive, both roots are real.
If negative, complex. If discriminant is zero, double the root.

Compute roots:

$$x1 := \frac{-b + \sqrt{d}}{2 \cdot a}$$

$\overline{}$ singularity $\overline{}$

$$x2 := \frac{-b - \sqrt{d}}{2 \cdot a}$$

Below is the computer's output:

$x1 =$
$x2 =$

Figure 2.4b *(Continued)*

need to design programs before writing code. The trivial example of finding the roots of a quadratic equation stretches the argument for designing before coding. For the design of a large data base of equipment problem reports one can see that one has to think about the forms in which data are reported, the commonality in the forms, the amount of data, the types of analyses that need to be made, and the kind of reports that will be drawn from the system.

Given the advantages of 4GL, you may ask why we still care about the third generation. 4GL programs tend to be much slower at execution time, sometimes by a factor of 100. Apart from speed, they are certainly unsuitable for embedded software applications since it is impractical to provide the overhead of a 4GL environment in an instrumentation system. Also, productivity during development may not be as great as the supplier of proprietary 4GL tools advertise. (There is a paucity of comparative experiments, but an experiment in which the same application was programmed in COBOL and dBase III showed an improvement of only 15 percent using dBase III.)[3] We predict that we shall be living with both the third and fourth generation languages for quite some time.

Programming in 4GL is sufficiently different from programming in 3GL that we can say it represents a different *programming paradigm*. The designer's approach to the problem is different (in using a 4GL DBMS, for example, data structure is all that counts), the tools are different in kind, and the runtime environment for the application is of a different type—different, in fact, for each proprietary DBMS. For that matter, programming in LISP represents a different paradigm from programming in any other 3GL. Another programming paradigm that readers should know of is *object-oriented programming, or OOP.* More often, it is referred to as *O-O programs.*

2.6 Object-Oriented Programming

Let's assume that we are involved with a real computer program, one containing several different applications for finding the roots of a quadratic equation. We would take our toy illustration and recode it as a procedure, or subprogram, by modifying the way we enter the routine and return from it. This would permit the routine to be used (called) at arbitrary times. Each call would provide the coefficients for the procedure to operate on and placeholders for the returned roots. This is standard 3GL programming—a "main-line" program and its associated procedures, many of which call other procedures. Each procedure supplies a method for solving a particular type of problem, but the code that calls the procedure supplies the data for it to operate on.

O-O programs comprise objects, not procedures. Each object contains its own data and one or more methods for operating on the data. Objects communicate with each other by passing messages back and forth. As a figurative example, "Status reporter, tell the monitor that the printer is ready for another job." Objects represent real things: the icons on a screen, the machines on the factory floor, the operators of the machines. Related objects are grouped into *classes*. In designing an O-O system, one starts by defining the classes needed to perform the necessary processing and then specifies objects as *instances* of classes. In specifying an object, certain characteristics of its class are *inherited*, making it unnecessary to redefine the characteristics of the class. Objects can even be created during execution of the system in response to the system's input. Objects, themselves are classes, and may give rise to further classes. Figure 2.5 depicts the inheritance of vehicular properties.

Proceding with Fig. 2.5, we could, for example, choose to specify the manufacturers of wagons, then their models, and finally models with various option packages. A vehicular object in 1920 might have been a Maxwell butter-and-eggs wagon with windshield wipers and electric headlamps; a wagon able to start, stop, and turn.

O-O represents a very different way at looking at the construction of software. We did, after all, call it a unique paradigm. One of the salient features of the O-O paradigm is that it lends itself to the reusability of classes and their instances. The objects that might have been generated for correlation of accident frequency with automobile characteristics can be used anew for a fine-grained state motor vehicle user tax program. In that sense, we might consider an approach to analyzing a problem for an O-O application to be one that favors composition, rather than the conventional decomposition processes. But we'll leave that for later chapters. Reusability is perhaps the one feature of O-O most often cited when software management decides to adopt the paradigm.

What does all this have to do with quality? It means that in order to ensure the quality of O-O software, we need be concerned not only with latent faults, compliance with requirements, code readability, and the like, but also whether classes are specified in as general a manner as possible so as to promote their reuse.

The brief survey of O-O we have presented may suggest that O-O is O-O is O-O. Not quite. No two O-O environments provide the same view of programming. One can specify the characteristics of each environment in terms of its eponymous programming language. We'll mention a few just to point out how O-O languages can differ.

Many consider Smalltalk, which evolved at XEROX PARC between the early 1970s and 1980, the archetypical O-O language. Others trace

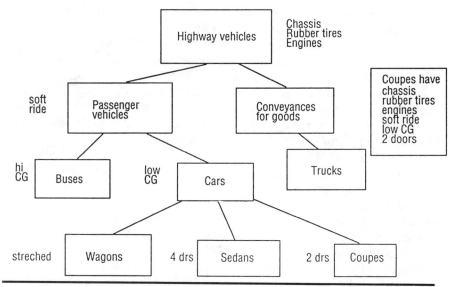

Figure 2.5   Vehicular objects.

the beginnings of O-O to Simula-67, developed in Sweden. (The 67 refers to 1967.) Perhaps the most used O-O language is C++, based on C. Unlike Smalltalk, C++ permits an object to inherit from more than one class. If Fig. 2.5 had a class called "Boat," an object Hovercraft could have been created from "Boat" and "Sedan." Flavors also permits multiple inheritance, but is built on a foundation of Lisp, not C. Ada is often thought of as a language for O-O primarily because of its Package construct, which can loosely be construed as a class. However, for reasons too technical to get into here, Ada is less object-oriented than the other languages noted. Readers interested in knowing more about O-O would do well to read the book by Khoshafian and Abnous.[4]

2.7   Systems Software

We have introduced assemblers, compilers, and interpreters as programs that, themselves, support the work of programmers. We have also alluded to "environments" for developing and running 4GL programs. These programming tools fall under the general rubric of systems software—the software used to invoke and run application programs and programming aids, control the devices normally thought of as part of the computer system, often monitor the execution of applications, and perform other useful tasks. Systems software makes the computer hardware invisible to the user. One of your authors used a UNIX operating system for two years without ever finding out what hardware the software was installed on.

We need to talk about operating systems, since the operating system is the software "platform" seen by programmers and end-users alike. Before getting into operating systems, however, we shall mention another programming aid that indirectly affects quality. We noted earlier that real programs comprise many individual procedures (to keep things simple, we ignore O-O). Procedures and their associated main-line program need to be welded into a whole, into a *program load*. The tool that does this is called a *link editor*. Link editors assign to the main-line and each procedure specific sets of locations in memory and replace dummy addresses used for calls with real addresses. Certain procedures, such as that referred to in the C code example as <stdio.h> or the FORTRAN example as SQRT, will be found in *libraries*. During the linking process, link editors extract the necessary routines (and sets of constants) from the libraries. To simplify configuration control of object code, all procedures are likely to have been placed in one or more libraries at *linktime*. Thus, in addition to their primary function of generating program loads, link editors become part of the configuration management process.

Loaders are companions to link editors. To handle programs so large that they must be segmented into *overlays*, loaders are often required to be in memory, or at least standing off-stage on disk during program execution. Readers who have used personal computer operating systems may have noted a slight delay before they get a response to certain operating system commands. If the delay isn't inherent in the amount of processing required, what is happening is that the program (or segment) required to execute the command is being loaded into memory.

End-users have learned to take advantage of the support provided by modern operating systems. So too, programmers. Programmers use operating systems to invoke the various tools they use: compilers, linkers, loaders, librarians, file managers, design and code analyzers, test beds, and still others. Increasingly, they also have *software development environments* to manage their tools and steer data output from one tool to the input of another. Software development environments, based on DBMS technology, also provide hooks for quality assurance. One can use the environment to learn project status, derive programming measurements, and track the correction of problems.

In modern programming environments, each programmer, or perhaps each pair of programmers, has a terminal—anything from a dumb terminal to a powerful workstation—connected to a central computer. In the familiar *client-server* type of network, all the controlled files are on the central computer (server), as are most of the software tools. This centralization, once again, works to the advantage of quality assurance. Any processing done locally (by personal computer or workstation terminal) is likely to be fairly rudimentary processing to the end of reducing data traffic on the network. For example, a programmer may build a file of program statements at the terminal, and then transmit the file to the server for compilation. Results of compilation, almost assuredly a file of error messages if this is the first attempt at compilation, are transmitted back to the terminal for display.

Operating systems can be layered. Many PC users are familiar with Windows, which operates under the DOS operating system. Windows, itself, fits our very general definition of operating system software. Windows serves also to illustrate another feature found in some software systems: When operating on a 386 or 486 computer, Windows 3.1 provides the capability of *multi-tasking*. In multi-tasking systems, the computer can execute several programs concurrently. Now that doesn't mean that a given machine cycle can be used to help perform a processing task in each of two or more programs. Rather, using one technique or another, multi-tasking shares the resources of the computer among two or more programs. In one task, the user may fill in the cells on a spreadsheet while in a second task the computer is chomping away at Bessel functions or sorting long data files. In fact, make that three concurrent tasks: spreadsheet, Bessel functions, and sorting. Here is a more pertinent example of multi-tasking: a programmer can analyze the results of one test while the program under test is subjected to another set of test data. When tests take a long time to run, this is one way of shortening test schedules.

Windows also provides an example of a *graphical user interface* or *GUI* (pronounced "gooey"). We are told that the left hemisphere of the brain responds better to images than to words, while the obverse holds for the right side. Or perhaps it is the other way around. Whatever, visualization help programmers perform certain tasks. And, if GUIs are useful to help end-users find their way around complex operating systems, they are equally useful to programmers. Interlisp, an interactive Lisp environment, had a GUI in the early 1970s. Smalltalk-76 (yes, that means 1976), an early O-O environment, had a GUI. All to the purpose of using both sides of programmers' brains. One can fashion one's own GUI with Windows or MacIntosh computers as the program development platform.

More importantly, graphics can come into play in portraying the structure of a program, the flow of data in a system of many processing tasks, the relations among the states of a program, or the results of tests. Recall that programs comprise a mainline and many procedures, and that procedures call procedures. Trying to grasp the broad picture of the relations among procedures is difficult on a large system. Figure

2.6 shows the relations among procedures (the *call graph*) for a small program involving 16 distinct procedures.

The programmer who has an analyzer that can produce the graphic depiction of the call graph is well ahead of the programmer who can rely only on the indentation conventions of a completely text-oriented analyzer, as in:

```
main
 getdata
  filea
   poplate
   seeknew
    statreport
     waitout
  errorhandler
 freetoken
 journ
  poplate
  statcheck
               . . . and so on . . .
```

With multi-tasking software and GUIs we seem to have come a long way from the language translators with which this discussion of system software started. All play an important role in the productivity of programmers and the quality of the software they produce. If technology is intrinsic to TQM, we cannot downplay the role of systems software in producing quality software.

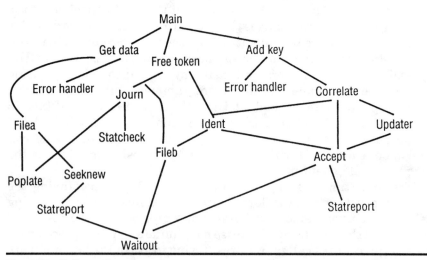

Figure 2.6 Call graph.

We must recognize that not all computer software is developed using the same set of systems software, nor even the same generic types of software. As there are many hardware environments and work place environments for software development, so are there many software environments. The people who develop software are not all of a kind, nor are the management strategies under which they work. Software is built in many ways: some tied to the characteristics and application of the software being developed, some to historical origins, and, to an astonishing extent, some to chance.

2.8 Summary

1. Whether small enough to fit on a printed circuit card or large enough to consist of thousands of microprocessors, computers do no work of any kind until their electronic circuits are programmed to follow a specific sequence of operations.

2. Computer programs consist of sequences of instructions coded in digits of the binary number system.

3. Since long sequences of binary instructions are difficult for programmers to work with, assembler languages for programming came into being. These allow programmers to use alphanumeric mnemonics for instructions and the naming of data. To execute programs written in such languages, the programs must be translated into binary code by programs called assemblers.

4. Compiler and interpreter languages (the third generation of programming languages, or 3GL) are one step further from binary, but closer to the problem being solved. 3GLs are more efficient and less-error prone in programming. The programs are translated into binary code by compilers or interpreters.

5. Regardless of the language used, code is but the implementation of a design. Most design decisions are captured in programming design languages (pdl), although some programmers continue to use the once ubiquitous flowcharts.

6. A fourth generation of programming languages (4GL) allows the programmer to specify what is to be computed rather than the computational steps the computer must follow. 4GL are mostly, but not exclusively, associated with data base management systems (DBMS).

7. 4GL programs run much slower than those written in 3GL. However, they take less time to prepare. Certain 4GL also have interfaces to encourage some programming by end-users.

8. Object-oriented programming (O-O), while still in the third-generation, represents an entirely different approach to programming. Encapsulating data with the algorithms that operate on them, objects in O-O can bear a one-to-one correspondence with objects in the real problem domain.

9. O-O has gained great interest because of the potential reuse of objects once they are programmed.

10. Assemblers, compilers, and other programming tools are at the less complex end of the systems software spectrum. At the other end we see operating systems; some capable of dividing computers into concurrently operating tasks, some capable of supporting graphical user interfaces.

11. Operating systems familiar to users of personal computers are similar to the ones used by programmers—may even be identical.

References

1. FORTRAN, *DoD supplement to American National Standard X3.9-1978*, MIL-STD-1753, 1978.
2. Sammet, Jean E. *Programming Languages: History and Fundamentals*, Prentice-Hall, Englewood Cliffs, NJ, 1969.
3. Misra, S. and Jalics, P. "Third-Generation versus Fourth–Generation Software Development," *IEEE Software*, July 1988, pp. 8-14.
4. Khoshafian, Setrag and Abnous, Razmik. *Object Orientation: Concepts, Languages, Databases, User Interfaces,* John Wiley and Sons, New York, NY, 1990.

3

The Life Cycle
of Software

In the last chapter we discussed the preparation of a program to find the roots of a quadratic equation. If there were distinctions between "concept," "requirements definition," and "design," they were blurred by the small effort required for each. For programs of that size, indeed of tenfold that number of statements, one would speak of the "writing" of programs, not of formal development processes. The specifics of how the program will be used are obvious, the requirements are tacit within the context of the program's use, and the design is but a few minutes— or at the most, hours—of analysis and thought. Moreover, some design probably will take place concurrently with the writing of code. If the program is to be used by no one other than its author, testing will be highly informal, consisting of one or two test cases for which the answers are easily arrived at without the use of a computer.

Even within a larger reference, it may be appropriate to consider the program as being written, rather than developed. Consider Sam, who needs a program to solve a system of linear algebraic equations. He knows how to solve them, may even know how to program the solution, but doesn't have the time to do the job himself. It is necessary for Sam to have someone else do the programming. The conceptual work has already been done. Sam has arrived at a system of equations to be used as the model for scheduling the use of his company's manufacturing equipment. But now he has to write a brief specification for the performance of the program he wants. In the specification, he defines the maximum number of equations, the fact that they are linear, how he will want to input the coefficients of the variables, and the accuracy he requires.

Sam gives the specification to Nancy who now analyzes it. Nancy's first thought is to use the manufacturing DBMS (data base management system). Surely, Sam plans to draw his coefficients from tables currently in the DBMS. Why not program the solution directly in the DBMS 4GL? As it happens, Sam's data came from the DBMS, but Sam likes to juggle the numbers to play what-if games. There is nothing left for Nancy but to do her analysis the old-fashioned way.

To determine which appears most applicable in terms of computation time and accuracy, Nancy researches the several classical methods (triangular elimination, Gauss-Seidel, etc.) for solving systems of linear equations. She recognizes that the program must test for independence among the equations. She has to choose formats (integer, floating point, single or multiple precision) for the coefficients and variables appropriate to their numeric range and the required accuracies. She also thinks hard about an easy way to enter the coefficients, and arrives at a method she believes will minimize the likelihood of incorrect data entry.

She then proceeds to translate the selected method of solution into an algorithm, incorporating logic for trapping outrageously incorrect input data and dependent conditions that would preclude a solution. For her own convenience, Nancy sets down the algorithm in the form of pseudocode (another name for pdl). With the pseudocode in front of her at her keyboard she writes code to implement the design directly into a computer text file.

Next she calls for a compilation. As she expected, the compiler tells her of several errors she had made that made it impossible for the compiler to correctly process the program. All the mistakes were in data entry (a great programmer, Nancy is a dreadful typist), none in the logic of her intentions. She quickly fixes the errors, recompiles (successfully, this time), links to standard input and output library routines, and tests the program to her own satisfaction, using test cases that she was reasonably certain would encompass the range of data. The test cases revealed one bug. Nancy quickly traced the patently incorrect result to the range she had used for matrix subscripts, changed the code, recompiled, relinked, and retested. All went well, and she turned the program over to Sam with a brief explanation of how to use it.

With Nancy's help, Sam's approach to the scheduling problem is so successful that he is promoted to chief corporate analyst. His first assignment in his new position is to assess the company's strategies for marketing penetration. After some research, he discovers that the strategies in use are based solely on a single set of premises about the plans of the several competitors, with no thought given to the responses that might be appropriate to other possible, if less likely, competition moves. An inveterate card player, Sam realizes he is in an N-player game and remembers having once read about a theory of games that could be applied to economic behavior. For all his talents, mathematics of this kind is not Sam's long suit. However, he discovers that two fellows in the IS department, John and Oscar, know a great deal about it. John and Oskar now set out to find a way to model the competitive environment, using gaming strategies along the guidelines stipulated by Sam.

In time they arrive at a conceptual approach, which, of course, will require a new computer program. John and Oskar now are the ones to write a software requirements specification, which Sam, as their "customer," reviews. This is a larger software problem than the last one Sam was concerned with, and it is not only Nancy, but three of her associates as well who are assigned to implement the specification. When they are ready, the program prepared by the four is tested twice, once to their satisfaction and again with test cases submitted by John and Oskar. Still more work remains: program development of this magnitude represents a considerable capital investment, the kind that is made in the expectation of recurring return, with the consequence that the documentation prepared by the programmers is more formal, better suited to the purpose of making future changes.

The program to find the solution of the system of linear equations, like that for the quadratic equation, was *written*. It was informally introduced to the programmer (Nancy), and its potential use was limited. The programmer was able to complete the task without coordination with other people, and any problems inherent in the program were expected to manifest themselves quickly. The gaming problem represents a program that was *developed*. It involved three tiers of persons concerned with the program, coordination within two of those levels, and a likelihood of much future use.

Another way to view software development is to evolve it from the quintessential code and debug to a full project status. Accordingly, we first define *programming* as the translation of an algorithm (or procedure) from natural or mathematical language or a diagram into computer language, and the process of then making the translation work. We now incorporate programming in the definition of *solution development,* which we define as determining the algorithm and programming it. Finally, we have *software development*:

- Analysis of the role to be performed by the program (concept)

- Solution development

- Evaluation of the program against the role conceived in the first step

- Documentation sufficient for the users' needs and for maintenance throughout the life cycle

For programs that are *written,* there is little interest in software quality assurance. The interest of a few people and little investment is involved. Problems will attract attention before creating serious consequences and will easily be solved. Code death will occur shortly after birth.

It is programs spawned by software development that are our concern, and, while each is different, the various activities that must take place during their life cycles have much in common. One can develop a hierarchical classification of software development activities, and we shall implicitly do so throughout this book. For example, we can refer to development testing, which in turn we can divide into unit testing and integration testing.

For now, let's look at the top level of just about anyone's hierarchy. As it happens, the activities at the highest level are largely sequential. Accordingly, it is customary to equate these activities with *phases.* Moreover, it is customary to depict the phases by a *waterfall chart.* There is, of course, no agreement on exactly what the phases are. Figure 3.1 reflects one of the more common waterfalls.

Although Fig. 3.1 is entirely linear, we speak of its depiction as a life cycle. The cyclic part is implied, not drawn. Each time one goes through a major modification of the software, one starts once again with concept and analysis and ends by placing the software into operation and perhaps performing minor maintenance tasks until the next major modification. Again and again.

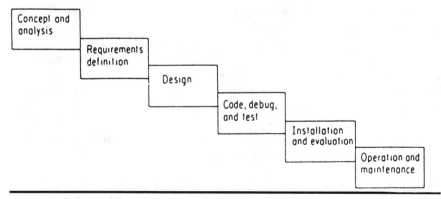

Figure 3.1 Software life cycle.

3.1   Concept and Analysis

Certain problems are obvious candidates for solution by computation, often through well-established techniques; payroll, mailing lists, and inventory control are among those that come to mind immediately. Others are less obvious. Sam's marketing strategy assignment, improving the image of a dull photograph, and operating an urban rail transit car are representative of the less obvious. If a computer is used for one of these tasks, an analysis of the overall problem must be made, a role for the computer must be established, and, in many cases, the functions of other elements of the solution (sensors, controls, people) must be determined. Conceptually, the assignment to a computer of a system task or group of tasks may be reached without much understanding of how the assignment will be executed: "It seems reasonable to leave this to a computer"; "this sort of thing has been done by computers before"; "It will boil down to a lot of arithmetic"; and so forth. Analysis is required to verify that the use of a computer is a well considered one and to determine just how the computer will be employed.

Analysis can take many forms and extend to many depths. For Sam's problem, analysis was a matter of researching the current marketing position, determining the kernel common to all the strategies, and then reading as much as he could about game theory. The program itself was the analysis tool that would prove the feasibility of the approach. The final system included both the program and Sam, using it interactively with various input data sets.

Consider, though, a large telephone system requiring a discrete set of traffic handling strategies which permit automatic rerouting of excessive loads between cities. If the concept is to embed these strategies in a computer equipped with on-line control of the telephone switches, you must consider simulating them in an off-line mode well before continuing the development cycle. This type of telephone traffic program is going to be large, costly, and must serve a large number of customers. Once scarcely wants to wait until test or evaluation to discover that the selected method is inadequate. Therefore, it is customary to carefully simulate the effect of the processing rules that will ultimately be programmed and to analyze the results of the simulations.

Although the simulations will themselves be performed in a computer, the simulation program can be much more modest than the final, operational program. It is not necessary to program each processing algorithm in detail (indeed, many will not even be known at simulation time), but simply the effects that the key parts of the program are expected to produce. Also, there is no need to work out the details of the interface between the computer and the rest of the system. It is sufficient to assert that status messages will arrive at a given rate and that external switches will respond to commands from the computer.

Once the computational task has been determined, it may be necessary to ascertain the amount of computer power that will be required. Obviously, this is not the case if the company's powerful mainframe computer is available and the problem to be solved is patently simple. However, if the problem is of a magnitude significantly greater than is customary, thorough analysis of machine requirements is a quality issue.

For embedded applications, this analysis is almost always a must. The computer (or computers) to be used will be dedicated to the task, and one wants to specify hardware appropriate to the job, as best it can be sized at this early stage. The analyses must take into account memory, input-output, and computational speed requirements. Since the last two of these are a function of machine architecture, and since there is so great a variety of architectures now available, doing the job properly is no small matter. Also, there may be constraints of weight, power and heat dissipation, space, and the physical environment in which the processor must operate. Finally, if there is a decided preference for a specific programming language, one must confirm that a compiler capable of generating object code for the embedded computer is available for installation on the computers used by the development staff.

3.2 Process Models

Referring back to Fig. 3.1, the activities starting with the requirements definition and ending with code, debug, and test are the essence of software development. Indeed, to many, the software development life cycle comprises these and only these activities, which means we ought to have a special name for the way this part of the software life cycle is implemented. We do. It's called *software development model,* sometimes *software process model,* and sometimes *programming development model or programming process model.* Regardless of name, the exact model adopted by a programming shop and the way it uses the model bear directly on the quality of the software produced.

Top-down process models

The model most often written about is the *top-down model.* In the most doctrinaire view of the model, requirements are completely defined before any design is started. Design, itself, is divided into two (sometimes more, but we'll go with two) stages, each sequential. Usually called *top-level design* or *preliminary design,* the first stage refers to the allocation of the requirements to hierarchically connected groups. The elements of the lowest level tier contain the requirements for each of the major code segments. Detailed design, similar to the design effort we have previously described, for the various segments comes next. Then code, then test. This is the classic waterfall software process model: rapids amidst the cascade of the software life cycle.

We call this the *classic waterfall,* not because it has stood the test of time, but because it has inspired many magazine articles and several how-to-do-software standards (e.g., the early, now obsolete, MIL-STD-1679A). It is a model for a consummately manageable software process. Unfortunately, the classic never works. Designers are aboard the project while systems analysts or engineers are still defining the external specifications for the software. The designers are there because if we waited until the requirements model is complete to hire or assign them, we should never get the job done. Once aboard, we cannot afford not to use the designers. We have a similar situation with the entry level programmers to whom we want to assign detail design and code, an independent test team, and others. Besides, marching along in a lock-step formation stretches out the total time to complete the project.

Inevitably, even where management has declared allegiance to the classic waterfall software process, the several phases overlap. In less doctrinaire versions of the waterfall, the overlaps are managed ones: you can start preliminary design on any discrete section of the requirements model that appears to have stabilized, even while other requirements continue to be defined. Similarly, detailed design can start on any defined section of the top-level design, and code can be written and unit tested on any segments for which design is complete.

The modified waterfall can be applied to quite nearly all programs that will end up implemented in a 3GL. In 4GL, code and design are intertwined to the point that it is hard to distinguish detailed design from coding. Within the context of the unique characteristics of the 4GL, however, the problem can still be split into hierarchically layered sub-problems in a top-level design process.

As reasonable as it looks, even the modified waterfall doesn't quite capture the essence of programming large systems. Programmers want to—need to—get to the crux of the programming problem early (assuming there is one, and there nearly always is). Taking a map-making application as an example, programmers may need to know how efficient a likely graphics format will be before they can design around it. The easiest way to find out may be to experiment with the format. Produce one or more graphic files and write some code to work with the data. In short, experiment.

Imagine that you have just moved into a new place. In late winter you start planning a kitchen garden for your yard. You know the family's preferences for vegetables (up on tomatoes and broccoli, down on lima beans, etc.), so you have no difficulty fashioning a requirements model for the garden: a harvest of two bushels of green beans, one of bell peppers, and so on. For your top-level design, you estimate you will realize the required harvest with so many rows of green beans, of bell peppers, of tomatoes, etc. Detailed design consists of deciding which varieties offered in seed catalogues you will plant. Spring awaits the equivalent of coding: turning over the soil and planting, the better part of three weekends to implement your ambitious garden. Not until you notice the absence of fruit on your squash plants do you find out that nobody in your part of the state has ever been able to get a satisfactory harvest of squash. It's too cold, or too wet, or too something. And you have two rows of squash.

The experienced gardener knows to experiment with a few plants of each desired kind. Find out how well they'll do. The gardener may lose a season, but three weekends of all gardening and no play will not have been wasted. Similarly, we need to let programmers approach problems from an organic point of view. We need to let them look ahead to implementation details that may affect the entire shape of the project.

We prefer the term *preliminary design* to *top-level design* simply because it seems to suggest more latitude in what one does early in the project. Preliminary design would seem to embrace the idea of experimenting at the time when experimentation does the most good.

Process models incorporating bottom-up activities

The opposite of a top-down process model is a *bottom-up model*. Top-down is essentially a process of decomposition: moving from a description of a problem into a description and implementation of a solution. Bottom-up is a composition process. You start with very detailed pieces of the solution and work them toward a composite solution. LISP programmers often find bottom-up detailed design and code a natural part of the process. Unlike most languages, processing in LISP doesn't modify data, it generates new data. Generating new data is most easily done in LISP by recursively defining the new data in terms of the old. When the required operations involve several data sets, the operations are encoded as nested recursive function subprograms. The surest way to do the job is to start with the function of least data scope. Then figure out the function of next higher data scope in terms of the first function. Then do the next higher function and so on.

Elements of bottom-up also enter into any modified top-down process when experimental code finds its way, after some modification, to the final product. It is patently impossible to start with a set of miscellaneous coded and tested procedures and hope that they will drift together to form an acceptable response to the defined requirements. As a formal model, composition strategies use a bottom-up process as part of a larger process. Assume that one has a number of software modules left over from previous projects; the corporate parts inventory, if you will. To demonstrate how sections of the requirements model or elements defined during preliminary design will be satisfied, these *reuseable* modules can be bound together with some new code and executed.

We are most likely to see this form of composition where O-O is the programming paradigm* in place. Objects, with their encapsulated data and methods, lend themselves to this kind of reusability. Several process models directed to O-O have been proposed. The fountain model,[1] which takes its name from the fashion in which it has been depicted, explicitly takes into account the iteration that accompanies early identification of system objects even as analysis of the problem continues.

System evolution

As we know it today, the U.S. Constitution is only as old as the last amendment. At the time of its initial ratification, the Constitution provided a framework for government sufficient to get things going. Ever since, we have been amending the framework to provide a more suitable reference for our society. Similarly, one can start with a rudimentary solution to a computational problem and gradually amend the solution by adding new functions or objects. In a sense, this is a bottom-up process in which we iterate the waterfall life cycle of Fig. 3.1 step by step.

Using a 4GL, it is attractive to limit the initial programming to those functions that frame the structure of the data and what users may do with the data, correct any design that doesn't quite do the job, add more structure and more reports, correct those, and so on until the system is declared complete. (Of course, it will still be modified no less than if the "complete" system were fully programmed *ab initio*.) The process allows both early correction of major shortcomings and early, if partial, utility.

Deciding to let a system evolve would seem to make things easier for management, but evolution also imposes its own burdens. To avoid

---

*Programming paradigms are programming conventions often tied to a group of languages. Without going into detail here (more in Chap. 5), we'll simply say that the differences among paradigms are like those among cultures—European, Samoan, East Asian, etc.

redundant data structures and code, one needs to have a good idea of what the final product will look like at all stages. Indeed, if a significant amount of top-down thinking doesn't precede the start of design, each round of evolution is likely to be marked by reworking all or part of what had been done before. Of course, this is not all bad. Careful reworking often results in something better than the original.

The spiral model

With the reduction of risk as their main objective, TRW has developed a life cycle model with stages (called *rounds*) that loosely map into the waterfall. Yet at the same time, each round takes on a series of activities that conceptually parallel those of the waterfall from analysis through implementation. For example, the round that includes software product design also includes risk analysis, prototyping (more on prototyping in Sec. 3.3), design validation and verification, and generation of an integration and test plan. For this reason, we include the spiral model under the rubric software process models, although it is really an alternative to the life cycle waterfall of Fig. 3.1.

Barry Boehm (once of TRW) notes that each round begins with an identification of objectives, alternative means of implementation, and constraints imposed on the alternatives.[2] The objectives identified are those already familiar to software engineers: performance, functionality, accommodation to change, etc. Alternatives can include new design, reuse of existing design, buying from an outside source, or whatever applies. Constraints are also familiar: cost, schedule, interface, etc. The spiral model is not specific to any one programming paradigm or analysis method, nor does it exclude within appropriate rounds elements of any of the other software process models discussed here. Managers who take the view that quality (as a discipline) is the management of risk should find themselves very comfortable with the spiral model.

Other process models

Certain proprietary methodologies can be thought of as unique process models. Two popular ones are Jackson System Design coupled with Jackson Structured Programming[3] and the Warnier-Orr[4] approach to development. Both are well-suited to IS applications. These are decomposition (top-down) methods, but rather than emphasizing the decomposition of functions or real world entities, they emphasize the decomposition of data.

More popular in the U.K. than elsewhere, the Vienna Development Method (VDM)[5] is an example of a little-used family of formal process models that start with formal specifications—formal in the sense that the required system behavior is couched in a formal, mathematically based language. The object here is to generate a product that can be traced mathematically back to its external specifications.

"Provable" processes such as VDM would seem appropriate to applications requiring extremely robust software, but we must note that they are not easily installed in the typical programming environment. At the very least, their application requires intensive training—although any change to the process should be accompanied by training—much of which will be lost if the trainees do not have a good grasp of discrete mathematics. Most programmers do not. Moreover, provable specifications are unlikely to be understood by the customer or user, and as we shall see, the software requirements model should be the basis upon which customers and producers agree to the programming that will be performed. If one uses a language for defining external specifications that is unintelligible to customers, an intermediate specification is called for. Beyond entailing additional cost, a nonprovable go-between means that we still have to cope with the inability to prove that the requirements model will meet customer needs.

This brings us to discussion of the major activities of software development processes, starting with first things first, requirements.

3.3 Defining Requirements

As we have noted, once the computational task is roughly defined and the methods generally understood, it is necessary to specify precisely what the program or programs are to accomplish. Perhaps we need not specify everything before we start designing, but any design that we undertake should be performed to well-understood objectives. In short, before doing any software design we want to perform further *system-level* design, with a software requirements model as the tangible output. The model may take many forms—text, diagrams, demonstration programs (prototypes)—but it must be sufficiently explicit and complete to serve as a departure point for design.

The people who generate requirements models are often not the people who will implement them. Ideally, we would have different people handle each aspect of software development. If the artifacts of development (requirements, design, code) must be handed off to new people, we have a built-in or organic mechanism for catching errors. Nowhere is this more important than in the definition of requirements, and it is common for requirements to be defined by people different from those who will implement the requirements.

In the commercial and, to a large extent, systems software milieu, this is normally attended to by *system analysts*. For embedded applications, software requirements are prepared by the same system engineers who also specify each of the other elements of the system. That is, they will have already roughly determined the function to be performed by each part of the system, including the computer, and now they must (possibly with support from the programming team) prepare detailed specifications for these functions.

The line between "requirements" and "design" is not easily drawn. One wants to draw an analogy to hardware, where one can say of an electronic amplifier that, given a stipulated input power, it must produce a certain output level at a specified maximum amount of distortion. How the amplifier will perform its function need never enter into the specification. And, indeed, for many computer programs it is possible to state, in the most specific of terms, what it is that needs to be done without saying how the program is to be designed. Where we encounter trouble is where only the system designers understand the processing method that will produce the desired result. Here, the system designers must specify, in addition to input-transform-output, the very means of effecting the transformation.

A scientist, examining a dull photograph through a microscope, observes certain correlative properties and conceives a mathematical technique for capitalizing on these to enhance the photograph. Further thinking develops the idea of using a new kind of fine-grained scanner to quantify the image and enter it into a computer where it can be processed by the new technique. The software requirements specification the scientist will prepare will specify input-transform-output, but the transformation cannot simply be named; details of the method must be supplied since only the scientist knows them. Yet, is not the method part of the design?

The kernel of the concept we are dealing with is the separation of system design from program design: keeping the problem space from intruding into the solution space. We want the requirements for the program design clearly documented so that programming personnel will understand what it is they must do. From a practical point of view, we are left to drawing the line at the point where requirements go no deeper into the stipulation of methods than is necessary to serve as a departure point for design. Whatever compromise to the division of church and state we are required to make, it remains that:

> To the extent practicable, the specification says what is to be done, and design determines how it will be done.

The rule serves yet another purpose. One use made of the specification, perhaps the most important from the aspects of software quality assurance, derives from its representation of tangible evidence that further software development effort will have direction. If a specification cannot be produced, further investment is obviously unwarranted. Thus, the specification, regardless of who produced it, can be the basis for a management decision, and the less design effort it contains the more timely that decision will be.

Earlier, we said that the requirements model is the basis of agreement between customer and producer. If text, with or without supporting tables and diagrams, is the only means practical to communicate the specifications, there is nothing for it but for the customer (or Marketing Department or user) to plow through the material and try to relate it to his needs. Of course, the customer probably had given the producer something in writing. But what the customer wrote is not the sort of thing that one can design to. Now the customer must see how the specification writers responded to the customer's stipulated needs. It is rather like the translation from a marketing specification to a technical specification.

It is unfair to ask a customer to wade through a technical specification and agree that it says all the right things (although the military is quite willing to do so, and insists on doing so in its acquisition procedures). Moreover, producers really do not want to depend on the willingness of a customer to analyze specifications thoroughly and knowledgeably. One can make things much easier for the customer. In the process, one also makes it easier for the designers (they're not that big on going through a specification bound to text, either), and perhaps more important, one gets the specification produced in much less time than by ordinary means. We are talking about *rapid prototyping*.

Rapid prototyping

In the physical world, a *prototype is* a working model of what the designers hope will be the final product. It may be a scale model (typical of aircraft prototypes) or it may lack finishing details (typical of tennis rackets). Whatever it is, construction is that intended for the production model. In the software world, a prototype is constructed differently. Not only is it scaled down in the sense that it may be only partly functional, but it is written in a language different from that of the implemented final product. Languages for prototyping are selected for the speed, relative to that of the "production" language, in which the model can be constructed; thus the term "rapid prototyping."

A software prototype captures the software team's understanding of the customer's needs and demonstrates how the team intends to satisfy those needs. Rapid prototyping is most useful when the customer has not plainly and completely specified his needs in writing—the usual case.

Consider a marketing specification for a computer-aided design (CAD) system for laying out motherboards: promises of a brave new world of computational features, interfaces with everything in sight, and exceptional ease of use. To design the program, the software people must translate the promises into something tangible. Interfaces are already defined, but the means of laying out printed wiring, lands, and the like; the displays; the on-line help features; and all the functional details that go into such an application need to be made explicit. The software team puts its collective head together and comes up with a large set of point-and-click commands, standards for representing the appearance of motherboards and the parts that mount on them, and an on-line help screen. Using one or another language in which they can quickly program, they put together a working model able to show the graphics, the graphical command file, a handful of commands that they have implemented, and enough of the help features to give the sense of the on-line hand-holding they propose. The prototype is run in the presence of marketing personnel and a major customer,* all of whom get a chance to try out the prototype.

"We like this." "Yeah, that's real good." "I think you have to go through too many menus to get help." "That's not the term we use in designing printed wiring boards." "Hey! Nifty! I can't do anything like that with what I now have." And so on. Enough feedback for the software team to know where it is on the right track, where to correct. A second prototype is constructed, a second demonstration, and by the third prototype a de facto software requirements model has been produced.

Figure 3.2 depicts the process. If the prototype were to end up as the first release of the product, we would have an evolutionary life cycle model. But the prototype will not, because it is written in a language unsuitable for the final product. The prototype will serve as the requirements model for design, code, and test, after which it will be put to rest until the time to consider adding new features for the next release.

Rapid prototyping has found its way into many applications. Any number of IS applications have been coded in 3GL for the sake of operating efficiency, based on requirements models coded in 4GL. An object-oriented DBMS was used for the prototype of a CAD system for VLSI circuits.[6] The first Ada compiler certified by the DoD was actually a prototype written in New York University's highly expressive SETL language. (SETL stands for set-theoretic language.) The last place we

---

*For the best assurance of customer satisfaction, "the customer" would include actual designers of circuit boards.

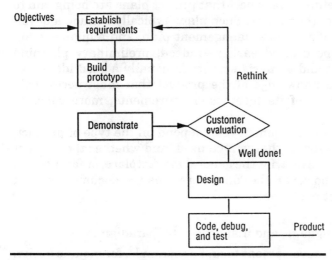

Figure 3.2 Rapid prototyping.

should expect to see rapid prototyping used is in the specification of real-time software. Yet this, too, has been accomplished using PSDL *(prototype system description language)* with a base of reusable software components coded in Ada.[7]

One last advantage of rapid prototyping is worth noting: the test cases (as distinguished from sitting at the keyboard to tinker with the prototype) used to demonstrate the prototype can be reused to check out the final product. They may not be sufficient to cover the entire scope of needed tests, but to the extent one has them, testing to the reused test cases ensures validation to the technical specifications.

We summarize the advantages of rapid prototyping:

- More thorough customer involvement
- Greater customer satisfaction
- Increased likelihood that designers will understand the technical specification
- Improvement in the cycle time to produce a technical specification
- Less likelihood of validating to the wrong requirements

Planning

Requirements models define what specifications designers will design to. Certain plans also define the job of the designers. While requirements are being defined, we expect that project plans are being laid to cover the balance of the project. Such plans typically include a development plan, a configuration management plan, and a quality plan. These plans can be drafted earlier—indeed, preliminary planning during the concept and analysis activity is usually a good idea—but with the increased knowledge of the product that must necessarily accompany definition of its technical requirements, more concrete plans can be drawn.

The contents of a development plan depend on the type of product, the programming process that will be used, and whether the product is produced under contract, for the general marketplace, or for internal users. In general, however, the following items are documented as a guide for all project personnel:

- Programming language, and if appropriate, paradigm.
- Definition of each development task. For example, for module design we would expect as a minimum a definition of task input, task output, reviews, and the tools that should be used.
- Major test activities, documentation, and required tools. (May be documented in a separate test plan, sometimes in the quality plan.)
- Form in which design decisions will be documented.
- Measurements and analyses.
- Any planning required to support the delivered product.
- Who is responsible for what.
- A project schedule. This may well be a separate document.

Much of the development plan of course, will be derived from documented standard practices. A development plan can refer to the standards, instantiating them for the project where appropriate.

The configuration management plan also will be derived from standard practices. The plan should, however, contain no less than:

- Numbering scheme for software and documents
- Identification of controlled libraries and what they are used for
- Tools unique to configuration management
- When items go under control
- How controlled items get changed
- Dissemination of change information
- Who is responsible for what

The quality plan also reflects standard practices. The salient items for a quality plan include:

- Product and process evaluations
- Method for tracking matters requiring correction
- Use of data and analyses relating to quality
- Outline of the qualification procedures that will be followed
- Quality interface with customers or users
- Quality interface with software suppliers, if any
- Who is responsible for what

Later chapters will discuss these plans in greater detail.

3.4 Design

Personal Processor Power (PPP) is a manufacturer of home computers. PPP's market niche lies in the ease with which the public can use its computers, and they make no attempt to be compatible with any other computer design. Each computer comes bundled with a small set of applications that PPP thinks represent the rationale for buying a home computer: word processor, address book, checkbook maintenance, and recipe card file. PPP's business strategy is to offer a number of application programs for which it charges high prices. The technique is not quite to "give away the razor to sell the blades," but by continually adding to the list of applications it can develop each computer purchaser into a source of recurring revenue. Typical of these program products are:

- Bill-paying optimization tactics
- Christmas card address generator (outputs onto gummed labels)
- Pantry inventory control
- IRS 1040
- Little League player statistics package

The marketing department, on the basis of a nationwide survey, advises PPP to invest in an applications package to allow lonely customers to play games with their computer. The project is approved, and the product development department is given the task and funding to produce a program that will, at the user's discretion, play backgammon, bridge, or craps.

The product analysts draft a requirements specification describing the general rules for the displays it wants to see on the CRT, the techniques for user interaction it believes will best simulate the real-world game play, and, under the "applicable documents" paragraph of the specification, lists Hoyle as the source for game rules.

The specification is, in effect, the work order for the software design group of the product development department. Nothing in the games package is similar to work they have done before, so they find a top-down decomposition process a good place to start. Their first impression of the specification is that the work to be done is too much for one person to accomplish if the program is to be ready in time to meet the marketing department's goal of the holiday season. They divide the package into three major sections, each corresponding to one of the games, and a fourth section, Executive control, to do little more than offer the player a choice of games and provide a means of storing the status of any game if play has to be interrupted. The design team now has a scheme for partitioning the work as shown in Fig. 3.3.

In addition to taking a first cut at partitioning the problem, the designers also define a task to investigate techniques for generating appropriate graphical displays. One person is immediately assigned the task, which has to do with such things as forming icons (e.g., chess pieces), backgrounds (e.g., chessboard), and updating the display in response to mouse input.

Returning to the partitioning problem, the design team now analyzes each of the three main sections. Craps, they believe, will be a fairly modest program, and needs no further thought until they are ready for detailed design. Backgammon and Bridge, on the other hand, seem much more formidable. Adopting the tactic of divide and conquer, they proceed to decompose these two games into compartmented processes or segments. This allows each of these games to be handled not as a single problem of great complexity, but as the aggregate of several smaller problems they can get their arms around. The result is seen in Fig. 3.4. Note that neither Fig. 3.3 nor Fig. 3.4 represent a

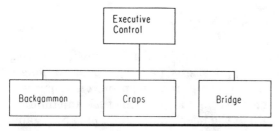

Figure 3.3 Zeroeth iteration of game hierarchy.

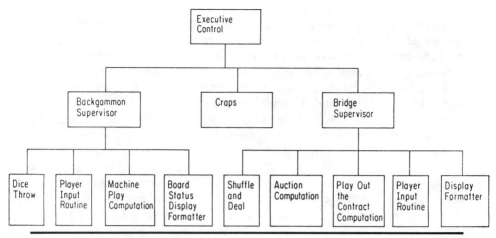

Figure 3.4 First iteration of game hierarchy.

procedure calling sequence. The boxes on the diagrams depict tasks and certain hierarchical relations that the designers will have to respect in their detailed design. Actually, in Fig. 3.4, they could have just as easily shown the Backgammon supervisor on the same line as the other four elements, all five under a box simply reading "Backgammon." Either depiction will result in the same code.

In Fig. 3.4 we see the game of backgammon, as it will be implemented for a computer, divided into five separate parts: a supervisor to maintain continuity, a component to simulate the throw of dice, code to input the player's choice of the moves that can be made with the player's simulated throw of the dice, software to determine the computer's best play based on its simulated dice throw, and a component to display the current game status. The four parts are not of equal magnitude with regard to programming difficulty or (anticipated) size, but, as viewed by the designers, they are of equal hierarchical rank.

Similarly, Bridge has been decomposed into six parts. Shuffle and Deal will be used to initialize each hand. Auction computation will have to bid for three of the chairs at the table, including the human player's simulated partner. Once bidding has closed, the computer will have to be equipped either to play declarer and one of the defenders, both of the defenders, or declarer and both of the defenders. This last implies that the human player's partner has won the auction, with the result that the human player will be dummy to three computer-simulated players. In their conceptual study, the product analysts had given considerable thought to the merit of this. They finally decided that a public accustomed to being told on the telephone "Hi, my name is Bill. I'm a computer. If you have a touch-tone phone, press 1 now ..." is ready to passively follow any sequence of computer instructions. Thus, the computer will have to play a variety of roles after bidding has closed and the contract is to be played out. The Bridge Supervisor will keep a running score, remember who is vulnerable and who is not, and so on.

Finally, there must be a way to input the player's bids and choice of cards to be played; and a display for showing each bid, the player's hand as dealt and as diminished during play, dummy, and the cards played each trick by the other "players."

At this point, the game problem has given way to a dozen or so smaller ones, but two of them, Machine play computation and Play out the contract computation are still too complex to be grasped with a certitude sufficient to allow detailed design to proceed. A further decomposition to the next hierarchical level is required, leading to the diagram of Fig. 3.5.

Let's assume that with this second iteration, the top level designers have decided that the principal parts of the program have been defined adequately for the purpose of those programmers who will perform the detailed design for each of the components. Although finished with partitioning the problem, the top-level designers have more to do. They need to specify what each of the components is supposed to do. To a large extent, the component specifications can contain references back to the technical specification, apportioning parts of that document to the defined components, but certain details are now known that did not appear in the technical specification. For example, Display Com-

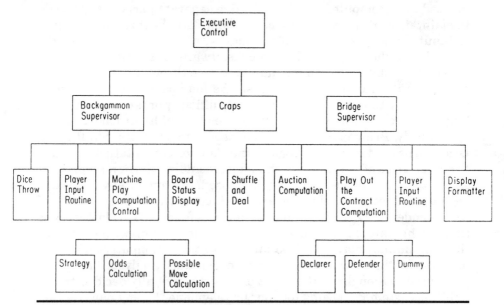

Figure 3.5 Second iteration of game hierarchy.

putation will benefit from the work done by the designer assigned to graphical matters. (Remember her?)

Even as they were decomposing the problem space into multiple compartmented solution spaces, the designers were roughing out data structures. Chess, for example, would need an 8-by-8 matrix containing a code for the piece located in each square. They settled on an alphanumeric code. B or W followed by 1 through 7 (empty, pawn, ... king). Bridge would require a 4-by-13 matrix to contain all the hands. Again, an alphanumeric code for each entry: N,E,S,W for the "player" and 1 through 14 for the card (played, deuce, ... ace). By the time the designers had finished decomposing the problem to their satisfaction, they had also designed all the system data.

As they continue to work with the temporarily frozen hierarchical design, the team notes a requirement common to all three games. To Throw the Dice for either Backgammon or Craps, or to Shuffle the Cards for Bridge, a random function generator is required. The designers decide to make this a utility, available as a *procedure* (or *subroutine*) *call* or as a *function call.** As many utilities as possible are identified during preliminary design, but others may well be added later as designers talk with each other. A requirements specification is prepared for the random function generator.

Bridge took the most thought. Before the top-level designers were through with Bridge, they had passed the requirements specification for Craps to the detailed designers. By allowing them to dig into the details of Craps at the earliest possible time, they should be able to be reassigned to Bridge when it is ready for detailing.

By the time PPP started to implement the Craps specification, the document was able to refer to interfaces with the utilities that had been identified, to the mechanism required to write the status of Craps (actually, just the player's bankroll) to disk if play were suspended before the player went broke, and to the work done by the analyst looking into graphics. (Remember her?) Ideally, PPP would like to have seen the specification for the Craps component include the complete interface with any graphics data elements and utility routines. To do so, however, would be to wait another few weeks, impairing the efficiency of staff deployment considered necessary to ship product before the holidays. The Craps designers will have to play it loose on the graphics interface, staying in constant touch with the analyst and reading all the E-mail she sent out. Such is the inefficiency entailed by the bottom-up use of inchoate graphics data sets and utility procedures, but it happens all the time.

---

*Functions are similar to procedures, but return a single value. For example, executing $x := (\theta)$ results in the function subprogram *sin* returning the value of the sine of θ and assigning that value to x.

The early pages of this chapter dealt with some of the activity that goes on during detailed design. However, Nancy's design of Sam's linear algebra problem did not serve to introduce the concept of *modularity*, the division of a program into articulated procedures (subroutines, or most generally, subprograms). We do so now.

The small team assigned to Craps met to identify the individual computable elements of a craps game. As it happens, none of them had ever played it. For PPP, which was learning the hard way that an effective quality system requires effective alignment of personnel and tasks, there was nothing for it but to send the whole team to Las Vegas for a few days of education.

In the mornings, after a night of intensive education, the team would gather to discuss what they had learned. They arrived at this list of major computable functions:

- The House—Rather like a main line program, it would determine the next major function needing execution according to house rules.

- First roll—Enter bet, roll the dice, end if craps or a natural, calculate odds otherwise and permit bet behind the line to be entered.

- Subsequent rolls—Roll the dice, end if craps, end if point is matched, repeat if neither.

- Adjust bankroll, taking into account initial and supplementary bets.

- Verisimilitude—Messages like "Okay Big Spender, move over for the next guy," interruptions for a hostess icon to appear with a tray of drinks, and similar effects to enhance the player's fantasy.

The team decided to make each of these a separate procedure. Recalling Chap. 3, a procedure is a set of declarations and executable statements that can be invoked by code elsewhere, and on completing its task returns control to the code that called it. By writing a set of procedures rather than one monolithic program, they expected to produce a program more understandable and more easily modified. Their strategy for identifying the separate procedures was simple, unlike the more thoughtful strategies found in Chap. 5, but appropriate for the simplicity of the problem. In any case, what they wanted was a set of procedures that had as little to do with each other as possible. In this manner,

> each procedure could be coded with the programmer's having minimum knowledge of how other procedures worked, could be modified with minimum likelihood of affecting other procedures. In short, the programmers intended to build a modular program, one whose parts were largely independent of each other.

These parts, along with the connection to utilities noted earlier, and their connections are shown in Fig. 3.6.

Before leaving the topic of design, let's consider how PPP might have approached the game package if they employed the O-O paradigm. Let's assume they already had a random function generator that issued a new integer when given a message to do so. Let us further assume that they had an inventory of graphic primitive objects—parts that could be used to build up more complex icons. For example, if they had a cube that could respond to messages to rotate (perhaps something originally designed for a CAD program) they could form new objects by inheriting the characteristics of the cube and adding new data in the form of dots.

Given these parts, PPP might have decided that it needed such Craps objects as bankrolls, messages to the player, a "table" on which to place bets, and a stickman to decide the outcome of each roll. At this point we might note that O-O objects, unlike callable procedures, retain their state between activations. Thus the stickman could hold such information as the point that the player is trying to make. Rolling the dice would mean getting two integers from the random function generator, and using the two integers to determine the number of rotations of each die. (Message to die object: "Wherever we last left you, rotate 11 times.") To make things more realistic, PPP might have added

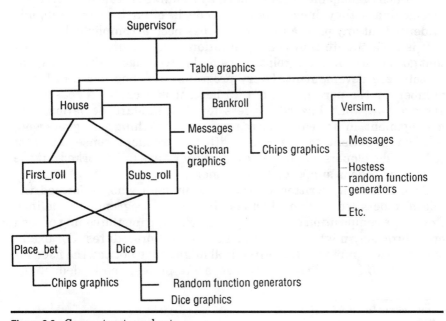

Figure 3.6 Craps structure chart.

forward motion to the die object and rotation in more than one axis at a time—all subject to additional random messages. Of course, not only do the dice have to rest with a graphically readable result, but the stickman needs to know the result.

Without laboring the illustration with further detail, let us jump to object definition. Each time the programmers need a new object, they look at the objects (as classes) that exist,* consider what is useful to inherit, and—for subsequent applications—define the new object in as much generality as they can, even if it means that the object they really need has to be further defined as a daughter of the new one.[†]

3.5 Code, Debug, and Test

In a sense, coding is the most prominent phase of software development, generating the first output that is unique to computer software. The analysis phase is common to any development effort, hardware or software, and design is patently analogous to the "black-box" design phase of systems engineering. Even for detailed design we can find patterns outside of computation: the schematic and logic diagrams of electronics engineering, or the process of determining the best method of extracting the meat from a 4 pound lobster.

Also, for the small programs that we exclude from our concern, but with which management personnel may be familiar from data processing seminars they have attended, code is often the first tangible evidence that any programming work has been accomplished.

It is unfortunate that code generation is so prominent. The effort that goes into coding is a relatively small percentage of the total spent on software development. Every programming shop has a different number for the percentage, but 15 percent is probably a reasonable average (we won't hazard a guess for the standard deviation). Yet management, in its search for reassurance that things are going well, is often impatient to see code, with the frequent consequence of software developers writing code before they have fully worked out the design the code is supposed to implement.

Code is usually written by the programmers who performed the relevant detailed design. Just as the Craps programmers defined Craps as a composition of several procedures, during the coding of each procedure they might have defined additional procedures. For example, the programmer coding First_Roll might have noticed the need for the same 10 lines of code in two separate places, one to deduct the

---

*Bottom-up thinking.

[†]Top-down thinking.

initial bet from the bankroll and the other to deduct a bet placed behind the line. Both could be replaced by a procedure call (the amount of the bet input by the player at the appropriate time), and the 10 lines revised to fit the form of a separate procedure.

With the ubiquitous terminals (including desktop computers and workstations) now found in programming shops, programmers generally do their coding directly on the keyboard. After getting a successful compile, the programmer runs the first test case, one of several of the programmer's own device. A cautious programmer might be content with a first test case designed simply to determine if the procedure completes its task, correctly or incorrectly, and returns to the right place. Each test case may well result in disappointing results. This requires debugging.

We distinguish between the terms *debug* and *test*. They are used in conjunction with each other so frequently that the phrase *debug and test* has the ring of an old vaudeville team or a brokerage firm. Nevertheless, each of the words has a distinct meaning. *Debug* means the removal of faults discovered by the test. We might extend the meaning of debug to include special tests run to help diagnose the reason that a planned test did not succeed. *Test* means execution, or set of executions, of the program for the purpose of exercising the code. (We'll go into detail on test purposes in Chap. 7.) That a program was executed with no evidence of error is no proof that it contains no errors. Program errors are sensitive to the specifics of the data being processed.

Low-level tests

It is impossible to predict whether a program contains a particular fault or not. However, there is a class of fault that can be depended upon to affect the accuracy of mathematical operations, and one objective of testing is the measurement of the effect. These errors are those of truncation and rounding off; the one resulting from the evaluation of functions (e.g., sin x) by a finite approximation to an infinite series expansion, and the other attributable to the finite word length available for arithmetic operations. These are not programming errors in the sense of mistakes. If the measured errors are no greater than those predicted during the detailed design analyses, the programmers are satisfied with the test results.

In contrast to measurable errors that reflect mathematical limitations rather than programmer laxity, there are programming errors that the programmer wants to find and eliminate. Finding errors can be simple or difficult, depending on the subtlety of the fault. Simple ones can often be found by studying the code or by comparing the code to the design documentation. The more intractable ones require the use of diagnostic aids. The most common of these are *trace* aids and *source level debugging* provided by the systems software, and additional program statements inserted by the programmer to output certain suspect variables. The last can be combined with either of the first two. With only limited selectivity, trace routines output the results of every computation made by the program. Source level debuggers provide much greater selectivity, allowing the programmer to see the values taken on by selected variables during execution.

In the days of assembler language programming, the only tools a programmer was likely to have were *breakpoint* and *dump*. Breakpoint outputs the contents of all the machine registers and status flags and dumps output selected blocks of memory. The programmer would incorporate the breakpoint or dump instructions in the program, submit the program to a computer operator for assembly and execution, and then await the results. After a wait of anywhere from a half-hour to a day, the programmer would pore over the pages of octal or hexadecimal numbers provided by the computer. Plainly, one had to carefully plan each debug run to get the most out of it. In contrast, today's programmers are casual about designing test runs, perhaps running four diagnostic tests an hour, each with easily interpretable results.

The level at which tests are conducted varies from shop to shop. PPP might well choose to have each of the procedures shown in Fig. 3.6 separately tested. To go below that level would probably represent overkill. The lowest level at which one plans tests is generally called either *unit test* or *module test*.

Testing a module requires that it be executed, and further requires that it be given some input data to be processed. If the module is a monolithic program, no special provision is needed to cause it to be executed. If it is a procedure or group of procedures, however, as indeed most modules are, it will not execute until it is invoked by other code. A program to call the module, provide input to it, and output the results is called a *test driver*. Test drivers must be programmed as part of the software development effort. A driver may be given the capability of generating and reporting a number of test cases, or it may have the limitation of only a single, static test. The choice depends on the difficulty of generating dynamic tests and on the plan for the tests that will follow.

Testing is not the only way to discover faults at the module level. In one of several types of review formats, people can manually find faults in code. Many programmers today also have access to *static analysis* tools, a mechanized technique for finding faults. Both of these are discussed in greater detail in Chap. 7, which also covers reviews and automated analysis of design artifacts. While few have suggested that one forgo all module-level testing, reviews and static analysis have the potential of finding more faults than dynamic testing. They can also find defects that testing cannot. For example, consider this dialogue:

"Suppose you found a wallet containing a million dollars. What would you do?"

"No question about it. If it belonged to a poor person I'd definitely return it."

The computer analogy is found in

```
BEGIN
 TOTAL := 0;
 FOR I WITHIN RANGE OF 1 TO 10
 ADD BEANS (I) TO TOTAL;
 IF (I > 11) THEN CALL ERROR_HANDLING
END
```

Here, THEN CALL ERROR_HANDLING can never be executed. While seemingly harmless, errors like this account for code that tests will not exercise. A subsequent change to the program, perhaps to fix another error, may now make it possible to execute the statement (or in the more common instance, group of statements), leaving executable but previously untested code in the program. Although tests will not find this kind of an error, reviews or static analysis can.

Integration and top-down testing

The integration of software parts into a working whole implies not the trivial linking process, but the testing required to demonstrate that the whole works. Using a graphic model, integration is the act of testing the edges of the modules after module-level tests have checked operation within the edges. Although conceptually useful, the trouble with the model is that one might infer from it that integration tests are themselves trivial; modules span finite space, while edges occupy none. However, this belies the usual experience, where integration consumes more workhours of effort than the sum of all the module tests. The problem decomposition described earlier was presented as a means of devolving a complex, often multifaceted, problem into small problems, each easily grasped in its entirety. In integration, no matter how careful the earlier design, the complexity of the problem is reconstituted. This is not to imply that careful design does not have a favorable effect on integration; it certainly does. But even with the most quality-driven design approach, it remains that integration is often the greater part of testing.

In theory, PPP could simply link the small main line of its game package with all its procedures and start running tests. People have actually tried to do this. However, doing so inevitably results in a program that bombs out (as the expression has it) as soon as the figurative switch is closed. That's okay. We do not expect software to work the first time. The problem is that it is exceedingly difficult to find out why the program bombed out when the pieces were imploded in a single step.

Which leads to the universal technique of incremental integration, for which we have two diametrically opposite classic techniques: bottom-up and top-down. (Sound familiar?) If PPP favored bottom-up integration, they would first integrate each group of procedures that comprises one of the blocks found in Fig. 3.5. Next, for each of the three games they would integrate all the game's procedures (i.e., testing at the level of Fig. 3.4). Finally, they would integrate the three games into a complete system. In brief, they would build a pyramid, as pyramids have always been built, from the ground up.

Top-down integration, by contrast, is a decidedly odd way to build a pyramid. Taking a fairly canonical view of it (we'll talk about a variant in a just a bit), PPP would start with Executive Control, linking it with substitutes for the three games and any utilities directly invoked by Executive Control. These substitutes, called *stubs*, are relatively simpleminded replacements for the routines whose names they bear, responding to calls from Executive Control with predetermined rote responses. A driver may still be required to provide test stimuli for some applications (not for the games package, which is user-driven), but no driver is required to invoke modules under test. The mode of operation here is quite the opposite of bottom-up integration: stubs replace modules invoked by the module under test. In our example, Executive Control does little beyond offering the player a choice of games and storing game status. We see more of the test methodology as we head toward the bottom of the pyramid. The game stubs are replaced, perhaps one at a time, perhaps all three at once, by the Backgammon and Bridge Supervisors and by the Craps procedure that Executive Control directly calls. Each of these, however, requires that the routines they call be stubbed off.

Recall that Craps was the first game scheduled for completion. We would expect that if PPP uses top-down integration, they would integrate all of Craps before the other games were ready for testing. Working top-down, just as in the bottom-up integration model, they have the option of integrating the several parts of the system at different times. At any rate, at each step stubs are used to substitute for the procedures immediately subordinate to those in the program load.*

The games package, we noted, requires no driver to provide input stimuli. If, as in the general case, a driver were required, PPP would probably want to integrate input routines as quickly as possible, skewing the integration sequence as necessary. This would permit a greater variety of input at less programming cost. For the games package, PPP will want to integrate the code that produces screen output as quickly as possible to simplify the evaluation of test results.

In this canonical model of top-down integration, you may wonder if the integration test for Executive Control would be any different from the unit test of that module. Not really. The integration tests might well be used to replace the unit tests. Indeed, the integration tests performed for any module upon its introduction to the system may be the de facto module-level test of the routine. In pure top-down testing, one does not do separate module-level testing. Before discussing a variant of the canonical model, we need to look at the relative merits of top-down and bottom-up testing.

One of the arguments raised by top-down advocates is that stubs are easier to construct than test drivers. Sometimes. Except for stubs that do little more than return as soon as they have been called, the size and complexity of stubs can easily approach, and sometimes surpass, that of drivers.

In most software, control more or less monotonically decreases from the capstone of the pyramid to the bottom layer of blocks. If one wants to expose the conditions of program control to as many variations as possible, it makes good sense to start at the top and work down. In this fashion, the upper modules get more exercise than the ones that have less influence on program flow. Alternatively, one may want to exercise the computational kernels at the bottom as much as possible. Put them in place at the start and work upward. As each block is cemented in place above the bottom ones, the hierarchically disadvantaged modules may get new stimuli. Pure top-down testing can make it very difficult to fashion test stimuli that will exercise a low-level module with input capable of covering the module's input domain.

More often than not, top-down testing departs from the canonical model to incorporate elements of both top-down and bottom-up integration. A hybrid strategy calls for modules to first be tested in a stand-alone or stand-in-a-group mode, and for the tested modules to be linked into program loads incrementally built from the top down.

---

*During the test, a program load consists of actual product code along with such stubs, drivers, and dummy data required for the test.

Glenford Myers[8] calls this modified top-down testing. Although it requires both drivers and stubs, it requires no sacrifice of test objectives addressing quality.

How much testing?

Much has been written on the topic of what represents adequate testing. Tests themselves are but jabs and thrusts used to sound the invisible structure of a program. Every now and again a weakness becomes manifest, and the defect is brought to light. The cumulative number of defects found at any point gives little clue to the number remaining. Yet somehow one must determine when it is appropriate to terminate the test phase.

"When" often depends on the type of program. For programs concerned with the processing of input limited in the number of discrete variations of the data environment, each test is concluded when each of the test conditions stipulated in the test procedure has been satisfied. This is typical of a process control program, where, although the input data may vary widely in range, there is normally but one set of measurements being processed. It is also representative of most mathematical programs dealing with continuous variables. It certainly is not typical of compilers, nor is it of programs developed to perform discrete simulations, process IS data, interface with personal computer users, or make real-time air traffic control decisions. For most software, the number of data conditions that differ in kind as well as degree is too great to be totally delineated in a test procedure. For programs as these, one could do worse than evaluate the rate at which faults are found in response to stimuli.

Figure 3.7 depicts the pattern of fault discovery that may be anticipated during test, once all the pieces are in place. Normal start-up

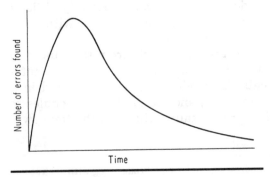

Figure 3.7   Fault discovery rate.

difficulties may preclude the rate of testing that will be obtained later. So at the beginning, we will see few faults found per unit of calendar time. As testing becomes more efficient, we find an early peak in the fault detection frequency rate. Assuming the number of new faults introduced by the corrections is small compared to the number discovered, the rate of discovery thereafter should decrease in a generally exponential manner. There is considerable evidence that the rate of decrease is predictable enough to permit quantitative conclusions to be drawn from the discovery rate data. We shall return to this in our final chapter.

As drawn, the number of new faults becomes asymptotic to a fault-free condition. At some point, after several days or weeks of fault-free performance, testers are tempted to conclude that all the faults that testing will uncover have, in fact, been found. Testing is over. It is also possible that for a variety of causes—complexity, weak structure, inadequate controls—the rate at which the fix process introduces faults approaches the rate at which faults are removed. This situation prepares the ground for a decision to terminate further testing even though the program is known to have defects. This may sound like heresy to quality managers, but is fairly common in software, provided no serious faults are still being uncovered. This is why IS software and the software used on personal computers is often delivered with *undocumented features* (known bugs with documented workarounds).

Qualification

The testing we have discussed thus far is often called *development testing*. It is the testing that developers perform to demonstrate to themselves that they have successfully performed the task assigned them. They have gotten the bugs out of the system, they have found out how accurately it can perform certain operations, and they have demonstrated compliance to requirements as they understood them. Integration may have been planned and conducted by staff other than those responsible for design and code (nevertheless, members of the development community).

Qualification is quite another matter. *Qualification* is the formal process of demonstrating that the software satisfies its purpose. Test cases are designed based on both the technical specification and any specifications from which the technical specification derived. Qualification may be as simple as subjecting the production code to test cases used earlier to demonstrate a prototype. Alternatively, qualification may require test cases citing chapter and verse of the external requirements, test scripts to ensure that the test cases are carried out as planned, demonstration with voluminous amounts of data, and formal demonstration of correct operation not only with respect to the input domain but the output domain as well. Qualification may also entail using the software in-house before releasing it to others. For example, a DBMS destined for the general marketplace may first be used by an appropriate department within the producer's company. This is called *alpha testing*. Qualification of a product produced for a specific customer may be witnessed by that customer (acceptance testing). The customer may even use the software as part of the qualification process.

In all but the most informal programming shops, qualification is planned and conducted by people apart from the development group. Likely qualifiers come from the Quality Department, Customer Service, and Marketing. The important thing is that the test cases must be designed with respect to external specifications, to the exclusion of internal specifications, and that the testers' observations must remain uninfluenced by knowledge of internal processing details.

3.6   Installation and Evaluation

Software is seldom used where it is built. A compiler developed in the shop of a software publisher may be transported to hundreds of offices throughout the world. The compiler may have to work on hardware platforms and under operating systems other than the ones used by the publisher, and will almost always be used with a number of different sets of peripheral equipment. A telephone switch containing a million lines of code may be installed in 100 different exchanges, each with its own set of interfaces to other exchanges and long-distance carriers.

The first installation of a program in conditions representative of its real service life often is accompanied by operational difficulties. These may be traceable back to defects originating in code, design, the software specification, or even the concept. In some cases, the problem can be attributed to incorrect or vague documentation. In any event, before it is possible to determine how well the program performs its function, it must be made to play as its designers intended it. This is analogous to the earlier debugging process, except debugging tools have little to do with it.

We also have programs that perform precisely as specified, yet still do not satisfy the service environment. The user manuals may be poor. Backgammon may lose too easily to most players and Bridge bidding decisions may be viewed as too conservative. The telephone switch may exhibit an unforeseen failure mode if another switch in the network fails. An IS application that ran fine on a mainframe may run too slowly when reinstalled on a local area network.

For such large-scale embedded software systems as telephone switches, the software producer will attend or even control each installation. For most software, however, installation is up to the software's new owner. To reduce the likelihood of releasing software of doubtful quality to the general marketplace, software producers usually precede general release with a provisional release to a relatively small group of users who get the software before their colleagues (or competitors) in exchange for providing the producer with evaluation information. This practice, called *beta testing,* is almost universal for systems software and for updates of applications programs.

The beta testers are the final judges of the usability of software, supporting documentation, and sometimes software support. The practice of beta testing, which predates our current awareness of TQM by a decade, has served the purposes of both final evaluation and market research. Beta testers not only complain that some things are too hard to do or do not work as advertised, they also advise the producer of new features they would like to see in the next release.

Beta testers may provide enough negative feedback to send the product back to the drawing board for further work, leading to a second and perhaps a third beta release. Products have been known to remain in beta test for over a year. This is a costly way to ensure the quality of software, but it speaks well for the commitment of management to satisfy customers.

Software, like any other product produced for a specific customer will, of course, be subject to whatever contractual stipulations exist to govern installation and on-site evaluation. Generally, the price includes whatever the producer believes support during installation and fine tuning after evaluation will require. Explicit warranties to cover the product after acceptance are seldom seen, however.

3.7   Operation and Maintenance

Unlike toasters, automobiles, and tennis balls, large computer programs tend to live forever. They may change a bit from year to year (DOS, DOS 2.0, DOS 2.1, DOS 3.0, and so on) as new features are added or the software is adapted to different hardware or software platforms, but code laid down at a product's inception is likely to remain largely intact through two decades or more of product evolution.

We call the subject life cycle phase *operation* or, as here, *operation and maintenance.* From a software management point of view, operation is a matter of providing customer support. When customers have problems in installing or using software, problems that may or may not be derived from bugs, we have the responsibility of providing support. *Support* takes many forms, but the primary means of support is usually an easily identified telephone number. To keep customers satisfied, the person who answers the call (we're not referring to humanoids who talk the caller through a labyrinth of touch-tone choices) should be able to solve most problems on the spot. The customer service staff should also be able to identify the programmers in the back room who can handle more recondite problems, and, if unable to transfer to the correct programmer, should arrange to have the programmer call the customer.

Increasingly, telephone support is being augmented by electronic bulletin boards. Among the several advantages to the producer, a bulletin board allows immediate posting of notices that, when read by the user directly after logging on, may obviate the user's need for conversation with the customer support staff. This is a classic case of reducing cost while increasing customer satisfaction.

The extent that a product will require customer support depends not only on the complexity of the product, but—especially a few releases down the road—on how well the product has been maintained. And maintenance is a big part of programming. Estimates vary, but maintenance accounts for as much as 70 percent of all programming costs. "Maintenance," however, is an umbrella term covering several types of programming activity. In 1976, E.B. Swanson provided a classification scheme for maintenance that has gained wide acceptance in the industry:

- Corrective
- Adaptive
- Perfective[9]

Corrective maintenance is the easiest to understand. It is not uncommon for faults to remain hidden until prompted by an input data set never before presented to the software or by a combination of data and operational modes. Some of these faults may even be known to the designers, but left in for one reason or another. "Let's not worry about that one, Fred. Who's going to open with a bid of four diamonds?" Unfortunately, within a week of receiving his game package from PPP, Eli, recently returned from a Mediterranean cruise in which he had learned the new Minoan bidding system, did just that. Instantly, the monitor of his PPP computer started displaying lines of gibberish. Eli reinitialized, repeated the bid, and got the same response.

The customer service rep assigned to Games (her cue is the response to "Press 4 Now") had to refer the problem to the programming staff. Assigned problem report #42, Eli's difficulty resulted in the following actions:

1. A caveat was printed for insertion in the user manual, "Opening bids of four diamonds may result in an unpredictable response," and

2. A fix was planned for Release 1.1, scheduled for the following January.

More generally, the problems reported by users derive from faults not previously known to the authors of the program. If the problem is adequately documented by the user, it can be recreated in the programming shop, the essential step that must be taken before the cause of the problem is found. For most software, it is simple to recreate the problem. For embedded software, it may be necessary to maintain a complex hardware test fixture to provide operational support, and even then the programming staff may have difficulty if the problem reporter was unable to capture the exact circumstances attending the incident reported.

Adaptive maintenance is the response to a change in a program's operating circumstances. A word processor sold to personal computer owners is modified to operate under Windows. A CAD drawing package, originally designed to work on minicomputers is modified to work on file servers connected to workstations with high-resolution monitors. An inventory control system, programmed for one DBMS, gets all new system calls to work on the DBMS just adopted as the company-wide standard. Software for an airborne fire control system has to be revised when the Air Force decides to install the same system on a second type of fighter plane. A telephone switch designed for the telecommunications protocols of a European PTT is modified to work in an emerging African country. In brief, adaptive maintenance has to do with modifying software for new operational environments. By one reckoning, adaptive maintenance accounts for a quarter of all maintenance dollars, beating out corrective maintenance, which accounts for a fifth.[10] The most costly maintenance category, perfective, consumes 55 percent of maintenance costs.

Perfective maintenance is the name given to enhancements of all kinds: New features, old features made more convenient, old features made more useful. Caller identification is added to the software of a telephone switch. A new radar is added to the library of an electronics countermeasures system. A general ledger program can now accommodate LIFO as well as FIFO. A Danzig tableau optimization feature is added to a spreadsheet. PPP adds the doubling cube feature to Backgammon. Packaged along with other improvements, the ability to select text blocks either backwards or forwards is added to a word processor.

Perfective maintenance, and often adaptive maintenance as well, require the full set of activities depicted in Fig. 3.1. Thus, does the "software life cycle" become a cycle.

From a pre-TQM perspective, management's top priority in the quality of maintenance programming is preserving the viability of product. Poor maintenance can cause gradual product degradation: crumbling software structure, inconsistent data, increased fault density, outdated documentation. From release to release, the product gets buggier, more costly to maintain and support, and more troublesome for customers to use, as in Fig. 3.8. The product is barely maintainable. Moreover, word has gotten around and few customers bought the latest release. The company announces they will terminate support next March, yielding marketshare and revenue from development long since written off. All because the product cannot be kept current.

TQM dictates that we should give customer satisfaction our maintenance priorities. Accordingly, while we cannot afford to let up on maintaining the longevity of the product through quality programming practices, we need also consider the time it takes to fix a problem once reported, the time it takes a user to install a fix or new feature, and the distribution of a fix not just to the customer who reported it but to all affected users. Going further, we need to make it easy for our customers to tell us the enhancements they would like to see in the next release, perhaps the next three releases.

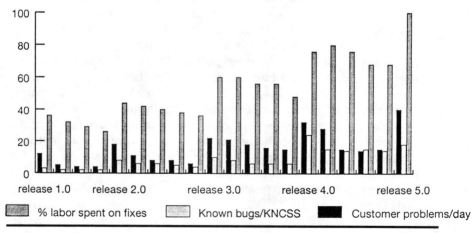

Figure 3.8 Software out of control. (Note: KNCSS = thousands of lines of noncomment source code.)

3.8   People Who Program

One of the seven categories of criteria for the Malcolm Baldrige National Quality Award—Category 4, "Human Resources Development and Management"—is entirely given over to people.* From the foregoing survey of the life cycle of software, it should be evident that the software business is archetypically people-intensive. The reader who has had little firsthand exposure to software may be curious about programmers. We shall say very little, however, since generalities, shaky under the best circumstances, seem especially difficult to apply to those who toil in the vineyards of software.

For example, consider education. If we were interested in accountants, we could be reasonably confident that most had degrees in accounting; if clergy, we could expect degrees in divinity. But programmers? The designers of systems software may have any degree conceivable, math and computer science being favorites, and perhaps none. Applications programmers in IS frequently have bachelor's degrees in business or math; many are graduates of technical training schools. More recent entrants may have degrees in computer science or, rarely, software engineering. Scientific programmers have degrees in the physical sciences, math, or engineering. Usually. The education of programmers of embedded software shows a distribution similar to that of the scientific programmers, except that since these people often become deeply involved in the systems aspects of the problem, their employers tend to prefer to hire engineering graduates.

As we forewarned, these are the grossest of generalities. We know of programmers with education in music, botany, and medieval history who are doing quite well in the field. Whatever their education, good programmers have to have an aptitude for reasoning.

In some organizations, most frequently large ones involved in IS, programming people are horizontally segregated. That is, requirements are defined by systems analysts, design—or at least preliminary design—by program analysts. The term *programmers* is reserved for those doing detailed design and writing code. Testing is performed by the *program analysts,* and in-house evaluation is left for the *systems analysts.* For an entirely different view consider embedded software: we are likely to find systems engineering writing the technical specifications and homogenous (except for titles reflecting experience) programming teams organized to do everything else, except that we may find separate test teams for integration testing.

Of the largest professional organizations serving the software community, three dominate. The Data Processing Management Association

---

*"People" is an old-fashioned word meaning human resources.

(DPMA) appeals mostly to those in IS. The Association for Computing Machinery (ACM), with a scholarly quarterly among its many periodicals, draws heavily from academe, although scarcely to the exclusion of industry and government. The Computer Society of the Institute of Electrical and Electronic Engineers (IEEE) publishes the greatest number of papers and articles directed to software engineering.

Software engineering is one of the two major influences behind software quality assurance. (To the extent that it is congruent with TQM, the other is the quality discipline.) We have used the term *software engineering* several times now without defining it, and if any term needs definition this one does. So to it. The term was coined by Frederich Bauer in 1967 at a Brussels meeting of the Study Group on Computer Science established by the NATO Science Committee. At the meeting, Bauer, according to a letter[11] he later wrote, used the phrase "'software engineering' in contrast to software tinkering." He was subsequently charged by the NATO Science Committee to organize an international conference under the title "Software Engineering." The conference, held in 1968 in Garmisch, West Germany, turned out to be a landmark in the development of programming as a discipline.

We still use software engineering as the catchall phrase to mean a systematic approach to computer programming, treating both technology and the management of technology. Unfortunately, software engineering has also come to mean:

1. The programming of embedded software.
2. Good programming.
3. Real good programming, and sometimes,
4. Just plain programming.

We use it in this book only in the sense of a programming discipline.

Some computer programmers spend their entire careers within one programming paradigm, using but one programming language. Most, however, migrate to a different language every now and again, and a few pull up stakes and move to a different paradigm. Programmers usually learn new languages on their own, but languages are sometimes taught in seminars; especially such "hot" languages as C++ or Ada. In moving to a new paradigm, programmers usually feel more comfortable if guided by a seminar or university course. For example, a programmer may learn C++, a language that supports O-O, but may not have the visceral feel for using the language within the O-O paradigm. Seminars are also the usual way to introduce a new process model.

With modern programming practices and a marketplace that has grown with unprecedented swiftness, programmers have collectively overrun society with the fruit of their ingenuity and energy. The fruit does, however, occasionally harbor worms, the subject of the next chapter.

3.9 Summary

1. The computer programs that present problems of control and quality are those programs that are important to people at a distinct remove from the programmers and that hold the promise of much future use. Such programs require the coordinated efforts of several groups of people.

2. Concept and analysis is the name we give to that phase of software development in which the requirement for computation and a rough notion of the role that software will play are introduced.

3. Several process models are in use to describe the overall approach to defining technical requirements, designing, coding, and testing.

4. Process models start with the most abstract solution (top-down models) or the most concrete (bottom-up models) or some combination of both. Some models use iteration, and some are tied closely to specific programming paradigms.

5. Customer or marketing requirements need to be translated into technical specifications to which programmers can design. There is a tendency, often understandable but troublesome, to blur the distinction between requirements and design.

6. Among other advantages, rapid prototyping enables customers to have direct input to technical specifications.

7. Project plans commonly are prepared to cover development (including testing), configuration management, and quality.

8. Dividing a single complex problem into a set of simpler problems underlies all design strategies. The division is accomplished during preliminary design, along with much of the required data design and (often) some experimentation.

9. Actual design of the components identified during preliminary design is accomplished by a detailed design activity, which leads directly to coding.

10. The generation of code, although only one of many activities of software development, is given an untoward amount of attention by management, who often view it as the first real output of the programming process.

11. Tests reveal program faults. Debugging is the process of finding and removing those faults.

12. Individual program modules may be first tested separately, in small groups, or when added to an evolving software structure.

13. Regardless of the method of module testing, software systems are put together piece by piece in an incremental integration test activity.

14. It is not always possible to eliminate all the bugs in a program. In the process of fixing old problems, it is even possible to introduce new ones at the same rate at which faults are removed.

15. In many cases, testing is concluded only when the rate of fault discovery approaches zero as a limit.

16. Qualification is a formal test activity to ensure the readiness of software for release.

17. Certain software products require programmer support when the product is installed.

18. In a process called beta testing, producers provide a sample of the marketplace with a provisional release of the product, which the users evaluate in the course of normal use.

19. Software maintenance may be divided into three categories: corrective (removing latent faults), adaptive (accommodating new operating environments), and perfective (improving or adding to product capability). The sum of all three accounts for the greater part of all programming costs.

20. Despite a great diversity of backgrounds of the people who develop software, they form a professional community.

21. Software engineering, the name given to the treatment of software development as a programming discipline, underlies software TQM.

References

1. Henderson-Sellers, Brian and Edwards, Julian. "The Object-Oriented Systems Life Cycle," *CACM*, Vol. 33, No. 9, September 1990, pp. 143-159.
2. Boehm, Barry W. "A Spiral Model of Software Development and Enhancement," *Computer*, May 1988, pp. 61-72.
3. Jackson, Michael A. *System Development*, Prentice-Hall, London, 1983.
4. Orr, Ken. "Introducing Structured Systems Design," *Tutorial: Software Design Strategies*, IEEE Cat. No. EH0149-5, 1977, pp. 72-82.
5. Jones, C.B. *Software Development: A Rigorous Approach*, Prentice-Hall, Englewood Cliffs, NJ, 1979.
6. Gupta, R., *et al.* "An Object-Oriented VLSI CAD Framework," *Computer*, May 1989, pp. 28–37.
7. Luqi, Berzins, V. and Yeh, R. "A Prototyping Language for Real-Time Software," *IEEE Transactions on Software Engineering*, SE-14, No. 10, October 1988, pp. 1409–1423.

8. Myers, G. *Software Reliability,* John Wiley, New York, NY, 1976, p. 184.

9. Swanson, E.B. "The Dimensions of Maintenance," *Proc. Second Int'l. Conference on Software Engineering,* IEEE, 1976, pp. 492-497.

10. Ramamoorthy, C.B. *et al.* "Software Engineering: Problems and Perspectives," *Computer,* October 1984, pp. 191–209.

11. *DACS Newsletter,* September 1979, RADC/ISISI, Griffiss AFB, New York, NY.

4

The Problems

We have seen that computer software is produced by well-defined disciplines, presumably executed by bright, clear-eyed men and women. Moreover, computer programs are inherently precise and contain no mechanical or electrical parts that can degrade in performance. What can possibly go wrong?

4.1 Defects

Unfortunately, just about everything. As a starter, let's consider latent defects. Of course, we do not expect that latent defects in software will take the form of latent defects in hardware. Nor can we expect that they will yield to a procedure appropriate to cracks in castings or the temperature coefficients of resistors. Yet, latent defects do exist in software. When the bank teller breaks the news to Mr. Zygote that his $100 check can't be cashed because his current balance is less than $100, and Mr. Zygote distinctly recalls depositing within the week $1500, we have to suspect the presence of a latent defect. Software troubleshooters will immediately wonder if the spelling of Mr. Zygote's name might not have placed his account at the very end of the long list maintained by the bank. This, in turn, should raise the question of the boundary performance of some of the algorithms employed in posting or sorting daily transactions. Never mind, Mr. Zygote has a problem, and likely as not that problem is a latent defect in the computer software used by the bank.

It is the tradition of computer software that latent defects are called by any name but that. The usual designations are "bugs," "errors," or more euphemistically, "software problems." Small matter. They exist, and, indeed, are likely to continue to exist despite the efforts of quality assurance. TQM can be instrumental in markedly decreasing their number, but it is unrealistic to assume that defects can be entirely eliminated. This may appear to be a surprisingly tolerant attitude; one scarcely consonant with the historical goals of the quality community. However, as a fact of software life, no degree of quality control can assure that a computer program, save for the most trivial, can ever be placed into use totally free of "bugs."

Figure 4.1 is a model of a fairly simple computer program. The small boxes represent processing nodes of any given complexity, anywhere from the addition of two numbers to the calculation of the harmonic frequency of an airplane wing. The small clockwise arcs about each node represent program switches, or jumps around the processing nodes, with the switch settings determined by previous calculations. That is, the node either is entered or it is not, the choice being the result of some other computation within the model. The large counterclockwise arcs represent the potential for iteration, or "looping." Each group of four processing nodes may be iterated, jumps and all, up to six times; the exact number once again a function of the calculations within the model. It can be shown (and is highly recommended as an alternate to doodling during a dull staff meeting) that the number of unique paths from the one end to the other is approximately 10^{17}. that is, the model, simple as it is, is capable of generating 10^{17} discrete states.

Now, 10^{17} is a very large number. One way of appreciating its size is to say that we shall test each of these paths at the rate of one path per microsecond, or, if you will, 1 million paths per second. This may sound unrealistically optimistic, considering that we need to set up each test and record the result, but we'll go with the number anyway. At this 1-microsecond rate, in order to be ready for next week's scheduled delivery of the software, we should have started testing

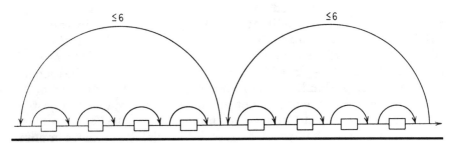

Figure 4.1 Program model.

sometime during the reign of Alexander the Great, roughly 2300 years ago.

Thus, we can see that the number of paths that computer software can produce is too great to permit the testing of each and every one. Simply put, no technique of product inspection can guarantee the absence of latent defects.

In brief, we cannot test computer software to the full exposure it will receive from the data (read, "real world") environment. Nearly all of the possible end-to-end processing sequences will have to go untested. It should not be surprising that some bugs will persist even after final qualification testing. What actually is accomplished is the testing of the main branches of the program. In our model, we might expect that the straight through (no jumps, no loops) processing will be tested; that each jump will be tested individually; and that each half of the model will be tested with some iteration, but with a given set of jump conditions. These tests will suffice to remove all but a few of the potential errors. It is these few that remain as latent defects. As we shall see, one of the main thrusts of a software quality assurance program is to reduce the number of defects that get into the code.

4.2 Usability

Latent defects are not the only problem. Many a program has been prepared and released that simply did not do the job expected of it. Perhaps the program was hard to use, required more thought than the operator was equipped to provide, or more knowledge than he was supplied with. Or even worse, it may have provided results that only represented part of the problem. If the inventory control system of a department store doesn't accommodate exchanges, because no one ever told the programmers that it ought to, how long will it be before reports of merchandise on hand are no longer current?

In the world of embedded software, we have further concerns, not the least of which is speed. We might look at a program that is intended to steer a cruise missile. If the sensor inputs (loran, inertial guidance, or whatever) occur at the rate of 10 input data sets per second, but it takes three-tenths of a second to fully process them, we can only hope that in the two-tenths of a second that the latest positional input must be ignored, the missile will not have drifted so far off course that the computed corrections will be to no avail. An otherwise splendid program, perhaps, but too slow to be of any real worth.

Software can satisfy all the technical specifications set forth for it, but fail to satisfy its customers. Perhaps we need another category:

grudging usability. One of the programming environments we use allows one to temporarily jump out of the interpreter/execution mode of operation into an editor mode. This is certainly better than exiting the interpreter, fixing up the code using some arbitrarily selected editor that offers no language-context assistance, and then reinitializing the interpreter to try another test run. Although it is much less convenient than the familiar BASIC environment, which allows the user to revise code at any time, the subject editor is a full screen editor, superior (in theory) to BASIC's line editor. However, the commands are not related to the keyboard in any rational manner. One would expect that the ctrl key, for example, would be used with a family of functions (say, select, cut, and paste). Not so. Each subset of the repertoire of commands is scattered across the keyboard. As a result, using the editor is slow and error-prone.

How we use the environment is illustrative of how customers cope with barely usable software. We get around the problem by running both an external, but friendly, editor and the interpreter in a multitasking environment, easily switching between the two and reading in the edited code library on each switch back to the interpreter. This is, however, at the expense of language-context editing aids. There seem always to be workarounds for awkward software, but contrived solutions do not lead to customer satisfaction.

Perhaps the acid test of usability in interactive software is whether the user needs to refer to a manual when using the program. Few systems pass the test, and we are not at all certain that every kind of application lends itself to reference-free usage, but it seems that few software producers ever bother to think about it.

There are any number of ways that a computer program can be inadequate to perform the needed job. Most of the ways have been explored. The archives are full of programs that were much admired for their design concepts, but never quite became useful.

4.3 Maintenance

Programs, when found to be responsive to the real application and when finally free of all bugs, can still develop problems. We have seen that software is frequently subjected to a continuing life of modifications. However, some programs are more easily modified than others. A program that is poorly documented or reflects "clever," rather than straightforward, programming techniques is hard to understand. The defects that can be introduced to code that isn't understood can be out of proportion to the significance of the modification itself. One can easily imagine the task of trying to change a program that the programmer doesn't fully grasp. Yet, modifications, or maintenance, is generally performed by programmers other than the ones who originally did the design or wrote the code. Indeed, only about six months need pass between program release and first modification before even the original programmer is hard put to change code that is poorly documented or designed with obscure logic paths.

In addition to insufficiently descriptive documentation, we have also the problem of documentation that is no longer current. As the program is revised, the documentation must be revised with it so that it and the code are always in agreement. This also applies to comments within the code. It is not at all rare to find obsolete comments that mislead rather than guide.

Finally, we have the problem of finding that a change made to one function of a program unwittingly affects other functions as well. While this can be a consequence of difficulty in understanding the program, it is equally likely the result of a nonfunctional software architecture; nonfunctional in the sense that the several modules do not reflect independent performance. Modularity is not a matter of mere program segmentation. It should reflect the division of a program into a set of smaller programs (indeed, into several hierarchically related sets of smaller programs) in a manner wherein each individual program, or module, performs a unique function. In this way the set of modules will exhibit the quality of maximum mutual independence.

Unfortunately, this paradigm of modularity is not universally encountered. A maintenance programmer, altering the logic within one module which was known to perform some function, finds that the performance of another, seemingly unrelated function has been inadvertently altered. Worse, the maintenance programmer doesn't find out, but a user of the program does. The authors can recall a program that computed an optimal routing for the interconnections of a back panel of a printed wiring board cage. A year or two after constant use, the program was modified to operate on a back panel of a somewhat different physical configuration. Mostly, the change involved a different scheme for identifying connector pins. Following this small change, made entirely within one module, it was found that electrical ground was no longer routed to the boards. On examination, it was learned that the altered module, which presumably only related pin identifiers to physical dimensions, also had the miscellaneous role of assigning the ground connections. Although this was properly documented, it (understandably) escaped the notice of the maintenance programmer, and the program was revised in a manner such that the secondary function could no longer be invoked.

Whatever the reasons for the difficulties encountered during program maintenance, the results are likely to be costly. Under the worst

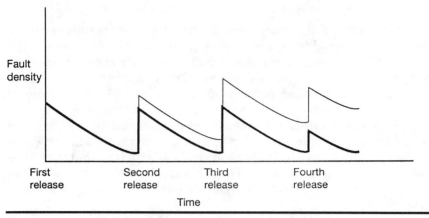

Figure 4.2 Winning and losing battles.

conditions, the modifications made to a program not well-suited to change, or the modifications badly made to a well-constructed program, can in time cause the program to become erratic in performance or quite nearly impossible to modify further. With a large program, it is not unreasonable to expect that a small number of new bugs will be introduced with every major modification performed. In time, however, these defects, as were those latent in the program when it was initially released for use, will be fixed. The heavy line of Fig. 4.2 approximates the expectations of the incidence of bugs over the life span of a program. If, however, the program is one that is difficult to modify, or if the modifications are uncontrolled, the light line may result, with the inevitable and costly consequence of premature code death when the only sensible management option remaining is to scrap the program and start over again.

4.4   More on Obsolescence

Software construction, documentation, and maintenance practices are not the only causes of early obsolescence. The very language in which the program is written may also doom its years of use. As we saw in the previous chapter, programs often are required to operate on computers or under operating systems other than the ones for which they were originally designed. For example, the land development firm of Nemo and Ahab in 1980 purchased a minicomputer of modest capability to produce topographic maps of their development sites. With the machine, they bought a software package to compute and plot not only the contours of the land, but also to superimpose the planned streets, canals, and clubhouses of their grand designs. By 1990 the business of

Nemo and Ahab had grown considerably, and they were no longer dealing with sites of hundreds of acres, but were acquiring huge tracts of ranchland for conversion to homesites and shopping centers. The old computer was no longer adequate, and the purchase of a new machine was indicated. One problem arose, however: The software was partly coded in the assembly language of the old computer, and no upgrade currently offered by the computer manufacturer could execute that code.

Had the software been written in any of several compiler languages, the system could have been made to work on the new machine. The manufacturer had taken the precaution to make the new operating system (in this sense, software platform) downwards compatible to the old one, which meant that the compiler language part of the program could be recompiled for the new machine. This was small comfort, however. Nemo and Ahab still had the assembly language code to deal with.

By this time, the upper tier of personal computers could not only provide the computing power required, but also could provide the power at far less cost than any upgrade offered by the manufacturer of the old computer. Moreover, several third party software publishers were selling systems capable of the topographic processing required. The solution looked obvious: buy a high-powered personal computer (at less cost than that of the minicomputer 10 years earlier) and buy an entirely new applications package (at three times the cost of the first one). Though obvious, this solution entailed two problems: the data files produced by the old software would not play with the new software, and Nemo and Ahab would have to shoulder the cost of retraining its staff in the use of the new system. Still, there was nothing for it but to buy a new computer as planned, buy new software as unplanned, maintain two systems (so that old data files could be kept current while new tracts went on the new system), and lose the staff for a week while they took expensive in-house training provided by the software publisher.

Now wise to the ways of software obsolescence, before ordering the software Nemo and Ahab asked the publisher the language of the system. They were assured that every last line of code was written in C, thus giving them the comfort of knowing that they would be able to avoid a second painful upgrade in 2005 when they planned to purchase the whole of Arizona.

The matter of providing machine and operating system transportability isn't quite so tidy as simply specifying an appropriate 3GL or 4GL. As Chap. 2 noted, programming languages can acquire dialects so that a program written in one dialect may have to be modified somewhat before being processed by a compiler for another computer or operating system. Worse, a program written in a 3GL can still be written in a manner that reflects certain machine characteristics. We once bought a program, written in FORTRAN, to perform reliability predictions. The program had been developed for a computer of 60-bit word length, and with an internal character representation that allowed 10 alphanumeric characters to be packed in one computer word. Files of component failure rates were cleverly constructed to group component data in sets expressed mostly in efficient word operation for the matching of component data to circuit use. Unfortunately, we had to run the program on a computer that packed four characters to a word. Thus, even though the program was written in a language compilable on both computers, major modifications had to be made to the program before we could use it. This could have been avoided had the program not been so cleverly constructed, but had conformed to the sense of the FORTRAN standard of the American National Standards Institute.

4.5   Configuration Ambiguity

No discussion of software problems would be complete without examination of the question of what it is that one has actually tested when one has tested a program. Testing takes place in the late phases of the software development cycle, well after considerable opportunity has arisen to make a number of changes to the design of the software. The prevalence of design changes during development is especially common in large programming projects, where, despite the thoroughness with which the software is initially designed in the large, the subsequent detailed design effort may reveal some inconsistencies or omissions within the overall design. Some of these may show up during detailed design, but others will await the start of testing to be found. Thus we find that a given module, having been previously tested with satisfactory results, is modified somewhat when a second module does not properly run in concert with it. This, by-the-by, can happen in either top-down or bottom-up testing. As it turns out, in our hypothetical case it is simpler to modify the first module than the second. However, a similar problem arises in the testing of a third module, and once again it is easier to modify the first. Eventually, there are several versions of the subject module to be found on various disks or tapes; each of which had at one time been the "authorized version." At this point, in any subsequent testing, the opportunity is present to include one of the earlier versions in the program load about to be tested. The situation is further compounded when one considers the periodic generation of backup files of source programs. Which version got copied?

While software documentation may lend itself to inspection by perusal of the contents, for all practical purposes the programs themselves are invisible. All that one sees is the medium on which the program is stored. This is not to say that source programs cannot be dumped onto a screen or printer and then read, but one cannot, when looking for the floppy disk that contains the latest version, pick one up and know with any certainty that it is, in fact, the correct edition. This is especially the case if its cardboard jacket bears only the legend "Module D310, Latest Version." Of course, it is more likely that competent software professionals would have labeled the jacket "Module D310 Rev C," or "Module D310, Mar 2, 1991, 3:45 PM." Even this offers no assurance that whoever is about to use the module knows the identification of the latest version. A day-shift librarian preparing a program load for testing recalls that D310 Rev C was current yesterday, and pulls it for recompilation with other modules. Unknown to the librarian, the night-shift found it necessary to modify the module 12 hours earlier, and the current version is now D310 Rev D.

Thus far, we have only discussed source code. In actuality, the building of program loads is more typically based on relocatable object files, with only one or two newly compiled source files. This makes the problem even more difficult, since relocatable files are normally strung together in a "library" on a single disk, with the consequence that picking up the correct disk really implies picking up the current (latest authorized) version of each module. In theory, this should make matters easier. In practice it does, but only if the status of the library is updated each time one of the individual components is... This practice is one that is easily, though unintentionally, circumvented. Moreover, it is one that does not readily lend itself to auditing.

In brief, it is possible to run an entire test sequence successfully, but uselessly, because the program tested may not be the basis for the next series of tests, or may not be the program that had passed previous tests. Software quality processes, as we shall see, are deeply involved not only with test planning and the testing itself, but with finding a practical means of verifying that the tests performed reflect the capabilities of the software finally delivered to the customer.

4.6   Department of Silver Linings

Summing up, we see that computer software can easily be the source of problems to its users and owners. It can, at delivery, be laden with latent defects, or can be endowed with them later. It can be nonresponsive to the real needs of its users. It can be short-lived even though its need remains. There may even be a question of what it really is, or to what tests the delivered product was actually subjected. There must be a solution, and in fact there is. It starts with the next chapter.

4.7 Summary

1. The number of distinct end-to-end paths inherent in computer programs is so great that 100 percent testing is impossible. Thus, programs are frequently put into service with latent defects that may surface unpredictably.

2. It is not uncommon for programs to be designed without regard to all aspects of the customer's operational environment.

4. A program written in a language unique to the computer or operating system on which it was initially intended to run will be prematurely retired when the platform has to be upgraded.

5. Loss of configuration control is all too easy, with the result that the program placed into service may not fully represent the software that was tested. Configuration control of software is especially difficult because code is awkward to inspect.

The Quality Solution

5

Prevention

This part of the book will deal with the quality solution to software problems. Consonant with the precepts of TQM, the quality solution has three elements: the people who produce software, quality-oriented technology, and a set of managerial techniques and practices directed to predictable and controllable development and maintenance. Moreover, the quality solution is rooted in prevention. In interpreting the third of Deming's 14 points for software, Richard Zultner put the matter succinctly: "Cease dependence on mass inspection (especially testing) to achieve quality.... [Inspection] does not produce quality. Quality must be built into the system—or it doesn't exist.... Quality comes from improving the system development processes, thereby preventing errors."[1]

Figure 5.1 emphasizes processes. Even in a prevention-oriented program, one cannot assure the quality of software by adding gussets to stiffen it, by derating its power dissipation, or by expediting deliveries with a next-day messenger service. Quality must be built in, and the only way to do so is to ensure that all activities of the development and maintenance processes are organized to that end.

> Above all, development and maintenance must be practiced within a coherent methodology, or systematic framework of smooth flow between tasks.

Moreover, the quality solution must incorporate measurable artifacts of the result of each activity, milestones if you will, where one can verify that the work done thus far is consistent with the ultimate goal of customer satisfaction. In the absence of a systematic approach to

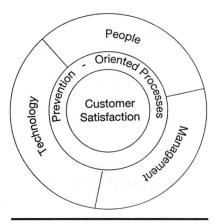

Figure 5.1

software, milestones are meaningless, and without milestones, multi-faceted processes cannot be managed.

In Part 2 we said that there is more than one correct way to write a program. There is also more than one way to develop a systematic approach. In Chap. 5 we concentrate on technological approaches to the prevention of defects and the retention of managerial control that are in some respects parallel, in other ways complementary. As a group, they represent solutions to those aspects of analysis, design, and coding that are the most critical to quality.

Since this is a book on quality management, we go into technological issues only to the depth necessary to explain their connection to quality. Not only do we keep matters as simple as possible, we make no attempt to touch all bases of technology or to recommend a single narrow course to follow—the first is far too broad in scope even for a book devoted to software engineering, and the second represents a naive presumption.

Since we are introducing not only Chap. 5 but the Quality Solution here, please note that we continue to restrict our focus to quality matters in Chap. 6. Chapter 6 is devoted to configuration control, a prerequisite for software quality in the "paper" stages of development, during testing, and throughout the operational life of software. Chapter 7, a tacit admission of the limitations of prevention, discusses the means used to achieve purposeful, effective, and controllable detection of software faults. Chapter 8 deals with the tools required to implement approaches toward prevention, control, and detection. Tools are scarcely separable from software engineering, and are referred to in all chapters. However, we treat tools separately so that the other chapters can focus on broader approaches to quality, rather than the specifics of how they are supported by tools. Chapter 9 wraps up the quality solution by focusing on management issues.

5.1   The Discipline of Software Development

In the earliest years of software engineering, Edsger Dijkstra, in connection with the software of a multiprogramming system, defined an ordered sequence of machines—A(0) through A(n). A(0) represented actual hardware. The others were virtual machines. He described the software:

> The software of layer i is defined in terms of machine A(i), it is to be executed by machine A(i), the software of layer i uses machine A(i) to make machine A($i + 1$).... The total task of creating machine A(n) has been regarded as the machine A(0) and in the dissection process this total abstraction has been split up in a number of independent abstractions.[2]

This, the introduction of the concepts of levels of abstractions, amounted to defining processes at one level in terms of those at the layer immediately adjacent to it.*The bottom layer is that which is machine-dependent. The top layer is the most abstract in terms of hardware. Knowledge of the contents of any layer is concealed from all layers below it. The idea behind Dijkstra's levels of abstraction was to attack a very complex problem in a manner that would permit layer-by-layer verification of the design correctness. Dijkstra's levels of abstraction applied not only to a means of grappling with the complexity of design, but to testing as well. In another paper[3] on the system, he implied that it was possible to structure the design so that the tests for each layer would completely test the performance applicable to that layer.

We can translate Dijkstra's concept to a classic example of systematic software development; one that leads monotonically from the greatest degree of abstraction (statement of the problem) to the state of no abstraction (executable code). A more popular name for this example is *top-down development.* In recent years, we have demonstrated that bottom-up sequences of activities also can be incorporated in a coherent methodology. The key is that each activity is defined so that its purpose is plainly understood (meaning that it yields measurable artifacts) and cannot be omitted without losing some part of the chain of traceability from customer requirements to customer satisfaction.

To a large extent, specific approaches to the prevention of defects differ from one programming paradigm to another. Moreover, certain paradigms are closely tied to but a few languages. To provide a general discourse on prevention, we'll restrict most of this chapter to topics common to most paradigms (although we *do* discuss aspects of several),

---

*Niklaus Wirth, another noted software engineer, at about the same time defined *Stepwise Design Refinement*, a seamless process of decomposition that descends through layers of abstraction.

specifically those topics that directly bear on quality. As we have previously noted, we make no attempt to touch all software engineering bases; just enough to provide a scaffold with which one can construct prevention-based quality management.

If software development is to provide traceability from requirements to customer product, the evolving product will, at any arbitrarily observed moment, have the shape fashioned by preceding tasks. Each new task gives the shape further definition. It's a bit like planting a field. You start by marking out the boundaries with hedgerows, irrigation or drainage ditches, fences, or the like. The furrows left by plowing define the orientation of the future crops. The seeds sown provide the field's final specificity. This top-down approach to agriculture is not alone. The affluent farmer could germinate the seeds in peat pots under glass. Now we have both top-down and bottom-up farming. If we were to deal with another kind of agricultural problem, a kitchen garden rather than a farm field, we could dispense with seeds altogether and buy immature plants from a nursery. Moreover, the outline of the kitchen garden can be marked by a flower border; say, marigolds to keep certain insects away. There are many ways to grow broccoli, but every approach to a good harvest has its own structure.

So too with software. We have many ways of developing software, but those based on prevention have a considered structure. We're going beyond software development models, as discussed in Chap. 3, and are addressing the technology that goes into individual tasks and ties the tasks together.

In Sec. 3.2 we had defined programming paradigms as sets of conventions often tied to groups of languages. Extending the definition a bit, we can describe a programming paradigm as the set of intellectual processes that, in the aggregate, defines the process of software development and gives the programming product its structure. For the most part, programming paradigms are thought of in terms of design and coding processes. Although one can use a requirements definition process entirely disassociated with most design paradigms, in many cases, the process of defining the external specifications of software products (the requirements model) is tied to the design process. The Vienna Development Method mentioned in Sec. 3.2 defines a single paradigm extending across the entire development process. PAISLey[4] is used within another inclusive paradigm, wherein specifications are transformed into code. So we like to think of the entire process of software development in terms of paradigms, even though we shall discuss the elements of development within the context of development models found in Chap. 3.

Any number of schemes have been used to classify paradigms. For example, one paper implicitly defines two major categories of design paradigms: those taking a modeling point of view and those taking a task-oriented point of view.[5] O-O is an example of the former, in contrast to most software development. While we have always considered development directed toward LISP programs an example of something called the functional paradigm, a recent survey[6] of a dozen paradigms or paradigm families speaks of both an *operational* functional paradigm (the one we had in mind) and a *definitional* functional paradigm, which attempts to do away with the need to sequence functions. The distinguished computer scientist R.W. Floyd did not explicitly define categories of paradigms in his 1978 Turing Award Lecture,[7] but he contrasted familiar paradigms such as structured programming with algorithm-based paradigms (e.g., branch-and-bound), state-machine paradigms where the computational state is represented by the values of stored variables, and others. He also posited a family of paradigms in which solutions would be given in one language, would produce a less abstract solution in a language of a lower hierarchical level that would produce yet another solution, which would in turn...

We need go no further into the business of paradigm taxonomy for the point to be clear: there is not one but a number of different technological approaches to producing software. To a great number of practicing software professionals, development means defining the requirements, breaking down the requirements into a set of functions (or in O-O, entities), writing the code (or *reuse* what one can), and getting ready for test. But look at the family of paradigms that Floyd posited. While we still do not see the paradigm embracing many hierarchical levels of language, we do see it at two levels, for example, as in the aforementioned PAISLey and in several Macintosh code generation tools. In the Macintosh tools, the higher order language is graphical (the GUI component), the lower order language may be either object-oriented (e.g., C++ or Object Pascal) or procedural (e.g., standard C and Pascal).

Quite plainly, a software development process that starts with a graphical language to produce a standard 3GL or O-O program is going to differ in a number of respects from a process that employs the popular technologies of 10 years ago.

Whatever paradigm or combination of paradigms is used, it must serve the purpose of prevention. Moreover, if the owners of the process expect to be able to improve the process over time, they must formalize the way they go about their work. To go about developing or maintaining software in an unplanned and lightly considered (read undisciplined) way provides no baseline for a program of quality improvement. So

> The first step in quality improvement often is the formal adoption of a development and maintenance methodology.

5.2 Specifying the Problem

Experience has shown that incorrect, incomplete, or vague specifications of software requirements are the most common cause of major design rework and schedule slips. Specifications may be incorrect for a variety of reasons, among which the most prominent are:

- Misinterpretation of customer requirements (Board of Education of a city in Quebec needs bilingual interactive dialogue; developer in Miami provides English and Spanish)
- Customer not knowing own needs
- Inadequate analysis of the operating environment, including available computing resources (computer has 16 Mbyte of memory, but operating system can only address 4 Mbyte)
- Conflicting requirements (specified accuracy of pattern recognition requirement requires processing more data than permitted by execution time constraint)
- Initial system state misstated (space vehicle *not* at rest when Doppler navigation algorithm invoked)

Some causes of incomplete specifications:

- Insufficient analysis of the operating environment (16-bit data bus assumed; 8 bits provided)
- Inadequate analysis of user profiles (messages in computerspeak unintelligible to operators of process control system)
- Unavailable interface information (a development constant: "We'll have it next week")
- Negligence in following up on all details (speed is one of the inputs, but is it in meters per second, knots, or furlongs per fortnight?)

Vagueness results from:

- Customer uncertainty about purpose ("We think the teachers will find it useful for remedial reading; but, who knows, maybe for spelling drills.")
- Casual documentation of specifications
- Inappropriate template for specifying by example (DBMS specifications for current holdings of investment bank were prepared by modifying specifications for warehouse inventory control)

- Ambiguity (specified allowable error of ± 1 milliradian, but that included instrumentation error; programmers thought they had it all to themselves)
- Negligence in providing full detail

The completeness and, to a lesser extent, correctness of a requirements model can be judged by playing the specification against a number of operational scenarios. Scenarios may take into account input data, user options, the reactions of software or hardware with which the subject software will communicate, or whatever else is appropriate to the problem. These walk-throughs are labor-intensive and offer no guarantee of completeness. Nevertheless, they are worth the cost. Many instances of vagueness can be identified by subjecting each discrete specification to an examination of its testability. How can we fashion a test of the complete product to show that we have satisfied the requirement? A process-driven method designed to capitalize on this is to require the test team to agree (by sign-off) that the specifications are testable.

Few cases of incorrectness will be caught by walk-throughs. More may be found by having the customer review the technical specifications prepared by the analysts. We score a bit higher at finding cases of incomplete specification when we play through scenarios, and even higher on finding vagueness by examining testability. The best way to avoid propagating specification problems into design is to prevent them.

We keep coming across the fallacy that a definition of requirements prepared by the customer can communicate everything required by developers. A customer specification may be sufficient to permit you to prepare a bid, but not enough to do the job. Analysts need to talk directly with customers, preferably at customer locations. They can get enormous insight into the way a software product will be used by spending some time at a representative site and watching people or machines do their jobs. For interactive software, technical specifications need to take into account some basic principles of usability. A Bellcore staffer has identified[8] the following *usability heuristics,* which we see as falling into three categories:

Use simple and natural dialogue	Minimize user memory load	Provide shortcuts
Speak the user's language	Provide feedback	Provide clearly marked exits
Be consistent	Prevent errors	Provide good error messages

Each of these can be translated into the specifics of the subject software. The term "prevent errors" is vague, but when applied to a specific application, can be made testable. To take a classic, if trivial example, where numeric input is required, any other kind of input is trapped and a message such as "34.5 percent is an invalid unit price" is output.

Rapid prototyping

Nothing beats rapid prototyping where you can apply it (most places) for building correctness and specificity into a requirements model. Completeness also gains. Section 3.3 contained an overview of rapid prototyping as a life cycle event, but the techniques of building prototypes are another matter.

The construction of prototypes ordinarily is a simpler matter than that of production software. You do not have to be concerned with using a programming language conducive to maintainability. Except when used as a test bed to try out new features added to an existing system, prototypes are rarely maintained. Accordingly, if the prototypers, for whatever reason, preferred not to use O-O or a 4GL, they might use the arcane, but expressive APL language or, perhaps, an expressive language seldom encountered but known to them, say, SETL. Moreover, design decisions often do not have to be recorded for the use of future maintenance programmers. This makes the business of documentation and its library control trivial.

Efficiency is rarely important. This means greater latitude not only in language selection, but in the environment in which the prototype will run. For example, one may be able to demonstrate features of the final product by prototyping the features in BASIC and running the model in an interpreter mode. As another example, one might fashion a model data base and draw reports using a point-and-shoot programming mode. If the only question is about the content and format of the reports, never mind how long it takes to run or how much memory it takes.

All of this applies to prototypes that will be thrown away—prototypes intended only to demonstrate specific features of the production software to make certain that both designers and customers are in agreement on the specifications of the features. If so, they had better be thrown away. There is always some danger that the prototype code will be used as an interim product, and somehow, interim products sometimes find their way into production use. An improbable, but documented example, is a prototype ocean surveillance terminal that saw action on a U.S. Navy ship during the 1986 Libyan incursion.[9]

The O-O paradigm offers advantages for the construction of rapid prototypes. O-O is well-suited to modeling what is most likely known at the start of the effort to define a requirements model; namely, real life entities. Also, if "rapid" is the essence of rapid prototyping, O-O is recommended for the task because of the way it lends itself to reusing existing code. Using a composition model, it may be possible to rapidly construct a demonstration program composed of existing objects.

The use of O-O for rapid prototyping is not restricted to standard O-O languages such as C++, Smalltalk, Flavors, and the like. Object-oriented data base management systems have also been used for this purpose and not just for modeling production DBMS. Staff at the University of California have used one system (OODBMS) to model a CAD system for VLSI designs.[10]

When a prototype has served its purpose and been declared acceptable as a model for all or part of a production system, it can without further effort be declared the *de facto* requirements model for the features demonstrated. Still, perhaps to better define the external specifications of the product for future maintenance activities, one can document the prototype in any of the usual requirements documentation methods. Which brings us to the ways, other than prototyping, of representing requirements models.

Common representations of requirements models

Even in the early 1990s, we most often find the definition of external specifications in the form of prose, page upon page of text, with amplifying tables or charts here and there. These specifications are costly to prepare and often difficult for readers to stay awake through. It's not just the Proustian length of endless pages of specifications that make for painfully dry reading. Still, text can be correct, complete, and specific. Moreover, by labeling individual requirements with unique numbers (usually paragraph numbers), one can provide the basis of a traceability mechanism to ensure that requirements get designed, coded, and tested.

A digression on traceability.   One such mechanism is the *system verification diagram* (SVD) scheme devised a number of years ago at Computer Sciences Corp.[11] The basic element of a SVD is a *thread* or stimulus-response pairing of a decomposition component as depicted by Fig. 5.2. Note that the thread contains a reference to a paragraph in the requirements specification. Threads can be identified at all levels of decomposition, but as a practical matter one is unlikely to want to go beyond those components identified during a preliminary design activity. Each thread can be associated with the modules that implement it. When tied to the *thread-at-a-time development model,*

Stimulus	Thread label	Response
	Function	

References to specification

Figure 5.2 Basic SVD element.

which describes the way a system is incrementally built, the SVDs carry through to validating the test cases used to demonstrate the functionality provided by each build. Figure 5.3 is a portion of a SVD decomposing a navigation function. (For simplicity, Fig. 5.3 omits stimuli and responses.)

Although the SVD was devised with embedded software in mind, the scheme is not at all limited to such applications. Thread-at-a-time software construction in popular in IS applications and the use of SVDs has been demonstrated there, too.12 Although we have never seen a SVD applied to a requirements representation other than text, we can see no reasons why the references under each thread cannot apply to other forms of documenting what a system is required to do.

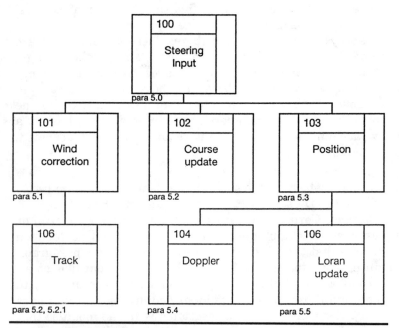

Figure 5.3 System verification diagram.

State diagrams.   All computer programs define a set (often an astronomically large set) of states. The states are, of course, hierarchically related. The ones at the highest level are often prominent features of the external specifications of the software. Depicting the states and the conditions under which the program transitions from one to the other can be a succinct way of defining at least part of the program's requirements. For example, consider a regression test system, one that runs a package of tests on a product after it has been modified. If any of the tests produce different results from those found in previous tests (benchmarks), the modification has produced unwanted and unintended side effects. Figure 5.4 illustrates the several states of the system, including the action of the operator.

Note that one of the states, *test load*, involves the operating system under which the regression test system runs. Moreover, *operator action* is reached only by an *abend* (abnormal end) produced by the operating system. Further, *wait* is entirely an operating system state. State diagrams are excellent means not only for clearly and simply depicting the major phases of a program, but also for portraying the interaction of a program and its environment.

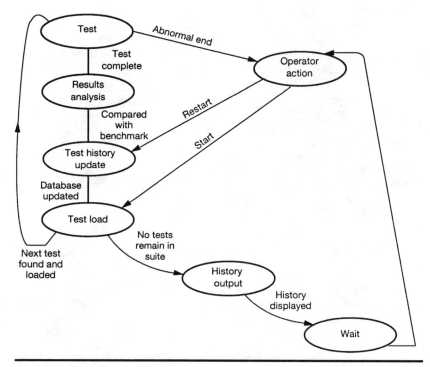

Figure 5.4   State diagram.

State diagrams can be hierarchically nested or *leveled*. For example, in Fig. 5.4 *test* may itself consist of several states; say, *stimulus application, wait,* and *response phase.* These would be shown in a second diagram.

Data flow diagrams.   Unlike state diagrams, which reflect a partitioning of operating conditions, data flow diagrams, usually abbreviated DFDs and sometimes called *bubble charts*, depict the partitioning of the processes needed to satisfy customer requirements. The network represented by a DFD contains all the processing elements of the system and the flow of data among them. Like state diagrams, DFDs can be leveled, with each process expanded into a DFD of its own. Each of the second level DFDs can be expanded into a third level, and so on.

In Fig. 5.5 we see the processes set in place when someone enters into the production floor terminal a request to get a batch of chips. The rectangles are data sources or sinks for the network, or as in the case of Production Department, both. Bubbles are processes, and files are bounded by parallel lines. The withdrawal record entered by keyboard

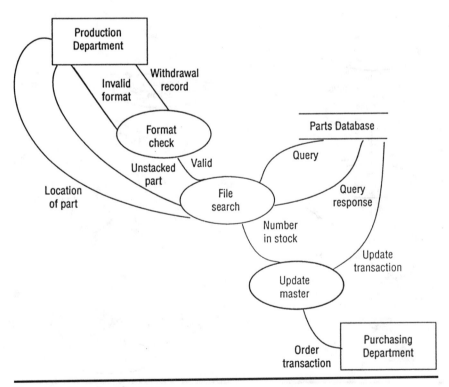

Figure 5.5 Data flow diagram.

is scanned for validity and sent on to form a query of the parts file, after which the stores location of the chips is returned to the terminal so that the parts can be withdrawn. Also, the parts file is updated to reflect the withdrawal, and if the number remaining is less than some predetermined minimum, an order is drawn to raise the number to a predetermined maximum. Incorrectly entered withdrawals yield an error message, as do withdrawals of parts not normally stocked.

We just used a lot of words, and our words still are not as clear as the illustration. That's the beauty of pictures. Graphics may not easily be processed (as can pseudocode) to provide consistency checks, generate test cases, and the like, but they make communication with customers much easier than words.

Of the several tools used in the popular *structured analysis* method of translating customer requirements into concrete requirements, the DFD is the most significant. While not new—the classic text on it being Tom DeMarco's 1978 book[13]—structured analysis continues to gain adherents, especially for IS applications.

We digress for a moment to note that we might view structured analysis as a unifying paradigm, at least in the sense of the tasks of requirements analysis (and definition) and preliminary design, since the same processes used to analyze customer requirements carry through to defining the elements of the solution. Indeed, in Fig. 5.5 we see the problem domain already partitioned into three processes. We have said that requirements specifications state *what* needs doing, while design specifications state *how* customer needs will be met. In a unifying paradigm, however, the line between the two is more arbitrary. O-O is another unifying paradigm, this time encompassing detailed design and coding as well. The advantage of seamless development (i.e., using the same tools, language, and thinking for all tasks) is obvious.*

Data dictionaries.   Data dictionaries are electronic coffers holding detailed information about each data element. When used with DFDs, data dictionaries define the data flows and data stores of the network.

When we say that data dictionaries are coffers, we do not mean to imply that they are warehouses into which one can push pallets full of data. On the contrary, they have structure. DeMarco writes of definitions in terms of the familiar constructs of sequence (concatenation of data), selection (either this or that), and iteration (repeating a data element).

---

*The several tasks involving development of an O-O program do not lend themselves to exactly the same tools and thinking. Reference 14 describes several methods for O-O analysis and O-O design in current use, each using models of the program not required for other tasks.

Here are some examples:

- Sequence: *part_status* is *part_number* and *number_in_stock*, where *part_number* and *number_in_stock* are separate data elements.
- Selection: *customer_status* is *promised_shipping_date* or *shipped_date*.
- Iteration: *flight_manifest* is iteration of *passenger_name*.

These constructs are, of course, combined. Also, iterations can be nested for data just as they are for program procedural flow.

Like DFDs and the artifacts of O-O, data dictionaries play a role in a unifying paradigm. At the time requirements are modeled, not much is known about the data of the system. Data entirely internal to the system generally are not known at all. But even as DFDs can be further developed or decomposed (leveled), so too can data dictionaries become repositories for decomposed data—that is, data partitioned into constituent parts. For example, *flight_manifest*, originally no more than an iteration of *passenger_name*, gains in specificity when *passenger_name* is expanded into *last_name*, *first_name*, *initial*, *address*. *Address* later is expanded into *number*, *street*, *town*, *state*, *zip_code*, and *country*.

Entity-relationship diagrams. ER diagrams, as they are familiarly called, also transcend the fuzzy line between requirements modeling and preliminary design. However, the diagrams have found their greatest application in communicating between customers and designers. If we regard entities in the real world as abstractions of data elements, the ER diagrams can be seen to model the way the objects of a system interact with each other. ER diagrams have utility only as a tool for ER modeling, initially the work of P. Chen.[15] ER modeling, however, has been used in conjunction with other forms of structured requirements definition. Chen's models had three classes of objects: entities, attributes, and relationships. Entities are the prominent objects of a system: address lists, inventories, people, and so on. Attributes describe entities by adding such details as length, quantities, names, and so on. Relationships associate the entities. Recall the inventory control DFD of Fig. 5.5. More realistically, production would order all the parts for an assembly, and the system would use the bill of material for the assembly to identify the parts required. Figure 5.6 is an ER diagram relating parts needed on the production floor and parts in stock.

Although the ER model worked well for communicating between customers and designers, it was less successful for more detailed analysis of customer requirements. For example, the model could not

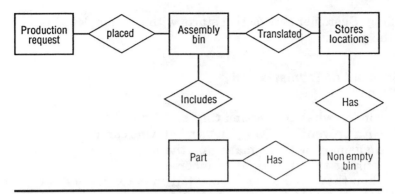

Figure 5.6   Entity-relationship diagram.

easily reflect the decreasingly abstract view of data that should emerge through stages of analysis and design. For this, one needs to be able to regard the entity *communication* as a generalization of *telephone_call*, *fax*, *data_transmission*, or *letter*. The Extended Entity-Relationship (EER) model was devised to provide this and other capabilities. Yet another unifying paradigm that starts with requirements modeling, the procedures and semantics of EER have been shown[16] well-suited to modeling the design of relational databases.

A tip from quality function deployment

Quality function deployment, or QFD, as it is popularly known, is a schema for projecting customer values onto producer activities and work groups. A Japanese invention,[17] QFD helps to clarify objectives to meet customer-oriented goals. QFD calls for partitioning objectives down to activities remote from stipulated customer requirements: data collection and analysis, design priorities, management reviews, and all the other activities likely to enter into satisfying the customer view of products and services. According to Richard Zultner,[18] leading software firms in Japan began applying QFD in 1982.

With the precepts of QFD in mind, we think it useful to note that when translating customer requirements into a technical specification, one should not only determine the customer's priorities, but should take care in making certain that they are reflected in the specification, the planning that is done at the time the specification is prepared, or both. If availability or safety is important, this is the time to think about fault tolerance, the length of time required to reboot, and the like. If data conversion is critical, the specification should include data migration criteria. If the product is directed to the general marketplace, alert the customer support department to the need for 1-800 type hand-holding. Customer satisfaction starts with the complete specification of the problem.

5.3 Refinement of Estimates and Staffing Plans

You may wonder what cost estimating and its corollary, staffing, have to do with prevention. TQM, that's what. One cannot have total quality management without managing the deployment of people, without ensuring that the right number of the right people are available when they need to be. A shortfall runs the risk of ill-considered development decisions made in the vain hope that things will all work out and the schedule will be made. Too many staff too soon runs the risk that people will be designing without a basis for design, and many managers consider it a career-limiting move to back off from work already accomplished even if the wrong work was done.

Planning, no less than development, is incremental. Preliminary plans are drawn and executed when a project is conceived, whether in the form of a response to bid on a contract or in the form of a new or modified product for the general marketplace or internal users. The software may be entirely abstract when proposed, but since the developers expect to be paid in hard cash and the customer or management needs to know the cost and the lead time, estimates are required. The product becomes a bit less abstract when a requirements model is produced and so, too, the planning. When enough is known about the product to further refine estimates—say, when most of the preliminary design work has been performed—it's time for another planning estimate. And again when most of the detailed design has been done. Thereafter, plans can be refined on a periodic basis, updated to reflect testing experience. However, in the earlier development tasks it is wrong to call for periodic replanning, rather than replanning on the basis of an updated view of the product.

Software managers must have an extra optimism gene, for the great majority of projects have been underestimated. The result is a succession of schedule slips, along with a relaxation of such quality-oriented efforts as reviews, design for reuse, and the documentation of design decisions. At some point, given scant credible information (such as that which comes from reviews and documentation) to assess progress, the real cumulative schedule slippage is more easily conjectured than reckoned. At some point the slippage becomes irrecoverable. Historically, that point is when senior management or the customer first becomes aware that the project is in jeopardy. One of the goals of a software quality assurance process is to make potential slippages visible in time for such remedial actions as increasing staff, taking a phased approach to feature release, using overtime, shuffling staff to place top performers in the trouble spots, eliminating bottlenecks by replacing the host for the programming environment with faster machines, or installing more effective debugging tools. But even alert monitoring, the best development technology, and the best people cannot prevent one from building in slips simply by understaff

The reasons that software slippages can easily become irreversible are several, complex, and superbly explained in F. Brooks's classic book, *The Mythical Man-Month.*[19] We will simply summarize his thesis by quoting Brooks's Law: "Adding manpower to a late software project makes it later."

Does it make sense, though, to refine estimates as time goes on? Is the greater accuracy of the later estimates relatively unimportant, since some of the funds have already been spent and pages in the calendar turned? Sure. But until a point is reached well downstream in the development cycle, the milestones that represent time to stop and take stock, time to verify the latest level of software specificity, and time to re-estimate the cost-to-complete occur at the natural intervals for adding staff. This is illustrated by Fig. 5.7, where the width of each rectangle represents the staffing level. The figure also shows, in a gross

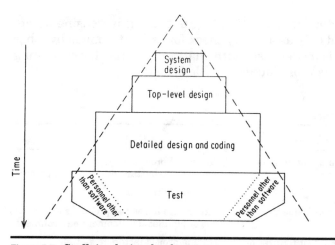

Figure 5.7   Staff size during development.

sense, that the closer the project is to completion, the more rapidly funds are expended.

Some may argue that no more workers are required for test than for detailed design and code. This is frequently true. However, for most projects, certainly for embedded software, the test phases often involve people other than the programming team, quite possibly customer representatives or a sample of inhouse users. In any case, we have pyramidal staffing as a function of time, from which it is clear that the earlier that estimating errors can be detected, the better the opportunity for appropriate staffing and cost control.

Plainly, we want to focus on the techniques for estimating at or near the start of a project. The product is then at its most abstract, which gives estimating the aspects of a black art; and of all estimates in the course of a project, the early ones exert the greatest influence on quality. Estimators need to account for the two independent sets of factors listed in Table 5.1.

Estimators in the early stages of a project use a variety of techniques. Some estimate simply by analogy. If the subject release is similar to the preceding in planned fixes and new features, the cost should be about the same. Where analogy cannot be applied, a composition technique is commonly used: break the project down into a number of discrete tasks (work breakdown structure), estimate the cost of each, and add all the costs. The detailed costs, of course, should take into account the cost drivers listed here. One advantage of the composition technique is that the people responsible for the various tasks can be asked to estimate their own costs, thereby placing responsibility for estimating with process owners.

The parametric model for estimating is gaining increasing acceptance, even if used only as a sanity check for estimates made by other means. Parametric models use mathematical formulae for combining cost factors, such as those found in Table 5.1.

TABLE 5.1 Cost Influence

Problem attributes	Cost drivers
Amount of code or number of function points	Historical productivity, given a reasonably constant development process
Conceptual difficulty	Caliber of the staff
Stability of customer requirements	Experience in related problems and in use of planned development environment
Dependency on external test fixtures or real data files	Unique project factors (e.g., tight schedule)

Some typical popular tools based on parametric models are SLIM,[*] COCOMO,[†] SoftCost,[‡] and SPQR.[§] We should note that none of the tools, even the relatively simple COCOMO model, assume linear relations between the influences and cost. Among the typical tool outputs are development and maintenance costs, development duration, confidence level, quality analysis (based on environment factors), and staff allocation.

Judicious procedures for estimating the jobs of designing software, implementing the design, and supporting the product help to smooth the road for the people who will perform the jobs.

5.4 Designing for Quality

We have no shortage of ways to produce quality designs. The number of methods published in books, journals, and trade magazines threatens to exceed the number of designers active in the field. Perhaps the most interesting reading has to do with experiments in software engineering conducted by universities and industrial research laboratories, much of which is purported to have industrial strength. We make no attempt to plow through this fertile field, and we promise not to further fertilize it. With one exception, what follows are some general attributes of quality designs and related design issues. The exception is found under the rubric "decomposition." Here we discuss one of the best-tested design methods, *structured design*, used in conventional programming (i.e., methods apart from those tied to such inclusive paradigms as O-O or specific CASE-supported methods as the Jackson Development Method).

Simplicity

Good design means simple design, or at least as simple as the problem allows. Note that we did not say that to get a good design you should design simply. On the contrary, simple designs arise from complex thinking.

Complex software is difficult to evaluate, test, and modify. The intricacies of complex software also are good hiding grounds for bugs. We shall have more to say about measuring complexity in Chap. 12, but for the moment let's refer to a popular measure of control flow complexity—McCabe's cyclomatic (graph-theoretic) measure.[20] Essentially, the model equates the complexity of a program to one plus the number of its binary decision nodes. The higher the number, the harder

---

[*]Quantitative Software Management, McLean, VA.

[†]NASA-Johnson Space Center, Mail Code FR5, Houston, TX.

[‡]Reifer Consultants, Inc., P.O. Box 4046, Torrence, CA.

[§]Software Productivity Research, Inc., 77 So. Bedford Street, Burlington, MA.

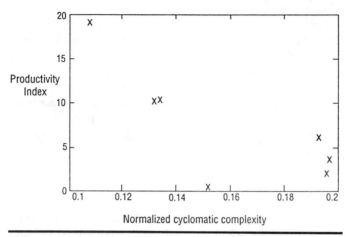

Figure 5.8 Maintenance productivity versus complexity.

it will be to live with the program. Over the years, a number of attempts have been made to independently validate the model, most of them successful. An example is found in the scatter plot of Fig. 5.8, which plots a maintenance productivity index against the cyclomatic numbers, normalized to thousands of lines of executable code, of the programs maintained. The specific maintenance activity of the plot is the addition of lines of new code to existing software. The productivity index is defined as the number of new lines (total) divided by the time (hours) spent in coding and testing the changes. The data apply to seven application systems.[21] Although Fig. 5.8 has few data points, it is fairly evident that maintenance productivity is adversely affected by control flow complexity. McCabe, incidentally, initially devised the complexity metric with maintenance in mind.

Programmers often argue that their products are complex because the problem is inherently complex. The assertion certainly agrees with our intuitive sense of complexity. Still, program designs can be more complex than need be. Quality software is no more complex than it need be. A prevention process demands simplicity.

As an example, consider the program Bill designed to compare two unsorted lists of names, deleting from the first list any names appearing in the second. He reasoned as follows: "All I have to do is go down the first list item by item, and for each item search through the second list to see if the same name appears there. If so, simply replace the name with a blank. When the program is finished scanning the first list, just compress it to delete the blanks." The result is shown in Fig. 5.9a, and it certainly looks simple enough. Unfortunately, compressing turned out to

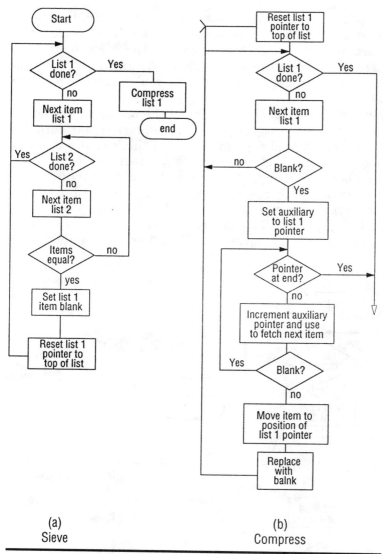

Figure 5.9 Bill's first design.

be more of a task than Bill had thought. When he expanded the block "compress list1," he discovered it metamorphosed to Fig. 5.9b.

During the review of Bill's design, Norma was disquieted by the total number of conditional branches in the program (the diamonds). Seven branches struck Norma as more than the problem warranted. Moreover, she knew that control flow complexity is loosely related to the total number of branches. Norma suggested that rather than replacing duplicate names with blanks, the program could just copy unique names to a third list, ignoring the duplicated ones. Back at the drawing board, Bill came up with the simpler design of Fig. 5.10, three branches as compared to the earlier seven. That evening, Norma and Bill had dinner in his apartment. But you've already seen the commercial.

There were other approaches to solving the problem that might have suggested themselves to Bill. In fact, even casual consideration of the problem would lead a programmer to think of the effect of using sorted input lists, of compressing by sorting (leaving the blanks at the bottom), and of other ways of scrubbing redundancy between two similarly structured lists. Superficially, such methods appear simpler (moreover, sorted lists would probably speed up the procedure), but analysis will show that they actually have more branches. The box on the diagram that says "sort" has a number of

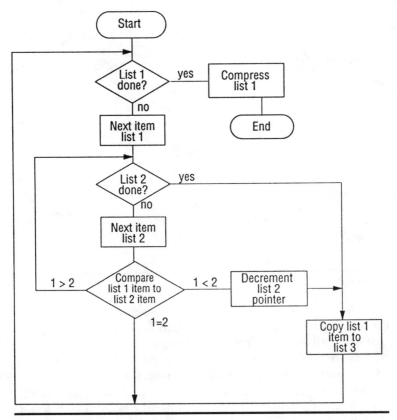

Figure 5.10   Bill's second design.

branches within it.* As Alfred North Whitehead said, "Seek simplicity and distrust it."

When we think of software complexity, we usually think mostly of control flow complexity. However, the complexity of data is just as important. We need to introduce the term *data abstraction*, which we loosely define as a view of data that omits details. At the machine level, we could speak of data abstraction in terms of structure types (vectors, arrays, and the like) rather than in terms of bytes. At a somewhat higher level, we can speak of a stack (a last-in first-out vector of dynamic length), which hides the details of the *type* vector on which it is based, or a coordinate transformation matrix, which hides the detail of its underlying *type* array. In terms of file structures, the abstraction of a structure of records and pointers is a tree of vertices and edges. Dealing with data at the most abstract level possible clarifies the essence of a design and makes the design, if not the resulting product, simpler.

Information hiding is another concept to make designs simpler. Formalized by David Parnas some years ago,[22] the idea is to keep the data used by a software component internal to it. Data exported to the component is "public" data, visible to (and alterable by) other components. Private or "encapsulated" data are independent of the way other components go about their processing. Each item of public data used by a component represents a hook into the rest of the system, effectively adding to the overall complexity of the component. Getting ahead of ourselves once again, we note that information hiding abets modularity, the independence of software components.

Parenthetically, we note that O-O derives from abstract data types and information hiding.

Thus far we have ignored individual data structures. The complexity of a data structure has to do with its layering and the heterogeneity of its contents. A vector in which each element points to another vector is plainly more complex than a single linear set of variables. A record containing seven different kinds of fields (name, credit rating, address, etc.) leaves more room for getting things in the wrong order than a record containing only customer names.

As with the control flow of Bill's program, we can make data more complex than they need to be. Consider a linked list of telecommunications messages. A record of one message followed by a record of another message followed by a record of yet another message and so on. This type of list is useful when messages have a variable and undefined number of records. Each record contains a pointer to the

---

*If utility sort routines that have stood the test of time can be used, we really should not have much concern for their internal complexity. But this virtue of reusable software gets us ahead of ourselves.

location of its successor in the message. To scan messages in various directions, each record also contains a pointer to the location of its predecessor (making it a *doubly linked* list). Adding a new message is simply a matter of adjusting pointers and filling empty space (space never used or last used by a message since disposed of) with records. Deleting a processed message requires only an adjustment of pointers. Figure 5.11 illustrates a section of such a list.

Plainly, the design required to process information contained in such a list is more complex than a more homogeneous structure. Moreover, handling the end of each link requires more processing than is immediately evident. The designers of the Thrillacom Company were so used to dealing with such lists that they might have been tempted to use the structure for the new product line, one dealing with a limited number of short messages of fixed, rather than variable, length. However, they recognized that they could use a simpler structure, so they loaded each message into contiguous cells of a file, and maintained a separate table containing the location of the start cell of each message. The design called for ordering the table each time a new message came in or was deleted. When a new message came in, the program could look at the table of starting addresses, find an empty one (they were all together), and place the new message there. The new data design is depicted in Fig. 5.12.

Complexity is not just a matter of complexity-in-the-small, as in our examples. We conclude this section with the observation made in a 1988 paper on complexity. Defining the external complexity of a module as a function of its interaction with its environment, the authors note that "...if a module is used in two different systems, its external complexity can be different, since it may have different amounts of interaction in the two systems."[23] In other words, we must be cautious in assuming that we shall get a simple result by designing a system comprising a set of satisfactorily simple components.

Modularity

Designers attempt to make a system as modular as possible, meaning that the parts have minimal interdependence. In the decomposition paradigm, problems are partitioned so that the designers working on each partition need have minimum communication with each other.

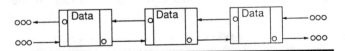

Figure 5.11 Doubly linked list schema.

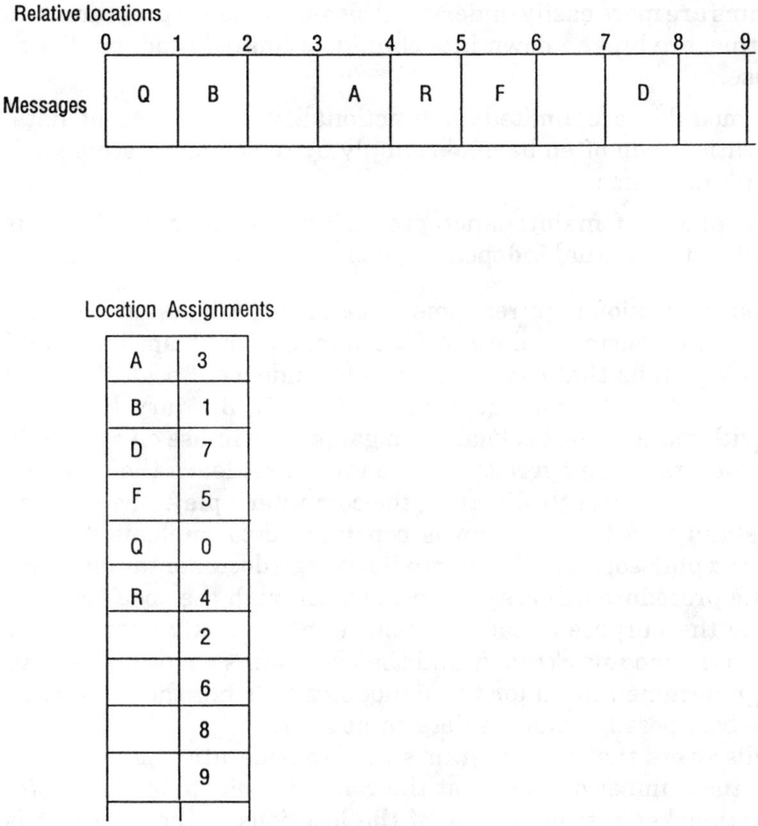

Relative locations

	0	1	2	3	4	5	6	7	8	9
Messages	Q	B		A	R	F		D		

Location Assignments

A	3
B	1
D	7
F	5
Q	0
R	4
	2
	6
	8
	9

Figure 5.12   A simple indexed data structure.

each partition need have minimum communication with each other. (This is not to say that they should not talk with each other frequently. The point is that they do not need to.) Modularity means more than just a way to make a project more manageable. We shall look at the effect of modularity on maintenance, testing, and component reuse, and then look at one widely used technique for achieving modularity.

Modularity and maintenance.   When we look at the structure of the product, which is what we look at during maintenance, we see not the earlier partitions but the set of procedures that, with the mainline program of most programming paradigms, constitute the product.

The connection between modularity and maintenance is threefold:

1. Programs are more easily understood by maintenance programmers when they are broken down into chunks of limited functionality or data use.

2. When modules are limited in functionality or the use of data, modifications can often be made simply by replacing existing modules with new ones.

3. The likelihood of maintenance producing adverse side effects is reduced as the mutual independence of the modules increases.

This last connection requires some explanation. Adverse side effects result from the sharing of data, the exchange of program flags, and other design details that compromise independence. Recall Personal Computer Products' Game program from Chap. 3. Mary has been charged with making the backgammon game, now in use on over 1000 home computers, more aggressive. She must first learn the methods and philosophies currently dictating the computer's play. She also has to understand how the program is constructed to implement these methods and philosophies. Turning to the design documentation, Mary studies the procedure call graph and reads through the specifications that define the purpose of each procedure. She quickly narrows her interests to the module *Strategy* and the procedures subordinate to it. The design documentation for these modules tells her the manner in which the best possible move is determined.

Mary discovers that the program's first consideration is always to minimize the number of blots that the computer has to leave. (A *blot* is a single marker resting on one of the locations of the board. It is vulnerable to capture if a marker of the other color can be moved to the location. A blot can be eliminated if the single marker is joined by another of the same color.) Mary wants to change this conservative play by coloring the decision with consideration of the poor strategic position that it may frequently create.

The three modules directly subordinate to *Strategy* are *Early_Game*, *Middle_Game*, and *End_Game*. Figure 5.13 extends part of Fig. 3.5 to show these, as well as the modules *Tree_Search* and *Weighting*. (Figure 5.13 ignores utility routines appearing in the actual call graph.) The complaint of conservatism had been applied to the middle part of the game, and it is to *Middle_Game* that Mary turns her attention. She finds that the most simple fix is to modify the processing of *Weighting* to lessen the penalty applied to those situations that result in blots.

She makes the change and runs some informal tests. After several days of making adjustments to *Weighting,* she link-edits the entire game system and sits down to match her wits with the computer. She wins three backgammon games in a row and is badly losing the fourth

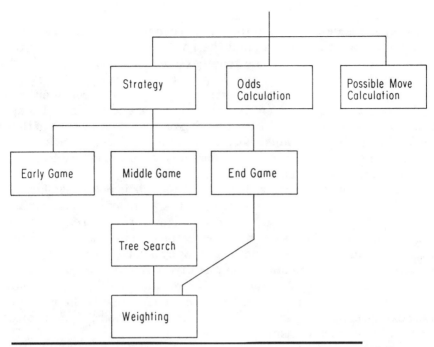

Figure 5.13 Backgammon detail.

when, only a few moves from winning, the computer makes a surprisingly inept move. Mary checks back through the results of all the evaluation reports made at the time of the initial release of the program and can find no report of a similar anomaly.

There is nothing to do now but study the end game processing. After considerable effort, Mary discovers the bug. *Middle_Game* had been designed to call the random number utility routine for the purpose of occasionally setting a binary program flag that, passed through *Tree_Search* to *Weighting*, would force *Weighting* into a rote response. This response, in effect, ignored all blots. It was hoped that the resultant move would be sufficiently uncharacteristic of the computer to puzzle the player. In her change to *Weighting*, Mary used the flag, but changed both *Weighting* and *Middle_Game* to make the flag a 5-valued performance modifier. What Mary discovered about the flag was that *End_Game* also used it, but for the purposes of establishing the rote response when blots were no longer significant to winning. Unable to properly interpret the revised states of the flag, *End_Game* blew the lead left it by *Middle_Game*.

In effect, despite appearances, *Middle_Game* and *End_Game* were not truly independent of each other, but were linked through other procedures.

Modularity and testing.   Among the purposes given in Chap. 3 for testing modules in isolation, we cited the potential for susceptibility to error conditions that cannot be readily tested except at the module level. Chapter 7 will go into this in greater detail. For our present purposes, as a rationale for unit testing, we may simply consider the number of interfaces between the input routines and the modules at the bottom of the hierarchy. The processing of input data by each of the intervening modules can make it time-consuming, at best, to backtrack from the driving conditions desired for the subject procedure back to the input data that will generate those conditions.

The unit test of a module, assuming the module is not overly large, should be exhaustive; when possible, to the point of exercising the module in each of the discrete states of data it can produce. At the least, every branch should be tested. If, however, the module is closely linked to others, as through common data areas or by a dependency on logical switches set by other modules, the test driver required to exercise it may be as large or even larger than the module itself. Under these conditions, the unit test in effect becomes the joint test of the module and the program used to test it. One then faces the choice of untoward costs in test support or insufficient testing.

Even in top-down testing, poor modularity can invite a visit from the programmers' two-headed *bête noire,*—cost and complexity. Prior to a module's entry into the evolving system, it is represented by a stub. The role of the stub is a simple one in theory: receiving the call intended for the module it is standing in for, it provides a return logically appropriate to the arguments with which it is called. These normally are rote responses. Again, in the presence of excessive module interdependence, the stub may have to perform a set of calculations based on the current status of common data areas or the status of other logical control indicators. In the extreme, the surrogate may approach its model in complexity, in which case it, too, may have to be unit tested!

Reuse.   When an automobile manufacturer adds a new model to the product line, every attempt is made to use parts originally designed for other models. The manufacturer saves the design cost, the tooling cost, and often the cost of training labor. A less obvious benefit is that the new model will include parts of known quality characteristics. (We hopefully assume that manufacturers do not reuse components known to provide an untoward number of problems for customers.)

Historically, software is built with few reused components. Yes, we have libraries of various mathematical subprograms, such as the extensive FORTRAN libraries, libraries for DBMS functions, and window/menu systems. We might remember, also, that the Unix shell, acting as a command interpreter, produces sequences of code that are recalled for similar functions. And we think of JCL (Job Control Language) procedures reused from job to job, or DBMS templates adapted for different queries. Indeed, the concepts of reusable software apply not only to program components but also to application generators, executable specifications (e.g., PAISLey), and software architectures.[24]

Nevertheless, it is to the reuse of program modules that we want to direct our attention. The analogy to manufacturing components demands that module reuse be placed among the prevention-oriented techniques of software technology. The reuse of software modules can create dramatic quality results. Consider a study of some 887 modules developed for flight dynamics software.[25] Among the modules were extensive and slight modifications of existing ones, existing ones reused with no change, and entirely new modules.

Figure 5.14 shows the fault rate incidence (classified as zero, medium, or high rates) for each of the four module groups. Looking at the extremes, only 44 percent of new modules had zero fault rates compared to 98 percent of the modules reused without change; 27 percent of the new modules had high fault rates compared to 2 percent of the reused ones.

Why are more modules not reused? Three reasons have dissuaded programmers from using modules prepared for earlier projects, or even for other parts of the current project:

- They have to know they are available
- They have to find them
- They have to know how to use them

The first reason implies that we need libraries of available modules that programmers can browse through. The second reason implies a

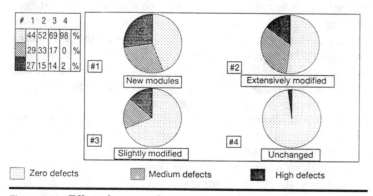

Figure 5.14   Effect of reuse and re-engineering on fault rates.

certain formality to the external specifications of the modules. The third reason tells us that the documented description (as in the prologue of the module's code) has to have an unambiguous description of the parameters of the module as seen by the calling program.

Modules designed to find new lives beyond the one for which they were initially destined should follow the precepts of information hiding. The more a programmer has to know about the innards of a module, the less likely its prospect for reuse. Moreover, prospects for reuse are increased if the public data can be expressed in terms of abstract data types, which lend themselves to browsing by tools. Information hiding and abstract data types? What do these suggest? Object-orientation, that's what.

Looking at O-O superficially, a group of interacting objects is likely to have members that can interact with the objects of another system developed under similar standards. Not surprisingly, the characteristic of O-O that receives the most attention is the relative facility with which it lends itself to module (in this case, object or class) reuse.

The study whose results are partially captured in Fig. 5.14 addressed both unchanged modules and modified modules. Modification, often called *re-engineering,* is a weaker but more common form of modular reuse. Generally, finding modifiable modules—those that come close to what you need—is a matter of programmers' memories. A programmer remembers having designed a similar module at an earlier time, or remembers that of a colleague's design. Most likely, the remembered module was no more than a couple of years old. Short of browsing tools based on formal specifications, programming shops should encourage re-engineering by maintaining a classified data base, including keyword-in-context descriptors, of module specifications.

MathCad, a 4GL (which we remarked in Chap. 2) makes re-engineering easy. For their Windows version, the publishers provide a set of on-line handbooks, complete with table of contents and index, for finding the publisher's own solutions to various kinds of mathematical applications. Using the table of contents or the index, the user finds a page of explanation and formulas close to what is needed. The user than pastes any part of the page to his document (normally in another window) and modifies it at will. This is rather like an updated use of a scientific subroutine library, but working with an expendable copy of the source code.

Plainly, only code or design segments independent of other segments in the system are candidates for reuse without modification. Put differently, modularity, which seems to affect so many aspects of software development, also bears upon the potential for reuse. Now that we all agree that modularity is a good thing, all we need to do is know how to achieve it. As it happens, "all we need to do" has preoccupied legions of software engineers for many years.

Decomposition. Various schemes have been developed to partition a computation problem into a set of maximally independent entities. None has achieved the popularity of structured design, especially in the United States. This is not to say that other methods, such as Jackson Structured Development and OOD, are not widely used, and any one could serve as an example of problem decomposition to the end of modularity. But we chose to use structured design's almost intuitive criteria for a well-decomposed system as our example.

In its entirety, structured design really has two parts: structured analysis based on the flow of data in a system, and the strategies of decomposition. Section 5.2, which had a brief discussion of structured analysis, noted that we could consider it a unifying paradigm, at least to the extent of its spanning the activities of requirements definition and preliminary design. The essence of structured design is that of a military commander driving a wedge to split an enemy force: divide and conquer. In our case, the enemy is the complexity of a large software problem.

The decomposition strategies of structured design are founded on concepts developed by Larry Constantine in the late 1960s. Central to these is the notion of module coupling and module cohesion. Modules are interdependent to the extent they are mutually coupled; modules are self-sufficient to the extent they are cohesive. Constantine and Yourdon list four influences on coupling.[26] In order of their effect on coupling, the four are intermodular coupling, the number of data items passed between modules, the type of information passed between modules (e.g., the flow of control information couples modules more than the flow of data), and the time at which connections between modules are made (e.g., binding at compilation time couples modules more than binding at execution time).

Constantine and Yourdon define seven levels of cohesion, starting with the least cohesive:

- Coincidental—Essentially, there is no commonality among the elements of a module.

- Logical—The elements of a module share a common class, such as all the output drivers of a system.

- Temporal—All internal processes are tied to a specific temporal event, such as initializing at boot time.

- Procedural—The elements perform several associated, but weakly related, sequential functions.

- Communicational—Like procedural cohesion, the module performs multiple sequential functions, but all on the same data set or with a common output data set.

- Sequential—The results from one internal process are the input for the next.
- Functional—Each element contributes to the processing of a single function.

Minimum coupling and maximum cohesiveness are qualitative goals. A somewhat more quantitative goal for a given module is to maximize *fan-in*, or the number of modules directly superordinate to it (above it). Where *module* and *procedure* are synonymous terms, the number of superordinate modules is equivalent to the number of modules calling the subject module. The higher the fan-in, the less the likelihood of code redundancy. The opposite number to fan-in is *fan-out*, or the number of subordinate modules. Heuristically, a fan-out of seven (more or less) is thought ideal, but fan-outs anywhere between two and 10 are common in well-designed systems.

Low coupling, high cohesion, maximum fan-in, and medium fan-out are perhaps the most prominent of the module level goals set forth for the iterative decomposition strategies of structured design. Constantine's original strategies were extended by G. Myers into a set of four types of decomposition: source/transform/sink, transactional decomposition, functional decomposition, and data structure decomposition.[27] Of these, functional decomposition seems to have become the most popular, and is often—as in Ref. 28—regarded as an integral part of the definition of structured design. One reason for its popularity is its simplicity: at each stage of decomposition extract, as separate modules, discrete functions from the modules already defined. This leads to functionally cohesive, loosely coupled modules. Functional decomposition also lends itself to the traceability of requirements model functions through relatively simple program call graph chains. Chapter 3's decomposition of the Games program loosely illustrates the thinking that goes into the first few iterations of functional decomposition.

We have gone into structured design only as an example of one systematic way of achieving modularity. As we noted earlier, other methods exist, some intrinsic to specific paradigms (e.g., object-oriented design and object-oriented structured design), some to development models (e.g., Jackson System Development). A prevention-based quality process demands that whatever method is selected, it should be purposeful, as seamless as possible, and supported by tools specific to the method.

Robust design and fault tolerance

When designers speak of software reliability, they often think in terms of software that continues to do what it is supposed to do when the operating conditions are as they had been specified. High reliability within these constraints may be of small comfort to users. The problem is that operating conditions are often not what designers are told they will be. The external specifications for software seldom address corrupted data files, erratic interfacing software, and fumble-fingered users. The robustness of software is the extent to which it can defend itself against violations of its external specifications.

The most obvious defense is the validation of all input; checks on data sanity, if you will. Checks are made not only of input to the system, but also of input to each procedure if erroneous input can escape earlier checks but may, nevertheless, cause the procedure to produce incorrect results or send the system into the ozone. As an example of the latter, a data reference index passed to a procedure (note the high coupling here) should be in the range valid for the file. This kind of defensive programming has been around for a long time, but remains conspicuously absent in many applications.

Sanity checks can also be applied to processing results. On final results, the checks can be used to warn the user of unreliable output. For example, two cells of a spreadsheet may contain small data entry errors, not noticeable in themselves, but capable of producing an out-of-range result when multiplied together. Testing the reasonableness of interim results serves a purpose only if an out-of-range check produces some action. Stop further processing with a warning. Better yet, by restoring any altered data to their state directly preceding the erroneous step, processes will be rolled back to the point where the error can be determined to have occurred. Note, however, that in systems of communicating concurrent processes, rollback is difficult to perform. Uncoordinated recovery points may require a series of cascading rollbacks in order to arrive at a state consistent with the several processes.

For real-time concurrent processes, where we have to deal with strict time limits, two schemes have been proposed to deal with fault tolerance.[29] If the system has cyclic synchronization points (as in a time slicing control mechanism), one can regress to the last of these points. The other scheme uses a watchdog timer to detect such errors as process hang-ups and infinite loops, and a backup scheduler to force the execution of critical tasks.

While on the subject of real-time processing, we should note that most processing errors produced by time-dependencies can be traced to sequences of external events other than the ones that were expected and for which the software was designed. Designers of real-time software need to be especially careful to avoid making unnecessary assumptions about the inviolability of specified time sequences. Where possible, real-time system designers should time-tag events at their source so that software designers can program sequence checks.

If we broaden our tolerance of faults to the point where we are willing to forgo the last N minutes of processing, we can guard against hardware faults by automatically backing up all data files every N minutes. The word processing program we use allows us to set the backup interval to whatever we want. On reloading the program after a power failure, we are given the option of retrieving the last backup. The same idea can be employed to defend against software faults so grave that files have been corrupted. A program to process sequential transactions can contain a task to periodically back up all the files and to journal or log the last set of transactions before backup. If the program is stopped manually or wanders on its own into the ozone, one reboots, loads the backup files, examines the transactions since the last known valid transaction, throws out the bad actor, and continues the job.

Although somewhat off the subject, we might also consider fault tolerance directed primarily at faulty hardware. One of the popular schemes in distributed telecommunications switches uses duplex processing modules. Output from the two modules can be externally compared, and both disabled if the output differs; or each can monitor self-checks made by the other. In the latter case, one has to be wary of the module that decides its mate is working improperly. How does one know that the checking module has not, itself, gone off the deep end? Figure 5.15 shows a scheme in which each module sends the other a series of verifiable logic checks. At the same time, each module reports its capability of making a judgment to the switch that selects the source of output to communicate with the rest of the system.

For example, Processor B determines that Processor A is out to lunch. Processor B sends a signal to the selector to disable A's output and enable B's output. Through simple logic circuitry, the disabling and enabling signals, however, can themselves be disabled if Processor B has failed to simultaneously send a signal saying that it has passed its own self-check. The system isn't fool proof, since, if really sick, Processor B might fool itself. But it comes very close to 100 percent reliability.

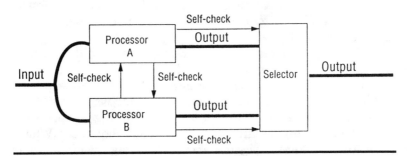

Figure 5.15 Hardware redundancy to tolerate faults.

An even more trustworthy system, used by the Stratus computer family, uses two pairs of tandem modules, with each pair feeding an independent comparator for continuous fault masking. The selector switch is fed by the outputs of the two comparators.[30] While highly reliable, this requires six processors (don't forget the two comparators) to do the work of one non-redundant or two duplexed processors.

For very critical parts of software systems, some designers have turned to design diversity, or *N-version programming*. *N* versions of the component are developed, each using a different algorithm. The two common methods to reconcile the results of the several components are:

1. To discard all and let the system coast if they do not agree
2. To use majority logic to select the presumably correct one (A farmer knows he has dropped his teeth in one of three identical sacks of seed. He has no scales. What procedure...?)

As an example, we might encode three distinct methods of extrapolating data: one based on classical polynomial approximations, another on a least-squares fit to the data, and a third using a Chebyshev approximation. In the best of worlds, all three are designed and coded by different people.

Design diversity may or may not actually increase the reliability of a system. Along with the cost of development, design diversity also increases the overall complexity of the software. In addition to having three versions, each of which may contain a bug that will one day bite the user's hand, we have also to reckon with the code that resolves the *N* results. As long as the jury stays out on this one, we should not expect to see a lot of application for design diversity.

5.5   Design Documentation

When we use the term *design documentation* we do not simply mean text. We refer to any means used to capture design decisions for the purposes of helping programmers understand the causes of test (and operational) failures and helping programmers make maintenance changes in the software at any future time. Secondary purposes of design documentation include a concrete basis for design reviews and tangible evidence that design has actually been completed. Document-driven development models, such as those implied by the family of IEEE software development standards and DOD-STD-2167A, promote the secondary purposes to a primary role. Such will not be our focus.

Unlike the documentation of behavioral specifications, customers do not have to understand design documentation. Thus, where appropriate, we can document design decisions at any level of design in forms other than natural language text, although natural language is uniquely useful for introduction (as in the prologues of pseudocode files) or for explaining the reasons for choosing a particular design approach.

Some of the popular methods for documenting preliminary design work follow seamlessly from methods used in analyzing requirements: data flow diagrams, state diagrams, data dictionaries, and System Verification Diagrams. Methods not likely to be encountered until preliminary design include:

- Hierarchical charts depicting the partitioning of the problem (such as Figs. 3.3 through 3.5)
- Indented lists, illustrated by Fig. 5.16
- Layouts of files and tables, as in Fig. 5.17, which is a graphical depiction of a data dictionary example from Sec. 5.2
- Tree structures of data, as in Fig. 5.18
- High-level pseudocode, as in Fig. 5.19
- Decision trees, as in Fig. 5.20

Data definitions grow with specificity in time. For example, we might guess that the first two columns of Fig. 5.17 were defined in

```
game
  backgammon
   supervisor
   dice throw
   player input routine
   machine play computation
    strategy
    odds calculation
    possible move calculation
  craps
  bridge
   supervisor
   shuffle and deal
   auction computation
   play out the contract
    declarer
    defender
    dummy
   player input
   display formatter
```

Figure 5.16 Component hierarchy.

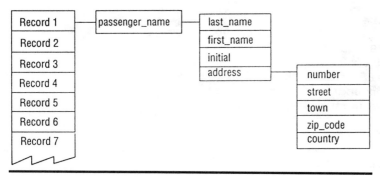

Figure 5.17   Layout of Flight_Manifest file.

problem analysis, and the last two in preliminary design. It remains for detailed design to fill in the number of characters in each field.

The preceding list included tree structures, yet another technique for documenting the decomposition of data. Figure 5.18 is a tree representing the flight_manifest file. Unlike the more conventional file layout diagrams, trees do not generally reflect logical assignments of records and fields. The more abstract view of data provided by trees conforms neatly with the idea of letting designers work in terms of concepts, rather than details, until they no longer can.

Pseudocode, the modern standard for outlining control flow, also can be used to help document the overall outline of control that emerges from preliminary design. Figure 5.19 is a nonexecutable program (pseudocode) that roughs out the overall control structure for a (much

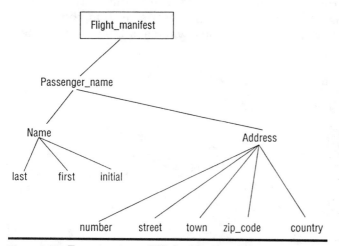

Figure 5.18   Tree structure of Flight_Manifest file.

```
procedure navigation
  while inertial indicates velocity do
    if GPS active
      then update inertial from GPS
      elseif Loran active
        then update inertial from Loran
        else warn pilot to use VOR input to compute LAT/LON
      endif
    endif
    if new LAT/LON manually input
      then update inertial with LAT/LON
    endif
    if flight director engaged
      then supply flight control inputs from inertial guidance
           system
    endif
    if altimeter differs from selected altitude
      then
        if jet
          then supply pitch change
          else supply power change
        endif
      endif
    end
  end
```

Figure 5.19   Pseudocode at a high level of design.

simplified) airborne flight director. At this, the highest level, the decision has been made to use inertial guidance to provide flight control input to ailerons, rudder, and elevator (for maintaining altitude during turns). To compensate for precession of the inertial system, the inertial system is updated by GPS computations, when available, Loran when

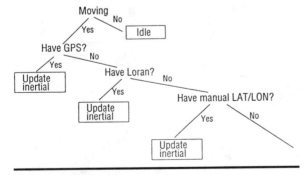

Figure 5.20   Decision tree.

not. If neither is available, the pilot has the opportunity to update the inertial system by manually entering the latitude and longitude of VOR beacons the aircraft flies directly over. Deviations from assigned altitude result in control inputs to the elevator servos (for jets) or in directed changes of power (for propeller driven planes).

Designers might choose to depict the decisions about how to update the inertial system in a decision tree, such as that of Fig. 5.20. Although decision trees lend themselves neither to easy updating nor to consistency checks and the like that pseudocode analyzers can provide, many designers believe the sense of the diagrams can be grasped more easily.

Structure charts (as in Fig. 3.6) or call graphs are likely to be produced during detailed design, although the first hierarchical levels may fall out of preliminary design tasks. (Recall that since we did not confine ourselves to any one exact development model, we have not specified a sharp distinction between preliminary and detailed design.) The detailed design tasks also lead to the evolution of a procedure use chart. For each procedure, one can see what other procedures call it and what procedures it calls.

Designers still occasionally use *truth tables* (a tabular form of decision trees especially useful if several predicates affect single decisions) to depict the conditions that should determine control flow. State diagrams, like that of Fig. 5.4, only at a more detailed level, are sometimes found useful for detailed design. You can see in the navigation problem the several states implied by the pseudocode: GPS used for update, Loran used for update, and so on. Of course, the contents of data dictionaries are given final form during detailed design.

The primary vehicle for capturing detailed design control flow is pseudocode, as in the example given in Sec. 2.4 and, at a higher level, in Fig. 5.19. Some designers still prefer to use flowcharts, like that of Fig. 2.3, even though they cannot be analyzed by machine. Indeed, flowcharts seem to be making a comeback, probably the result of CASE tools that make it easier to update them. Still, flowcharts produce a quality problem. Since they do not lend themselves to restrictions of form, they frequently spread amorphously into entangled networks that approach plates of spaghetti and meatballs in their intricacies. Worse, in trying to find one's way from one processing meatball to another, one often follows the pasta to an off-page connector; not at a logical functional boundary, but at a point dictated by the size and aspect ratio of the paper on which the diagram is drawn. Nevertheless, we must recognize that some programmers have much greater ability to understand concepts when presented graphically rather than verbally.

For either flowcharts or pseudocodes, we pause to address the venerable question of how detailed detailed documentation should be. We certainly do not want to see a one-to-one correlation between lines of pseudocode or flowchart symbols and production source code. That would be unreadable. Those given to quantitative standards at all costs have suggested that each line of pseudocode or flow chart symbol should represent an average of five instructions (except for those who advocate an average of seven or eight or 10 instructions). None of these magic numbers bears directly on the matter of readability or communication of design concepts or evidence of design completion. Another school of thought holds that each decision point, or branch, should be shown. This is a reasonable idea, except that taking a doctrinaire position on this may result in pseudocode cluttered with trivial IF-THEN-ELSEs at the expense of beclouding the important design decisions captured by the pseudocode. The same thing holds true for flowcharts. As a somewhat lame alternative along the lines of the Bauhaus school of design (less is more), we suggest that for each line of pseudocode or flowchart symbol, the form of the consequent code should be obvious; that is, that there should be no substantive latitude in the manner in which the design can be implemented in code by an experienced programmer.

For many design efforts, the allocation of computer resources also needs recording. How much memory per module? How much time—average, maximum, and standard deviation—per servicing each kind of interrupt? How much disk space for each file? For systems programming, we may get into register allocations, port assignments, and assigned uses of cache. Whatever resources enter into the picture, they need to be recorded and, where applicable, summed. Better to find out that the design calls for more computer than is available before the program files are rolled into the test lab.

The diversity of schemes for capturing design decisions suggests that software is an industry with few documentation standards. This is in sharp contrast to the hard goods industries where schematic and assembly diagrams, engineering parts lists, and bills of materials are much alike from one company to another; where the blueprints a machinist uses in one shop can be accurately interpreted by a machinist in another; where galleys differ little from one publisher to another.

We can attribute the lack of software documentation standards to the diversity of programming paradigms and development models, not to mention individual style preferences. But there is something else: if they are not copied—that is, manufactured in a production environment—most hardware designs are useless. This has driven the documentation of hardware designs. Software products, however, are cloned from the last development model, with the result that the heat has been taken off their documentation. Yet, the last, tested, proven development model is the end product of a lengthy and (presumably) orderly process of analysis, specification, design, and testing. If efficient, consistent, and informative documentation doesn't attend all phases of development, it is difficult to see how customer requirements can survive the entire process without compromise or complete loss. And then there is maintenance, for which the documentation represents a Rosetta stone for unlocking the mysteries of the program, without which the program will surely be short-lived.

5.6 Coding for Quality

A revolution in computer programming was started in 1966 when C. Böhm and G. Jacopini published a paper proving that the control flow of all programs can be realized using but three constructs: sequence, condition, and iteration.[31] The full import of the paper was not recognized until 1968 when E. Dijkstra published his short paper "Go To Statement Considered Harmful."[32]

The unbridled use of unconditional branches, or *gotos*, had for years produced program logic that was difficult to understand, impossible to formally verify, and since they can create logic topographies (in the sense of the then ubiquitous flowcharts) approaching that of the New York City subway system, an inexhaustible source of latent defects. The three Böhm and Jacopini constructs, illustrated by Fig. 5.21 in flowchart form, lit the path out of the tortuous subway tunnels. By restricting program branches to the two conditional types of Fig. 5.21, programmers could avoid the use of any goto statements.

Although Böhm and Jacopini addressed themselves to flowcharts, the translation to code was obvious. The term *structured programming* was coined to reflect the coherence of code free of gotos. Structured programming, now a *sine quo non* of quality for code written in 3GL, gained adherents at an astonishing rate. There was a problem, though: Few programming languages offered *if-then-else* or *do-while* (or such equivalents as *repeat-until*) statement forms. Which brings us back to the topic of programming languages and quality.

Today, many 3GL support structured programming. Pascal, one of the first, has been joined by C, FORTH, PL/1, Ada, and a host of lesser known languages. Even venerable FORTRAN and COBOL have been retrofitted for structured programming. LISP champions, by the bye, will tell you that their language was structured from the start. In LISP, every conditional branch has to be satisfied within the structure (outermost parenthesis pair) of the predicate. Structured programming has happily become a nonissue when it comes to selecting a programming language. Since many of the languages retain the goto, programmers can still write unstructured code, but that is a matter

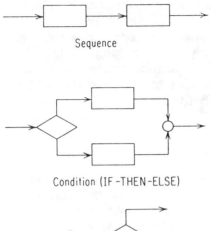

Sequence

Condition (IF-THEN-ELSE)

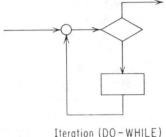

Iteration (DO-WHILE)

Figure 5.21   Böhm-Jacopini constructs.

for code reviews, which we'll take up in Chap. 7. With structured programming out of the way, we turn to other areas in which coding practices and programming languages affect quality.

Data typing

From the earliest years of programming, the forms of *constants* (in a semantic sense we do not usually consider these as data, but for the present purpose we do), *variables*, variables logically associated in *tables* and *files* have been found useful as standards. Later, certain types of data were defined: variables could be integers, reals (capable of taking on fractional values), complex (having imaginary parts), or Boolean (having but two values, true or false). Each type defined the attributes and storage requirements for each datum so defined. Some software engineers regard data typing as the data equivalent of structured programming. A language that requires the programmer to distinguish between reals and integers prevents the programmer from incorrectly attempting to read precisely 3.4 records from a file. Looking at it from a bit of a distance, data typing adds a measure of definitional redundancy to reduce programmer errors.

Most popular languages used for algebraic computation, such as C, FORTRAN and PL/1, differentiate between integers and reals, but then there is BASIC, which in its minimal form treats all data alike. At the other extreme, specificity gains when the programmer is permitted to define types of data unique to the program. To take one example, PASCAL comes supplied with the types integer, real, Boolean, and character. The operations permitted on each are those appropriate to the type. Beyond these, PASCAL allows the user to define new types. For example:

```
TYPE
  day_name = (sunday, monday ... saturday)
```

Having so declared the names of the days, you can use the PASCAL function ORD (short for order) to operate on a variable of the type *day_name*. Assume we have previously pulled from a file a datum *toll_record* of the type *day_name*, and we want to determine if it is a weekday record. We could use the statement

```
K := ORD(toll_record)
```

which will return a 0 for Sunday or a 6 for Saturday. Thus, for $K = 1$ through 5, weekday toll rates apply.

As another example, user-defined types also allow programmers to define sets of data with the future operations of disjunction (or union) and conjunction (or intersection) in mind. For example, if you've declared *tennis, golf, baseball, water_polo* to be the set of warm weather games you play with a ball, and *sailing, water_skiing, water_polo* to be your favorite water sports, then the conjunction of variables assigned to the two sets turns out to be the only water sport (*water_polo*) you play with a ball, and the disjunction yields the full complement of your summer recreation.

Information hiding

Section 5.4 introduced the term *information hiding. Ripple effect,* wherein several modules in the system are affected by a change to one, is related to information exposure. Limiting the amount of data available to each module reduces the number of assumptions of that module made by the other modules with which, either through direct interface or shared data, it interacts. Fewer assumptions reduce the ripple that can accompany a change to the subject module. Put differently, reducing a module's access to data reduces maintenance effort and the likelihood of adverse side effects when the module is modified.

Going a step further, hiding code and data from other modules makes it impossible for the interacting modules to get involved with the way the subject module implemented its specification. If a programmer does not have to know how a given, existing, module works, that module is more likely to be incorporated in the programmer's own design; that is, reused.

Much has been written about the way Ada hides data. Ada has a unique type of module called a *package*. Packages comprise:

1. External specifications of data and operations

2. Procedure bodies to implement the specifications

Both public and private data are found in a module's specification, but the latter are defined as private data types encapsulated within the (separately compiled) body of the module. You can do a lot worse than considering Ada if reusability is an important issue.

Object-oriented programming

Since we have already discussed the contributions that O-O can make to quality, we'll confine this discussion to O-O languages. Languages that support O-O fall into two classes: those that, beyond supporting O-O, require that the software exclusively comprise instances of classes, and those that are built on top of more conventional languages and allow the inclusion of code that does not conform with the O-O paradigm. Smalltalk and Eiffel are examples of the former class, C++ and LISP with Flavors, the latter. True believers in the O-O paradigm will be tempted to select the purer languages, but there are other considerations that enter into a language selection: data typing (languages in either class, such as Smalltalk and LISP, may do no type-checking), whether the language is interpreted (as in LISP with Flavors) or compiled (as in C++), the availability of tools for the language, and other considerations common to other paradigms—expressiveness, concurrency mechanisms, and the like.

One matter that must always be considered when migrating to O-O is just what kind of O-O one wants. We have talked about O-O as if it were a single paradigm. It would be more realistic to speak of O-O as a family of paradigms. Nearly everyone agrees that O-O implies objects, classes, and class inheritance. But some O-O languages extend the paradigm to include such other features as:

- Polymorphism—loosely, the use of generic classes tied down to specifics by parameters

- Encapsulation (essentially, information hiding)

- Dynamic binding—binding objects' methods to message selection at run-time, rather than compile-time

Not only is the sense of object-orientation a function of the features included in a given interpretation of the meaning of O-O, but the very sense in the way the features are implemented lends further diversity to the meaning of object-orientation. And all the diverse meanings are language-dependent.

What we come down to is that before a language is selected for O-O, a software shop must consider not only the more general attributes of languages (e.g., readability, expressiveness), but the features (and their shades of meaning) of O-O really wanted. Otherwise, O-O may well be a disappointment.

We digress for a bit to take up the special case of Ada. Many programmers regard Ada as a less object-oriented language than such languages as C++, Smalltalk, LISP with Flavors, Eiffel, and Object-Pascal. The primary area of disagreement has to do with inheritance. When thinking O-O, Ada's package structure is the equivalent of a class of objects. In the O-O paradigm, classes are derived from parent classes, in the process inheriting certain features. Ada has no explicit inheritance mechanism. However, generic (polymorphic) packages can be used to derive new collections of objects containing the operations of the generic parent. Though not as straightforward as the creation in other languages of new classes with inherited characteristics, this is a way of implementing the concept of inheritance.

Several books are available to provide a much fuller explanation of object-orientation at the code level than our broader subject permits. Two such books are found in Refs. 33 and 34.

Compiler or interpreter?

We touched upon this in Chap. 3. In terms of both memory and speed, compiled source code is more efficient than interpreted code. Interpreted code, however, offers programmers the opportunity to see how their code works almost instantaneously, has the potential (not always implemented) of letting programmers see the state of arbitrarily selected data at any time, and offers users of interpreted production code a variety of options. If the application is a system to monitor the vital signs of hospital patients, one would not build software that had to be interpreted. One might, however, provide Accounts Receivable with a DBMS that operated with an on-line interpreter to facilitate user-programmed queries.

Interpreters and compilers exist side by side in both the 3GL and 4GL worlds. Interpreters are hard to find for some languages (e.g.,

COBOL, PL/1), compilers for others (e.g., APL, FOCUS), so the choice of interpreter or compiler is intertwined with one's prioritization of language—indeed, paradigm—characteristics.

Expressiveness

The more easily programmers can express themselves, the less likely they are to make errors and the more likely they will generate easily maintained code. Expressiveness in a language is another way of saying problem-orientation, in contrast with machine orientation. Plainly, a language highly expressive for one set of problems is not likely to be expressive for other kinds of work.

One doesn't ordinarily associate expressiveness with conventional 3GL. However, a programmer developing a driver for a peripheral device may find C's mechanisms for setting and manipulating bits the very nub of expression. More generally, though, we think of expression in terms of computer applications. In that sense, DBMS languages are highly expressive for correlating large amounts of data, and application generator languages are highly expressive for narrowly defined classes of problems. Stretching the point just a bit, the handling of related asynchronous external events is facilitated by a language able to deal with concurrency, as in Ada's rendezvous mechanism.

Beyond the direct connections to quality noted earlier, expressiveness makes languages good candidates for rapid prototyping. The more expressive the language, the faster one can prepare a prototype.

Other considerations

We briefly discuss three coding practices that also influence the quality of the product: the use of magic numbers, initialization oversights, and the use of recursive procedures and functions.

Programmers should avoid the use of *magic numbers*—constants that show up in source code as if wafted in on a flying carpet. For example,

```
gnp := 0
i := 1
WHILE i <=50
  gnp := gnp + gsp(i)
  i := i + 1
END
```

might well add the gross product of all 50 states to form the gross national product, but it's bad code. Six years from now, when Martha's Vineyard and Nantucket secede from Massachusetts and are admitted as the fifty-first state, the GNP will be underestimated. An alert reader will advise the Commerce Department and a newly hired émigré programmer will be assigned the job of checking the program for error. Not knowing what the constant 50 represents, the programmer will be at a loss to find the problem. The following would have been proper code:

```
n_states := 50 ;50 is the number of states in the union
 .

 .
gnp := 0
i := 1
WHILE i  <= n_states
 gnp := gnp + gsp(i)
 i := i + 1
END
```

Failure to observe initialization standards often leads to error. In the previous example, our careless programmer remembered to initialize the value of gnp to 0, rather than depending on the compiler to do so. Some language specifications (e.g., C) include automatic initialization of certain variables to zero. Other language specifications (e.g., FORTRAN) do not. For some languages, certain compilers or interpreters initialize to a default, others do not. For example, some LISP interpreters assign all newly introduced variables a value of NIL. Mischief will break out when a LISP program lacking explicit initialization is prepared for one interpreter and later ported to a different LISP environment.

Recursion is a useful feature in programming for the same reason that it is in mathematics; it makes many things simpler to do and, in the process, more understandable. For our purposes, this means less prone to programmer error and more conducive to maintenance. In mathematics, recursion is employed wherever possible. The most familiar example of mathematical recursion is the calculation of factorials.

$$n! = n(n - 1)!$$

given that $1! = 1$

The equivalent in software is a recursive subprogram; that is, one that calls itself.*

```
FUNCTION factorial (n)
 IF n < 1 OR n = 1
  THEN factorial := 1
  ELSE factorial := n * factorial (n -1)
END
```

---

*A definition of recursion attributed to many sources reads: Recursion. *See* recursion.

The application of recursion to mathematical computation is obvious (Chebyshev polynomials, combinatorials, etc.), but recursion is also popular in other applications. For example, recursion is the easiest way to list all the source statements comprising the tree network represented by the game hierarchy of Fig. 3.5. Indeed, "pure" LISP (an acronym for "list processing") has no form for iteration, the natural alternative to recursion, leaving the programmer no choice but to write recursively.

Wisely applied, recursion adds to the quality of source code, but may use enormous amounts of memory and machine cycle times. Each recursion requires that the state of the relevant data be saved on a stack, requiring memory; and "unwinding" the chain of recursions once a terminating condition is reached (the THEN branch) adds processing time. In short, another trade-off. Most popular languages support recursion, some (curiously, FORTRAN, the most popular language for mathematics) do not.

Some concluding observations

Although source code (or more commonly, its binary derivative) is the product delivered to the customer, the thought given to the design behind the code has more effect on quality than the actual task of coding. Nevertheless, good design can be undone by poor code. It is fairly easy to define good coding standards. One has to put more effort into selecting the language(s) that will become standard for the shop or, as sometimes occurs, employed for a particular job. Rather than wrestle with the number of tradeoffs required, many shops choose languages by a curious default process: they use whatever most of the programmers are comfortable with or have been trained in. Of course, even that is better than a case we know of where the language selected for a new product line was the only one the newly hired software manager had ever used: BASIC for an instrumentation system.

5.7   Order in Progress

A cardinal rule in TQM is don't try to do everything at once. Moreover, things take time. An improvement made to a process seldom shows payoff as quickly as hoped for. The important thing is to keep your eye on the target (customer), develop a strategy for improving processes while at the same time letting the improved processes refine the strategy for further improvements, and piecewise implement the strategy. Developers need to determine their baseline process, recognize where it fails to serve their purposes, and adjust.

Specific to software, prevention starts with analyzing the paradigm in place and competing paradigms. Which offer the greater likelihood of satisfying quality criteria? After settling on a paradigm, analyze appropriate languages and development models. (Iteratively, the choice of paradigm may have been influenced by available languages.) An influence on choices we have not fully explored in this chapter, but left for Chap. 8, is that of tools available to support paradigms and languages.

A development model is mapped onto the agreed paradigm and fleshed out with specific identification of the activities that take place in each of its tasks. These tasks should be defined such that they lend themselves to demonstratable results. For example, each design task should produce artifacts capturing the decisions made in prosecuting the task. One way to determine if the process is working out is to review the output of each task to see if the work was done according to the defined process. If not, we might expect one of the following:

- The team has not bought into the process
- The process was not properly explained to the team
- The team was provided inadequate written description of the process
- The process cannot be followed

Whichever, the avenue for improvement is obvious.

The artifacts of development serve another purpose. Since they not only provide the tangible output of tasks but serve as the basis for further tasks, they are marked by sufficient detail to provide the foundation for both of the following:

- Verifying that the work performed derived directly from the results of previous tasks and did not introduce new concepts or approaches that have not previously been verified
- Validating consistency with the constraints and requirements of the problem being solved

Verification and validation are so often said as a single word that one forgets that there is a conceptual difference between them. Both connote traceability to the problem being solved; verification accomplishing this by assuring that the process of solution evolves step by step (although possibly iteratively); validation by providing direct traceability to customer requirements without concern of how the solution was derived.

We do not use verification and validation exclusively in the sense of a team of inspectors coming in and passing judgment on the work, although we know that many companies like to use independent verifiers and validators. Rather, we refer simply to the processes of verification and validation, which may lie either within or without the general process of software development. In that sense, peer reviews accomplish the purposes of verification and validation. Customer involvement in prototype evaluation, test planning, and technical reviews is another form of validation. However performed, verification and validation can find early evidence to confirm that projects are on the right course to meet customer needs. In the absence of these interim checks, we have too many examples of program development that missed the target; provided a solution, yes, but not specific to the problem for which development was funded. Flagrant examples are machine tool postprocessors optimized for the wrong machine features, or data base systems that took several minutes to respond to simple user queries. Subtler examples are programs that do not lend themselves to potential expansion or could not be deployed over the full range of computing platforms in the company. How one goes about verification and validation we leave for Chap. 7. In the present context, we are concerned simply with defining the process so that:

- Developers can determine if, in a given instance of the process (i.e., a development project), the process will lead to a satisfied customer

- Developers can reconsider and refine the process at the conclusion of each project

5.8 Summary

1. Software quality must be built into the process of developing software. Hence, the emphasis on prevention.

2. A prevention-based process requires a coherent methodology, or systematic framework of smooth flow between tasks.

3. Few programming paradigms, the intellectual processes that define software development and give the product its structure, apply to all development tasks. Nevertheless, prevention is closely tied to the technology inherent in paradigms, whatever their scope.

4. Software quality improvement often starts with the formal adoption of development methods founded on specific paradigms.

5. The most common cause of rework and schedule slips are incorrect, incomplete, or vague specifications of requirements.

6. Rapid prototyping is an excellent technique to avoid incorrect and vague requirements models.

7. Expressive programming languages are best suited to building rapid prototypes. Object-oriented languages are also good choices.

8. In addition to ordinary text, requirements documentation can take the form of system verification diagrams, state diagrams, data flow diagrams, data dictionaries, and entity-relationship diagrams.

9. Applied to software, QFD implies early consideration, in addition to behavioral specifications, of such matters as fault intolerance, data migration, and the like.

10. As a product takes shape, becoming increasingly less abstract, plans should be refined.

11. Planning, even if necessarily the least precise, is most important early in a project.

12. Early cost (and staff size) planning is usually done by analogy to earlier jobs, in a composition process based on a work breakdown structure, or by parametric models.

13. Primary considerations for design are simplicity, modularity, reusability, robustness, and fault tolerance.

14. Simplicity involves control flow, data design, and the independence of system components (also called modularity), each with its own attributes.

15. Modularity makes programs more maintainable by making them more understandable, akin to aggregates of replaceable parts, and less likely to produce adverse side affects of change.

16. Modularity simplifies the construction of software required to support testing.

17. Re-used or re-engineered modules tend to have fewer faults than new ones. Formal module specifications enhance the prospects of reusing modules. Tools, from fairly simple databases to elaborate browsers, capitalize on formal—even well described—specifications.

18. One of several popular methods for achieving a modular structure is that of structured design. In this method, modularity is seen as a function of coupling between modules, cohesion within modules, and modular fan-in and fan-out.

19. One view of structured design presents four approaches, of which functional decomposition is the most commonly used, for achieving low coupling and high cohesiveness.

20. Robustness is achieved through data sanity checks, rollback processes, and—for real-time software—time-tagged input.

21. Methods for tolerating faults include periodic backup and journaling, redundancy of physical modules, and design diversity.

22. In addition to text, techniques for documenting preliminary design decisions include those used for analyzing customer requirements, plus hierarchical charts and lists, layouts of files and tables, tree structures of data, high-level pseudocode, and decision trees.

23. Common methods for capturing detailed design decisions include structure charts, call graphs, pseudocode, truth tables, data dictionaries, and flowcharts.

24. Design tasks should include the documentation of required system resources.

25. In the interests of achieving code simplicity, nearly all new code follows the precepts of structured programming, which limits the allowable branching constructs.

26. The use of restricted data types reduces the opportunity for programmer error (type checking).

27. Encapsulating data within a module adds to the reusability of the module and the maintainability of the system.

28. Some object-oriented languages support O-O, others enforce adherence to the paradigm. Differences among O-O languages have spawned a family of variants of the basic O-O paradigm.

29. Some applications lend themselves to interpreted source code, while others require execution of compiled source code.

30. Maintainability, reduced risk of programmer error, and speed of coding increase with the expressiveness (for a given class of applications) of the programming language.

31. Among other coding practices that affect quality we find the use of magic numbers, initialization assumptions, and the use of recursion.

32. A prevention-oriented process has the following steps:

   - Baseline one's process.
   - Carefully analyze the paradigm(s) in place and competing paradigms.
   - Settle on and define the use of a specific paradigm or set of paradigms, including programming language or languages.
   - Map a development model, complete with a work breakdown structure template and assessable output from each task, onto the paradigms.
   - Build verification and validation into the process.
   - Refine the process at the conclusion of each project.

References

1. Zultner, Richard. "The Deming Approach to Software Quality Engineering," *Quality Progress*, November 1988, pp. 58-64.
2. Dijkstra, Edsger W. "Complexity Controlled by Hierarchical Ordering of Function and Variability," Conference of the NATO Science Committee, Garmisch, Germany, Oct. 1968. Paper reprinted in J.M. Buxton, P. Naur, B. Randell, *Software Engineering: Concepts and Techniques*, Petrocelli/Charter, New York, 1976, pp. 114–116.
3. Dijkstra, Edsger W. "The Structure of the 'THE' Multiprogramming System," *CACM*, Vol. 11, May 1968, pp. 341–346.
4. Zave, Pamela "An Operational Approach to Requirements Specification for Embedded Systems," *IEEE Trans. Software Eng.*, Vol. SE-8, May 1982, pp. 250-269.
5. Korson, Tim and McGregor, John D. "Object-Oriented: A Unifying Paradigm," *CACM*, Vol. 33, No. 9, September 1990, pp. 40-60.
6. Ambler, Allen, *et al.* "Operational Versus Definitional: A Perspective on Programming Paradigms," *Computer*, September 1992, pp. 28-43.
7. Floyd, Robert W. "The Paradigms of Programming," *CACM*, Vol. 22, No. 8, August 1979, pp. 455-460.
8. Nielsen, Jakob. "The Usability Engineering Life Cycle," *Computer*, March 1992, pp. 12-22.
9. Davis, Allan M. "Operational Prototyping: A New Development Approach," *IEEE Software*, September 1992, pp. 70-78.
10. Gupta, Rajiv, *et al.* "An Object-Oriented VLSI CAD Framework," *Computer*, May 1989, pp. 28-37.
11. Fischer, Kurt and Walker, Michael. "Improved Software Reliability through Requirements Verification," *IEEE Trans. Reliability*, Vol. R-28, August 1979, pp. 233-240.
12. Mathur, Raghubir. "Methodology for Business System Development," *IEEE Trans. Software Engineering*, Vol. SE-13, No. 5, May 1987, pp. 593-601.
13. DeMarco, Tom. *Structured Analysis and System Specifications,* Yourdon, New York, NY, 1978.
14. Fichman, Robert and Kemerer, Chris. "Object-Oriented and Conventional Analysis and Design Methodologies," *Computer*, October 1992, pp. 22-39.
15. Chen, P. "The Entity-Relationship Model—Toward a Unified View of Data," *ACM Trans. Database Systems*, Vol. 1, No. 1, March 1976, pp. 9-36.
16. Teorey, T.J. Yang, D. and Fry, J.P. "A Logical Design Methodology for Relational Databases Using the Extended Entity-Relationship Model," *ACM Computing Surveys*, Vol. 18, No. 2, June 1986, pp. 197-222.
17. Akao, Yoji. *Quality Function Deployment: Integrating Customer Requirements into Product Design,* translated by Glenn Mazur, Productivity Press, Cambridge, MA, 1990.
18. Zultner, Richard. "Software Total Quality Management (TQM)," *American Programmer* (Ed Yourdon's Software Journal), Vol. 3, No. 11, November 1990, pp. 2-11.
19. Brooks, Frederick P. Jr. *The Mythical Man-Month,* AddisonWesley, Reading, Mass., 1975.
20. McCabe, Thomas. "A Complexity Measure," *IEEE Trans. Software Eng.*, Vol. 2, December 1976, pp. 308-320.
21. Gill, Geoffrey K. and Kemerer, Chris F. "Cyclomatic Complexity and Software Maintenance Productivity," *IEEE Trans. Software Eng.*, Vol. 17, No. 12, December 1991, pp. 1284-1288.
22. Parnas, David. "A Technique for Software Module Specification with Examples," *CACM*, Vol. 15, May 1972, pp. 330-336.
23. Lew, Ken, *et al.* "Software Complexity and Its Impact on Software Reliability," *IEEE Trans. Software Eng.*, Vol. 14, No. 11, November 1988, pp. 1645-1655.
24. Krueger, Charles W. "Software Reuse," *ACM Computing Surveys,* Vol. 24, No. 2, June 1992, pp. 131-183.
25. Card, David, *et al.* "An Empirical Study of Software Design Practices," *IEEE Trans. Software Eng.*, Vol. 12, No. 2, February 1986, pp. 264-271.

26. Constantine, Larry L. and Yourdon, Edward. *Structured Design,* Prentice-Hall, Englewood Cliffs, NJ, 1979, p. 86, 108.
27. Myers, Glenford J. *Composite/Structured Design,* Van Nostrand Reinhold, New York, NY, 1978.
28. Song, Xiping and Osterweil, Leon J. "Toward Objective, Systematic Design- Method Comparisons," *IEEE Software,* May 1992, pp. 43-53.
29. Kelly, John, *et al.* "Implementing Design Diversity to Achieve Fault Tolerance," *IEEE Software,* July 1991, pp. 61-71.
30. Nelson, Victor. "Fault-Tolerant Computing: Fundamental Concepts," *IEEE Computer,* July 1990, pp. 19-25.
31. Böhm, C. and Jacopini, G. "Flow Diagrams, Turing Machines and Languages with Only Two Formation Rules," *CACM,* Vol. 9, May 1966, pp. 366-371.
32. Dijkstra, Edsger W. "Go To Statement Considered Harmful," *CACM,* Vol. 11, March 1968, pp. 147-148.
33. Khoshafian, Setrag and Abnous, Rasmik. *Object Orientation: Concepts, Languages, Databases, User Interfaces,* John Wiley & Sons, New York, NY, 1990.
34. Smith, David N. *Concepts of Object-Oriented Programming,* McGraw-Hill, New York, NY, 1991.

Chapter

6

Configuration Management

The word *configuration* applies to a set of computer software characteristics described in documentation and realized in code. *Documentation* takes any of the text and graphic forms described in Chap. 5, and *code* spans all of the levels the chapter describes. The configuration evolves during development in a series of *baselines*, or formal document and code software definitions. Even as the configuration develops, decisions made during the earliest sets of tasks change. The configuration of software is an endless story of change. *Configuration management* is the management of those changes.

It is not uncommon for configuration management to be regarded as a post-development activity. True, as a consequence of the absolute necessity of formal change control to protect the interests of software users, configuration management is most visible during the operation and maintenance part of the software life cycle, but it is an imperative during development as well. Development is when the rate of change is at a maximum. Configuration management activities during development differ in several respects from those during the operation and maintenance period; we will cover both.

We usually think of configuration management of software as a form of control that is necessary for large systems. Actually, even the smallest programs may require configuration management. Consider the first use of microprocessors by the Ajax Medical Instrument company for a sputum analyzer application. Ole Charlie wrote the program. We no longer remember whether he was an electronic engineer trying his hand at the programming of these new devices called microprocessors or whether he was the first programmer ever hired by Ajax. In either case, he was a one-man programming department.

Ole Charlie did some design on the backs of some proverbial envelopes, wrote the code, debugged it, burned the code into PROMs, and got the equipment to work. The envelopes and the program listings, stained with proverbial coffee, were stored in a drawer in Charlie's desk. Also in the desk was a floppy disk containing the source code and the binary program load. This was Charlie's *code library*. The same drawer also held the paper tape, punched from the floppy disk, used to operate the machine that "burned" the program into PROMs. This was Charlie's *production library*.

As time passed, more and more enhancements were made to the sputum analyzer, most of them accomplished by adding on to the program. Ole Charlie just kept adding to the material in his desk drawer. Any time a new change is required, Ole Charlie just opens the drawer, moves the bologna sandwich and thermos bottle aside, and pulls out his reference documentation. Last we heard, Ajax had taken out a half million dollar life insurance policy on Charlie. That's what they figure it will take to reprogram the analyzer if Ole Charlie has to be replaced. As he smilingly told the director of development one day, "Don't you worry none about what's in those programs, I got a top-drawer control system."

When we first told this story a decade ago, one could easily believe that there were Ole Charlies still about in industry. Indeed, we knew of several cases in the banking industry where only one person knew the current configuration, and that person wasn't telling. But today? Surely we have come a great distance from the laxity of Ajax Instruments. The fact is that not only do we still find Charlies in small companies, but the whole problem of managing change has been compounded by programming models that deliberately incorporate change through rapid prototyping practices and software evolution. Where once we could attribute the uncertainty of software configuration to job security (as the popular euphemism has it) or lax management standards, we now have to recognize that the control mechanisms of the past—too bureaucratic to serve the present—must be circumvented if software is ever to be delivered to the customer. Yesterday's paper-oriented control methods are today's equivalent of Charlie's top-drawer system.

The practical solutions for coping with present software configuration control challenges actually start with a concept borrowed from the old control mechanisms: fixing software characteristics in baselines.

6.1   Baselines

Baselines comprise collections of items under configuration control; that is, items for which any change requires formal approval. The items are the interim and final products of the development process. A popular school of thought holds that products do not need to come under control until they are placed in a baseline. We take the opposite view: when a new level of development maturity (or level of abstraction) is reached, the items that define that level should be placed in a baseline. Which brings us first to the question, when should an item go under control?

As long as only the item's author(s) are using it, and as long as they are not using it as input to another defined work task, we see no reason to put the item under control. For example, a data flow diagram and such supporting artifacts as a data dictionary can remain the "property" of their initiators until the time when design begins on the processing nodes of the diagram. At that time, however, the material must be frozen, with no changes permitted outside a defined process that can account for all necessary changes.

Baselines permit an instant appraisal of the status of a project. If all the artifacts of say, preliminary design, are complete and ready for use by lower level work tasks, we can speak of the set of artifacts as a preliminary design baseline. If we know that a preliminary design baseline exists, we know something about the amount of progress that has been made to date. (We don't know as much as we would like, of course, until we examine the content of the baseline.) But more than providing status, baselines also define the product at some stage of development. If, during integration we encounter a mysterious problem, study of the design decisions embedded in the preliminary design baseline may give us the necessary insight to solve the problem.

The military, in DOD-STD-2167A, define three baselines. They speak of establishing a *functional baseline* at the conclusion of system design, an *allocated baseline* at the end of software requirements analysis, and a *product baseline* established at the end of system integration and testing but before the final testing and evaluation activity. Since DOD-STD-2167A essentially requires contractors to follow a waterfall model, although with considerable latitude in the specifics of the individual tasks, it was fairly easy to define the three baselines as functions of activities that have discrete end points. In the waterfall, one does not proceed with any work specific to software until the overall system design has been completed. It's easy, then, to define the artifacts of system design as the functional baseline. One does no software design (well, maybe just a little that we can overlook) until a software requirements model has been specified. Finally, one does not test and evaluate parts of the system while other parts are still under development; hence, a single product baseline.

Plainly, if one were using an evolutionary model of development as described in Sec. 3.2, one would have not a single functional baseline, but a series of them.

The important thing about software baselines is that they are collections of everything we know of all or part of the product at specified levels of abstraction, thereby serving as defined departure points for further development or expansion.

Thus, one can establish a baseline for the preliminary design of Chap. 3's Game package and three more for the collections of material that define the design of each of the three games. Once a baseline is established, we know that changes to any material in the baseline may propagate to material in baselines or work products of less abstraction, and we are alerted to evaluate the effect of the change.

Baselines during initial development of a product should reflect the software development model in use. We do not need to be terribly clever to decide the reference points that will be manifested as baselines. Baselines, however, often do not end with delivery of the code and manuals contained in the first product baseline. A feature is added six months down the road, entailing new (baselined) requirements, new (baselined) design, and finally, a new product baseline. Since the new product does something different from the old, we give it a new version number. Ah, but two months later we respond to customer complaints by making it easier to use the new feature. We append a revision number to the version number. Version 1, revision 1 is actually a new baseline.

The linear sequence of versions and revisions is easy enough to deal with, but let's look at the problem of concurrent versions that must be supported. Figure 6.1 is a much simplified schema of the materials under configuration control for a newly released program.

Within weeks, the program is recompiled to operate on hardware or software platforms different from the first. Slight changes in the source code accommodate the unique properties of each platform, yielding the schema of Fig. 6.2.

Some time later, the first new feature is made available. This is released as a new version, but not shipped to all users. Perhaps it entails additional cost that everyone doesn't find worthwhile,* or perhaps the new version is designed to handle a new class of peripheral devices not installed by all customers. The new version may even

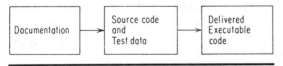

Figure 6.1 Initial release.

---

*Do you have the latest version of all the software you use on your personal computer?

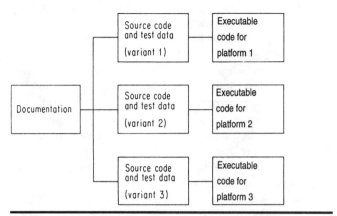

Figure 6.2   Source code modified for different platforms.

provide a capability peculiar to certain geographic areas. Whatever the reasons, the new version does not supersede the old. Rather, both continue to be supported. In time, there are other versions, each tailored to different platforms.

To make matters worse (we seem never to leave bad enough alone), each version will be subject to its own revisions. At any moment, we may have version 1, revision 6; version 2, revision 4; and version 3, revision 4. Each of these is a separate product baseline. Change to all must be managed. Moreover, for software intended for heavy industrial or defense use—say, a shipboard fire control system—each installation may have its own peculiarities. For example, the fire control system may require a configuration file to account for the exact armament and set of sensors on board.

To simplify things, many companies discontinue support for old versions. A company eager to maintain a high level of customer satisfaction will not do so, of course, if it still has many customers using the old versions. Further, it will not discontinue support without sufficient warning to give customers the opportunity to upgrade to a later version. Even where companies are able to perform the Herculean task of reducing the number of heads of their Hydra, however, they may still be left with a variety of different baselines to maintain.

6.2 Library Control

Software libraries comprise documentation and code files. Documentation files include descriptive text, pseudocode, and any graphics produced on a computer. Code files include prototype code, 4GL, 3GL, and binary code. In short, software libraries are as inclusive as they can be. They are the place to store baselines. Libraries do not have to be restricted to items under control, but once under control, all machine readable items are placed in libraries.

Typically, a project under development will have several code libraries. There may be a library for each programmer, entirely under the programmer's control, for the programmer's own code. Alternatively, there may be a library for each programming team. Sometimes, a common *development library* is maintained on a server and programmers download items to their network nodes. Write privileges to controlled items in the library are restricted to prevent their modification. Many companies have two libraries of controlled code, one containing source code and the other, often called a *production library*, containing binary code program loads.

The whole idea of documentation and code libraries is to ease the problem of configuration management. Indeed, control is quite nearly impossible without libraries. They are central to configuration management.

Libraries, especially documentation libraries, are often based on data base management systems. While there may be good reasons not to want all source code shared among the development staff, documentation must be available to all members. A library on a DBMS located in the server of a network provides each node of the network access to all documentation. In recent years, host-based data bases called *repositories* have attracted considerable attention. Along with code, data, and test results, a repository contains planning, analysis, specification, and design documents. Repositories also have interfaces with programming tools.

However the controlled items of a project are stored, we need to have evidence of the changes made to controlled items. Given an audit trail of changes, we can identify any unauthorized changes. And someone should, from time to time, compare the audit trail to the list of authorized changes. Few projects have not seen at least one change made with full intent to catch up on the "paperwork" that for one innocent reason or another never happened.

Audits

Library control procedures need to state how material is approved for entry into a library, how changes are approved, and how audits are performed. Among the techniques used for auditing, we have

- The examination of DBMS journals for evidence of "writes" to controlled files

- The examination of date stamps that indicate when a file was last written into
- Edition labels attached to documentation and code files

Where an auditor finds evidence of change, and the date correlates with approval of a change, it is appropriate to examine the contents to see if the change made is the same as the change approved. We do not mean to suggest that every change needs to be examined, but some percentage, perhaps selected based on sampling lot techniques, should be. The reason for the concern over unauthorized changes is not so much that developers will want to circumvent a change control system (if it is not bureaucratic, they have no need to), but changes are often made in anticipation of approval. Fine, especially to fix a catastrophic problem encountered by a customer or to get a system through another set of test cases, except that the emergency change may not be the one eventually approved. When the final form of a change is agreed upon and approved, we need to know that *some* change had previously been made.

Code control

As important as is control of documentation, control of code is even more important. Not surprisingly, the earliest forms of library control were devoted to code. In the days when all we had to be concerned about was 3GL, we could talk about source code control and binary code control. Things are a bit more complicated today. If we are using an application generator, we need to control the code that describes the problem to be solved. We still need to be able to control the binary code (at the very least, we need to make certain that customers get the correct updates), but do we need also to control the intermediate 3GL code produced by the application generator? Perhaps not, but we leave ourselves open to unauthorized versions if our procedures permit "massaging" (modifying by hand) the code to improve performance and we neglect to control the massaged code. So we now have multiple levels of control to be concerned with. We encounter this, also in paradigms employing specification transformations, which also produce product code.

Control of source code may sound like a formidable problem, but it yields easily to the use of such tools as DEC's CMS, SofTool's CCC, and Unix's SCCS, all of which allow backtracking to recreate any earlier edition of the code, thus enabling the ad hoc generation of change history. For example, SCCS has over 50 arguments available to specify a history report, including various ways of identifying a "delta," release number, date of delta, author, and the like. Code control can also be built into more comprehensive tools for recording change history, such as ProMod's ProMod/CM which is built upon the DEC system.

Unless one can afford the time to always generate executable systems from source code,* control of source code does not guarantee that the binary code tested or delivered derives from controlled source files. Compilers, however, can solve the problem by automatically transferring the edition identification of the source file to the binary file, thereby ensuring traceability.

Build control

Tracing binary code back to source code, at whatever level, is an essential part of ensuring the integrity of linked files (or builds) submitted for testing or rolled onto the figurative software loading platform. A program load comprises linked object code files, sometimes data files, and sometimes patch files.† To ensure that the correct edition of each (yes, even patch files can be controlled) is linked and loaded, load builders routinely use *load files*, or build lists on electronic media, to identify the components the linker should fetch from the libraries. Load files, themselves, can be given edition identification.

The often chaotic conditions of integration testing frequently get in the way of an orderly process of:

1. Compile
2. Load the object code in the object code library
3. Link

Let's consider what happens when a module is modified to fix a problem just encountered or perhaps simply to shed more diagnostic light on the problem. We want to rerun the test immediately, either to get the diagnostic information or to see if the fix really is a fix. What we would most like to do is simply list the components, including edition, in the link file and have a system fetch the correct object files from the library, and, if a correct object file is not in the library, fetch the source code, compile it, and link the on-the-spot object code with the other components. This is the kind of service provided by modern build tools such as UNIX's *make* utility, DEC's MMS, and Sage Software's PolyMake.

---

*Such *clean builds* are the rule for small to medium-sized systems.

†Binary fixes are plainly patches. But how about changes to 3GL code originally produced by an application generator? Bellcore's R. Erickson has a definition we like: a patch is any fix made in a language of lower order than the program's original language.

Plainly, where a build tool such as *make* is used (and such use is now the rule), control of builds is a matter of controlling build lists (or files or scripts). Such tools make it easy for programmers to follow code control procedures, and there is no reason to audit build lists during development testing. However, to ensure test traceability, the build lists used for qualification, alpha testing, beta testing, and official release should, themselves, be controlled and approved. If each customer gets a unique product—some components included, but not all, factory set binary switches, and so on—the control of build lists may seem impractical. However, recall that for a number of years automobile manufacturers have been able to deal with orders accompanied by a score of options. Their secret: it's all done in the computer. Well, we certainly ought to be able to do the same.

Edition identification

A variety of schemes has been used to identify the editions of code and documentation. One of the most commonly seen conventions separates changes in functionality from less conspicuous changes. *Version* numbers indicate levels of functionality or features. *Revision* numbers account for fixes, minor enhancements, and adaptation to updated platforms (e.g., a modification may have to be made to permit the latest version to take advantage of the latest version of Windows). This is the scheme we used to identify editions in Sec. 6.1.

Typically, our_product 3.2 means the second revision of the third version of our_product. Nearly always, editions of products are synonymous with releases, although editions have been produced that never got out of beta testing. Edition labeling of documentation and source code files is not quite as straightforward as that of final product. If source code file our_source is a constituent of our_product, we might like our_source to bear an edition label of 1.0 for the initial release of our_product. However, unless revisions to our_source keep pace with those of the product, it works to our disadvantage to keep updating the edition of our_source every time we produce a new release of our_product. No worry. Just keep the build lists current. However, the larger issue is whether it makes sense to give modules, at least at a level smaller than subsystems, edition labels that represent both version and revision. Usually one does not. Indeed, a common module label convention is the date; sometimes, for fast-moving programming staffs, date and time.

The latest wrinkle in the librarian's buckrum is the library maintained for the reuse of its components. If a component is reused without modification, it can be incorporated in the build list without any change of identification. If, however, it is re-engineered, it should be given a new name and edition label and placed in the library with other parts specific to the subject product.

Finally, let's consider the correspondence of documentation and code editions. If all code changes followed from changes in the documentation leading to the code, we would have no problem. The documentation and the code would have the same edition labels (unless dates were used for labels). Similarly, if final design details are actually filled in during coding (to the horror of top-down purists, but in deference to pragmatism), documentation and code would remain consonant. The fact is that many changes are made to code that do not reflect back to design documentation; simple fixes to coding bugs, for example. We cannot rely on consonant edition labeling, but then, we don't have to. What are data base systems for, if not to help us establish cross-reference correspondence among separate items?

6.3   Firmware

It may be a bit off the subject, but we need to consider maintaining records of the translation of software into *firmware*. Embedded software often ends up cast into ROMs (read only memory), PROMs (programmable read only memory), EAROMs (electronically alterable read only memory), and other types of firmware devices. For all but the smallest programs, individual ROMs (we shall use this term to cover all of these devices) do not have the capacity to contain the entire program, with the consequence that the operational program resides in an array of ROMs.

Consider that we need to transfer a program of 3000 sixteen-bit binary locations to a set of identical ROMs, each having 1000 addresses of four bits of storage. (The reader can scale up to a more realistic problem, but we want to keep the arithmetic simple.) Twelve ROMs will be required, and one of the many reasonable ways to do it is shown in Fig. 6.3.

To make certain that each ROM is inserted into the correct place on the circuit board that will physically house the program, it is necessary to label each ROM in a fashion that will be consistent with the interconnections of the board. In other words, we have to correlate the ROMs with the program load addresses output by the link editor.

The transform from program load binary words to individual ROM bit patterns is performed in a mapping program. A proper mapping program will provide hard copy correlation of the contents of each program load address to addresses within each ROM. This document must be controlled.

We need, also, a way of cross-referencing the unique identification marked on each ROM with the ROM references on the hard copy of the transformation map. If this cannot be accomplished by inputting the set of unique identifiers to the mapping program, the cross-reference

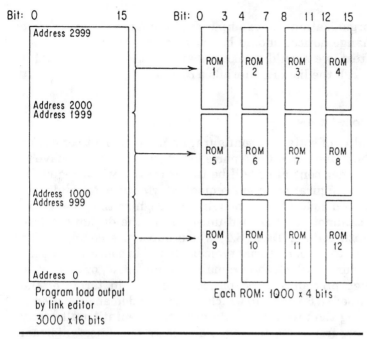

Bit: 0   15   Bit: 0   3 4   7 8   11 12   15

Address 2999

ROM 1   ROM 2   ROM 3   ROM 4

Address 2000
Address 1999

ROM 5   ROM 6   ROM 7   ROM 8

Address 1000
Address 999

ROM 9   ROM 10   ROM 11   ROM 12

Address 0

Program load output   Each ROM: 1000 x 4 bits
by link editor
3000 x 16 bits

Figure 6.3 ROM mapping.

will have to be made up manually and subsequently maintained under configuration control. There is no other way to make certain that the board is properly assembled in routine manufacturing operations, even when automatic component insertion equipment is used.

It is possible to perform the mapping and cross-referencing within the link editor. Given this degree of tooling, all the necessary information will appear on the load map, obviating the need for the additional controlled documents.

6.4 The Configuration Management Plan

Quality software never just happens; it gets planned. Among other plans, one needs to plan for configuration management. Specifically, what is required is early identification to all interested parties of the documents and program files that will be controlled, when they go under control, who controls, and how changes are controlled.

Since a configuration management plan must address the specifics of the project to be controlled, it is peculiar to that project. Nevertheless, it should be possible for most of the substance of the plan to be given by reference to a configuration management standard that applies to all software projects undertaken by the development or maintenance organization. For example, the format of software release notices and change notices should be uniform. Whether by reference or by explicit text, we should expect a plan to define the material it covers. We can call the list of materials a *catalog.*

Catalog of controlled items

With the volatility of software, configuration management cannot be as simple as the management of a parts list. Nevertheless, we have to know what is under control or will be under control when ready for use. Software configuration management starts with a catalog of documentation and code files, although we recognize that fine grain software items cannot be identified until late in the design process, possibly not until coding. Table 6.1, which subsumes coding under design, lists the classes of material typically found in control catalogs* and the period during which they remain under control, or subject to a formal change procedure. The periods are cast in terms of the baselines discussed in Sec. 6.1, to which we have added an *operational baseline*, meaning the product and its user documentation after any changes resulting from beta testing. The design baselines, informal compared to the others, depend on the specific software development model in use.

The catalog can be a good source for reporting status. That is, for each item (and note that the design, code, and certain other classes of material contain many items), you should be able to determine one or more of the following:

- Item identified, but nothing done so far (e.g., a module has been identified, but has not yet undergone design)
- Item in progress (can apply to design, code, plan preparation, or anything else)
- Edition label
- Change has been requested (with change request number)
- Change approved and in progress (with change request number)

One can add more information, such as names of people assigned, when assigned, when due, and the like. However, this information can also be recorded in various other management information systems.

---

*Recursively, the catalog includes the configuration management plan itself. The most likely change to the plan would be changes in the constituency of the Change Control Board. Putting the plan under control ensures that everyone will know of these.

TABLE 6.1

Controlled material	Functional	Allocated	Validation design	Product	Operational
			Baseline		
Development plan*	←———————————————→				
Quality assurance plan*	←———————————————→				
Configuration management plan*	←—————————————————————————→				
Measurements plan*		←———————————————————→			
System description specification	←—————————————————————————→				
Software requirements model		←———————————————————→			
Qualification plans		←—————————————→			
Data design			←———————————→		
Test specifications (including scripts)		←———————————————————→			
Design analysis documentation			←———→		
Design documentation required for maintenance			←———————————→		
Module call graph or tree structure			←———————————→		
Source code library			←———————————→		
Binary code library			←———————————→		
Patch files				←———→	
Build lists, starting with integration			←———————————→		
User manuals				←———→	
Deliverable or delivered program loads				←———→	

*These plans are often combined in various ways.

Quite possibly, one can incorporate the catalog in such other information systems, simplifying correlation between staff assignments and schedules and the status of changes.

Table 6.1 leaves vague the definition of design baselines and when items come under control. Section 6.1 provided the philosophy that items come under control when they are ready to be used as departures for further work. We would find it appropriate, in a waterfall model, to establish a preliminary design baseline for each subsystem of the project and a detailed design baseline for closely associated groups of modules within each subsystem. Other models require different approaches. For example, in a model based on object-oriented programming the baselining of the initial set of defined classes recommends itself, followed by the set required at the start of system level tests. However design baselines are defined, they must serve as useful reference points protected from modification performed without notice.

Control authority and responsibility

A configuration management plan describes the procedures for initially placing items under control, for submitting proposals for change, for approving changes, for broadcasting proposals and approvals to all concerned staff, and for broadcasting change completions. All these procedures come under the aegis of a *configuration control board,* sometimes known as a *software change board, change control board,* or other permutation of the key words. Whatever it is called, it has members, and the dramatis personae is likely to change during the course of a project. The plan names the members of the board. We consider plans that only identify the positions held by the board's members, when the actual people are known, mealy-mouthed. Staff may not know who Customer Service representative is, but they do know how to contact Ivy Planne, ext. 2946.

Most large companies have permanent configuration management organizations to house the clerical infrastructure required for configuration management. Where such an organization exists, it is likely to chair the change board, although others will hold seats. In early stages and after product release, Marketing may well be represented. Marketing may retain a seat on the board during development, but is unlikely to keep it warm. Customer Service should have a seat after release if the product is destined for the general marketplace. If there is a Program Management Office, someone from that office will want to be represented. The software project manager may want to sit on the board, or may choose to appoint a configuration control manager to have the job, or may do both. For small projects, we have seen vestigial change boards (perhaps splinter would be the better word) having but one member—a part-time configuration control manager. At the other extreme, we have seen boards comprising a full-time configuration control manager, the leader of each development team, the head of the test team, a representative from the quality function, and token representation from Marketing and Program Management.

Placing items under control should be a rubber stamp operation. A checklist shows that the item has the supervisor's approval, has been blessed by a successful review or other verification process, and is subject to no planned further work. An edition label is provided, the item is placed in an electronic library if possible, a copy in a file cabinet or microfiche if not, and an all-points bulletin broadcast on E-mail stating that the item is now a member of a baseline and available for perusal. Configuration status is also updated, of course. All this is clerical and, on large projects, a configuration control clerk is usually assigned to handle the business. The clerk, of course, will carry out other board procedures as well.

Boards usually meet at set periods, the interval between meetings dependent on the activity rate; frequently during development, more so during integration, perhaps only monthly at other times. Indeed, after release, a board may meet only in response to a request for a change.

When a product is ready for release, the board needs to be assured of the integrity of the libraries, the quality of user documentation, the quality of maintenance documentation (they may not hold up release, but will certainly insist on updating maintenance documentation to quality standards), and the adequacy and success of the qualification exercise. This requires an all-hands meeting with an emphasis on quality as perceived by the customer.

Entering a new item into the control system and releasing a product are end points in the configuration control process. What goes on in between, namely, the *change process,* is crucial to the success of configuration management.

The change process

The procedure for changing controlled materials needs to be markedly different for changes during the product and operational baselines and changes during the development of new products or new features. We tackle the more difficult problem first.

We had noted earlier that design baselines are less formal than others. By "less formal" we mean that all changes need to be accounted for, but one cannot always wait for the execution of the change process to make a change. Consider an Ada project involving a number of packages, each pursued by a different programmer. In the course of design, Linda, for subtle reasons not evident earlier, finds that she needs access to certain private data in Tom's package. Either Tom makes the data public or Linda has to duplicate much of the time-consuming processing performed by Tom's package. Making the data public changes the system data design baselined last month. Accordingly, Tom not only revises his thinking about the design of his package, but writes up a change request, asking the change board to approve a modification to the system data design. Linda and Tom continue to go about the business of designing their packages, and the change board advertises the request through E-mail. When the time runs out for any compelling objection to the change, the change board rubber stamps its approval of the request and broadcasts the change through E-mail. This is why we call design baselines relatively informal—they do not hold up necessary changes. But they do ensure notifying people of changes.*

Any large project will have many such approvals after the fact both during design and during integration of the code produced by diverse programmers. The most important role played by a change board during design is to make certain that everyone who needs to know is aware of a proposed change, and to make certain that the change is incorporated in the appropriate baseline definition of the evolving product. The formality of change request procedures and baseline control is maintained, but not permitted to be a bureaucratic impediment. Nevertheless, it is the responsibility of the configuration management functions to "Maintain all cross-references among baselines, change to those baselines, and forms requesting or authorizing those changes."[1]

All of these cross-references are relatively easy to come by with current data base software. Back in the days of paper shuffling, it was more common than not to find configuration management unable to keep up with the pace of change. But with everything on electronic media, including change request forms, configuration control clerks have no excuse. Still, we like to have the records audited from time to time.

The procedure for introducing changes to the product and operational baselines is more formal. Except for such emergencies as repairing a catastrophic latent defect in a shipped product, changes are requested in advance, weighed against various factors, and action to execute the request is made contingent on prior approval. Let's take a typical scenario. During beta test of a spreadsheet, over half the users have responded to one question by saying that the method for defining calculation formulas is much too cumbersome. The competition has been making a big thing of the simple point-and-shoot method of specifying formulas in its brand new release. Customer Service has filed a change request (problem only, no solution) and says to hold up release until a better method is incorporated. Development says they can simplify things, but it might take another three months. Marketing says that in three months the company will have lost its window of

---

*If everyone on a project were advised of every possible change, people would get in the habit of ignoring all such notices. Fortunately, E-mail systems have the capability of broadcasting to a variety of node pools.

opportunity to introduce a new product—a good setup for a table-pounding session. The paramount concern of the change board's chair—let's give the job to the configuration control manager—is to make certain that the change request has been duly processed and considered. Nevertheless, the configuration control manager finds that the major attention of the chair must be paid to negotiating a settlement without getting higher-ups involved.

Since the company is TQM-minded, Customer Service wins the day and the problem is handed over to Development with an assignment to report back within one week with the outline of a solution and its impact on cost and schedule. The "proposed change" part of the change request form is filled in by Development and presented to the change board one week later. The change is approved, Development is tacitly authorized to start working on it directly, and Marketing agrees to fund the change out of its budget if no one will report to the president that when the project was initially conceived it was Marketing who said not to worry about specifying calculation formulae since nobody really cares.

If this procedure appears deliberate, it needs to be. New product features or enhancements need to be carefully considered. A step-at-a-time approach is not intrinsically cumbersome. Emergency fixes to the product or operational baseline are something else. Like changes during design, fixes are often made before Change Board approval. Certain changes may, however, need more consideration than can be given by the programmer sent for on-site assistance. For example, an emergency fix to a local problem encountered with new telephone switch software may produce havoc in the trunk lines connected to the office. The change board needs to be among the first alerted to the problem, and will have to undertake the responsibility of getting assurance from Development that the proposed fix is carefully evaluated for adverse side effects.

Emergency fixes often take the form of patches (yes, even today) with a change to the source code to follow. The reasons for patching are several: field repairs without the development environment available to make a source code fix, inadequate time to reconstruct a complete system build (for very large systems, only), and recourse to the band-aid approach of temporarily bypassing the troublesome operation without actually fixing it. Whatever the merits of using patches, their use entails two rounds of change requests—one for the patch and the other for the permanent fix, which may well await the next revision release.

All change procedures and the conditions under which the procedures apply should be spelled out in the configuration management plan. The plan should note where electronic signatures are required, who is responsible for what, the electronic forms in use (please, no paper), and even the circumstances when technical staff can start to work on a requested change without approval. After all, we don't want the people most important to software quality feeling guilty about doing their job when, in fact, they have no reason to.

6.5 Distribution

Several problems can attend the distribution of software products to multiple customers or to different sites of the same customer. One problem occurs when all of the parts of the product do not apply to all the customers. For example, a large system may include components not needed or paid for at all installations. Consider a proprietary electronic CAD system with built-in libraries of available off-the-shelf circuit chips. A user of only MOS logic isn't going to want to pay for the updates to the ECL library or the TTL library, but to maintain customer satisfaction the MOS user must get the updates the user is entitled to. Many configuration control systems need to be able to maintain site configurations.

In this regard it is helpful to have the group of modules comprising an option to be a unique software configuration item, quite nearly a product baseline in its own right. The configuration control system would then have a list of such configuration items installed at each site, as well as data bases and libraries. This parts list approach makes bookkeeping easier.

The distribution problem gets more complicated when there are several versions, each with options, in the field. Now it is important to keep track of which installation has which version or option configuration. The installations will, of course, from time to time change their software configurations; to add capability, drop capability, reflect a change in the hardware configuration, and so on. Given this common situation, it is clear why we recommend, at least for large systems, placing installation configuration status under control.

One method of distributing updates, especially updates paid on a subscription basis, is to download the updates directly from the production library. Not only does this provide faster customer service, it permits distribution under the direct control of the data base that houses the site configuration data. The only quality concern we might have is that of transmission errors. Either the distribution transmission protocol should embody redundancy for error detection, as do today's common protocols; or the update, when received, should automatically "read back" to ensure its safe passage via telecommunications. In the excellent but imperfect environment of telecommunications lines, the quality of downloading is directly related to customer satisfaction.

6.6   Summary

1. Configuration management is the management of change, and software seems to be ever changing.

2. Baselines are defined departure points for further development, including new releases of product. Configuration management has often to deal with the concurrent support of a variety of releases.

3. Libraries for code and machine readable documentation are indispensable to the mechanical part of configuration management.

4. File managers and other simple software tools make audits of libraries fairly simple.

5. Code control has become simplified by tools that allow one to reconstruct the history of change. Tools also remove the potential of program loads containing obsolete or unauthorized parts.

6. Records need to be maintained to show the mapping from binary code to the contents of ROMs and the like.

7. Configuration management plans tell what material is controlled, how and when. The plans also identify the configuration control board (or change board) and the procedures for getting proposed changes approved.

8. The use of electronic media and E-mail have made it possible to explicitly permit changing controlled designs and code during development without waiting for approval. With data base cross-referencing, configuration control is possible without being a bureaucratic impediment.

9. Once a product is released, even for beta testing, formal procedures must be adhered to, even when emergency fixes are required.

10. To maintain customer support of certain products, configuration management must encompass records of installation configurations. The quality of downloaded updates must be ensured.

References

1. Bersoff, E. and Davis, A. "Impacts of Life Cycle Models on Software Configuration Management," *CACM*, Vol. 34, August 1991, pp. 104-118.

Chapter

7

Detection and Demonstration

After reading Chapter 5, the reader may feel that we have gotten so good at preventing software faults that we need have no concern for detecting them. Right. Analogously, we know so much about avoiding disease that we have no need for annual checkups. Prevention of software defects, indeed, has improved enormously. Where we might have expected 30 to 50 defects per KLOC in the mid-1970s, we now expect as few as five. But five is five too many to ignore. Worse, in a system of one million lines of code, five faults per KLOC multiplies up to 5000. And there is no way customers can ignore 5000 defects in anything.

Detecting defects (we use the terms *defects* and *faults* interchangeably when talking of programs themselves) remains a big part of the software business. Most of this chapter is devoted to the techniques of detecting defects and confirming that detected defects, in fact, have been removed. We not only address defects in code, but defects in requirements models and design as well. The earlier we can root defects from an evolving system the less it will cost us, since we can thereby prevent defects from propagating into further work tasks.*

Most of the interest in detection has to do with testing. Although testing is certainly neither the only nor best way of finding faults, we shall see testing get the greater share of attention. One reason for this is that once we get into testing we find ourselves dealing also with a second topic: demonstrating the product's capability to satisfy customers. Actually, there are several reasons why we test software. The most prominent purposes for testing are given in Table 7.1.

---

*Although it muddies the water, some software engineers go so far as to speak of early detection as a form of prevention.

TABLE 7.1 Seven Reasons to Test

1	Expose faults
2	Demonstrate that requirements have been satisfied
3	Assess the suitability of the product to customer needs
4	Calibrate performance
5	Measure reliability
6	Make certain that changes have not produced adverse side effects (regression testing)
7	Establish a level of diligence that can be referenced in the event of product liability litigation

The seventh reason may not seem to relate very well to customer satisfaction, but if we have indeed been diligent in testing, we have no fear of customers so dissatisfied they will litigate.

Detection methods fall into two basic camps: passive and dynamic. *Passive methods* do not involve execution of product code by a computer. *Dynamic methods* do. Dynamic methods are what we usually mean by *testing*. Passive methods have a major advantage over dynamic methods: when one finds a fault one has found the fault. A test failure only tells you that one or more faults exist. Now go and find them using diagnostic procedures.

The passive methods noted in this chapter include reviews of requirements models, design specifications, and source code; static analysis of pseudocode and source code; and formal verification. Still more methods exist, but they have thus far found little application in industry. A passive method that we think holds a great deal of promise is the analysis of formal specifications. The rigid grammar of formal specifications would seem to lend such specifications to validation (as an example, Stanford University's prototype Specification Analyzer).[1] However, as we noted in Chap. 5, formal specifications are yet little used in industry.

7.1 Testability

The effectiveness of the several detection or demonstration methods is influenced by characteristics within the product (or within the artifacts produced during problem analysis and software design). For example, in reviewing parts of a software design we shall want to see whether the design complies with relevant parts of the requirements specifications. Compliance will be difficult to ascertain if individual specifications are not clear, truly specific, and given with minimum interaction with other specifications. In short, if they are not *testable*. Accordingly, looking forward to detection at the design and code levels, we review requirements models with an eye to their testability.

The IEEE Computer Society provides two definitions of testability. In reverse order, they are

1. "The degree to which a requirement is stated in terms that permit establishment of test criteria and performance of tests to determine whether those criteria have been met."

2. "The degree to which a system or component facilitates the establishment of test criteria and the performance of tests to determine whether these criteria have been met."[2]

The first definition is related to the sense of testability we alluded to earlier. A good example of this kind of testability is found in the circa 1914 Army specification that reads something like this:

> The contractor shall deliver a flying machine capable of lifting two men having an aggregate weight of at least 300 pounds for a distance of 10 miles and at an altitude of at least 1000 feet. The flying machine shall be of sufficiently simple construction that a properly trained mechanic can repair it within a reasonable amount of time.

The first sentence is testable. The second is not. A software equivalent of a testable requirement is:

> "**5.3** The system shall provide the user with the capability of clicking on a unique icon to invoke each of the commands listed in the preceding paragraph."

We have no difficulty in determining if the design implements the specification, nor would we have a problem in determining—by examination—if the design and code follow through on the specification, nor would we have difficulty in designing a dynamic test to see that the specification is ultimately realized in code. Here is an example of a software nontestable requirement:

> "**5.3** The system shall provide the user with a friendly way of using the commands listed in the preceding paragraph."

Any review of the design that implements this specification would necessarily be subjective. Subsequent design reviews might well be objective, in that it may be possible to verify that more detailed design work did implement the first cut at design. But then, again, they may not, since even designs can be nontestable. Consider that a preliminary view of the product that will implement the nontestable interface specified, "The requirement of para. 5.3 will be met using a menu." What kind of a menu? Verbal? Graphic? With contextual cues? How selected?

Accordingly, in reviews of requirements models, we look for testability, and in reviews of preliminary designs we look for specificity.

The second of the IEEE definitions would seem to jog our sense of modularity. The more independent the parts of the system, the easier it is to set up tests of the parts. This is plainly the case in bottom-up tests, where the size of test drivers reduces with the extent of modularity. In top-down tests, our ability to see the effect of a given set of test data on the code just introduced to the system increases with the self-sufficiency of the code.

The IEEE definitions seem to favor a functional view of the product. If we look at the product in terms of data transformations, we might come up with a different view of testability. Let's consider a program structure as a set of processing nodes with interconnecting paths, as in the directed graph of Fig. 7.1. S. N. Mohanty[3] defines the testability T_{ij} of the node N_{ij} (the jth node at the ith hierarchical abstraction level) as

$$T_{ij} = A_{ij} \times P_{ij}$$

where A_{ij}, the *accessibility* of the node, is a measure of the number of nodes that have to be traversed, starting from the departure point, to reach N_{ij}, and P_{ij} is the probability of successful execution of the node. In this manner, we have the accessibility of any given node as the iterative function of the accessibility of the nodes separating it from the root of the graph.

The accessibility of N_{11} is, by definition, 1. The accessibility of N_{21} is the product of its likelihood of being selected (in this case, one-half) and the probability of the successful execution of N_{11}. The accessibility of N_{31} depends in a similar manner on N_{21}, while that of N_{32} depends on N_{21} and N_{22}.

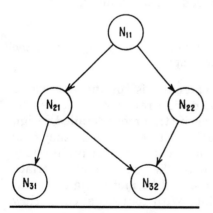

Figure 7.1   Node access.

Thus, testability is a function of the ability to reach a node based on the states created by the test stimuli, the success of other execution processes, and the success with which the node performs its processes. Mohanty goes on to use T_{ij} in the definitions of the testability of logical paths and the entire logical structure. For our purposes, it is sufficient to infer from these concepts that:

> The more defect-ridden a program is or the more involuted its structure, the harder it will be to probe its vital organs.

The concept of testability underlies much of one's overall plan for detection and demonstration. Indeed, one cannot develop a test strategy without knowing the level of testability (all definitions) expected from the prevention process.

7.2 Strategy

At the most elementary level, a strategy for detection and demonstration requires a plan to identify each detection and demonstration process one intends to use. A plan (commonly called a *test plan*) keys the processes to specific events (e.g., requirements review as the last step before defining the allocated baseline, integration test extended as each compile module passes its unit test). For each step or set of steps, the objectives should be clearly stated and the required resources identified. We like to see objectives couched in the set of reasons to test given in Table 7.1. Required resources may include computer time, special computer linkages, non-computer hardware (mostly for embedded applications), software tools, and people. The plan should state clearly who has responsibility for what. As with all plans, the plan may be reduced in size by reference to documented standard practices.

Strategies are also driven by product objectives. In terms of customer needs, how much should detection techniques be driven by considerations of safety, reliability, accuracy, usability, or other user perceptions? If we intend to continue adding new features, we need to find structural characteristics that can compromise the ability to maintain the product. Plans for product demonstration and fault detection will reflect these product issues.

Companies will do well to include checklists for test planning in their documented standards. For each generic test series, checklists—essentially laundry lists of candidates for inclusion in reviews—should cover such items as:

- Objectives
- Required resources

- Expected duration
- Responsibilities and authorities
- Source or reference for success criteria
- Risks
- Measurements (unless a separate measurements plan is prepared)
- Tangible outputs—reports, logs, etc.
- Relevant baseline
- Product documentation (e.g., user manuals) required

Test plans may appear costly to produce, but much of the bulk can be generated from boiler plate. Technology can also help to reduce the cost. For example, one may develop a query-by-example tool to walk the author through the preparation, perhaps even supplying entries from a multiple choice menu.

Black box, glass box

We have noted that strategies are influenced by the testability built into the structure of documentation and code. Another major influence is the distinction between *black box* and *glass* (or white) *box processes*. Table 7.2 lists four views of the difference between the two classes.

Although all four say much the same thing, the first carries an interesting implication. In designing test cases from the information in external specifications, you often find errors in the specifications themselves; this despite any reviews to which the specifications had previously been subjected. This "use" of specifications, which actually improves them, is an integral part of the comprehensive STEP (Systematic Test and Evaluation Process) of Gelperin and Hetzel.[4,5]

Recall Table 7.1's seven prominent reasons to test. All but the first and last are satisfied by black box testing only, although, in theory, glass box testing could enter into reliability estimations. The last of the seven requires one to archive the conditions and results of all defect

TABLE 7.2

Black box	Glass box
Test to external specifications	Test to internal specifications
Emphasize input and output domains	Emphasize program domain
Pretend no knowledge of the code	Test with full knowledge of the code
Functional testing	Structural testing

detection procedures, and makes no special demands on either black box or glass box tests other than that one extensively use both. Where the comparison between black box and glass box testing gets interesting is in the first item in the list—fault detection.

Glass box testing is primarily directed to the branches and paths in the structure of designs and code. Essentially, one wants to test as much of the structure as possible without regard to the functions implemented by the structure. The participants in a design or code review not only attempt to determine that the piece under review satisfies its external specifications, they trace the flow of data through various paths. In a dynamic test of code, test designers can attempt to do the same thing; that is, design test cases to exercise each path or each path of a given number of embedded branches. In fact, such is extremely tedious and seldom done even at the procedure level of code. For dynamic testing, the only practical way to perform exhaustive (or nearly so) branch and path testing is through the use of coverage analyzers.

Coverage analyzers report the percentage of execution of one or more of the following (listed in decreasing order of likelihood of exposing faults):

- Paths, usually of a given length as measured in terms of branch points traversed
- Branch-to-branch or decision-to-decision paths, actually a weak form of path coverage
- Statements

In addition to reporting the coverage achieved by the latest test, many coverage analyzers also provide a cumulative history of coverage. In using an analyzer, one establishes (in the test plan) a criterion for minimum coverage—say, 90 percent of all branch-to-branch paths. One designs additional test cases in the expectation of exercising more of the structure until the criterion is met. Some analyzers provide help in fashioning test data for this purpose. Representative tools, all of which are language sensitive, are TCAT,[*] Logiscope,[†] RXVP80,[‡] and the LDRA Test Bed.[§]

We had said that glass box testing is primarily branch and path testing, and then we threw in statement coverage—plainly an exception. One more exception is noteworthy—data flow analysis. The idea

---

[*]Software Research, San Francisco, CA.
[†]Verilog USA, Alexandria, VA.
[‡]General Research Corp., Santa Barbara, CA.
[§]Liverpool Data Research Associates, Ltd., Liverpool, UK.

here is that programmers cannot trust the correct assignment of a value to a variable if the path between the assignment and the use of the variable has not been exercised. Like branch and path coverage, practical data flow analysis requires a dynamic analysis tool. Unlike branch and path coverage, tools for data flow analysis have yet to achieve industrial strength. Keep an eye out for data flow analysis, though. It is a promising idea. Some experience in using a tool developed at the New York University Courant Institute makes for interesting reading.[6]

Glass box testing is found mostly at the level of module testing, partly because analyzers have difficulty in crossing module thresholds, partly because analyzers can only handle so much code at a time, and partly because if one knows that the goal of 90 percent exercise of all branch-to-branch paths has been reached at the module level, there seems little point in repeating the tests at higher levels. Especially in light of the fact that glass box testing will not reveal all faults.

The last statement sounds self-contradictory. If one achieved the (unrealistic) goal of 100 percent of whatever coverage method was favored, would that not mean that the program was exhaustively tested; that any possible fault must have been detected? No. A classic example was given some years ago by Goodenough and Gerhart:[7]

```
if (X + Y + Z)/3 = X
  then print ("X, Y, AND Z ARE EQUAL IN VALUE");
  else print ("X, Y, AND Z ARE NOT EQUAL IN VALUE")
```

Both paths can be taken without revealing the fallacy. In fairness to glass box testing we need also to include an example of the failure of black box testing to find a bug. Consider that we need to form the square of x, which we should code as

```
y:=x**2
```

but mistakenly code as

```
y:=x*2
```

In this example of *coincidental correctness*, we can easily see that if x is assigned the value of 2, the program will compute the correct value of y. Of course, as luck will have it, the statement, deep in the bowels of the program, will be executed only with a value of 2 during functional testing.

What we need to know is that a third or more of all faults can be found by either black box or glass box testing.* Alternatively, as few as

---

*Not necessarily the same faults, of course. For example, black box testing, unlike glass bok testing, can find unimplemented requirements; while glass box testing, unlike black box testing, can find "dead" code.

20 percent may be found by either technique. In short, both kinds of tests should be included in a strategy for exposing faults. We must use black box testing, in any case, if we are to achieve most of the objectives listed early in the chapter.

Getting back to Table 7.1

We shall need black box testing—and here we are speaking of dynamic testing—at all levels from the most detailed* to the completed system. Without setting objectives for each level of test, we are likely to plan more testing than we should ever be able to complete. Scarcely appropriate for prevention-based TQM! A reasonable approach to a black box plan defines for each set of tests objectives that reflect both the level of functionality reached by the software under test, and the objectives of Table 7.1.

Let's consider how we might plan a series of black box tests for a new system involving both hardware and software. Let's assume that we have chosen to follow a thread-at-a-time development process, wherein individual threads of product hardware and software functionality are integrated and tested separately. (See Sec. 5.2.) Figure 7.2 depicts both a set of four analysis and programming tasks and a set of four black-box testing tasks. Even as the four tasks in the upper part of the illustration decompose the problem, the four tasks in the bottom part incrementally construct and validate the solution.

The first thing we notice is that the testing tasks have specific functional objectives. Unit (or module) test will tell us if we have satisfied the external specifications of each module. Software integration will validate the response to the software part of each thread's external specifications, and thread integration will validate the external specifications for each thread. Finally, in the tests of the full system we shall learn how well we met the systems' specified requirements. So much for Item 2 of Table 7.1.

In designing test cases for each class, keeping an eye on both Item 1 and Item 2 of Table 7.1, we will attempt to test both within the mainstream of processing and without. That is, we will include test data to take care of all the special cases and the effects of out-of-range input. As an example of a special case, in thread integration of a system involving duplex processing units, we would include simulation of the hardware failure of one half of a duplexed pair. As an example of out-of-range input, again in thread integration, we will include erroneous input data. We will also include input that attempts to explore the upper limits of performance. For example, although the thread

---

*Unless we can trust correctness proofs. See Sec. 7.3.

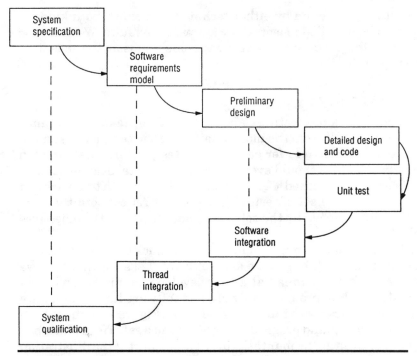

Figure 7.2   Verification objectives for testing tasks.

specification says that we need to keep up with data at an average input rate of one message per 10 msec., we will keep increasing the input rate until the system no longer keeps up. We expect the system will handle messages occurring more frequently than once per 10 msec., but we want to know by how much. Recall Item 4 of Table 7.1. We shall, for each class, calibrate performance to the extent the completeness of the piece under test permits.

When we correct the code during the last testing tasks of Fig. 7.2, we plan to rerun a portion of the tests previously run during the test series. Perhaps all. Such regression testing (Item 6) is essential if we are to trust our own testing process.

During thread integration and again during the system qualification tests, we will record the rate at which we get erroneous output (or outright failures). Of course, we expect none by the time we get to system qualification.* In any case, this will be the way we measure reliability (Table 7.1's fifth item). We may not only chart the improve-

---

*And if we get none it will be the first time.

ment in the pace at which tests fail, we may attempt to establish confidence limits on our assumptions of reliability, but we leave that discussion to Chap. 12.

In our scheme for thread-at-a-time embedded software, system qualification is the primary place to determine how well our system suits the customer's needs (Item 2) short of actual use in the field. For an airborne electronic countermeasures system, we shall have to await the results of tactical evaluation exercises conducted by the military. For a flight simulator, we can first use our own FAA licensed pilots to check out the system with emphasis on its verisimilitude with respect to actual flight conditions. If the simulator were produced under contract, we should later ask our customer to provide some trainees to determine its effectiveness. If produced for the general marketplace, we should ask Marketing to place the simulator in the hands of flight school customers and get their opinions on its suitability; in short, beta test the machine.

Plainly, processes other than those built upon thread-at-a-time embedded software development call for sets of test series different from the ones of Fig. 7.2. Whatever makes sense in terms of constructing a product, one should keep in mind the need to fashion tests that will meet all seven of Table 7.1's reasons to test. Understand, too, that a given class of test may be used to satisfy many of the items in the table, as we shall see in Sec. 7.4 under the rubric "Team Development Testing."

Detection effectiveness

We have a variety of processes for detecting defects, differing in both kind (review, dynamic test, analysis, etc.) and point of use (during preliminary design, in integration, etc.). To form a strategy employing different processes, we need to know what to expect from each with respect to the capability of exposing faults. The primary basis for our expectations should be our own history, for which we need measurements.

Let's define the effectiveness of a single instance of a detection process as

$$ E = \frac{D_f}{D_f + D_r} \times 100 $$

where D_f = defects found
D_r = defects remaining after use of the process

Assume that we perform a code review and find seven faults. A few months after the product is released we look through our archives and discover that seven faults attributable to the code of the module were found during module test, integration, qualification, beta test, and operation. This would yield

$$E = \frac{7}{7 + 7} \times 100 = 50\%$$

Let's look at a hypothetical project and give the project some hypothetical D_f and D_r numbers with respect to faulty code:

	E	D_f	D_r
Static analysis	30	216	720
Code review	70	505	215
Unit test	70	150	65
Integration	70	45	20
Qualification	50	10	10
Beta test	50	5	5

Since we know about the five faults remaining after beta test, we have to admit that customers found them. There may be more defects out there that remain to be found, but based on what we know we can further hypothesize an overall effectiveness of

$$\frac{931}{936} \times 100 = 99\%$$

Assuming we make no improvement in our processes, the six values for E listed above are what we can expect for our new project. We might want to compare our numbers with those we think are typical of industry. Using one set of industry numbers,[8] covering at least some of our detection processes, we find:

	Our E	Industry range
Static analysis	30	20–40
Code review	70	35–85
Unit test	70	20–70
Integration	70	20–70

which suggests that we're doing quite well. Still, there is room for improvement in the way we do our code reviews. Lest we get complacent, next month we'll benchmark against the world leaders in software defect detection.

7.3   Detection at the Module Level

We single out the lowest managed level of detection because of the variety of *practical* techniques available to it. Some of these, with extrapolation, apply also to higher levels—detailed design reviews are no different in kind from reviews of preliminary design—but we can most easily understand the techniques at the lowest level. The techniques we discuss are static analysis of detailed design and code, reviews, dynamic testing, and—while scarcely as widespread as the other three—correctness proofs.

Static analysis

As we now use the term, static analysis is a collective term to describe a number of techniques, implemented by tools, for providing insight to the structure of designs and code, and for exposing faults. Since every compiler checks for syntactic errors, programmers subject their code to some static analysis without being aware they are doing so. However, we are concerned here with analyses beyond those of compilers.

At the design level of modules, static analysis of pseudocode performs much like the syntax checking of compilers. The value here is that such checking can quickly reveal incomplete design logic or logic not fully thought through. Applied to a group of modules, static analysis of their design provides cross references of data use, mismatched module interfaces, and the like. Static design analyzers are now generally found as part of more comprehensive tool collections for software design, or CASE, and are covered in Chap. 8.

At the level of module code, typical output generated by static analyzers includes various combinations of the following:

- Number of each type of source statement used
- Number of unique operands
- Presumed use of operands (input data, table index, etc.)
- Uninitialized variables
- Unused variables
- Cyclomatic complexity measurement
- Improper nesting of loops and branches
- Infinite loops
- Violations of coding standards

When applied to a group of modules, output may include:

- Cross-references for operands
- Mismatched module interfaces
- Inconsistent use of common data areas

Static analyzers have become well known to software engineers, and are now available to support most current 3GLs. Static analysis is also the basis for test data generation and the instrumentation of code for coverage analysis. Any static analyzer that generates a *program* (sometimes, *control*) *graph* performs the first step need for test data generation and coverage instrumentation. Such test data generation, of course, is of the glass box variety; that is, based on the paths seen by the analyzer.

In recent years, we have seen an increase in the use of graphics by static analyzers. Using rectangles for nodes and lines for arcs, Fig. 7.3 shows a control graph for two basic control constructs as an analyzer might generate them, while Fig. 7.4 shows the control graph for the two constructs in combination. One of the first analysis systems to produce control graphs was Logiscope, which, among other graphic output, also produces call graphs for complete systems.

Graphic portrayal of the control flow of software, as in Fig. 7.4, but on the much larger scale of a typical module, provides the programmer with both an instant grasp of the structure and guidance for determining the extent of testing appropriate for the code.

Design and code reviews

It is difficult to overstate the value of reviews. Some years ago, in an attempt to persuade some skeptical programmers that they would do well to routinely review their designs and code, we made this offer:

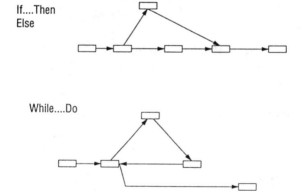

If....Then
Else

While....Do

Figure 7.3 Control graphs for primitives.

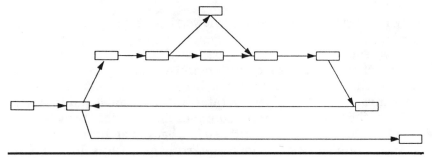

Figure 7.4   Control graph using two primitives.

"Take a group of modules that have already completed unit test, and conduct peer reviews of the code. If you don't think the reviews were worthwhile in terms of the number of problems you find, tell us and we'll stop bugging you about reviews." The programmers kept their part of the bargain, conducted the reviews, and found as many bugs during the reviews as they had previously found by testing.

Apart from conversion of the heathen, design and code reviews are one of the cornerstones of what some call "modern programming practice." Reviews take several forms:

- Formal inspections, as described by Fagan[9]
- Peer reviews of varying degrees of formality
- "Code reading" performed by an individual

The first two apply equally to code and design. The formality of the first is seen in Fagan's classic 1976 article, which described four roles: designer, coder-implementer, moderator, and tester. Inspections patterned after the Fagan model remain popular to this day, and with good reason: they are productive. Less formal reviews, often called *walkthroughs,* are even more popular, possibly because they require little training of the participants and possibly because they fall more easily into the modern mold of team programming. In these reviews, the author of the work under review explains, step by step, how the design or code implements its external specifications. The participants, apart from the author, usually include two to four fellow programmers, but may include others as well. One of the analysts who prepared the external specifications may be present to make an independent judgment of the satisfaction of those specifications. Someone from the test team may show up, especially if the test team is the next group to get the subject work. A software quality engineer may be present, most likely as a facilitator if reviews have only recently been introduced.

Finally, for very high level design reviews, the customer may be invited to participate.

Reviews should be directed not just to verify that external specifications are satisfied, but also to see if improvements can be made in the quality of the work. Has attention been paid to built-in defenses against invalid data, against operator errors, against faulty equipment? Can the module be made more reusable? Do data transfers get verified? Are all transactions recorded in a backup audit trail? Can the program get hung up waiting for an interrupt or a status flag? Can the piece be made less complex? These and their like are grist for the review mill.

Many companies make it their practice to have the author of the piece arrange for the review. Beyond dispelling any thought that it's normal for programmers to be dragged, kicking and screaming, to an inquisition, the practice puts the ownership of the process at its most grassroots level. Of course, in a thought-out quality process, a task cannot be considered complete until the work has been reviewed, and any good programmer is always interested in getting on to the next task.

Code reading, a precursor of code reviews, is still practiced. A single qualified programmer working in isolation goes through the code step by step, attempting to find errors. Perhaps one reason that we see decreasing use of the practice is that it's hard to find anyone willing to do it and even harder for the code reader, without the stimulation of discussion with others, to stay awake after the first page of code. Here and there, however, one comes across a person who actually enjoys code reading (the same person who still takes a cold shower every morning) and is good at it.

One of the most powerful techniques for finding problems and areas that can be improved is the use of a data flow chart to record changes in the state of data during execution. The technique can be used for design or code reviews or for code reading. Using the chart, which all participants help to fill in, lends focus while at the same time keeping everyone involved. Figure 7.6 depicts a chart, after completion, for a code review of the procedure in Fig. 7.5.* The purpose of the procedure is to compare two files of 80-character records. If the two corresponding records do not agree, the record number and contents of each are printed. However, to most concisely report that the two files are skewed by one record (a record deleted or added at an arbitrary location in one file but not the other), the program is to recognize that this has happened and recover from the skew.

---

*Both figures are taken from pages 107–109 of Ref. 8.

```
     procedure COMP (FILEA, FILEB)
     boolean var: AFLAG, BFLAG, AEOF, BEOF, SAME -- all flags
     integer var: AKNT, BKNT
     string array: A(80), ALAST (80), B(80), BLAST(80)
1    AKNT := 0
2    BKNT := 0
3    AFLAG := TRUE
4    BFLAG := TRUE
5    do while not AEOF and not BEOF
6       if AFLAG        -- don't read A if B is behind by 1 record
7          then
8             AKNT := AKNT + 1
9             call BININ (FILEA, A, AEOF)          --BININ reads 1 record
10            else AFLAG := TRUE                    -- but read the next
11         endif
12      if BFLAG        -- don't read B if A is behind by 1 record
13         then
14            BKNT := BKNT + 1
15            call BININ (FILEB, B, BEOF)
16            else BFLAG := TRUE                    -- but read the next
17         endif
18      call COMPRA (A, B, 1, 80, SAME)            -- are the current records
19      if not SAME                                -- the same?
20         then
21            print AKNT, A, BKNT, B
22            call CMPR (ALAST, B, 1, 80, SAME)    -- does current B record
23            if SAME                              -- equal last A record?
24               then AFLAG := FALSE    endif       -- don't read next A
25         else
26            call CMPR (BLAST, A, 1, 80, SAME)    -- does current A record
27            if SAME                              -- equal last B record?
28               then BFLAG := FALSE               -- don't read next B
29            endif
30      endif
31      -- save A and B before next iteration
32      call MOVE (A, ALAST)
33      call MOVE (B, BLAST)
34   endo
35   print AKNT, BKNT
36   end COMP
```

Figure 7.5

We might observe that this appears to be an expensive way to find faults compared to simply testing on a computer. However, reviews often find faults that testing does not, especially when the test cases do not exercise the actual boundary values encoded.

Another valuable review tool is the checklist. Each kind of review requires its own checklist, of course, but the essence of any checklist is to capture the objectives of the review. For example, a checklist used in the review of the design of a related group of procedures should include such items as:

FILEA: ABLE, BRAVO, CHAS, DELTA, EASY, FOX, HOTEL, INDIA, JULIET, eof

FILEB: ABLE, CHAS, DELTA, ECHO, FOX, GOLF, HOTEL, INDIA, JULIET, eof

Line	AKNT	BKNT	A	B	ALAST	BLAST	AFLAG	BFLAG	SAME	Print Output
15	1	1	ABLE	ABLE	UND	UND	T	T		
19									T	
33					ABLE	ABLE				
15	2	2	BRAVO	CHAS						
19									F	
21										2,BRAVO,2,CHAS
23							F			
27							F			
33					BRAVO	CHAS				
15	3	3	CHAS	DELTA						
19									F	
21										3,CHAS,3,DELTA
23							F			
27							T			
28								F		
33					CHAS	DELTA				
9	4		DELTA							
16								T		
19									T	
33					DELTA	DELTA				
15	5	4	EASY	ECHO						
19									F	
21										5,EASY,4,ECHO
23							F			
Line	AKNT	BKNT	A	B	ALAST	BLAST	AFLAG	BFLAG	SAME	Print Output
27							F			
33					EASY	ECHO				
15	6	5	FOX	FOX						
19									T	
33					FOX	FOX				
15	7	6	HOTEL	GOLF						
19									F	
21										7,HOTEL,6,GOLF
23							F			
27							F			
33					HOTEL	GOLF				
15	8	7	INDIA	HOTEL						
19									F	
21										8,INDIA,7,HOTEL
23							T			
24								F		
33					INDIA	HOTEL				
10							T			
15		8		INDIA						
19									T	
33					INDIA	INDIA				
15	9	9	JULIET	JULIET						
19									T	
35										9,9,

Figure 7.6 Data flow states during a manual "test."

- All necessary validity checks accounted for?
- Any implied changes to preliminary design?
- Can termination conditions for each loop be realized?
- Any violations in the conventions for nesting of loops and branches?
- Queues protected against interrupts?
- Initial conditions stipulated?

And many more.

Checklists should also account for ancillary information. Returning to our example of design reviews for groups of related procedures, we should want to make certain that the designer has estimated the use of computer resources, has run the pseudocode through the analysis system, and has identified any assumptions, limitations, and constraints implied by the design.

Many companies have taken the view that code reviews should take place before unit testing. Before the advent of modern source level debugging tools—especially those integrated with editors and code file management (see Chap. 8)—this view certainly made sense. Today, we would argue that greater overall efficiency obtains if one *first* debugs on the computer, and then conducts the review. Doing so avoids wasting review time in finding obvious mainstream process errors that the computer will discover very quickly. As a secondary advantage to testing first, the less likely the code will change after the review, the less likely the chance of undoing review recommendations.

The opposite side of the coin minimizes the importance of testing. A fairly recent proposal by Robert Britcher of IBM has extended the early concept of inspections to embrace a concept of correctness based on the attributes of *topology, algebra, invariance,* and *robustness*.[10] Topology, loosely the conservation of program space, is related to structured programming. Algebra refers to the traceability to preceding work. Invariance has to do with fixed relations among variables. Robustness is used in the sense we have been using it: the capability to tolerate errors external to the software. Viewing the program as a state machine, two or three inspectors attempt to answer a number of questions pertaining to each of the four attributes. Plainly, an inspection of this kind is far more structured than the reviews we have been talking about, but powerful in its potential. Similarly, the IBM Cleanroom[11] approach uses inspections based on verification. Here, an analysis tool prepares a script with questions such as "is loop termination guaranteed for any argument of the predicate on line 15 AND does the behavior spec on line 13 equal the behavior spec on..." for the inspectors to attempt to answer. These IBM approaches would seem to serve as a point of departure for our next topic.

Proving correctness

We have included proofs in this chapter because most software engineers, even though they have never used proofs, consider proofs as formal verification of completed code files. The truth is that proofs have seldom been used except as an accompaniment to program construction. In other words, if anyone is going to try to prove a program correct, it is the person who programmed it, and most likely in the course of writing the code. Even at that, the practice of attempting to prove programs correct is uncommon. We think the reasons are that proofs of any kind (and we shall touch upon three kinds) are tedious and error-prone themselves. Moreover, proof that code is correct with respect to its specifications is no proof that the specifications are correct. Nevertheless, proofs have much to recommend themselves, even if used only on modules crucial to safety, security, or reliability.

Axiomatic proofs. These proofs regard computer programs as mathematical objects built upon formal axioms much as we built a geometry, theorem by theorem, in our high school Euclid courses. We shall use the best known of the axiomatic proof methods as an example. Usually called *Floyd-Hoare* proofs, these start with a simple premise that we'll come to after some definitions. We define a program in terms of a theorem comprising the program text Q and assertions of the state of the program vector (loosely, the variables of the program) before and directly after its execution. Using Hoare's notation,[12] we write the theorem in the form

    P{Q}R

Now for the premise: if the assertion P is true before execution of Q, the assertion R will be true following Q's execution. Alternatively, if R is true following execution of Q, P must have been true before execution. By restating programs as theorems—in essence, translating programs into extensions of the first-order predicate calculus by replacing statements with assertions waiting to be proved—correctness is reduced to the proof that the input, output, and intermediate assertions are valid theorems. One selects assertions, expressed as logical predicates (i.e., assert A > B) based on the invariant relations among variables. A major problem is finding non-trivial relations that, if true before entering a loop, must also be true during and after the loop. In Floyd-Hoare proofs, such relations, or *loop invariants*, are found using R. W. Floyd's method of inductive assertions.[13]

For all but the most trivial programs, the proofs are tedious to the point of pain. Some help is provided by automated theorem-provers, but not enough to make the use of the proofs a common practice. Pages

154–170 of Ref. 8, which demonstrate a Floyd-Hoare proof on a toy problem, also discuss theorem provers.

Algebraic proofs.   If the axiomatic proofs regard programs as theorems, algebraic proofs regard them as equations. In the algebraic method of London[14] the prover operates directly on the text of the program, explicitly asserting the relations among program variables, as in the axiomatic proofs. Thus, directly following the statement controlling iterations of a loop (e.g., `while K < E do`), you may need to assert `W = 1/2 ** K, B = DEN * W/2`, or whatever should be invariant at that point of the program. The trick is to prove the validity of the assertions using reason and algebra. Of course, one still has to find good loop invariants, and the reasoning and algebra—actually the symbolic execution of the program—are not trivial matters. Nevertheless, you're at least dealing directly with program text and not with theorems based on the text, as required for axiomatic proofs.

Pages 151–154 of Ref. 8 contain an example of an algebraic proof in the mold of the "Informal Proof" model presented by Elspas et al.[15] The disadvantage of such algebraic proofs is not that they are any less a proof—indeed, they can prove loop termination directly, which axiomatic proofs cannot—or that they are less vulnerable to human error, but that they do not lend themselves to automatic theorem proving. So the net result is that algebraic proofs may be even more labor-intensive.

Functional proofs.   The University of Maryland has developed a model of correctness derived from the early work of Harlan Mills[16] that it uses in its introductory computer science course. The external specification for a program is formally expressed as a mathematical function, and the proof consists of proving that the function the program implements is the same function. We use Zelkowitz's[17] notation to define:

- [a], the function that computes the same value as the program a
- f, the specification function

The formalism lends itself to three different activities:

1. Verification: if p is a program, show that $[p] = f$
2. Program design: develop p such that $[p] = f$
3. Reverse engineering: find a function f such that $[p] = f$

Although some heuristics are provided as an aid, the third activity is accomplished by hypothesizing a solution and using the first two activities to show that it is the correct solution. Zelkowitz provides simple examples for verification and design.

The formalism of the methods, for all its rigorousness, is fairly easy to follow. As an example, the Pascal code:

```
if bool₁ then funct₁
else if bool₂ then funct₂
```

would satisfy the specification, in the notation of the algebra of sets:

$$(bool_1 \rightarrow funct_1) \mid (bool_2 \rightarrow funct_2)$$

Evaluation of a string of such (Boolean) predicates goes from left to right, ending (as in Lisp) with the first true predicate. If none are true, the expression evaluates to *false*, and none of the design functions (*funct_i*) are invoked.

The straightforward premises of functional correctness does not imply proofs or designs having but few steps. Indeed, the number of lines of proof will greatly exceed the number of lines of code, although the University of Maryland has developed software providing limited automation to help the student. The important thing is that students are learning to approach programming from the point of view of correctness. Moreover, the Computer Science Department of the University of Maryland has considerable influence in the software engineering community. We might well expect, especially with further automation, that their view of functional correctness will eventually become common, especially where safety is of paramount importance to the customer. Recall that we concluded the discussion of reviews with the remark that the IBM Cleanroom uses inspections based on verification. In fact, their verification model is a close kin of the University of Maryland's functional correctness model. In short, the IBM Cleanroom has demonstrated that proof of correctness, at least in the sense of functional correctness, can be used as a routine practice in industry.

Unit test

As it happens, inhabitants of the IBM Cleanroom have enough confidence in their mathematically designed and verified code to "forgo programmer testing (debugging) of code..."[11] Most programmers, however, need to continue the practice of testing individual procedures or groups of closely related procedures. Whether tested in stand-alone mode (bottom-up testing) or directly after being added to a new build of the system (top-down testing), programmers want to find out if their code does what they expect it to do, and to find out why it does not.

Whether or not coverage criteria are specified (see Sec. 7.2), unit tests are primarily oriented toward the glass box. True, the programmer will design test cases to demonstrate that the code under test—let's call it the *module*—satisfies its external requirements. But the programmer will also want to see if the code conforms to the design of the module, likely designed by the same programmer. In this sense, most test runs are directed to finding where the code does not conform, or where the design itself was in error. Bugs are expected, and usually lead to ad hoc diagnostic test cases, supplements to the planned test cases. In short, unit testing is mostly a debugging activity.

Although unit testing should be under the control of the programmer who prepared the module, we expect to see planned test cases prepared as early as the module design activity. Moreover, the design review should include review of the test cases. Review of functionally oriented test cases is the fastest way to determine the designer's understanding of the requirements for the module. Any of several forms may be appropriate to the documentation of module-level test cases, depending on the size and character of the project. We have seen where a statement of the purpose of each test, a reference to the requirements model for the system, and simple listings of the range of input data and results were sufficient for each type of test. At the other extreme, detailed test scripts or procedures may be necessary to augment the test case descriptions, especially if the means of conducting the test are not immediately apparent from the description. However documented, test case designs should always include expected results. For tests directed to exercise specific paths, it may be appropriate for the programmer to simply identify the paths, specify the input required to get to the path, and stipulate the method used to confirm the path was taken and fully executed.

Determining the input data that will force execution of a path is frequently difficult, which helps explain why stand-alone, or *in situ* testing remains favored by most programming shops. In pure top-down testing, wherein unit test is conducted with the module operating *in loco* in the evolving system, such input may be very difficult to synthesize. Consider a module, at some hierarchical remove from the input modules of a system, that takes a given path based upon two variables, g and n.

Figure 7.7 depicts the branch to the path in question as a node with the module. The two variables that force the branch are each doubly transformed from four input data. Moreover, the transformations are not necessarily the result of straightforward algebraic operations. That is, the functions in each node might be conditional propositions. For example, the function $H\,(c,f)$ might be:

if c has occurred and f has not
    then $g = 1$
    else $g = 0$

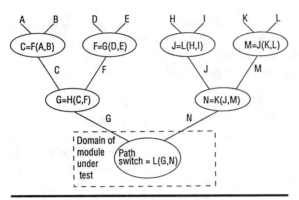

Figure 7.7 Transformation of input data to test stimuli.

Producing the required *g* and *n* from the eight input variables, as one must do if the module is tested *in loco* with the modules hierarchically above it, is far more demanding than simply synthesizing the variables for a test of the module *in situ*. This, of course, is simply another way of saying that program nodes (including the path selection decision points) are most testable when within an isolated module.

As we have noted earlier, some static analysis systems include test case generators to produce input data specific to exercising individual paths. These lend themselves more easily to module testing than testing of a full system, another reason to favor *in situ* module tests. Similarly, various CASE tools help select data for functional tests of modules. We'll return to this in the next chapter.

Parenthetically, we note that of all the paths most likely to go unexercised, none are so likely to be ignored as those associated with error handling. Programmers are dutiful about putting in traps for certain errors (e.g., checking for zero divisors), but they don't always bother to test them. "What the hell, it's never going to be used anyway." Also, the fact that an error is trapped is no assurance that corrective action can be taken. We recall one programmer whose code contained a trap for an illegal data condition, but who, baffled by the appropriate action to take if the prohibited condition arose, simply coded a program halt. The comment he placed before the halt instruction was "Drop back 10 yards and punt."

In addition to testing to the structure of the logic at the module level, one might consider the value of testing to the structure of the data. If the module uses a linked list, attempt to delete the first and last entries of the list. Attempt to pop an empty stack. In a data base system, for example, it is appropriate to exercise each type of data element. In an inverted index flat data base, try to retrieve records using each field as the key. In a relational data base attempt to dynamically form new tables keyed on any column appearing in two or more tables.

Whatever methods we use to select test data, we seem always to worry about the adequacy of our test cases. Mutation analysis[18] can provide the desired confidence, but the limitations of available mutation test beds restrict our use of the technique.* Dynamic coverage analyzers will tell us the exact percentage of the structure that has been exercised, but we may not be confident that we recognized something that went wrong in the execution of a path accessed not by study but by machine. Testing over the full input domain is certainly called for in unit testing, but in attempting to go beyond the specified input ranges we may not be able to recognize every kind of illegal combination of input. If we think we have a problem at the module level, wait until we get to integration testing.

7.4 Team Development Testing

We just got to integration testing. Also testing of the full system as a dry run of qualification testing. Also integration of embedded software and product hardware. What they all have in common is that testing is no longer the responsibility of the individual programmer, but the responsibility of a team. The team may include, or even fully comprise, developers, but often the testers are entirely independent of the developers. The larger the project, the more likely we are to encounter a fully independent test team. However constituted, independent teams are the people most likely to have the responsibility to plan, design, run, and analyze development tests beyond the unit level.

Integration

If unit testing is performed *in loco* as in pure top-down testing, the line between unit testing and integration vanishes, except that the programmer responsible for the latest module to reach the integration test team will likely be on hand during its exercise. Since the modified top-down testing regimen is the most popular, the one in which unit tests are performed *in situ* before being linked in to a new system build, we'll confine the discussion of integration to this model.

Given separate unit testing of all modules, we can in theory view integration as the testing of the interfaces among the modules. Superficially, this suggests that only the linkages between modules need be exercised. In reality, the faults that one finds are often faults in the

---

*Mutation test beds repeatedly insert small bugs in the code, and for each such bug rerun the set of test cases, at least one of which should identify the presence of a bug. If, for a given mutant, no test results reflect the change, we lose some of our confidence in the adequacy of the full set of tests.

conceptual interfaces. That is, integration reveals faults created in preliminary design. Recall Fig. 7.2, which suggests that the fault-finding aspect of integration derives from an attempt to verify against preliminary design. Actually, the design itself may be verified as well. During preliminary design we decided to put a table in our data base containing all the faults found by customers. The table would contain problem report numbers attributed to each of the several releases of the product. When determining the preformed reports that would be drawn from the data base, we decided on a report that would list the total numbers of *unique* problems opened against each release. During integration we discover the totals displayed by the report were far in excess of what we expected. The reason: the dummy data used to check out this and other reports contained instances of the same problem reported by several customers—a realistic circumstance understood by the testers but one not made explicit in the description of the table used by the developers.

Test teams need to start planning their tests early in the development phase. While developers are working to amplify the detailed design, the testers should have determined the resources they will require, laid the groundwork for the measurements they will make, and set up tentative integration paths—the sequence in which modules will enter into the system. Later they will devise specific test cases, increasingly functional (as contrasted to structural) as the system evolves and entirely functional by the time all parts are on line.

Apart from the bottom-up, pure top-down, and combination modes of integration, the very form of integration varies with the product. For a monolithic program, integration means welding a number of procedures and tables of constant data into a whole. A system of many individual processors with different task assignments may require integration similar to that of the monolithic program for each (if each is large enough) plus integration of the processors into a complete system. Another system may require checkout of a newly designed data base, programs to populate the data base, and programs to generate reports from the data base; possibly also with checkout of a newly minted query language or common user interface. A monolithic real-time program may require separate integration of each task before integration of the tasks with resident monitor software. Now complicate it even further by making it a real-time program embedded in an instrumentation system, so that we can talk about hardware/software integration as well.

These are only a few of the types of integration that one might be concerned with. What they have in common is that all must be planned, with resources and test specifications—possibly including test scripts—on hand when needed. One of the problems that testers have to deal with is that they seldom know just when a new piece will be ready to join the system. Although integration paths may be planned in the interests of test efficiency, the pieces necessary to complete path a, scheduled to be tested before path b, may not be ready before all of the path b pieces are in the starting gate. Integration testers need to be flexible, to replan on the spot, to develop new test harnesses in a hurry. The tester who complains that it is now May 4 and module qwerty was supposed to be ready April 27 runs the risk of getting qwerty thrown over the wall (delivered without adequate testing and updated documentation). Better to integrate module asdfgh if it is available.

Unfortunately, modules too often are thrown over the wall. Configuration management practices can help prevent this by insisting that modules enter into integration only from a controlled library to which access is blocked until modules are truly ready. Nevertheless, the orderly, incremental growth of a system is impaired if unit development falls behind schedule. Consider Fig. 7.8 where, in a monolithic program, we have module Bravo subordinate to Alpha, and Charlie and Delta subordinate to Alpha.

Depending on Bravo's response to being invoked by Alpha, Alpha may again transfer control to Bravo. Further, Bravo, depending upon its interim computations, may call either Charlie or Delta. In each of the lowest three modules we symbolically indicate three data flows that must be taken to properly check out module interfaces and system functions. Each time Alpha invokes Bravo, the potential exists for implementing any of 18 data flows. In Fig. 7.8 the stubs for Charlie and Delta might have to be quite ambitious if Bravo's marriage to Alpha is to be properly consummated. Barring other constraints, it would be productive to add Charlie and Delta to the system directly after Bravo has been integrated, holding off some of the Alpha-Bravo interface tests until Charlie and Delta are on the scene. Thoughts as these underlie integration planning, but all plans go awry when unit development falls behind schedule.

> It is crucial that team testers be kept current of any changes to the schedules for module development. They can adapt, but they need to be forewarned.

Let's return to Table 7.1. The primary objective of integration testing is getting the system to run, at least to the partial satisfaction of Item 2 of the table. In the process, many faults—Item 1—will be exposed. Periodically, sometimes after a fault in a previously integrated module has been found and corrected, a set of test cases will be run to make certain that the correction did no unwitting damage. So integration testing involves regression testing—Item 6. All integration test activity is recorded, adding to the record that underlies Item 7. What integra-

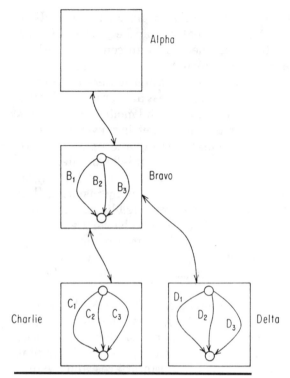

Alpha

Bravo

Charlie

Delta

Figure 7.8

tion testing does not do is fully demonstrate the satisfaction of requirements, assess suitability, calibrate performance, or measure reliability.
These await the pronouncement that the system is integrated and
ready for further evaluation.

System development test

We include "development" in the above rubric as a reminder that the
software (and possibly hardware) are still "owned" by the development
staff. Not until they have done their best to wring out all faults and to
determine what it is that has been built should they be asked to
officially submit the product for qualification.

The line between system development test and integration is fuzzily
drawn. As we noted a few lines ago, the test team says the software is
running (possibly with product or interfacing hardware) and ready for
more interesting testing. More interesting? What could be more interesting than the moment of truth when a system first produces recog-

nizable product? Here's what: testing over wide stretches of the input and output domains, both within and without the stipulated limits.

In the interests of customer satisfaction, it is seldom sufficient to state that a program has been demonstrated to be in conformance to its external specifications. Certainly, a program that processes an alphabetically ordered file of names to print mailing labels in order of zip code can be demonstrated to do its thing, given a suitable sample input file. And surely a navigation computer can be demonstrated to produce a position fix within the stipulated tolerance and within the maximum elapsed time. We can even test the mailing list program's capability to handle the maximum specified input file size. We can test the navigation program at the four corners of the "rectangle" formed by the minimum and maximum longitudes and latitudes over which it was specified to operate.

However, it is impossible to explicitly specify all operational conditions. It is implicit, but not otherwise specified, that the mailing list program operate even when Wm. Zygote's zip code is the highest numbered code in the input file. Yet it is possible that the program contains a flaw that shows up only when the last input name is also the last that should be output. And if the test designer anticipated that, did the designer also anticipate testing to see if all goes well when Abner Aaronson's name is associated with the lowest zip code and appears first in the input file? Was the performance specification explicit enough to specify both an odd number of input records and an even number? Probably not; this is an implicit requirement for a sorting program, and, interestingly, a surprisingly frequent source of error. Similarly, the navigation program specification cannot include delineation of every potential combination of raw measurement input that produces a position fix within the stipulated geographic bounds. Yet, some of these may produce results out of tolerance with respect to accuracy owing to geometric dilution of precision.

A common strategy to reach all across the spectrum of input and output is the use of random data, copious amounts of randomly generated input. Some software engineers decry the use of random data, believing that one can deliberately select a sufficient, if far fewer, number of test points to accomplish the same thing. We do believe in boundary testing, and we shall get to it shortly, but we believe also that random testing should also be performed wherever the character of the product permits it. Only random testing has the capability to exceed the imagination of the development staff—including the test staff—thereby providing a domain of points exhibiting singular performance greater than that deliberately explored.

In any case, system tests must certainly include deliberately determined test points. Actually, if random testing is used, these need only be tests at the boundaries of performance. To calibrate performance, we record the average time it takes for a server/client network to respond to a keyboard return command, given 25 active terminals, 50 terminals, 75 terminals, and so forth. We record the accuracy of our aforementioned navigation systems at the extremes of latitude and longitude, and we also analyze the mathematics of the navigation solution to find such other "interesting" points to measure as places where the region of error is elongated. In a telecommunications system we record the length of an input queue as we gradually increase the data rate; and, if applicable, record the rate at which we started losing data. Using a bit of code instrumentation for a pattern recognition system, we record the maximum length to which chains grow for various types of images. We test a program for laying out circuit boards by populating every available component and connector position and increasing the number of interconnections. As the board gets increasingly dense, we record the ratio of incomplete to complete connections as a measure of performance. Whatever the application, there are boundaries of values, volumes, capacities, and stresses that system tests should explore.

The aggregate of all these measurements satisfies Item 4 of Table 7.1, the calibration of performance. During the course of these tests, no one should be surprised by intermittent interruptions caused by previously unexposed bugs. With an aggressive pursuit of prevention, there ought not be so many bugs that one is left with a significant rate of fault detection by the time performance has been demonstrated and the envelope calibrated. Starting with the first of the planned system tests, we might expect a decline of fault incidence as in Fig. 7.9, a record of the disruption of testing by faults

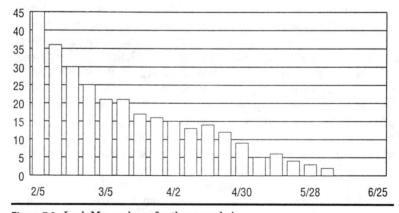

Figure 7.9 Look Ma: no bugs for three weeks!

serious enough that they could not be left in the system. Had the fault incidence data started with the start of integration testing, the overall shape of the data would more likely have followed the general shape of Fig. 3.7.

In Fig. 7.9 we see that no new serious faults have appeared in the last three weeks. Does this mean that none are left? Maybe. We'll never really know, although we'll feel fairly confident if nothing further shows up in the first few months after release. In any case, management has no problem in declaring the product ready to undergo scrutiny for qualification.

Suppose, though, that the fault incidence during system testing was more like that of Fig. 7.10. Here, we have run weeks of demonstrations of mainstream performance, boundary tests, and tests with random input, and we still find new bugs popping up, although none during the last week. Given intelligent and scrupulous attention to prevention, odds are that a high percentage of the new bugs result from bad fixes of other bugs. Either an old bug was not completely fixed or the fix created a problem elsewhere. Example of the first: the comparison of two values is made by a "greater than" relational. An integration test discovered that it should have been "less than," the programmer having thought the problem through backwards. Late in system testing a condition comes up wherein the correct result requires a "less than or equal" relational. Example of the second: a common data area is made one datum larger as a simple way of compensating for incorrect indexing in one of the routines that uses the data. Much later in testing another routine that uses the data is invoked for the first time since the change was made, and fails.

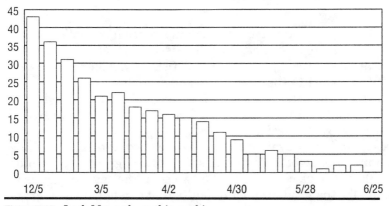

Figure 7.10 Look Ma: no bugs this week!

Getting back to the trend of Fig. 7.10, we should certainly like to keep exercising the system to evaluate its reliability and decide whether it's time for development to give up its ownership of the product. In short, it's time for a quality management decision. The decision will be influenced by two factors: the type of product we're dealing with and the calendar. We deal with the second influence first. If the product is late and the customer or the conditions of competition exert great pressure to release as soon as possible, we shall have a tough job convincing management to hold off until we get some more good weeks under our belt. As for the role played by the product, medical instrumentation or nuclear powerplant control software make safety imperative. Certainly, we have insufficient data to feel comfortable if *our* lives were at stake. No release yet. At the other extreme, if we are producing contact follow-up software for telemarketers, the worst that will happen is we shall be very red-faced if one or more serious problems showed up during beta test.

In Chap. 12, we talk about statistical models for establishing confidence in the belief that there are no more than some given number of serious faults remaining in the product after weeks or months of test, but the models do not really lend themselves to determining whether there are zero defects left. The fundamental question is:

When can we stop testing?

There is, of course, no simple guideline to help managers make the decision. The influences of application and schedule (possibly, also, cost) must be taken into account. Statistical models may provide help if safety or reliability requirements are not paramount, but they often are. There remains, however, one more technique that managers can use, one that directly attempts to answer the question of whether enough testing has been performed.

Seeding.   Seeding is related to the tagging procedures followed for many years by state fisheries. In what is also referred to as the capture-recapture process, a number of fish in a lake are netted, tagged, and returned to the lake. A second fishing expedition nets a new catch, and the ratio of tagged to untagged fish is noted. The estimate of the total number of fish is formed by dividing the size of the second catch by this ratio.

The programming equivalent of tagging uses two testers. Each finds a certain number of defects. Alvin finds a set of a bugs and Betty finds b. The number of bugs common to the two sets (the tagged fish) is c. The estimate for the total number of faults that existed at the start of testing is

$$N = \frac{a \times b}{c}$$

The tagging model requires two programmers operating independently for some period of time. The result is an estimate of the number of faults requiring removal. This has value for estimating the remaining amount of testing that will be required, but it does not help us to gain confidence in the tests that have been conducted. For that, we turn to a variant of tagging: seeding. In seeding, a number of faults are deliberately implanted in the code at the start of system testing. To determine the effectiveness of the tests, we can interpret the previous equation, $N = (a \times b)/c$, as follows:

N = estimated total number of real and seeded faults
a = number of faults that had been seeded
b = total number of faults exposed during testing
c = number of seeded faults that were exposed

In Chap. 12, we'll see where application of probability theory can yield a given confidence level that the number of true faults lies between two limits.

Both the simple estimate of N and the more involved one in Chap. 12 are only as good as the seeds are randomly distributed. We have no presumptive way of determining this. We can, however, postulate a qualitative test of the presumption of randomness. Consider the ratio:

$$R = \frac{b - a}{N - a}$$

After many bugs have been exposed, when we should expect that the total number of exposed faults exceeds the number of seeds, R should approach 1. Randomness presumes that seeds are found more or less in proportion to the total number of exposed faults. If we calculate and plot R for each batch of detected bugs, as in Fig. 7.11, and find that we can pass a line through the scatter diagram of the pairs (R_1,b_1), (R_2,b_2) . . . (R_n,b_n) with a high correlation coefficient (perhaps .95 or higher), the presumption of randomness would appear reasonable.

Failure to match the complexity of seeded faults with that of real ones will also impair seeding effectiveness. More on this in Chap. 12.

Before leaving system testing, we should note that even more conscientiously than in integration testing, regression tests need to be run after changes. In integration, changes are made at so frequent a rate that it is

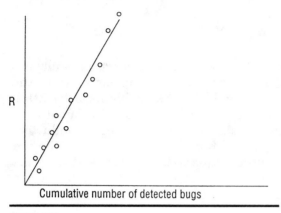

Cumulative number of detected bugs

Figure 7.11

impractical to rerun a representative subset of previously passed test cases after each change. Early in system testing we would recommend running regression tests at the end of each day. As the rate of fixes goes down, it should be practical to run regression tests after each modification.

7.5   Qualification

1. The customer's witness of the producer's qualification test series
2. Several hours or days of hands-on operation by customer personnel

In addition to code, the product one qualifies may include documentation required for future maintenance, user documentation, and data. What gets included depends on the external specifications and the product's application. Finally, qualification of certain products may entail extensive user testing. With all these variables, one thing remains constant: the product should be under the control of people not in a position to make any modifications.

Controls

We do not mean to imply that modifications are prohibited. If the product should utterly fail in the midst of a series of tests, remedial action is mandatory. What we mean is that any changes to the configuration must be approved using the configuration management procedures established for the project. Moreover, qualification may be the last chance before product release to confirm that documentation is consistent with code. The military likes to use the term *functional configuration audit* for the exercise of determining that neither ambiguity nor inconsistency attach to the delivered programs and their documentation. Whatever one chooses to call it, company practices should document the procedures that provide such confirmation. The procedures, of course, should be little more than recall of the trail of configuration management actions and audits that attended development.

Evaluation of quality

We qualify against external specifications. A product may well satisfy all of its external specifications yet leave us dissatisfied with its quality. Sometimes the problem lies with the specifications. A real-time program operating with a radar system worked marvelously in the laboratory, but was discovered to overload intermittently in a real environment. The problem was isolated to the noise filtering algorithm. It handled the specified noise spectrum successfully, but the customer's specification did not accurately reflect the physical world. A critical path program for project management, written for a specific hardware/software platform, ran impossibly slowly. It seems that no one told the programmers that the software operating system left it up to the application program to manage the computer's cache memory.

We have also cases where the specifications simply are not sufficiently comprehensive to cover all the ingredients of product quality. For example, the specification for a network application could not stipulate the maximum time to respond to a keyboard return. Response depended upon the network software, the number of on-line workstations, and the data traffic on the network. While awaiting a response, the clerical users, doing repetitive work, would continue to fill the input queue with undisplayed keyboard input. When a string of characters suddenly showed up on the screen, many users were thrown out of their nimble-fingered stride, resulting in erroneous input. Had this been foreseen, the programmers could have provided an interface requiring screen cues for the entry of each field.

The quality of user documentation, whether for personal software or such complex systems as telecommunications switches, can only be judged by the users. Apart from out-and-out errors, what is obvious to the writer may be obscure to the user. The same thing with help screens. How often have users of personal software asked for help in the context of a specific key position only to be told what the key does? This they know. What they don't know are the circumstances under which the key can be used to accomplish what they really want.

In short, apart from showing compliance, the qualification process needs to address the larger issue of quality in whatever context appears appropriate. One of the more common ways to do so is the use of alpha testing. Another is beta testing. Both follow the judgment that the product is sufficiently robust to be released for such tests.

The alpha and beta of testing

Alpha testing is use of the product by the producer's own employees. Plainly, alpha testing is not performed by a company that specializes in airborne fire control systems. But alpha testing is practical for spreadsheets, DBMS, accounting systems, and even instruments to record and correlate blood sugar measurements. Every company uses spreadsheets, DBMS, and accounting systems, including the publishers of such software. And odds are that the company manufacturing the blood sugar equipment has a few diabetics on its staff.

The way alpha testing works is simple: integrate use of the product in daily work (or health monitoring) activities. The company's managers all use release 2.5 of its spreadsheet. Before the outside world gets it, the managers are asked to use release 3.0 until further notice. Each user is asked to call ext. 369 with any comments or questions. Questions, especially requests for help, are important, since they relate directly to usability. Of course, the answerer must decide if the requestor was simply too lazy to look in the manual. At the conclusion of the trial period—a matter of several weeks—the alpha testers are either interviewed or asked to complete a questionnaire. The results may lead the product's managers to submit change requests to the change board, in which case look for a substantial delay of the release date. (Who said that quality doesn't cost?)

If alpha testing can apply to a software product, beta testing nearly always can as well. The scenario is the same except that the users come from the customer community. A 1-800 number, questionnaires in self-addressed stamped envelopes, and a longer test period are the main differences. The customers are selected based on the expectation that they will use the product extensively, and on their cooperation in beta tests of previous releases or products. Well, sometimes Marketing wins its plea to have a beta copy sent to the people at Omega since they are raising an awful fuss about the product's being three months late and THEY NEED IT NOW. Just make sure that the Omegans get all the caveats appropriate to a beta release.

More than once, we fear, software producers have released beta copies before the completion of alpha testing. Indeed, we know of one product that was release for beta testing with no alpha testing whatsoever. It's scarcely in the interests of total quality management to have one's customers be the first to know of a product's deficiencies. At the other extreme, we know of companies that have gone through several cycles of beta testing for the same product until they were finally satisfied that they had got it right. And the "window of marketing opportunity" be damned.

Regression testing

We remarked earlier that strict configuration control practices do not prohibit changes from being made. During formal qualification testing, change requests may result from the exposure of serious faults (one always wonders how they escaped earlier tests) or even from the awareness of grave operational deficiencies. Back to the drawing board to make some new (controlled) changes, and back to square one of the qualification tests. And we do mean square one. Repeat all. Not only that, it is necessary to repeat many of the system tests conducted while the product was still under the control of development staff, at least a subset of those tests that provide intensive testing of the data flows affected by the change.

Automatic regression test systems help to make regression testing practical (read, likely to happen). These tools run a battery of tests in succession, comparing the results with a controlled benchmark, perhaps the result of the first successful set of runs. Regression test systems have greatest applicability for those products wherein all test stimuli can come from disk or tape, and wherein all responses can be logged on the same media. Still, even where outside world stimuli are required, one can often build tools to control external data generators and capture the data output by the program.

7.6 Independent V&V

Much of detection has to do with shortcomings in the fidelity with which the work of one task is implemented by a successor task. Many software engineers call this *verification*. Demonstration of compliance with the prime set of specifications is called *validation*. Collectively, the two processes are known as V&V. Barry Boehm provides a succinct distinction between the two: "Verification is doing the job right and validation is doing the right job."[19]

Customers, especially government agencies, who perceive a high degree of risk in the development of new software occasionally hire independent contractors to perform their own V&V activities; hence IV&V. The software contractor delivers copies of all in-process documentation to the IV&V contractor, often provides the IV&V contractor with office space, and invites the IV&V contractor to witness tests (as well

as comment on test specifications). In turn, the IV&V people are
expected to find anything that may be incorrect. And they often do.
Over a four year period, according to a report published by the National
Research Councils'Aeronautics and Space Engineering Board, IV&V staff
assigned to NASA's space shuttle program have found 15 software defects
of a severity that could have lead to the loss of a shuttle or its crew.[20]

Understand that the space shuttle contractors all had internal V&V
programs. Indeed, there seems to be some question that at least some of
the defects were actually found by people in the employ of the software
developer, IBM, which also argued the severity assigned to the faults.
Whatever the number of defects actually found by the IV&V contractor,
and whatever the extent to which they were potentially life-threaten-
ing, it remains clear that NASA felt that IV&V was a necessary form
of insurance. Expensive insurance at that: between three and four
percent of the total cost of developing the shuttle's software.

In dealing with software suppliers, industry also has recourse to
the use of IV&V contractors. If risk containment is a paramount
concern—whether with respect to safety, reliability, even schedule—
the price of insurance may be worth it. However, under no circumstances can one consider the use of IV&V an acceptable substitute
for confirming that the supplier has an effective software quality
process in place.

7.7 Summary

1. Passive fault detection methods are more direct than dynamic (or
   actual product test) methods. Nevertheless, both are required.
   Only passive methods can be applied to artifacts of analysis and
   design tasks.

2. Quality demands that we address several distinct testing objectives. (See Table 7.1.)

3. Testable specifications permit the design of tests to demonstrate
   the product satisfies its specifications. Testable software products
   also facilitate the design and performance of tests. At the most
   detailed level, the testability of a processing node is a function of
   the ease in determining input data that will exercise the node.

4. Testing falls into two classes: black box and glass box. In the former
   we deal with the external specifications of the product, in the latter
   with the internal specifications.

5. Glass box testing of software is mostly at the module level, and to
   fulfill our expectations for it, requires the use of automated
   coverage analyzers.

6. To meet all testing objectives, we require a strategy based on discrete testing tasks, each of which has specific verification or validation goals.

7. We can calculate the effectiveness with which we use the diverse detection methods, and we can use the calculations in our quality improvement processes.

8. Automated static analysis of both module design and code is a standard passive detection method. Design and code reviews of varying degrees of formality are even more widely used. With the use of any of several aids, reviews can be as effective, and often more so, as unit testing.

9. Formal verification, or proofs of correctness, are time-consuming and, themselves, error-prone. However, automated aids are making these passive methods increasingly useful to industry.

10. Unit, or module test, leans toward glass box testing.

11. Integration, or the construction of a system from its parts, is mostly left to test teams, members of which may or may not have been involved with the design.

12. Integration is performed incrementally, adding modules bit by bit, until all are in place and the system is producing output.

13. Once the system can produce output under a variety of circumstances, test teams evaluate its operation over the full range of input and output and assess its ability to defend against illegal input.

14. Both carefully designed test data and random input have a role in system testing. The latter are particularly useful in evaluating reliability.

15. The deliberate insertion of faults—or seeding—helps to determine when one has run enough tests of a system.

16. Products are considered qualified when they have demonstrated they satisfy their external specifications, can be maintained, and can be supported for customer use.

17. Where applicable, products are used in-house before release to customers, a process known as alpha testing. Where applicable, products are used by selected groups of customers before release to the general marketplace, a process known as beta testing.

18. The government often uses independent verification and validation contractors to decrease the likelihood of faults in software produced under contract.

References

1. Neff, Randel. "Specification Analyzer Symbolic Interpreter," *IEEE Software*, May 1990, p. 57.
2. ANSI\IEEE Std 729-1983, *IEEE Standard Glossary of Software Engineering Terminology*, IEEE, New York, NY, 1989.
3. Mohanty, Siba N. "Models and Measurements for Quality Assessment of Software," *ACM Computing Surveys*, Vol. 11, No. 3, September 1979, pp. 251-275.
4. Gelperin, David. and Hetzel, Bill. "The Growth of Software Testing," *CACM*, Vol. 31, No. 6, June 1988, pp. 687-695.
5. Hetzel, W. *The Complete Guide to Software Testing*, 2nd ed., QED Information Sciences, Wellesley, MA, 1988.
6. Frankl, Phyllis and Weyuker, Elaine. "An Applicable Family of Data Flow Testing Criteria," *IEEE Trans. Software Eng.*, Vol. 14, No. 10, October 1988, pp. 1483-1498.
7. Goodenough, John and Gerhart, Susan. "Toward a Theory of Test Data Selection," *1975 Internatl Conf. Reliable Software*, IEEE Cat. No. 75CH0940-7CSR, pp. 493-510.
8. Dunn, Robert. *Software Defect Removal*, McGraw-Hill, New York, NY, 1984, p. 20.
9. Fagan, Michael E. "Design and Code Inspection to Reduce Errors in Program Development," *IBM System Journal*, Vol. 15, No. 3, 1976, pp. 182-211.
10. Britcher, Robert. "Using Inspections to Investigate Program Correctness," *IEEE Computer*, November 1988, pp. 38-44.
11. Dyer, Michael. *The Cleanroom Approach to Quality Software Development*, John Wiley & Sons, New York, NY, 1992.
12. Hoare, C.A.R. "An Axiomatic Basis for Computer Programming," *CACM*, Vol. 12, No. 10, October 1969, pp. 576-583.
13. Floyd, R.W. "Assigning Meanings to Programs," *Proc. Symp. Appl. Math.*, American Mathematical Society, Vol. 19, 1967, pp. 19-32.
14. London, Ralph. "Certification of Algorithm 245 [M1] Treesort 3: Proof of Algorithms—A New Kind of Certification," *CACM*, Vol. 13, No. 6, June 1979, pp. 371-372.
15. Elspas, Bernard, *et al.* "An Assessment of Techniques for Proving Program Correctness," *ACM Computing Surveys*, Vol. 4, June 1972, pp. 97-147.
16. Mills, Harlan. "The New Math of Computer Programming," *CACM*, Vol. 18, No. 1, January 1975, pp. 43-48.
17. Zelkowitz, Marvin. "A Functional Correctness Model of Program Verification," *IEEE Computer*, November 1990, pp. 30-39.
18. Martin, Rhonda. "Mothra Uses Mutation Analysis," *IEEE Software*, May 1990, p. 56.
19. Boehm, B. *Software Engineering Economics*, Prentice Hall, Englewood Cliffs, NJ, 1982.
20. Gruman, Galen. "In the News," *IEEE Software*, November 1992, p. 106.

8

Tools

Programming tools have been around since the pre-Cambrian days of programming. The earliest recognizable ones were assemblers and loaders. Compilers, automatic linkers, and utilities to chain simple operations followed in due course. File managers, elements of operating systems that we are barely aware of today, soon followed to help programmers catalog and retrieve source and binary files. Simple diagnostic aids such as break and dump and snapshot provided necessary relief from the mysteries of assembly language debugging. All of these primitive tools addressed the simple mechanics of translating source code into working programs. Programmers, busy providing useful software to the paying customers, found it difficult to find funds to improve their own lot. It was a clear case of the shoemaker's children.

It was not until the early 1970s that programmers began to have access to tools a notch above the most austere level of functionality. Among the first were simple static analyzers and compiler pre-processors, both supplementing the capability of compilers to find logic errors, symbolic debuggers, and aids to producing documentation. Hopeful software engineers thought the latter would solve the seemingly intractable problem of getting programmers to document their work—a perennial problem of the early days, as the lack of time to do a proper documentation job only added to the natural inclination of most programmers to avoid writing anything but code. This second generation of tools operated on artifacts after they were produced, rather than contributing to the creative process.

Tools that directly entered into the design process had to await the 1980s. These tools, even today not all in universal use, were mostly stand-alone tools. That is, the output of one tool seldom fed into a second, nor did two tools often share the same project data. Some sharing took place in the Programmer's Workbench,[1] operating on early versions of UNIX. Many software engineers considered this a major jump in development tooling. Nevertheless, the tools one could have installed back then seem modest by present standards.

Today, the emphasis is on integrating, in one fashion or another, the great variety of tooled capabilities that were developed during the 1980s. It is in the integration of tools that we see their real potential to build quality into software products. Having tools operate on a common body of data (only one of several aspects of integration) precludes the opportunity for information disconnects. To take a simple example, the programmer's ability to navigate directly between compiler or static analyzer and editor leaves no doubt about the edition of code subjected to the analysis or compilation process.

You may expect management to jump eagerly at the acquisition of sophisticated tool systems. They seem to offer not only improved quality but improved productivity. However, the migration from the simplest of tools to the most capable has been impeded by three factors: cost, disappointing productivity increases, and culture. We'll take these in turn.

Costs are not inconsiderable, especially when you include the cost of training and acculturation. The per-copy cost of tools runs between $500 and $1000 at the low end and 10 times as much at the upper end. But including such other costs of ownership as workstation acquisition, training, upgrades, and maintenance, the actual cost of a $2500 tool may, over five years, run to $40,000 for a small staff.[2] Of course, with programmer salaries what they are, the cost need not seem formidable if it can be recaptured through increased productivity. Users of the Excelerator CASE product, surveyed by the producer (Index Technologies) several years ago, reported an improvement in productivity of nearly 40 percent in the analysis and design tasks of development.[3] However, we have much anecdotal evidence to suggest that significant productivity improvement is not a necessary concomitant to the introduction of CASE. Run-of-the-mill graphics capabilities, offering little more support than plain vanilla drawing packages, may produce neater data-flow diagrams, but the cost may be two hours of mousing around rather than the 30 minutes required to scribble on paper. Moreover, software of too much generality may produce diagrams no more easily modified than those done by hand. Thus we find that increased productivity may be more illusory than real. In a study roughly contemporaneous with that of Index Technologies, tool use improved productivity only 3 percent in a study of 22 NASA projects.[4] More modern tools, especially integrated tool sets, should provide a far better return in terms of productivity, but the memory of 1980s disappointments continues to reverberate in the cautious chambers of software engineering.

If modern tool use is to be sold, it will have to be sold on its contributions to quality.

We mentioned a third restraint on tool acquisition, acculturation. One shouldn't buy a basket of tools and then adopt a development model to fit the tools. It doesn't work. The way to tool one's business is to find the tools that fit the model and methods in place. Sure, some bending of the model may be required, but that is scarcely the same thing as attempting to turn one's programming culture upside down. As it happens, many tools support a variety of methods.

Despite the slow adoption of advanced tools, the programming community itself remains keenly interested in them. And, indeed, the capabilities now offered seem wondrous to those who have toiled in the programming vineyards since the pre-Cambrian days. In a survey[5] of readers of IEEE Software to determine which of some 18 subjects the readers were most interested in seeing published, CASE was the most popular, although beating out the Languages/programming category by only a nose.

Before going into more specifics on tools, we need to wade through a bit of taxonomy for collections of tools. We can become bewildered too easily by such locutions as *software development environment, CASE, programming environment, integrated project support environment,* and other flavors of the month. In the sense of software tools, we can loosely define an *environment* as one in which tools share project data—or at least permit multiple users to share the data pertaining to a given tool—and offer some common features in their user interfaces, if only in the use of the underlying software operating system (or software platform). Readers interested in the taxonomy of environments will find two different, but interesting, views in Susan Dart *et al.*[6] and Perry and Kaiser.[7] For our present purposes, we need to recognize only four kinds of environments:

1. *Language-bound environments.* Tools under these are specific to languages. The support provided must be in the back end (see Sec. 8.2), but may extend to the front end (see Sec. 8.1). Examples: Interlisp, C++, and the Smalltalk environment.

2. *Method-based environments.* These are the ones to which the term CASE is most often (if narrowly) applied. Each applies to one or more specific development paradigms. They generally apply to the front end of development, but may extend to the back end. Examples: Excelerator, Software Through Pictures, and Teamwork.

3. *Toolkits.* These tool collections provide a set of basic functions that communicate with each other through the file system of their host software platform. Modern ones have provisions for tools to share information. Examples: UNIX Programmer's WorkBench and the APSE CAIS for Ada.

4. *Integrated open environments.* To one extent or another, these apply to all development activities, provide common user interfaces, and permit sharing of product information among the tools. These will be discussed in Sec. 8.4. Examples: Hewlett-Packard's SoftBench, Atherton's Software Backplane, and Digital Equipment Corporation's FUSE.

Apart from the type of environment in which they may fall, we find it easier to discuss programming tools within the separate contexts of the front-end and back-end of software development. We use the term "front-end" to refer to those development activities that take place from the start of a project through the end of design. By "back-end," we mean activities involving actual program code.

8.1 Front-End Tools

The tools used in the specification of requirements, analysis of requirements, and design are the ones most likely to bear the appellation CASE, although if CASE is truly to mean computer-aided software engineering, we have no problem in using the word to describe back-end tools as well.*

Before actually mentioning any tools, we note that we have not attempted to present an inclusive catalog of off-the-shelf tools and their suppliers. For one thing, the number of tools is so great we can scarcely claim to know much of any of them beyond a small sample of the population, although the names of most are familiar to us. Secondly, suppliers constantly change and improve their offerings, so any catalog becomes obsolete within a year. Where we mention commercially available tools, we do so only to provide evidence that we are talking about industrial strength here-and-now, not future harvests from current research. With the disclaimer behind us, we move into the topic of front-end tools.

To a large extent, and for historical reasons, many have seen front-end tools only as documentation generators. The emphasis on documentation has been particularly important for military contractors required to comply with the data item descriptions cited in the standard for software development, DoD-STD-2167A. CASE suppliers such as Meridian Software Systems (Promod), Index Technologies (Excelerator), CADRE Technologies (Team*work*), Interactive Development Environments (Software Through Pictures), and Yourdon (Cradle) provide support for the generation of compliant documentation from

---

*Rather than front-end and back-end tools, some prefer the terms upper-CASE and lower-CASE.

the various diagrams and text files used in the pre-code stages of development. Apart from DoD requirements, all of the front-end tools supply documentation of one form or another, much of it graphic as in data flow diagrams and entity-relationship diagrams.

Tools produce documentation by providing any of several facilities: context-sensitive drawing packages for diagrams, templates for text documentation of specific formats, processors to translate designated information into such templates, and software to draw upon related files for producing composite reports. However generated, the quality of documentation produced by modern CASE tools is improved by its traceability to the work of the actual analyst/designer.

Attractive as their capability of capturing design decisions may be, the greatest value of front-end tools is the guidance they provide to analysts and designers and the continuity they provide to the several levels of abstraction that mark the early stages of development. In this view, documentation is not only faithful to the work of the originator, *it reflects actual design processes.* To take but one example, Software Through Pictures, which supports several methodologies, incorporates design rules for each. The core of the system, a relational database repository for all tools, provides communication among individual functions. While inherent features include automatic documentation, analysis of data dictionaries, such packaging considerations as fan-ins and fan-outs, and the tracing of requirements, the system provides editors and diagram interfaces for several methodologies: DeMarco/Yourdon structured systems analysis, Jackson data structures, entity-relationship modeling, and others.

The user interface for most modern front-end tools is graphical. The GUIs resemble those of the MacIntosh or Windows, which, in one variant or another, underlie several of the interfaces. Thus, apart from graphical editing, a programmer can view simultaneously, say, entries in a data dictionary and a data flow diagram citing the entries. This, in itself, reduces error. However, the systems themselves provide any number of consistency and syntactic checks. Typical checks include

- Specification of processes or diagrams before subordinate ones are specified
- Compliance with labeling conventions
- Consistency between diagram labels and the data dictionary
- Connections to other diagrams or the outside world
- At least one input or output data flow for a data store

Screen prototyping tools have demonstrated their worth by permitting users to agree and freeze the screen designs early in the process.

By automating the "what-you-see-is-what-you-get" (WYSWYG) philosophy, these tools have dramatic effect on productivity.

A recent study[8] of 12 tools supporting data flow diagrams found tools incorporating as few as 6 different checks and as many as 13. Additionally, front-end tools can report fan-out ratios, the number of defined entities, and other data pertinent to the methodology. Such statistics help one to grasp the scope of the unfolding solution.

For object-oriented technology, tools that identify inheritance relationships are proving invaluable. ObjectMaker, for example, provides drawing and analysis support for a variety of O-O methods. The tool checks the consistency of the model and depicts the relationships among classes and objects.

For data bases, schema design and conceptual-to-logical model translations would be incomplete without some form of data dictionary and data base analysis tool. Linking these to the DBMS has also proven useful, as has the integration with DBMS and applications generator 4GLs.

In addition to supporting analysis and design methods, front-end tools, through their output, can be coupled to back-end operations. For example, both Excelerator and KnowledgeWare provide back-end application generators to produce COBOL code from information captured and created by design and analysis tools. We shall return to more complete life cycle environments in Sec. 8.4, where we shall see that the current trend of front-end CASE is to open architectures; that is, user-extensible systems capable of interfacing with tools produced by other suppliers or in-house toolsmiths. However, in most programming shops of the early 1990s we find little communication between front-end and back-end tools.

8.2   Back-End Tools

At the beginning of this chapter, we noted that the earliest programming tools had to do with code: assemble (later, compile), link, load, and debug. We still need such tools, only now we expect much more help from them. Just as few of us choose to drive a car lacking a heater or interior lighting, except between garage and antique show, programmers now demand help in writing code, debugging it, and designing test cases. Many programmers also expect their tools to help them visualize their code.

Basic capabilities

The most elementary programming tool is an editor. In programming's *ancien régime*, programmers penciled their source code on preprinted forms, handed the forms to keypunch operators, and received a deck of punched cards in return. That's if they were lucky. The keypunch clerks might be busy doing the payroll, in which case the programmers had no choice but to do their own keypunching. Today, programmers expect not only to be able to enter their code directly from a terminal, workstation, or desktop computer keyboard, but to be able to edit the code on the screen using delete, replace, search, and other features of word processors. Indeed, the only significant word processor features not necessary for coding are word wrap-around and such print options as font changes and graphic insertions. On the other hand, context-sensitive editors, not to be found in word processors, may provide symbolic replacement, automatic indentation and prompting. As an example of the latter, by blinking the innermost left parenthesis not closed by a right parenthesis, one of the LISP* editors we use reduces the likelihood of leaving a statement with unbalanced parentheses.

Programmers not only expect helpful editors, they want the editor and other basic tools (e.g., compilers and linkers) to be supported by file management and a host of utility functions. In the toolkit environment model, this translates into the expectation of an operating system complete with a comprehensive command file. The best known of such operating systems is UNIX, which, despite its current use as a general platform, had its beginnings in support for software development. However, any modern general purpose operating system can form the basis for program development. The same operating system, of course, also serves as the platform for front-end tools. In addition to UNIX, Digital's VMS, IBM's mainframe MVS, MS-DOS, OS/2, and the MacIntosh operating system are examples of systems found extensively in software development environments. The last of these, of course, provides graphic support, while graphic adjuncts (e.g., Windows) have become a common means of providing GUIs on other machines.

As we noted in Sec. 8.1, GUIs not only provide an attractive alternative to command-driven interaction, they provide programmers with depictions of program graphs, decision trees, and other graphic representations of the structure of code. Using windowing techniques, GUIs can simultaneously provide different views of a program. For example, the Smalltalk environment (obviously a language-oriented environment) can allow the programmer to view an object's code while browsing through a collection of objects.

Source-level debugging

We have been discussing the most basic of back-end programming tools. Now add interpreters, compilers, and their run-time support

---

*Lots of Irritating, Silly, Parentheses.

systems. Once entered, edited, and compiled (or interpreted), code gets tested. As we noted in Chap. 7, the first tests are really debugging runs. In the interests of both productivity and quality, bugs will be found more quickly and with greater certainty (i.e., with less likelihood of programming incorrect fixes) if the programming environment includes source-level debugging capabilities. Source-level debuggers, once rare, now common, permit programmers to request the values of variables as they appear in the source code, set breakpoints using source code identifiers, change the values of data, and perform other operations entirely within the reference of the source code. Only rarely do you find a programmer who has to dump memory and then use a sheath of compilation output and link maps as the Baedeker for tracing the route home to source code statements. Like the other basic programming tools we have mentioned, source-level test beds are directed as much to quality as to productivity.

Things are a bit different if the hardware host of the programming environment differs from that of the program's target machine, as when debugging a microprocessor-based instrument control unit on a VAX. This requires that the test bed be capable of capturing and interpreting the microprocessor instructions to emulate their operation. Alternatively, the test bed might simply compile the code for the host machine and run it directly. This, of course, requires ultimate source code portability, a constraint that doesn't always work for embedded software.

Environments that accept source code and interpret commands for a foreign target have to deal with three variables: programming language, target processor, and hardware/software hosts. Microtec Research's Xray/DX analysis tools, when augmented by Microtec's emulation and simulation software, handle C, Pascal, and FORTRAN; most of the commonly encountered microprocessor families; and a variety of hardware/software platforms.[9] Although few systems are as versatile as Microtec's, most producers of embedded software should be able to find a system that will at once run on an in-house platform, accept the language of the source code in use, and run target code.

Build tools

We have discussed build tools in preceding chapters. Most of the ones we have seen, both off-the-shelf and homegrown, are based on UNIX's *make* utility. Version control is assured by the tool's capability of finding and compiling source code if the object code library does not have the latest edition as identified on the build list. The *make* superstructure is usually a matter of programs that allow the tool to work with unique production and development libraries and special build-list conventions.

Build tools, as distinguished from relatively primitive linking loaders, have become fairly common; witness to the years of struggle to ensure the configuration correctness of test loads and customer deliveries. Build tools reduce manual operations somewhat, but their greatest effect is on quality.

Coverage-based test beds

Section 7.2 discussed coverage-based testing. The test beds employ one of three basic methods. The most common uses a static analyzer as a preprocessor to instrument source code with soft probes (e.g., system calls) prior to compilation, as in Fig. 8.1. The probes, strategically placed (as at the first statement of a sequence construct) report their "activation." Or don't. Matching the probes that reported with those that did not, the test bed can determine the paths or branches executed, as well as examining calls and linkages to other programs.

Alternatively, if code execution is simulated, execution flow can be deduced from the execution of the simulator which, when combined with source code data still in the system, will produce execution reports in source code terms. In our earlier reference to the Microtec test bed,

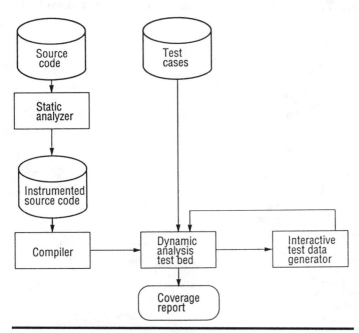

Figure 8.1 Coverage-based test bed.

we hadn't mentioned that its features include coverage analysis, but it does in this basic way.

The third method we know of is relatively primitive: One creates a dummy memory map by zeroing out n locations in memory, where n is the size of the target program. Then, by one means or another, one traps the program counter such that at the execution of each instruction the corresponding zero in the dummy memory map is replaced by some other value. A post-processor with access to the load map, the compilation maps, and the source code later backtracks to individual source statements to flag the statements exercised.

Regression test systems

As we noted in Chap. 7, automating the execution of regression tests greatly increases the likelihood the full set will be run, producing a corresponding increase in the confidence that changes to the program under test have not produced adverse side effects.

Figure 8.2 recalls Fig. 5.4, a state diagram for a hypothetical regression test system. Figure 8.2 outlines the basic software components of the system: a controller to load the next test in line, run the program, record the results in a format permitting comparison with a benchmark execution against the same input data, and output a report of any differences. The sense of regression testing is not simply to

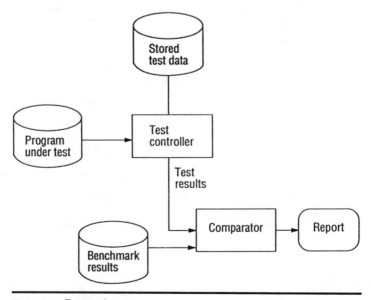

Figure 8.2 Regression test system.

determine if a change to a program causes tests that had previously passed to now fail. The regression test system must flag *any* differences in results, since any difference might be a symptom of unintended effects of the change.

The marketplace offers several off-the-shelf regression test systems. For example, SMARTS from Software Research, Inc. (San Francisco) contains tools to manage suites of tests, mechanize repetitive test activities, and automate test execution and evaluation. Among other widely known companies offering tools for regression testing, we find Digital Equipment Corporation (DEC/Test Manager), and Control Data Corporation (Automated Testing System).

Using another approach to the simplification of regression testing, numerous tools exist for recording and playing back test scripts consisting of user keystroke files. While a less ambitious method of automating regression testing, this approach does ensure consistent playback.

Test case generators

Based on 165 questionnaires returned by attendees at a testing conference, the principals of Software Quality Engineering determined that 13 percent used test data generators* for unit test, 17 percent for system test, and 11 percent for acceptance test.[10] Despite the contribution they can make to quality, completely automatic or interactive test data generators are not yet the rule.

Test data generators come in two flavors. In the first, static analysis of source code identifies the input required to exercise discrete parts of the structure (e.g., individual decision-to-decision branches). This is the kind of test data generator found in coverage-based test beds. It is fine for the purpose of increasing the amount of the structure tested, but, since its information comes only from the code itself, it cannot generate test data that will help determine if the code is the right code. Only functional testing can do that. The second approach to automatic generation of test data has as its input not source code but the specifications to which the source code was written.

Test data generators that analyze specifications plainly need to have the specifications prepared according to some formalism. The tool must be given unambiguous and decipherable definition of functions, external events, and valid data ranges. To reduce the scope of the problem, the tool can be given the capability of partitioning functions into equivalent classes. Test cases are members of the same functional class if:

---

*Technically, a test case is a set of test input data accompanied by identification of the intended actions and expected results. Software engineers usualy use the terms "test data generator" and "test case generator" interchangeably.

- The same input variables are relevant to each
- The same types of transformations will result
- The same output variables are affected by each

Iteratively, subclasses are formed by using the same definition. For example, inquiries of the status of a file of items (e.g., manufacturing parts) form one class. This class is divided into two subclasses: valid and invalid inquiries. Invalid inquiries include those that are unrecognizable (e.g., soup) and those for items not yet inventoried. Another functional class comprises transactions that modify the file. This in turn divides into the subclasses of invalid transaction classes (e.g., input codes for which there is no identified transformation), inventory additions, withdrawals, and alterations. Each of these is further subdivided...

The result is a finite set of domains, each a candidate for a unique set of test data. Functional partitioning also fits neatly with boundary value testing, since the derived domains separate valid input from invalid input, and within the former implicitly define range limits.

If the transitions among system states are specified, data can be devised automatically to test the correct sequencing of states. For example, a test can be fashioned to make sure that a feature is not invoked before public data it requires have been assigned values. Similarly, dependencies on the sequence of external events can be confirmed, as in checking operation against invalid sequences of interrupts. Indeed, simply by permuting the order of events within related classes, such sequence tests can be accomplished even when valid sequences are not defined.

We know of one off-the-shelf test case generator that uses these techniques (and a few more), namely, T, which meshes with specifications produced by Team*work* front-end tools.* T++, an enhanced version, is suitable for O-O software.

Performance measurement and evaluation

We seldom have occasion to care about the time it takes a word processor to respond to a character delete command. For many programs, however, time is of the essence; not just the obvious candidates, real-time programs, but even IS applications having highly repetitive operations. Compute time is but one measure of the quality of performance, and we shall touch upon some others. The end purpose of all such performance measurement is not simply to assign a quality score, but

---

*T is produced by Programming Environments, Inc. of Tinton Falls, NJ, and Team*work* is a product of Cadre Technologies, Inc. of Beaverton, OR.

to supply the data necessary for tuning software to a higher level of user satisfaction.

Typical measurements include:

- Time to respond to a query
- I/O channel utilization and disk latency
- In an on-line data base system, percentage of time spent by each report generator, data base input routine, and other applications
- For any program, average number of calls to each routine per hour of execution
- For networks, various traffic and loading statistics
- Average time expended by a given procedure for each call
- Virtual memory swapping statistics (how close is system to thrashing?)
- Connect delay statistics for telephone switches
- Extent of parallelism in concurrent systems

Many measurements are taken directly by the operating system. For example, IBM's mainframe MVS can report the number of times a given program was used during the month, the average time it was on-line, and the like. All virtual memory operating systems can report swapping statistics. Novell's FConsole, which runs on their network software, reports packet size, disk read, disk write, and other statistics vital to network management. Telephone switches collect data important to measure network performance. In another approach, hardware monitors take measurements by plugging directly into circuit or memory cards.

Of course, even when the software supplier can provide measurement software, one often has the option of using third party tools. For example, several suppliers sell network measurement software for Novell networks.

For many systems, measurements can only be made through the use of third party or in-house tools. For example, Carnegie Mellon University's Programming and Instrumentation Environment (PIE),[11] given a possible n parallel computations in a system, reports the fraction of time there was but one computation, two parallel computations, on up to n. For a given interval of time, PIE reports the amount of parallelism throughout the interval. Backing up these reports, PIE provides various fine-grained statistical graphs to identify exactly what is going on during the intervals reported.

Generally, where performance measurement is important, developers should think about incorporating key probes directly into the software rather than depending on external tools. In a real-time system, for example, it is easier to equip the software with the capability of periodically logging the size of an input queue than to instrument a special test bed to do the same thing. Moreover, built-in instrumentation can be handy for diagnosing field problems. If built-in performance instrumentation degrades performance by the microseconds required to perform and log the measurement, one can encode software switches to disable the measurements when not needed. Of course, even soft switches require at least one Boolean evaluation, but that's a matter of nanoseconds. Finally, compile time switches can be used to provide measurements up to the point of software release, and then turned off for production code.

8.3   Management Tools

We include in the management tools category those aids that help project managers maintain schedule and cost budgets, unambiguous editions of software destined for test or customer deliveries, adherence to project standards, and deliveries unsullied by faults once thought to have been corrected. We also include tools to measure attributes of product quality other than performance.

Cost/schedule/fault tracking and prediction

Section 5.3 addressed the issue of prediction and tracking. In the course of the section we noted several off-the-shelf tools implementing parametric models of cost, schedule, and fault generation. You can also use homegrown tools tuned to parametric values derived from experience. For example, you may know that work performed for a given customer always contains an unusual number of faults because of the magnitude of changes ordered after the contract is signed. A parametric multiplier for rework (resulting from both directed modifications and faults) can be applied to schedule dates and staff size for applicable work tasks. A spreadsheet is a good vehicle for combining the ingredients of a parametric model and deriving estimates of schedule, staff size, and likely numbers of faults.

If estimates based on analogy work well for the manager, one needs to maintain experience of previous projects in an accessible form. The obvious vehicle for storing past triumphs (and their opposite number) is a DBMS, but then, a DBMS is a basic management tool of many project management uses.

Project planning and accounting

Project managers deal with resources, discrete tasks and the way they relate to each other, and estimates and actuals. All of this is pretty much standard stuff, no more applicable to software projects than to highway construction. Still, it's surprising that software managers, of all people, rely no more heavily on tools for help than do civil engineers. Much of the business of project management revolves about the task structure, or *work breakdown structure* (WBS), so we start there.

A WBS organizes work tasks in much the manner that a program structure chart organizes a program. Subordinate to an element of the structure, *Detailed Design*, we may find the tasks *Monthly Report Design*, *Year-to-Year Report Design*, and so on. The WBS does no more than organize the work that needs to be done in iteratively divisible packages. Program planning starts with a WBS, but at the time of planning, some downstream WBS items remain unidentified. For example, at the start of the project the requirement to design a *Monthly Report* was obvious from the marketing specification. However, division of the design effort into *Inflow*, *Outflow*, and *Variance* won't be known until some time during the design cycle. In short, a WBS will get modified, and computers are the preferred hosts for anything we expect to modify.

Of course, modification isn't the prime reason to place the WBS in a computer. One wants to be able to assign resources to each task, to schedule its start and duration, and to determine its expected completion date. In short, the WBS itself should be a resource feeding other management tools.

Once tasks are in a computer, they can be assigned start and expected completion dates. Next, resources (for software development, mostly staff) can be assigned each task and aggregated, as in Fig. 8.3.

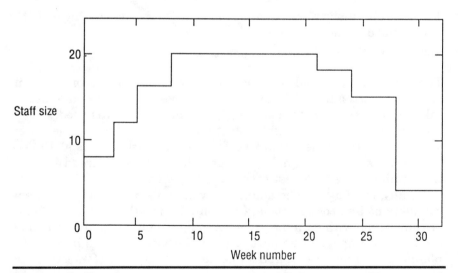

Figure 8.3 Staffing plan.

Total staff per task is useful, but individual names from the personnel data base are even more useful. Even more useful, for the case of people assigned part-time to parallel tasks, is the assignment of names and hours per task. We find this capability in any number of project management software packages available on personal computers.

Gantt charts remain the most popular way to depict the start and completion dates of overlapping tasks, although many managers find critical path charts (e.g., PERT) not only capable of revealing subtle effects of task dependencies but excellent means for displaying task start and completion dates. Completing a project requires successful execution of a diverse set of sequences of interdependent tasks (or routes). With parallel tasks, the project team may simultaneously transit a number of sequences (or routes, as they are often called). Determining the longest (timewise) route is not always obvious.

Figure 8.4 shows a project plan emphasizing the most conspicuous software tasks: development of a requirements model, preliminary design, implementation (detailed design and code), and testing beyond the unit level. The numbers above each task box represent the estimated time in weeks.

In the sense of critical path analysis, however, the topography looks quite different, as shown in Fig. 8.5. Here we see that it is not the implementation and test tasks that determine availability for alpha test, as suggested by Fig. 8.4, but the path having to do with documentation and training. Rather than letting the tail wag the dog, the project manager will do well to divide the user documentation task into two parts:

1. The preliminary work needed to prepare both the training diskette and the documentation

2. The final documentation preparation

This way, the disk and the final documentation can be prepared in parallel, shortening the total path. What we have is remedial action taken in plenty of time because the appropriate tool was used.

Parenthetically, we might note that test sequences, alone, often present a formidable candidate for critical path analysis. Project control tools can be invaluable in supporting the use of thread analysis in planning achievable test programs.

Finally, one ought to be able to show actuals both in terms of task completions and cost. Cost data accumulated in the computer should be compatible with both the project management and payroll systems. Actuals are important as part of the data base that will be used for planning the next project and for demonstrating the cost effectiveness of quality improvement measures.

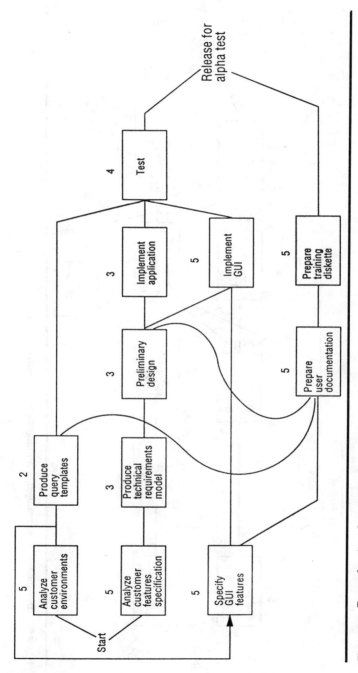

Figure 8.4 Dependencies of project tasks.

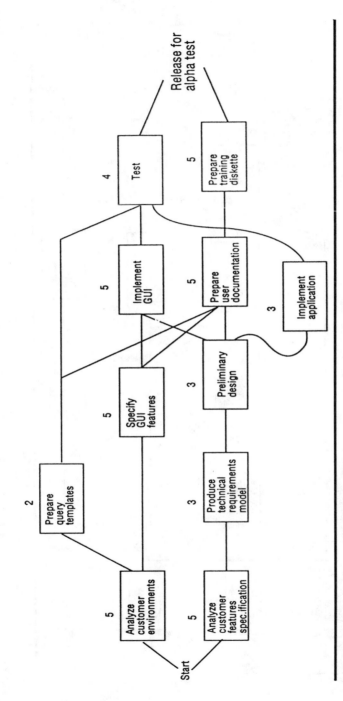

Figure 8.5 Dependencies rearranged to highlight critical path.

A number of project management tools are available for personal computers to handle cost accounting against specified work packages. Actually, we should like to see all the items we have discussed, except for payroll, handled in a single system with a common user interface language. One such system is the Project Workbench, produced by Applied Business Technology Corp.

Configuration management

Chapter 6 could not avoid discussing configuration management tools, since it is only through tools that you can manage libraries of documents and code and be certain of the contents of program builds. We need not repeat the material of that chapter. However, we should note that beyond the literal management of the artifacts of programming, configuration management tools support other aspects of management. For example, status is automatically updated when an item is entered into a library. As another example, object managers manage inheritance relationships that cannot always be expressed as hierarchical parent/child relations.

We should also note that the basic tool for library management remains the mechanism for managing data, most commonly a DBMS or object management system (OBS). The integrated tool environments discussed in Sec. 8.4, with their sophisticated data management technology, all have ample provisions for configuration management.

Audit

The data base of any programming environment is an audit tool, at least with respect to status and version accounting. For example, if one wants to know how many of the identified modules have been designed down to the pseudocode level, the answer can be found in the entries of a library, dictionary, or repository. To determine if the latest description of a software component has been updated to the latest system description, just look to the dictionary (or alternative base of data). If the dictionary itself doesn't have the material, it should have a reference to where it can be found. Auditing is made much easier when everything is in one place: No need to wander from office to office, pulling folders out of file cabinets and, at that, wondering if the latest edition made it to the file cabinet.

Although there are limits to how much one wants to put in the project data stored in the computer, certain notes are appropriate. For example, if the proposed release requires changes to module *alpha*, a note identifying the changes can be attached to the *alpha* descriptions. Before the advent of modern tools, we would place such notes in the

unit development folder (literally, that) for the module. Unit development folders contained everything applicable to software elements at
the lowest level of management. They were a great idea, provided
people replaced material pulled from folders, and certainly made
auditing easier. But not as easy as computer-based data.

Problem and correction logs

At the very least, logs of identified problems and their closings (corrections) should be maintained in a data management system of one type
or another. Better yet, if you have an environment repository, the
problems can be copied (or indexed) from a composite log to the
applicable software item. Thus, when auditing the descriptions of
alpha, you may find a still-unresolved problem.

Problems reported by customers can be kept separately, but copied
to the composite log, or simply identified by a special code. Problems
that were encountered in development are of less interest once the
product is fielded. We want to know about them as part of a quality
improvement program, and we may have to refer to development
problems when investigating a customer problem. The problems reported by customers, however, are what we most often pull from the
log, whether to draw an agenda of product improvements or to correlate
reports from different customers.

Measurements

Measurement tools start with data acquisition and end with reports.
Data acquisition falls into two categories: manually entered data and
data derived from other entries in the dictionary or repository.

Every terminal, desktop computer, or workstation connected to a
central computer or file server can serve as the entry device for minutes
of reviews, fault descriptions (found in testing), classified daily totals
of faults found in testing, and the like. The same terminals or computers serve for the manual entry of change requests, customer problem
reports (perhaps remotely entered directly by the customer), labor cost
data, and other information that needs to be stored for reasons other
than measurement but enjoy a second life when drawn upon for
inclusion in systems of measurement data. Templates or query-by-example screens can be used for all manually entered data to ensure
completeness and correct format. Other derived measurement data
come from structural measurements made by analysis tools.

A powerful measurements system does more than simply regurgi-
tate individual data reports. It permits the interactive user to correlate
data from several reports. If all the data are in a RDBMS, it is simply

a matter of a query to form a report (as in Fig. 8.6) to show the ageing of problems reported by engineering change requests, customer reports, and customer service. A number of such queries should be preprogrammed, cataloged, and made available for users. Of course, users can always fashion their own queries in a 4GL such as SQL.

Certain measurements yield directly to tools. Many editors and compilers report lines of source code. A preprocessor to strip out comments can provide lines of non-comment source code. Many tools (e.g., Verilog's Logiscope) generate cyclomatic complexity measures. In hours one can write a program to tally bean-counting fault data reports to show fault modality, fault detection effectiveness, and other factual input for quality improvement (see Chap. 9).

Several tools have been developed to package common product measurements under a single umbrella. For example, Knowledge-Ware's Inspector has five categories of measurements for COBOL code: size (as in LOC), static analysis measures (recursions, dead code, and the like), weak control flow (as in the use of GOTOs), the extent to which the code follows the rules of structured programming, and complexity.

8.4   Tool Integration

Most CASE systems have been *closed* (also called *closed-end) environments.* Language-bound environments and method-based environments traditionally have been self-contained tool sets capable of working with

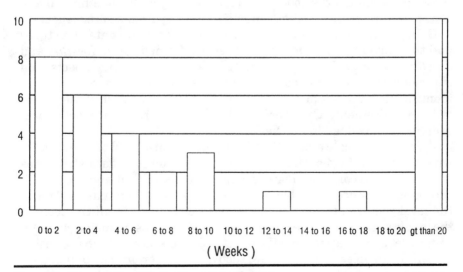

Figure 8.6   Open problems dating from time of report.

no alien tools except through the importation and exportation of data files. Few of the older toolkit environments had facilities for any direct sharing of data among tools, although the UNIX Programmer's Workbench backend environment was a notable exception. Sharing information is not the only characteristic of an integrated environment. We have also to consider the relations among the tools and between each tool and the process in place. The action, so to speak, in the direction of tool integration is focused on *open* (also called *open-end) architectures* as the means of enabling the integration of tools from multiple suppliers into a coherent set. Open environments, however, are but a contrivance to permit integration. First, we need to understand what we mean by integration.

Levels of integration

As we noted earlier, integrating tools mean more than just finding a way for them to share data. At the lowest level of integration, we can speak of integrating tool *doesthis* and tool *doesthat* simply by having the two operate on the same software platform. *doesthis* exports its output data and *doesthat* imports the data to use it. With the two tools having nothing else in common, *doesthat* must manipulate the data to fit its own purposes; not entirely satisfactory from the aspect of efficiency. At the next level up, both tools use common data formats and operations codes. Let's assume that *doesthis* and *doesthat* deal with text documents. At this level of integration, *doesthis* places a special code (ASCII something-or-other) at the start of each new paragraph, and *doesthat* recognizes the code. We're now dealing with something analogous to a word processor that can import directly from a spreadsheet.

Going up an integration step, we deal with common data structures and the conventions under which they are formed. Both *doesthis* and *doesthat* work with a data structure identical in all respects and sufficient for the tasks of each; say, records of three fields: requirement identification, requirement description, and identification of the source of the requirement. The special codes at the start of each new paragraph are embedded in the fields.

We go up the scale again, this time to a semantic level of integration, where the meanings of the operations on the common data structures are themselves common. For example, all tools will cut and paste with the same sequence of keyboard or point-and-shoot commands. This is the level required to have a user interface common to all the tools in the environment. This level of integration entails a major jump in "interface" specifications and the effect of the specifications on the design of tools. In an object-oriented view, such as the Atherton Backplane, data objects and control objects are coupled in a messaging scheme.

Brown and McDermid have published an excellent outline[12] of integration levels, in which they define the highest to be that in which nonoverlapping, specific, jobs are specified for each tool. This, of course, implies that the tools support a specific development method. We have such tools now in the method-based environments defined in the introductory paragraphs of the chapter. However, none currently extends over all elements of development. In the discussions that follow, unless noted, we shall talk about integration below the method level, since that is where we currently find the greatest promise of tool integration for the entire software lifecycle.

A user's view of integration

Programmers take a pragmatic view of the extent to which tools are integrated. We draw upon the four aspects of integration seen by Thomas and Nejmeh[13] to identify integration in terms of user perceptions.

1. Presentation:
    a. Similar look, touch, and feel of user interface (e.g., similar screen formats, same technique for selecting highlighted object).
    b. Similar concepts (e.g., all tools involved in library control present the relations among controlled artifacts as a tree diagram).
2. Control:
    a. Tools provide services needed by other tools (e.g., if a search algorithm used by a language-sensitive programming editor is also used by a document browser, the user performs searches in the same way). As a corollary, well-integrated tools use services provided by others.
3. Data:
    a. Information can be exchanged among tools (e.g., a user should be able to cut data used in one tool, paste it into the data used in a second tool, and have the second tool understand the data).
    b. Updating duplicated and derived data for tools that operate concurrently should be automatic, not something the user has to think about. Put differently, the context of each tool should be saved when another tool is invoked.
4. Process:
    a. Tools should support the user's task in the user's language (e.g., a source level debugger should communicate with the user's source code and not the source code that a preprocessor might have [invisibly] generated from the user's code).
    b. Tools specific to a given process model should enforce the standards of the process (e.g., if the process calls for a static analysis of freshly compiled code before execution, the debugger should not accept the code unless it has been submitted to the static analyzer).

Note that process integration, in this user's view of integration, partly corresponds with the method-oriented level of integration proposed by Brown and McDermit. We do not expect to soon find this in environments that come close to covering the entire span of development activities. But maybe next year?

Perhaps we can summarize the concept of tool integration in terms of an environment in which the user can use common mechanisms to navigate between inherently consistent views of the program, its documentation, its quantified characteristics, its configuration status, its behavior under test, and the like, at each step adding or deriving new information about the program. Such an environment, schematically depicted in Fig. 8.7, is usually described in one word: *seamless*.

Parenthetically, we note that it seems fairly certain that comprehensive, seamless, systems of tools will be based on hypertext, which follows the lines of entity-relationship models to permit users to navigate from one object to another in contextual ways, on repositories, or on both.

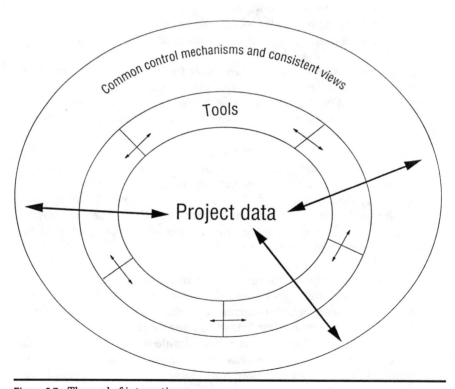

Figure 8.7 The goal of integration.

Common interfaces

From a mechanical point of view, integration is a matter of the interfaces among tools and between tools and the host platform. Integration—especially integration of tools from diverse vendors—would be accelerated if there were a standard tool interface. Several have been proposed and may yet come into common use. Plainly, a single interface would permit the broadest choice of tools for one's environment, but two or three standards would be better than none. We make passing mention of three prominent candidates:

Perhaps the archetypical interface standard is that of Europe's Portable Common Tool Environment (PCTE).[14] In the PCTE concept, tools are stored in a repository from which they are executed as processes. Software suppliers are currently building tools to operate under PCTE, both in the States and in Europe. Also, we understand that Hewlett Packard is re-engineering its SoftBench (of which, more later) for the PCTE.

The IEEE Computer Society has drafted a standard for tool integration. The standard, P1175/D11,[15] addresses four techniques for exchanging information among tools: tool-to-tool, via the file structure of the host platform, transfer based on communications protocols, and the use of a repository.

As part of the Ada Programming Support Environment (APSE), the Ada Joint Program Office has developed a proposed standard for the tool interface. With nested acronyms that only a programmer would tolerate, the standard is known as CAIS (Common APSE Interface Set).[16] CAIS has much in common with PCTE concepts, but its mechanisms also provide for access restrictions for confidential and secret information.

Off-the-shelf systems

We conclude the topic of integration by pointing out that there currently exist a surprising number of software product lines that exhibit the characteristics of tool integration in terms of the user's perceptions as we have described them. None of the available systems is capable of satisfying more than a portion of the tooling described in Secs. 8.1, 8.2, and 8.3. But, at some sacrifice of the user's view of integration, current open architecture systems can accommodate other tools to cover all software development activities. Truly integrated, comprehensive, environments lie in the future. Nevertheless, present offerings can substantially contribute to the quality of software products. We give four open architecture examples to indicate the present state of tool integration.

Software through Pictures, available from Interactive Development Environments, is an open architecture product line directed primarily to front-end development tasks. We have remarked a few of the features in preceding sections. We shall not list all the features, but as an example of integration we note that the system uses a consistent "mouse-and-menu" user interface for each of its nine graphical editors (dataflow diagram, data structure, entity relationship, control flow, control specification, state transition, structure chart, transition diagram, and an object-oriented editor). A multi-user, object-oriented data dictionary connects all tools.

Preceding sections have also commented on the KnowledgeWare product line. The repository-based architecture permits windows for four different virtual workstations (for planning, analysis, design, and construction) to be simultaneously open on a PC running on an OS/2 platform and connected to tools running on a mainframe. Coherent tools serve each workstation, but more significantly, all four workstations present look-alike interfaces. Moreover, users can cut and paste between windows and can use OS/2's Hypertext to navigate through documents.

Hewlett Packard (HP) SoftBench permits the user to click on any of six virtual workstations or other tools installed on the user. All Soft-Bench tools permit a window to be resized, moved, and focused on an icon. An example of how the programmer can stay in one mode of operation while running the system is found in the use of the graphical browser for developing C++ O-O programs. The tool allows the programmer to specify and analyze objects and the relations among them. Pulldown menus permit the definition of inheritance relations for the generation of new objects. Once the classes have been defined and methods have been programmed, the same pulldown menus are used for the development of programs employing them.

The FUSE product of Digital Equipment Corporation uses a graphical interface based on an environment (OSF/Motif) similar to that used by SoftBench. Programmers can switch between tools by clicking a mouse without losing the context of the task. Thus, if the compiler finds an error, the source code comes up on the editor tool with the faulty lines of code annotated. In the editor screen, the programmer fixes the code and submits for a recompile. Similarly, the programmer can click on an object in the graphical depiction of the call graph to bring up the corresponding source code. FUSE contains a variety of tools essential to the iterative back-end tasks of code entry (or edit), compile, debug, analyze, and measure performance, all within a consistent set of graphical idioms. Also, the open architecture permits front-end tools to be incorporated under the FUSE umbrella. One of many third-party tools that has been configured for FUSE is the aforementioned Software through Pictures.

These tools, and others like them, are available now, can be simultaneously used by multiple programmers working on the same project, and can form the linchpin of a quality improvement program. The four tools we have used as examples are wedded to no specific development method, although support for programming languages is an understandable restriction.

8.5 Summary

1. Powerful tools are costly, and their contribution to programmer productivity has been disputed. Although the trend toward increased tool integration will greatly increase productivity, the chief argument for acquiring tools is their favorable effect on quality.

2. Tools must fit one's software development model, not the other way around. The tools at a programmer's disposal constitute a programming environment for implementing the model of choice.

3. At one time, front-end tools, which are used for analysis and design, were thought of mostly as documentation aids. Modern ones, however, are an integral part of the design process.

4. Graphic interfaces (GUIs) permit programmers to simultaneously view different aspects of the evolving code and more easily find errors. Modern tools incorporate a number of their own consistency checks.

5. Back-end (or code-oriented) tools are indispensable. Only in recent years have these tools offered such quality aids as source-level debugging, traceable library control, coverage-based testing, automatic regression testing, and generation of test data from specifications.

6. Management tools include those for project prediction, planning, accounting, control, configuration management, auditing, problem tracking, and the measurement of products and processes.

7. We can speak of tool integration at several levels. From a user's point of view, integration is a matter of common means of presentation and control, common data, and conformance (or integration) with the user's programming process.

8. Open environments allow users to add their own or third-party tools to those included in the supplier's tool set. Open environments are the key to comprehensive tool integration. The number of off-the-shelf open environments is rapidly increasing, and software managers can currently choose from a variety of powerful and effective systems.

References

1. Ivie, Evan. "The Programmer's Workbench—A Machine for Software Development," *CACM*, Vol. 20, No. 10, October 1977, pp. 746-753.

2. Huff, Clifford. "Elements of a Realistic CASE Tool Adoption Budget," *CACM*, Vol. 35, No. 4, April 1992, pp. 45-54.
3. Chikofsky, E. and Rubenstein, B. "CASE: Reliability Engineering for Information Systems," *IEEE Software*, Vol. 5, No. 2, March 1988, pp. 8-16.
4. Card, David, *et al.* "Evaluating Software Engineering Technologies," *Trans. Software Engrg.*, SE-13, No. 7, July 1987, pp. 845-851.
5. Burgess, Angela. "From the Editor," *IEEE Software*, Vol. 9. No. 2, March 1992, pp. 6-9.
6. Dart, Susan, *et al.* "Software Development Environments," *Computer,* November 1987, pp. 18-28.
7. Perry, Dewayne and Kaiser, Gail. "Models of Software Development Environments," *Trans. Software Engrg.*, SE-17, No. 3, March 1991, pp. 283-295.
8. Vessy, Iris, *et al.* "Evaluation of Vendor Products: CASE Tools as Methodology Companions," *CACM*, Vol. 35, No. 4, April 1992, pp. 90-105.
9. Chang, Rob. "Xray/DX analysis of embedded applications," *IEEE Software,* May 1990, p. 55.
10. *Executive Summary and Selected Highlights, 1988 Survey on Software Test Practices*, Software Quality Engineering, Jacksonville, FL.
11. Lehr, Ted, *et al.* "Visualizing Performance Debugging," *Computer*, October 1989, pp. 38-51.
12. Brown, Alan and McDermid, John. "Learning from IPSE's Mistakes," *IEEE Software,* March 1992, pp. 23-28.
13. Thomas, Ian and Nejmeh, Brian. "Definitions of Tool Integration for Environments," *IEEE Software*, March 1992, pp. 29-35.
14. "Portable Common Tool Environment," *Tech. Report ECMA-149,* European Computer Manufacturers' Association, Geneva, Dec. 1990.
15. *A Reference Model for Computing System Tool Interconnection, IEEE P1175/D11* (draft), IEEE Computer Society Press, Los Alamitos, CA, 1991.
16. *Common APSE Interface Set*, DOD-STD-1838A, Ada Joint Program Office, Department of Defense, 1989.

The Quality Process

Chapter 1 made little distinction between *quality programs* and *quality processes*. Programs have start points and end points. Processes have only start points and continuously repeat themselves. Admittedly, the distinction is slight, but we raise it to highlight the emphasis placed by a quality process on the improvement of software quality. This chapter discusses the application of quality processes to given projects, but also focuses on the improvement in the software process underlying all of a company's projects.

As we said in Chap. 1, we see the principles of total quality management (TQM) as the key to productive, effective software quality processes. Let's call our goal "a mature process for software." Let's go a step further and state that achieving the goal requires us to address four primary objectives: customer (or user) satisfaction, project control, reduction in the cost of quality, and a process for continuous improvement (see Fig. 9.1). The fishbone schema of Fig. 9.1, by the bye, was inspired by the ubiquitous Ishikawa cause-effect diagrams.[1]

We have selected the four objectives shown on Fig. 9.1* as the ones management is most concerned with. Project control and the satisfaction of customers and users is obvious. Indeed, customer satisfaction

---

*Figure 9.1 is not a true Ishikawa diagram. Devised for manufacturing processes, Ishikawa's diagrams had five main control points—man, method, machine, measurement, and meterial—which plainly do not apply to our interest in objectives and goals.

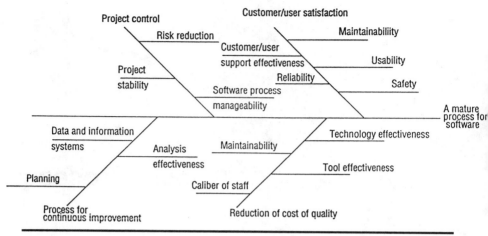

Figure 9.1

is the end purpose of TQM. Reduction of cost of quality (COQ) is obvious once we define COQ as the costs associated with preventing, finding, and fixing faults. Reduced COQ means a reduced development time cycle and greater profit (or, to a nonprofit programming shop, less drain on budget). The fourth objective, a process for continuous improvement, is a bit subtle. We feel that it is not enough to reach some specified level of quality. One must continue to take measures to reach higher levels. If you can get from here to there, you can also get from there to a point beyond. And another beyond that.

Although Fig. 9.1 identifies the first-order constituents of the four objectives, we have gone one step deeper than that in Figs. 9.2 through 9.5. Each of these fishbone diagrams, which capture the spirit of cause-and-effect implicit in Ishikawa's diagrams, explodes one of Fig. 9.1's objectives. Using the term we used for data flow diagrams, state diagrams, and similar development artifacts, the set of six figures represents a *leveled* illustration of a mature process for software. (We use the word *leveled* as we did in discussing dataflow and state diagrams to describe the unfolding of detail as one goes through levels of abstraction.)

In Fig. 9.2, we see five contributors to customer/user satisfaction: reliability, support, maintainability, safety, and usability. Not all of these apply to all users, of course. Take safety for example. Only the most paranoid user of a word processor is likely to fear getting hurt by it. On the other hand, safety is paramount to the controller of a medical life support system. Most of the items in Fig. 9.2 are self-evident from the substance of Chaps. 5 through 8. We note, however, that testing effectiveness, which contributes to attaining both reliability and safety, has a somewhat different meaning in each of the two contexts. With

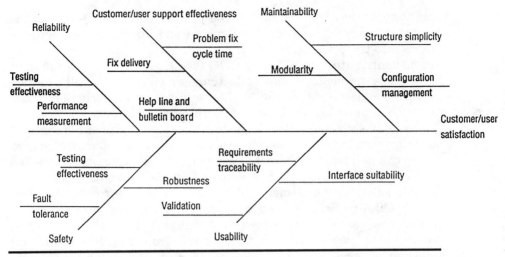

Figure 9.2

regard to reliability, testing effectiveness has most to do with ridding the system of bugs. For safety, the emphasis of testing needs to be on ensuring that the right thing was tested, and that analysis of possible faults was sufficient to ensure that the behavior of the system in the presence of such faults was evaluated.

Figure 9.3, given to the objective of project control, also introduces nothing not covered by preceding chapters. However, we shall see in

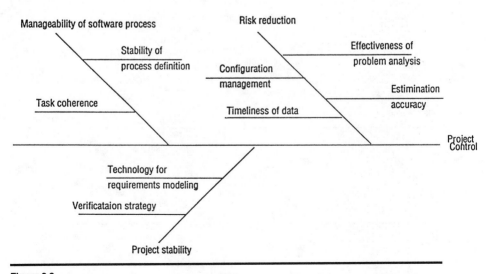

Figure 9.3

this chapter how the stability of the process definition—that is, the local standards that govern development and maintenance—actually enters into project control.

The contributors to reducing COQ (see Fig. 9.4) are also familiar. For brevity, under technology effectiveness we combined all pre-code activities under "analysis and design" and under "construction" those (other than detection) having to do with code.

Unlike the other detailed diagrams, Fig. 9.5, which details continuous improvement, introduces new topics. Most of the topics are covered in this chapter, with the balance (planning and self-assessment) treated in the next. We do not mean to suggest that the rest of this chapter is devoted solely to the elements of Fig. 9.5. Chapter 9 rounds out Part 3, The Quality Solution, by building onto the topics of Chaps. 5 through 8—a management view of integrated quality processes. Nevertheless, we start with a new topic from Fig. 9.5—data and information systems—a prerequisite for processes for continuous improvement.

9.1   Management by Fact

While everyone understands that intelligent decisions are rarely made solely on the basis of anecdotal information or the feeling in the seat of one's pants, few have given much thought to the system that provides the data* that form the foundation for most management decisions. Such systems have four major elements:

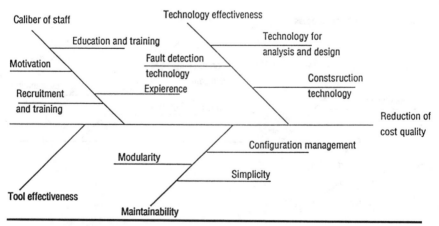

Figure 9.4

---

*For brevity, we shall use data to mean both quantitative data and other information.

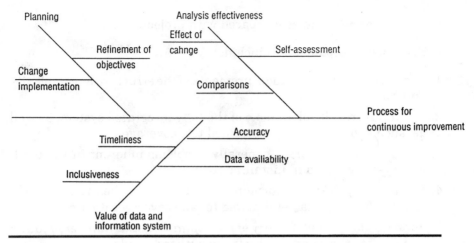

Figure 9.5

- Collection of data
- Storage of data
- Analysis of data
- Dissemination of data and analysis results

We discuss each of these in turn.

Data collection

Let's start by looking at the diversity of data required for TQM. We have three basic categories to consider, project data, product data, and process data. In the following examples of data for each category we have gone beyond raw data to include a few simple examples of processed data, such as tabulations.

Project data, used during the course of bringing a product or a new release to market, include:

1. *Status of each defined task*—including, as appropriate, such fine-grained data as the number of performance functions thus far resolved in design, percentage of test cases designed, etc.
2. *Current estimate of required system resources*—memory, time to execute certain functions, etc.
3. *Test data*—for system level tests, number of test cases attempted and number passed.
4. *Cost to date*—and as compared with projections.

5. *Staff on hand*—and as compared with projections.

Examples of product data include:

1. *Structural data*—such measurements of the structure as complexity and component size.

2. *Test data*—results of all tests of the fully integrated system, as well as such summary data as attained test coverage.

3. *Customer / user reports*—generally, problems inherent in the product or encountered in installing the product.

4. *Frequency of faulty performance* (at the risk of theatricality, we'll call this failure data)—tabulated to take severity into account.

5. For each component, *history of recompilations and number of faults* found after the component left the authors' hands.

6. *Customer calls for assistance* by the month or quarter.

7. *Customer responses to questionnaires* addressing desired features and the perceived quality of product.

8. *Number of known faults of each severity class* in the system—a corollary is the number of undiagnosed test failures or customer problem reports.

Process data, all of which derive from the compilation of data from individual projects, include

1. *Cost of labor* for each work breakdown structure task required to bring products and their releases to market.

2. *Effectiveness of fault detection processes*—see Sec. 7.2.

3. *Tabulation of detected fault sources*—as attributed to development tasks (requirements analysis, code, etc.).

4. *Tabulation of fault modes*—number of faults attributed to static logic, I/O, etc.

5. *Software development environment response time*—statistics indicating delays in compilation and similar operations.

6. *Response to customer requests*—statistics on the number of requests handled directly by the person staffing the telephone line, fault ageing, and the like.

7. *Customer responses to questionnaires* directed to support.

These data come from diverse sources: minutes of review meetings, test operations, simple tabulation forms (as illustrated by Fig. 9.6) labor time records (via the cost accumulation system), status reports, static analyzers, and other tools discussed in Chap. 8, LAN management software, questionnaires, and the like. Much of the information can be entered directly from keyboard at the point where the data originate. For example, the obvious place to enter test data is from a terminal in the test lab. Figure 9.6 illustrates a screen into which presumed fault information can be entered. We say "presumed" because certain information, such as the source of the fault, may be less than certain. The illustration shows both the "buttons" (bold outline) that the tester clicks on* and the pull-down menu that results. When clicking on "report complete," the tester is told of any data not yet entered and is asked if this is okay. This gives the tester the opportunity to go back and "fill in the blanks" or to defer completion until further analysis is done. Thus, if no diagnosis has been performed, several of the fields will necessarily be incomplete. However, to permit subsequent updating, the tester, on exiting the screen, is given the number assigned to the report.

Data collection aids, such as that of Fig. 9.6, should be tailored to the product, development model, or both. While the three severity levels of Fig. 9.6 may work for computer-aided design software, they would be difficult to interpret for DBMS software. (What would "results out of tolerance" mean in that milieu?) Similarly, the types of tests displayed in the test type pull-down menu reflect a specific development model. But it should be plain that even under the most

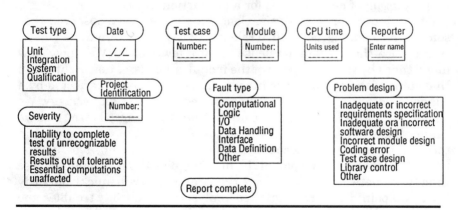

Figure 9.6 Test data collection screen.

*Alternatively, the buttons might be fields in a menu that the reporter clicks on to bring up a follow-on action or a list of choices.

chaotic of circumstances, integration testing, one can painlessly—if not effortlessly—collect fault data.

Data storage

We should like to say that all data can be stored in one place. A RDBMS, for example, is the obvious vehicle to permit one to correlate problems found in testing with problems encountered by customers. However, much of the data—especially product structural data—derive from tools and get stored by the tool in a repository of one kind or another. Cost accumulation data derive from labor time records and are stored in the data base used by the Comptroller's Department. At least some of the customer support data may have to be compatible with a data base under the control of the Marketing Department.

In short, one may have to deal with several data bases, at least until the time when it is feasible to consolidate them. Certain RDBMS permit one to join tables from two different data bases, which simplifies things a great deal. In any case, with all the data stored one way or another on the computer, one has the foundation for a data and information system. Data stored only on paper are unlikely to get much use.

Analysis

Some data require no analysis to provide insights to management. Consider Fig. 9.7, a history of the backlog of approved requests for the programming of new features for a production control system.

Other data require analysis. Consider that we have observed that some of the modules included in release 4.2 have been recompiled many times since their original release, others few times. (We know how many times by the extensions of the modules' labels.) This might mean that some of the modules are inherently unstable, easily affected by a change in other parts of the system or—worse—just plain buggy. We should want to investigate these further, but with limited resources we cannot hope to investigate all modules. At what point (measured in terms of the number of recompilations) should we defer investigation to a later date? A simple plot of the number of modules recompiled less than twice, between three and five times, and so on will quickly identify the cutoff point for further detailed analysis of potentially troublesome modules. Called *Pareto analysis** by quality engineers, the technique has many uses in separating the "vital few from the trivial many" (in J. Juran's words). Figure 9.8 makes it obvious that we want to look

---

*After the economist Vilfredo Pareto, who early in this century postulated that 20 percent of the population controls 80 percent of the wealth.

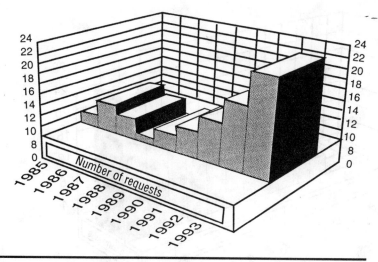

Figure 9.7 Backlog of approved requests.

first at those modules that have been recompiled 12 or more times. Similarly, if we were looking to streamline a product by simplifying the complexity of individual modules, we might plot the number of modules at different levels of complexity.

As another example of the need for analysis, let's look at the information contained in customer questionnaires. Depending on what one is looking for, all the information found on questionnaires may not lend itself to simple tabulation. How does one tabulate responses to "Please tell us of any suggestions you have?" These must be directed to the appropriate department and analyzed there. Even responses that can be tabulated need to be analyzed. We can form a histogram of the responses from customers to "How many hours of elapsed time did installation take?" but we should want also to calculate the mean and standard deviation of the responses to know whether we need to do something to simplify installation.

Some analyses take considerable effort. Determining the response time of the software development environment, for example, may mean correlating network traffic statistics during given intervals with the activity logs of the terminals on-line during the interval. No easy task, and one requiring certain analyzer insights. Most analyses, however, can follow cookbook procedures.

A common problem with the analysis of data is that the interval between the collection of raw data and the availability of analysis results makes the results obsolete by the time they are received. If analysis of test results includes subjective decisions, as in tests dealing

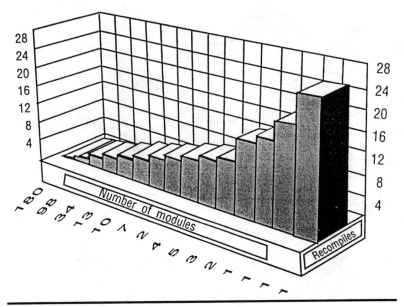

Figure 9.8   Module recompilation statistics.

with the readability of screens, one runs the risk that the pass/fail test status trend will always be running behind real time, reducing the options for remedial action if testing runs into trouble. Analysis procedures should be streamlined and mechanized as necessary to preclude the possibility that data will go unused.

Analyses are not about to happen unless they are planned to happen and someone is assigned to make them happen. Simply put, analysis has to be part of the data and information *system*.

Dissemination of data and analysis results

A system for data and information is of no use if the data and the results of analysis are not available to the people who can use them. Ordinarily, this is no problem if there are enough terminals to access the data and the results. We have never understood programming shops that do not provide each programmer and manager with an individual terminal, whether smart or dumb. (The terminal, that is, not the person.) From their terminals, programmers and managers should be able to simply query the data base(s) to get the reports they want. However, they need to have some kind of on-line catalog to learn of the data and results available to them. This is often overlooked, leading to data base users wasting time trying to find the right way to query information that doesn't exist.

Another way to help ensure the availability of data and results is to provide prepackaged queries. Our programmers and managers are certainly capable of fashioning their own queries, using SQL or some other 4GL, but the need to do so has to exert a dissuasive influence on the use of the data.

On counting beans

Before leaving the subject of data and information systems, we need to address one more item, and we do so by returning to the systems of data and information systems.

The four elements of management by fact just addressed—data collection, storage, analysis, and dissemination—have to be integrated into a system. Before changing something in the data collection procedure, one must consider how the accuracy of the data will be verified, how the data will be stored, what analyses will be required (and who will do them), and how the data or results will be made available. In doing so, one starts by answering the question, "Why are we doing this?" That is, one identifies both the intended use of data and the intrinsic value of the data or results.

We question, then, the interest in "quality factors" or "quality indexes" or other numbers that arise from some complicated formula based on both hard data and judgments. We certainly understand that one would like to attach a number to the entire process—say, something on a scale of 1 to 10—since that would simplify management decisions. But we remain unconvinced of the value of the number formed by the sum of the dollar investment in software tools and the percentage of code reviewed, divided by the size of the programming staff; or similar formulas actually proposed, some of which contain ordinals (judgments on a scale of 1 to 10) multiplied by cardinals. Compared to data on agricultural production or semiconductor yields, software process data are slippery enough without bending them with arithmetic outrages. Management by fact is a necessary part of total quality management, and we ought not confuse fact with numerical fancy.*

9.2   Staff Involvement

Figure 9.4 noted that the caliber of the staff is a function of native ability, education and training, experience, motivation, and upgrade of native ability through improved recruitment and screening. In Sec. 3.8, we addressed education and training. We can add little beyond the

---

*For that matter, we must recognize that software process data are there only to support the decision-making process, not to predicate decisions.

commonplace on experience and recruitment screening practices, save to note that the most valuable types of experience are:

1. The use of specific languages and tools
2. Participation in similar projects

Motivation is another matter, however. We mean not simply motivating programmers and managers to do a good job, but inspiring them to join in improving the development process. Participative management—most commonly implemented by quality teams (a.k.a. quality circles and a variety of other names)—is used widely to help staff get involved in process improvement. Here, teams are given assignments to find better ways of doing things. Many teams have taken matters into their own hands and have proposed their own assignments. The findings of the teams—and they usually come up with something worthwhile—are used to finetune or even overhaul some part of the process.

For example, a team might be asked to investigate the availability of front-end tools capable of being plugged into the back-end tool open architecture in use. The team comes back with a short list of recommended tools, evaluation copies are obtained, and the team proceeds to use the tools. The team members compare notes, and prepare a report (written, oral, or both) of their hands-on experience. This leads to the acquisition and installation of new tools and a concomitant change to the standard development practices. Or it doesn't. If it doesn't because the team didn't do its homework and present the necessary supporting data, that's one thing. It's quite another thing if management backs off from an implied commitment to the team, in which case it can forget about getting further help from arguably the most valuable source available for process improvement.

Deming's fourteenth point for management says to put everybody in the company to work to accomplish the transformation. This requires reaching people. A technique, often called *Management by Walking Around* (MBWA), seems to work particularly well for programming projects. Despite the name, MBWA is not a way of managing, but a way of communicating. Let programmers see management, let management inquire not what, but how programmers are doing the task at hand. This often raises the topic of how the job might be better accomplished. Good programmers have native creativity. Anything that can stimulate that creativity to improve the process should be considered. Quality teams, MBWA, seminars in which programmers on one project tell others about their project and how they are going about it, communications between teams; these are all stimuli to get the creative juices running.

Although we hope that it is never necessary, we also need to enable staff to be heard if they know they are pursuing a losing battle. We recall an incident many years ago when a small staff of programmers was assigned the job of documenting the technical problems encountered on a large programming project contracted to a software supplier. After two months of learning that their reports were simply being filed, counted as increments toward the solution (bean-counting of another kind), but not used as the basis for directing the supplier, the most outspoken of the unhappy group loudly proclaimed that the whole effort was no more than a charade. Unfortunately, for purposes that border on the criminal, the manager he said this to refused to take action. Six months later the project was finally abandoned at the cost of additional millions of misspent dollars.

It is not enough to assure programmers that they will be heard, they must be allowed to honestly assess the results of reviews and tests. Peer reviewers should never be pressured into saying that previously identified inadequacies had been rectified when, in fact, the result of changes leaves work that one still cannot take pride in. Testers should never be pressured into saying that code is ready for qualification tests when, in fact, they know that it contains highly unstable modules despite having been massaged through the planned series of development tests.

Finally, customer support people should be empowered to send a customer necessary fixes, even if it means sending a freebie software update, without awaiting approval from a higher-up.

9.3   Project Control

Figure 9.3 says that the ingredients for project control are manageable software processes, stable projects, and risk reduction. The last may be regarded equally as an objective of project control, rather than a contributor to it. We have elsewhere discussed the elements of each of these ingredients, with the exception of the verification strategy found on the project stability part of the fishbone. We address that here, as well as a technique of project control alluded to in other sections of the book, trend analysis.

Rites of passage

Whatever one's development model, each of the defined tasks may be viewed as an opportunity to verify that development is proceeding in an orderly fashion; that is, that the work done in the task is:

- Traceable through preceding tasks back to the agreed upon requirements model
- The result of adherence to the prescribed software process standards

To take advantage of the opportunity, the definition of each task needs to include criteria for satisfactory completion, or *task exit criteria*. Following this precept, we speak of customer sign-offs on the demonstration of rapid prototypes, review minutes with closed action items, evidence of the use of static analyzers, and evidence of satisfactory test results as common criteria for deciding whether the subject work should be passed down to the next task in line. The use of the word "evidence" implies that someone checks to see that the evidence is acceptable. If the work resulting from a task lends itself to the use of analysis software and a review, the analysis results should be available to the reviewers before the review meeting. The pro forma checklist for the review should contain an entry for acceptable analyzer results. For code, we recommend that code be reviewed after the completion of static analysis and unit test. The pro forma checklist for code reviews should contain entries for acceptable results from both analyzer and active test. At one time, we would have argued that code should be reviewed before testing, but with modern test tools the effort spent in unit testing—which is mostly debugging, anyhow—is relatively modest.

In addition to the work—requirements modeling, analysis, design, construction, and testing—performed directly on the product, project control must also address the design of test cases and (if necessary) test scripts, user documentation, customer support, and any other tasks found in the plans for the project. All must be reviewed with respect to the requirements model and the development standards, and in many cases the customer environment as well. Some reduction of review effort is possible when test cases are automatically generated from specifications.

Project control requires more than evidence that the work has met its criteria for acceptability. Project control requires also that the responsible manager sign off on the work's acceptability. For each task, we recommend a simple form listing each of the acceptance criteria and ending with the manager's signature. Figure 9.9 illustrates criteria appropriate for code units. For clarity, Fig. 9.9 shows a form more applicable to paper than machine. Machine forms, of course, are preferred, and are now possible using either signature facsimile mechanisms or a file write protocol requiring the manager's restricted password.

Note that Fig. 9.9 avoids the doctrinaire position that code may not be sent to integration testing if any item requiring attention remains

---

Code Acceptance Sheet

This form must be completed and signed by the appropriate manager before the code is copied into the integration test library.

Project identification: _ _ _ _ _ _ _
Module identification: _ _ _ _ _ _ _
Author: _____
Review held and minuted: Yes_ No_
Action items in minutes closed and verified: Yes_ No_
    If no, explain:

Design documentation updated on _/_/_
Analysis and test results placed in repository on _/_/_

Signed: _____   Date: _/_/_

Figure 9.9   Form for accepting code.

open. As a practical matter, one may want to pass the code to integration even though some corrections await verification. We can take a chance in the knowledge that if a further change is required, we can always perform regression tests to ensure that all planned tests will be conducted with the final version of the module. Or, perhaps, in the interests of efficiency, the minutes of a review call for revisiting the system software design to determine whether a function, common to many modules, should be designed as a system call or utility function. The recommended review may well take place, but the manager does not want to hold up further integration progress while the matter is being considered. Again, regression tests will save the day. We should note that waivers such as this must be expected if we want to avoid the bureaucratic demand that tasks be completed in a pre-defined rigid sequence.

The rites of passage may be viewed also as milestones in the progress of a project. As such they serve as hard status indicators, at least before tests of the full system are in progress. Once into integration testing, however, status becomes a matter of both unit construction (until all units have been submitted for integration) and experience with individual test cases.

Trend analysis

The composite status of module design is the sum of the status of all the individual modules: some still to be defined, some in construction, and some integrated. In Fig. 9.10, we see what a month-by-month chart

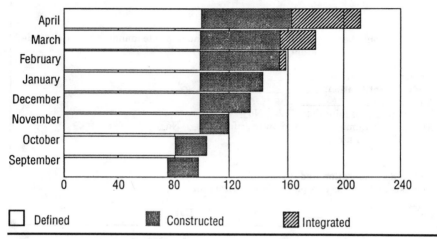

Figure 9.10 Composite module status.

of the completion of these tasks might look like, perhaps for a whole system, or perhaps for a discrete thread. Such charts, wherein one can easily ascertain trends, provide managers with quick comprehension of where projects are headed, even though the charts cannot account for differences in the difficulty of the items being counted.

Of equal importance is the trend of progress against plan. Figure 9.11 is an example of the trend of progress during any test phase

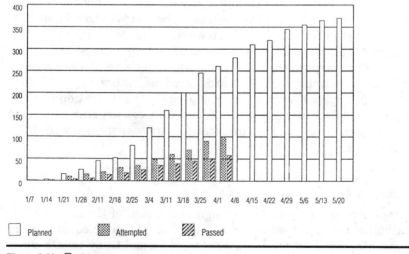

Figure 9.11 Test progress.

involving many test cases. The chart shows the cumulative number of test cases planned to be executed, actually executed at least once, even if unsuccessfully, and the number that have executed successfully. As we can see, things are going badly, and it appears that remedial action is required.

Figure 9.11 doesn't differentiate among the types of test cases. Some may be basic to operation, others probe system defenses, and still others explore performance at the boundaries. To estimate the date one will have a product capable of demonstrating basic functionality, it is best to also chart the number of functions tested against time and extrapolate.

Other simple trend analyses find their way into project management. Some examples include:

- Staff build-up—actual and planned staff vs. time.
- System resources estimated at various stages—e.g., memory at conclusion of requirements analysis, preliminary design, design of each thread, construction of each thread.
- Number of discrete functions resolved in design vs. time.
- Density of known faults from release to release.
- Backlog of requests for programming services (as in Fig. 9.7).
- Test failures vs. time.

The last is of unusual interest to us in that it is often used to estimate the date at which the failure rate will fall to some predetermined criterion for release. Figures 7.9 and 7.10 illustrate such charts. Note that there is no excuse for releasing a product that continues to exhibit severe failures.

At the risk of stating the obvious, let's not forget that trend analyses require of a data and information system timeliness, accuracy, and, at least, some processing of raw data.

9.4   Keeping the Books

Recall Fig. 9.9. One of the lines on the handoff form refers to closed and verified action items. Before he or she can check the appropriate box, the manager needs to know what the action items were, whether they were closed, and whether (and how) closing was verified. Following the review that resulted in the action items, the manager—perhaps a first line supervisor in charge of eight programmers and some 40 discrete manageable software components—has three things to do for each item: assign someone to find the solution, assign someone to verify the solution, and get confirmation of the verification. Let's assume there was only one action item, an incorrect interpretation and implementation of one of the module's specifications. The correction would normally be assigned to the module's programmer. The manager might want to take on the responsibility for verification, or might assign the matter to one of the reviewers. Either way, there are several points of action that can easily be forgotten in the presence of other pressing matters.

Let's assume that the one action item is the belated recognition by the programmer that a system function has been left out. The programmer designed, coded, and unit tested the function as part of the module, but (properly) wants to see the specifications changed. (Plainly, a quality-motivated programmer.) This action item does not apply to the module (and explains why the manager would sign off on it) but to a specification produced at an earlier time. The authors of the specification are still on the project, and they get the assignment. These days, however, they are busy preparing user documentation. They might forget.

Action items are tennis balls left on the other side of the net after serving a basket of balls for practice. Someone has to pick them up. Unlike tennis balls, which are highly visible, action items easily go unseen. In one form or another, a quality process has to incorporate a mechanism for recording the status of every action item on a project. Generally, records of the correction item log (a common locution) have fields for:

- Applicable software item.
- Reference for a description of the required action.
- Date the item was initiated.
- Change request identification, if applicable.
- Person(s) initiating the item.
- Activity in which item was noted—this will be useful for measuring fault detection effectiveness.
- Person(s) to whom action is assigned.
- Assigned date for completing the action.
- Action status—codes representing the last completed activity in the correction process.
- Person(s) to whom verification is assigned.
- Verification status—verified or not.
- Manager responsible for follow-up.

Figure 9.12 illustrates a small section of a report that one might generate from a log of action items. In this illustration, we see that the log has been sorted on the initiation date field. It could as easily be sorted on other fields to produce the information needed to track the open items.

Weekly, applicable subsets of open items are culled for each name on the log. Of course, in an on-line DBMS, each person can call for a report at any time. Another weekly report lists any items for which action or verification is overdue. So much for keeping the books.*

We think it useful to maintain separate logs for action items applicable to the product and those applicable to the process. By the latter,

IDENT	SOFTWARE ITEM	REFERENCE FOR ACTION	INITIATOR
p361.10	Borogove: prndriver	FR 233	J.S. Bach

DATE INIT.	INIT. ACTIVITY	CHNG. REQ.	RESP. MANAGER
1/3/94	final engrg test	E12.006	F. Couperin

ASSIGNED TO	SCHED. COMP.	ACTION STAT	VER. ASSIGNED TO	VER STAT
L. Spohr	1/12/94	D1	A. Scarlatti	

IDENT	SOFTWARE ITEM	REFERENCE FOR ACTION	INITIATOR
p145.2	Gryphon: exec	minutes, DR1.12	J.P. Rameau

DATE INIT.	INIT. ACTIVITY	CHNG. REQ.	RESP. MANAGER
1/3/94	prelim.design rev.		P. Hindemith

ASSIGNED TO	SCHED. COMP.	ACTION STAT	VER. ASSIGNED TO	VER STAT
A. Vivaldi	1/18/94	P	H. Purcell	

IDENT	SOFTWARE ITEM	REFERENCE FOR ACTION	INITIATOR
p361.11	Borogove: garbcoll (doc)	FR 234	J. S. Bach

DATE INIT.	INIT. ACTIVITY	CHNG. REQ.	RESP. MANAGER
1/3/94	final engrg	D17.001	G. Handel

ASSIGNED TO	SCHED. COMP.	ACTION STAT	VER. ASSIGNED TO	VER STAT
P. Glass	1/5/94	C	B. Bartok	V

Figure 9.12   Section of correction log, ordered by initiation date.

---

*Nevertheless, the human touch always helps in following up delinquencies. Section 9.7 recommends that the "touching" human be a software quality engineer.

we mean deviations from plans and the approved process. For example, if the integration test team consistently modifies test plans without approval, something needs to be done. Perhaps several things: improve the test planning process, streamline the change approval process, or increase the participation of the testers in test planning. In any case, process corrections pose problems different from those of product corrections, and the tracking needs to reflect the differences. Records of a process correction item log should have fields for:

- Applicable activity or activities.
- Reference for a description of the required action.
- Date the item was initiated.
- Person(s) initiating the item.
- Person(s) to whom action is assigned.
- Assigned date for completing action.
- Correction status—brief description of actions taken thus far, including "item dropped."
- Person(s) to whom verification, if applicable, is assigned.
- Verification status—verified or not.
- Manager responsible for follow-up.

9.5 Supplier Relations

Deming's fourth management point is to end the practice of awarding business to the lowest bidder. When buying off-the-shelf software, as in buying standard software tools, cost is less likely to influence the software professional than compatibility with the professional's process, specific tool features, or compatibility with existing tools. Too often, senior management rejects what appear as costly subtleties and applies pressure to buy on the basis of price. When awarding contracts for custom software, even software professionals too often are influenced as much by cost as by other factors.

Before we get to the cost of custom software—which, in any case, eventually will be reduced as suppliers are encouraged to "do things right"—we need to consider a potential supplier's:

- Related experience.
- Prospects for being able to continue in business.
- Quality process maturity.

- Customer support capabilities.
- Reputation for satisfying customers.
- Response to our specifications.
- Willingness to include us in the development of the product.

Using the usual vendor survey techniques, the first five items can be ascertained before giving a new supplier an opportunity to bid. For small projects, one may find it adequate to send a boiler plate questionnaire to the supplier and then follow up with a site visit. For larger projects, suppliers expect to have to visit us and pitch their corporate virtues. To confirm customer satisfaction, one obviously queries the supplier's present customers.

We do not claim that it is easy to assess the maturity of the supplier's quality process, but one can look for certain things. During a visit to the supplier, one can bring into play some of the assessment techniques of Chap. 10 to confirm that TQM precepts underlie the development process. Although in individual cases educational level is a notoriously unreliable indicator of programming talent, most companies can provide statistics on the education of the professional staff, which in the aggregate, has some meaning. The supplier can define the software development environment and list the tools proposed for use on the project, describe the development model in use, cover the test process, describe estimating procedures and how the project will be staffed, and, indeed, cover all the key points of this book. During the site visit, walk around and observe the space available to programmers, the number and type of terminals, and the space available for meetings.*

The willingness of the supplier to permit customer involvement in the project is most important in the translation of customer specifications into a requirements model and in the qualification of the product. We have addressed the customer's role in rapid prototyping and the review of requirements models. This involvement applies whether one is the customer or the producer. With regard to product qualification, when buying custom software, the customer is wise to insist on reviewing the supplier's plans for qualification and attending at least some part of the supplier's own qualification exercise. The alternative, performing acceptance tests after delivery, is more costly. Moreover, if deficiencies are observed, it is likely to be more difficult to confer with all the necessary supplier personnel to determine the best course of action.

---

*Also note the number of copies of this book in evidence.

Suppliers with whom one has a good standing relationship are the best kind. Suppliers with a product line and a large marketing budget will, from time to time, visit their customers and present their plans for the future. These show-and-tell events often are accompanied by an unstructured opportunity for the customer to reciprocate and thereby influence the supplier's plans with informal marketplace input. Suppliers of custom software will be pleased to comment on software elements in their "inventory" that with re-engineering may fit into their customer's systems and reduce cost. And, of course, suppliers know that there is nothing like good will to maintain a customer base.

Since most businesses do not annually purchase a great variety of off-the-shelf software, it is impossible to maintain a close standing relationship with many software suppliers. For most applications, off-the-shelf software acquisition means adding to an existing software base. This, in itself, tends to limit the number of off-the-shelf software suppliers. With regard to custom software, few companies buy a large annual volume of software built under contract. Again, one cannot expect to maintain a close relationship with many suppliers. Since software buyers seldom deal with a great number of suppliers, they have both opportunity and incentive to work out partnering relations with their suppliers. Too often, however, we see software purchasers act as though the new acquisition were up for grabs to the lowest bidder or cheapest seller. Not what Dr. Deming had in mind. In the last few years, following a Japanese practice, U.S. automobile manufacturers have cut down on the number of their suppliers in favor of partnering. Software purchasers would do well to follow suit.

9.6   Continuous Improvement

Deming's fifth point for management says that we should "improve constantly and forever the system of production and service." Translated into software development and maintenance, this means to improve constantly and forever the process of development, maintenance, and customer service. Returning to Fig. 9.1, we see what must be continuously improved. Customer/user satisfaction, project control, reduction of cost of quality, and the improvement process itself must be continuously evaluated, analyzed, and incrementally revised.

Improvement processes

Continuous improvement implies forever asking ourselves questions about the subprocesses and product/service elements found on Figs. 9.2 through 9.5. Looking at Fig. 9.2, the fishbone diagram for customer/user satisfaction, we focus on maintainability, the effectiveness of support,

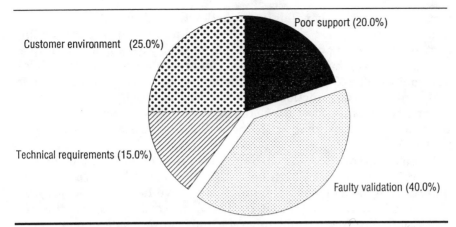

Figure 9.13a Root causes of customer technical problems.

safety, and usability. We ask questions of each. We have reason to believe that our software creates fewer problems for our customers than does that of our competitors, but we still get many complaints. Accordingly, we segregate two years' worth of technical problems reported by customers into four categories (as shown in Fig. 9.13a) and find that faulty validation accounts for 40 percent of all problems. Faulty understanding of the customer environment represents 25 percent, faulty understanding of technical requirements accounts for only 15 percent. At 40 percent, we make validation our first candidate for analysis, and look at the history of problems attributable to faulty validation. What we find in Fig. 9.13b is that we do a reasonable job in making certain that all functional requirements are validated (11

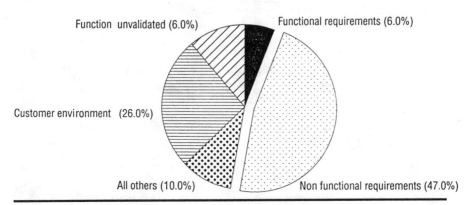

Figure 9.13b Validation problems.

percent) and correctly validating functional requirements (6 percent), and not quite so good a job at understanding how to account for the customers' working environments (26 percent). We appear to have a real problem in handling validation outside discrete functional requirements. The 47 percent of problems that have to do with something other than discrete functions—say, poor procedures for demonstrating reliability—certainly would seem to recommend themselves to improvement. We now analyze the procedures as in the fishbone of Fig. 9.14.

Going over the fishbone rib by rib, we are brought up short by the item in the lower left, highlighted by the use of boldface type. In determining possible out-of-bounds input, we have been looking at the built-in defenses against invalid data rather than the operational anomalies we could have gotten from our customers. Also, looking at the rib highlighted in the upper right, we discover that our procedures for trapping out-of-bounds output only work when the program actually fails, not when it produces out-of-bounds output that will cause some other part of the system to fail. We have found the root causes, and we are now on our way to finding and implementing solutions.

Incidentally, take note that in analyzing the validation of reliability we have said nothing about the upper left rib (reliability) of Fig. 9.2. Reliability, in this sense, is a matter of purging the product of latent bugs *as we understand them*. Validation, branching from the usability rib, has more to do with checking our understanding of requirements.

In the department of customer/user satisfaction, we look not only at customer problems, but at our own process of solving the problems.

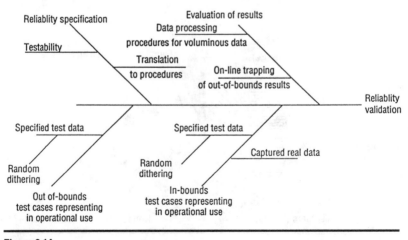

Figure 9.14

Looking along the support effectiveness rib, we see *problem fix cycle time*. Figure 9.7 charted a disquieting increase in the backlog of requests for features. One can find the same phenomenon in the backlog of problems requiring fixes. A chart of the correction backlog trend should be available to throw onto the table when we are ready to choke on the bone of problem fix cycle time. With the aid of Fig. 9.15, let's look at a hypothetical start to the fix process: the procedure for assessing problems, other than emergency ones, and placing them on the backlog.

Figure 9.15 appears reasonably efficient, thorough, and takes into account (how many companies do not!) the importance that attaches to problems solely by their being reported by not one but many

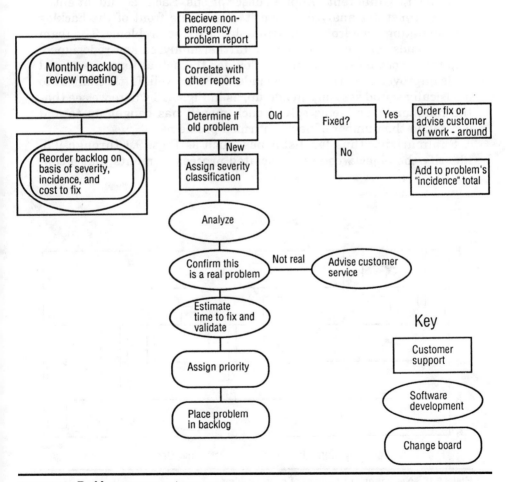

Figure 9.15   Problem assessment process.

customers. A quality team, with constituents from both customer support and development, is assigned the problem of improving cycle time. As the team looks at the process flow, they stumble on the software procedure for confirming that the problem is real. A confirmed problem is one that is both different from any others previously reported and truly a problem rather than a user's failure to follow operational procedures that no one else seems to have trouble with. (If enough people report the same thing, it *is* something that needs fixing.)

In talking about the procedure, the software members of the quality team realize that they have been trying to match symptoms from the problem history data base too literally. The result is that many times the same problem has been placed on the backlog more than once, each entry bearing different symptom descriptions. Each redundant entry, though, must get analyzed when it gets to the front of the backlog queue, taking time from that available for fixing problems. The team recommends that the procedure be further analyzed and redesigned. The team goes on to analyze the flow for the actual fix process, and finds improvements that can be made there, as well. Little changes to a basically sound system can add up, as in Fig. 9.16 where we see that the number of problems solved each month has caught up to and overtaken the number of new confirmed problems.

Summarizing thus far, fishbones, such as Figs. 9.1 through 9.5, identify the objectives and associated process elements that a con-

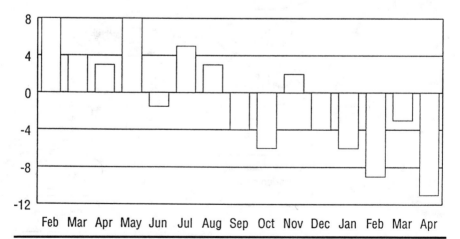

Figure 9.16 Net change in number of open problems.

tinuous improvement process iteratively and periodically re-examines, always to the end of finding refinements that will improve quality.

Figure 9.5 is the one that depicts, recursively, the influences on the process for continuous quality improvement. Of the three ribs, we earlier addressed the data and information system, we shall address planning in the next chapter, and we now turn to analysis.

Effective analysis

It happens that our anecdotal examples of the operations of an improvement process had mostly to do with analysis. Analysis, both of software processes (cued by the fishbone diagrams of Figs. 9.1 through 9.5 and Fig. 9.14) and results (as in Figs. 9.13a, 9.13b, and 9.16), forms the foundation of the improvement process. We need to give thought, then, to the quality of our analyses. We need to ask questions such as those found in Table 9.1.

If the answer to the first question is anything less than 50 percent, we may not be doing a very good job at analysis. Of course, the problem might be that the solutions to shortcomings are too costly or meet with resistance born of inertia. Absent such reasons, we need to find a better way of doing analysis. Make the fishbones more pointed to the current processes. Get more measurements to ensure that the correct things are being analyzed in detail. Get more anecdotal information from customers. Get more comparison data. Find out if teams are assigned tasks for which they have little gut feel. Analyze the team's effectiveness in the use of problem solving techniques.

Question 2 is an easy one to answer. Figures 9.7 and 9.16 are two parts of an answer. Figure 9.17, the favorable flip side to Fig. 3.8, contains three other indicators. Companies need to define the customer measurements that make sense for their product and its support, and having defined what makes sense, do whatever is necessary to get the data.

TABLE 9.1 How Good Is the Improvement Process?

1	What percentage of recommended improvements are actually implemented?
2	What effect have the improvements had in measurements made of product and service?
3	What effect have the improvements had in the perception of customers?
4	What effects have the improvements had in measurements of processes?
5	What effect have the improvements had in the quality level of the process?
6	What effects have the improvements had in the quality level relative to that of competitors and benchmarks?

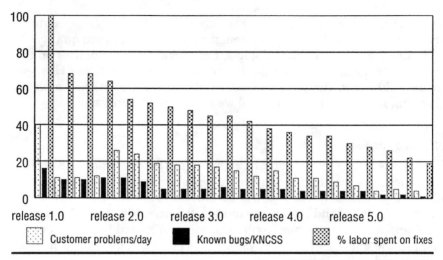

Figure 9.17 Improvement with product maturity. Note: KNCSS = thousand lines of noncomment source code.

Question 3 is not quite so easy to answer as question 2. Earlier, we had spoken of questionnaires and interviews. The questions must be formed so that the answers can be related to the process. To ask, "Do you find the product support bulletin board helpful?" cannot provide as useful an answer as "How many times did you use the bulletin board the first month you installed the program, and how often did it contain the answer you needed?" Let's assume that answers to the latter question average:

1. Four times a week, and

2. 30 percent of the time.

Four times a week is low (the product, after all, was a virtual reality system to place the user in any of the Senate sessions of ancient Athens), suggesting that the product is fairly self-explanatory. Thirty percent, on the other hand, suggests the bulletin board may not be very helpful. Fortunately, the questionnaire had a third question, "How many times in the first month did you call to speak with a service representative?" Since the average answer to that one was 50 times, we know that the product is not all that easy to use and that the bulletin board is plainly inadequate.

Questions, like our example, that rely on the customer's memory yield unreliable answers unless the customer is asked, ahead of time, to log certain data for future reference. In our example, the producer can record the number of calls for assistance or bulletin board log-ins.

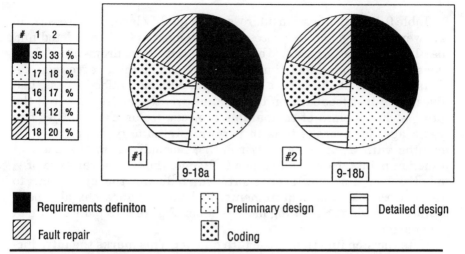

#	1	2	
■	35	33	%
⋮	17	18	%
☰	16	17	%
⋰	14	12	%
⧄	18	20	%

■ Requirements definiton   ⋮ Preliminary design   ☰ Detailed design

⧄ Fault repair   ⋰ Coding

Figure 9.18 Fault origins before and after analysis.

The producer can also include in the log-out protocol a question on whether the board provided all the assistance needed.

Like the third, the fourth question lends itself to hard data. Seldom quite as hard, however, and generally more difficult to get. Nevertheless, Sec. 9.1 gave some examples of measurements one can make of the development process.

Taking the origin of faults as an example, if we can see that analysis of fault sources has caused an overall reduction in fault density, we can assume that this part of the improvement process is going well. Let Fig. 9.18a represent the distribution of fault origins (by task) two years ago. Based on the distribution, we analyzed the way we modeled technical requirements and their use during design, with the result that we changed the scheme for documenting the dependencies among discrete functions. Figure 9.18b depicts the current distribution of fault origins. Not much has changed.

A quality team is empowered to reopen the study. Perhaps the method of analysis was faulty. Perhaps the measurements, which depend at least partly on subjective decisions about the source of faults, are unreliable. The quality team notes that programmers provide all of the source assignments, other than those for faults found in the reviews of requirements models and preliminary design. One of the team, herself a programmer, remarks that when a fault is found with no plainly discernible source, it usually is attributed to the requirements model. Need we remark that the programmers in our hypothetical company are distinct from the analysts who prepare requirements models?

Table 9.1's fifth question addresses the quality level of processes. To answer this we combine process measurements of all completed and partly completed projects. We need composite measurements of fault density, task completion times, schedule compliance, regression defects, productivity,* support cycle times, detection effectiveness, bad fixes, beta test feedback on quality, and whatever else goes into the process. For a class of comparable projects, let us assume that two years ago the average time to perform preliminary design was 4½ months with a variance of ¾ months, normalized on the basis of function points. Now the average is 3¼ months with a variance of ½ month. The time has been shortened, reducing the cycle time to respond to customer requirements, and the variance has also been reduced, making scheduling more reliable. Figure 9.19 plots the trend by quarter.

Note the step function at the fifth quarter. This marks the introduction (with training) of a new CASE system, an improvement directly traceable to an analysis performed by a quality team a half year earlier. High fives for everyone on the team! Maybe some more tangible recognition as well?

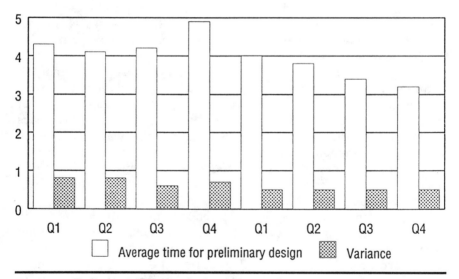

Figure 9.19   Preliminary design cycle time by quarter.

---

*Productivity directly influences quality. A company with high productivity can afford to concentrate on quality. The converse is also true: high quality means less rework. In any case, technology adopted to increase productivity also increases quality, and vice versa.

The last question of Table 9.1 calls for comparisons with competitors and benchmarks. Depending on one's business, it may be difficult to get information from competitors. Nevertheless, from time to time, one finds data in the journals and magazines of the professional software societies: not just bottom line data (defect densities and productivity measures) but defect distributions by process elements as well. We have seldom seen support data published, however. The data found in the literature are, of course, published with pride—the proof of the promise of new methods or tools. As such, they can be viewed as benchmarks.

Perhaps the ultimate benchmark, at least from the point of defect densities, is *zero defects*. In his forward to a book[2] on IBM's cleanroom approach to the development of software, Harlan Mills writes of two projects in which customers found no defects: a 25 KLOC real-time program developed for the 1980 U.S. census and a 65 KLOC program for an IBM typewriter. Mills also notes that the 500 KLOC space shuttle software, although exhibiting failures on the ground, has never had a failure in flight.

But why compare quality trends with those of other companies? The reason we do so is that improved technology and management methods has raised almost everyone's quality level. Even a company not committed to a conscious quality improvement process is likely to find its products—if not service—getting better. But this says nothing about whether the company's quality levels are growing as fast as they should. Comparison with others is the way to determine if one is lagging, leading, or staying abeam.

Risk reduction

Many managers have come to regard quality assurance primarily as an instrument for risk management, TQM even more so. So too, for TQM for software. Few industrial processes carry as much risk as the development and maintenance of software. Management has already demanded that exposure to software risk be whittled away. Know thine enemy. The primary software risks are

1. Delivering software that does not comply with the customer's expectations.
2. Underestimating the cost and duration of a project.
3. Exceeding time and cost budgets, even when realistic.
4. Misjudging the feasibility of a proposed project.
5. Building obsolescence into the product.
6. Staffing problems.

TQM offers solutions to each of these. For the first, we have to look at two sides to the problem: software developed under contract and software developed for the general marketplace. The prevention methods of Chap. 5 and the detection methods of Chap. 7 directly apply to both. For contract software, rapid prototyping reduces the risk that the customer will be surprised at the functions, features, and interfaces of the final product. For other software, our principal weapons are good use of customer information, as gleaned from questionnaires and interviews, and beta testing. Beta testing, to be sure, is somewhat after the fact. Beta test feedback may even lead to modification of the requirements model, but at least it reduces the risk of damaging one's reputation in the marketplace.

Section 5.3 addressed the estimating problem. As one might expect, estimates are least credible when we most need them: that is, when the work planned is unlike projects previously undertaken. We cannot divorce estimating methods from the size of the problem under consideration. Traditionally, lines of code, in one form or another, has been the metric for accounting for size. Code, however, is part of the solution space, not the problem space. Increasingly, managers have found that an alternative metric dating back to 1979,[3] *function points,* produces estimates with less inherent risk. Function points can be determined from requirements models. The number of function points is computed from the number of external input and output types (e.g., input and output screens), the number of logical internal file types, the number of files shared with other applications, and the number of queries used to generate immediate output. Before being summed, each of these is multiplied by a weighting factor, a composite of a number of influences (e.g., rate of transactions).

As it happens, investigators have attempted to determine the correlation, if any, between function points and lines of code. Capers Jones, for example, found that 106 COBOL lines, 80 PL/1 lines, or 40 FOCUS lines implement the average function point.[4] One after-the-fact way to validate one's ability to estimate function points is to perform the estimates for a number of previously executed projects and then determine the standard deviation in the ratio of production lines of code to estimated function points. A low standard deviation indicates good estimates. We note here that function point estimation is anything but a cookbook exercise, but the month seldom goes by when we don't find in the mail an announcement of a seminar featuring, if not dedicated to, function point estimation. Also, experience is important. In a study of function point estimation, the estimates of a group of 18 experienced analysts had a standard deviation of 11.1, while two groups of inexperienced analysts (11 in the first group and 9 in the second) had standard deviations of 34.5 and 30.6.[5]

However accomplished, estimating is not the end of the matter. Armed even with the best estimating procedures, tools, and detailed productivity measurements from preceding projects, software managers often find themselves directed to cut costs or schedule to meet budget, market, or operational needs. "Look here Sylvester, I can't give you more than $220,000 to do the job, and the warehouse gotta get the system by July." This situation leads to projects that start off understaffed, with explicit omission of such quality-oriented tasks as preparing a traceability mechanism for requirements, and end up overstaffed with products capable of performing only some of the expected functions. The first of the categories of the Baldrige Award criteria addresses leadership. From the CEO down, management must buy in to realistic estimates.

The third risk item, blowing realistic estimates, is also controlled by placing emphasis on prevention and early detection. Additionally, however, we have to consider:

1. The stability of external requirements, and

2. A gradual loss of project control caused by poor visibility of real status.

Rapid prototyping or customer/user acceptance of technical requirements models are two quality techniques to reduce the number of changes to the external specifications. When the going gets tough, meticulous observance of Sec. 9.3's rites of passage will ensure that management gets the warning afforded by credible status indicators to take remedial action in time to do some good. Trend analyses, also discussed in Sec. 9.3, are highly effective here, as well.

Perhaps the risk factor having the most devastating effect is the fourth, undertaking a nondoable project or undertaking a doable project using untried technology. Mercifully, this happens rarely. Software managers are leery of venturing into the unknown. This type of risk is controllable. If the project is scary-looking and unlike any other previously attempted,* the evolutionary process model (see Sec. 3.2) is called for. One attempts to identify the kernels of the problem, develop and evaluate those, and, iteratively, build upon satisfactory solutions. If at some point it appears that nothing good can come of this, the project can be abandoned without incurring further investment. The key is to properly identify the knotty elements and to limit the amount of functionality added in each round of development.

---

*Say, a multimedia system to make the musical semantics of string quartets intelligible to punk rock groups.

With regard to the use of untried technology, we recommend that one employ new methods and tools on pilot projects before essaying their use on large projects. Not uncommonly the two halves of the fourth risk item are combined. Analysts report that the best way to pursue a proposed, seemingly difficult, project is by using technology new to the company. We know of one company, set upon developing a process control system that could be operated with something akin to the single stroke simplicity of calculators, that decided upon O-O's dynamic binding as the only feasible technology for the product. Whether it was the only feasible technology, no one can fault it as an obvious candidate. Unfortunately, only a few people in the software department had ever used O-O. At that, the few had never used O-O in their present employment, nor had they ever used O-O for an embedded application. The project was abandoned before any production code was written, indicating a sensible risk-limiting decision. Unfortunately, the decision was made by management senior to that of the software department.

The fifth risk factor, building in obsolescence is limited in the initial release by scrupulous configuration management, preparation and preservation of development artifacts useful to maintenance, readable and portable code, and simplicity in the structure. Maintaining product viability release after release is a matter of equally scrupulous attention to configuration management, documentation, and readability; augmented by special care in preserving the structure of the product and the artifacts that attach to each modification.

Staffing problems usually come in two flavors: in general, failure to maintain the caliber of personnel, and in particular, failure to maintain staff for the life of the project. Reducing the risk of the first requires attention to training, continuing education (including seminars and conferences), and upgrading when the opportunity presents itself (as when expanding staff). Keeping project personnel on the job is less of a problem than it used to be, when the best way to distinguish between a programmer and a gypsy was that the programmer was the one colorfully dressed. Still, player drafts seem to happen periodically, and the loss of a key member of the project can hurt. To reduce this risk, divide the job up into small bite-size tasks, each of which has tangible output, and pursue projects using programming teams. Of course, a whole team can be drafted.

Changing software processes

We have come to the point of action of continuous improvement. Analysis has told us what to change and has identified a promising new policy, method, technology, or tool. Now do it. Here is what we have to keep in mind:

- The change may meet with resistance.
- The change may not work as we had hoped.
- Because of phasing, we may have to restrict the projects to which we apply the change, resulting in different practices among the set of concurrent projects.

Resistance can come from two sources, senior management and development staff. We don't expect trouble from enlightened management unless change entails a significant bump in costs or schedule. Changes expected to improve productivity as well as quality can be sold on the basis of a quantitative return on investment analysis. If we do not expect improved productivity, we shall have to sell the change on the merits of quality alone. Management favorably disposed to TQM will understand. Without quality leadership (recall Category One of the Baldrige criteria), the software manager or team of software and quality managers may have to enlist help from internal users and other functions such as Marketing. Whatever the case, if change must be justified solely on the basis of quality, the reward can best be presented in terms of customer or user satisfaction.

Resistance from technical staff is the more common, especially from those who do not like to change habits or learn new technology. On the other hand, if staff were not part of the analysis process, their objections may well be valid. No one knows the location of shoals better than the local sailors. But we have said before that continuous improvement processes can profit from the involvement of the affected personnel, whether through quality teams or other forms of participative management. Note also, that if the change comes primarily from a quality team the team members are the obvious candidates to sell the change to their peers. As an example, no one can get staff to buy in on the use of new tools better than the co-workers who can answer questions based on their experience trying out the tools.

Let's look at the danger of a proposed change not working as expected. This is real. Many companies rushed into O-O expecting immediate gains, only to find that the O-O paradigm represents a cultural change, not just new language capabilities. We have even more case histories of companies adopting CASE systems without recognizing that the software was less compatible with their processes than had been apparent. Recalling the preceding discussion on risk reduction, we strongly urge that changes, other than those affecting personnel policies or most measurements, be tried out on pilot projects. If possible, candidates for such projects should be small or inconspicuous. As a last, costly resort, one might consider experimenting with a dummy project.

Finally, we look to the phasing problem. We plan to start collecting fault modality data, starting with faults found in code reviews and continuing through all testing tasks. Of our four current projects, Alpha is in qualification test, Beta is in the last stages of integration, Gamma is partly coded and integrated, and the requirements for Delta are still being analyzed. If we can afford to wait for a pilot project to collect data from all fault detection processes, we shall have to wait for Delta. If we are willing to settle for partial data, Gamma is the best bet. At least we should be able to collect enough faults to draw some statistical inferences.

On the other hand, if we decide the major effort is in the development of data collection screens for our terminals, a pilot may not make much sense. We'll collect what we can from Beta, and wait for Delta for a full harvest. But Gamma? To minimize confusion, it's best to restrict the Gamma data collection until after all modules have been integrated.

Whether or not we go the pilot route, we shall have four concurrent regimens for fault modality collection. None on Alpha, data from some detection processes on Beta and Gamma, and the whole nine yards worth on Delta. This means that staff reassigned from one project to another will work under different process standards. Now, compound the matter with the likelihood that we shall have not one, but several, changes recently introduced. After all, continuous improvement should be carried out on a broad front.

It should be clear that one cannot attempt too many changes at any one time. Prioritize them, as we said some pages ago. Prioritize analyses beyond the preliminary ones, and prioritize implementation of those changes that further analysis produces. Keep the confusion down, a lesson learned by many companies.

9.7 SQA Organizations

Quality assurance for computer software does not require a separate function to implement a quality process, especially when we recall that one of the precepts of TQM is that the quality of a process ultimately rests with the owners of the process. Still, echoing an argument of Sec. 1.3, we recommend that SQA organizations be given a role in software TQM. Stan Siegel has put the matter succinctly. After noting that TQM is about "doing right things right," Siegel goes on to say that:

> ...The challenge is to figure out what things are "wrong" and then how to do them right so you avoid the other three possibilities: doing right things wrong, doing wrong things right, and doing wrong things wrong."[6]

This view would strongly suggest that TQM can profit from the full-time support of people dedicated to figuring out "what things are wrong." We posit that software quality engineers (SQE), the staff of a SQA organization, can help focus the quality improvement process without diluting the principle of process ownership.

The role of a software quality engineer (SQE) in analyzing what things are wrong leads to other ways in which the SQE can support the processes of software development and maintenance. Borrowing from Ref. 7, we find five hats for SQEs to wear:

1. *Analyst*—of measurements and processes

2. *Surrogate*—for the customer/user community

3. *Collector*—of data for measurements

4. *Peacekeeper*—keeper of the books, corrections tracker, etc.

5. *Planner*—of software quality programs

Analyst

SQEs are good quality team citizens. They are familiar with the use of fishbone diagrams, Pareto analysis, failure mode and effects analysis, and other quality tools directed to finding candidate processes for improvement. Not charged with any direct development tasks, the SQE can maintain an objective position in evaluating the results of current processes.

Apart from using analysis techniques within quality teams, SQEs are the obvious people to perform many independent analyses. Section 9.1 spoke of analysis as part of a data and information system. Most of the reduction of raw data into insightful measurements can be a matter of cookbookery, much can be totally automated. Still, someone has to do the cooking and call for the reduction of data by computer. The ideal person to do this is one involved in the quality of products, services, and processes, without the distraction of having to do the actual work. Hence, the SQE.

In the act of analyzing data, SQEs cannot help but make certain evaluations. For example, in tabulating the data for Fig. 9.19, the SQE cum analyst will observe that the process changes appear to have had a favorable effect. The SQE can bring these and similar evaluations to the attention of technical management in concise monthly reports, sparing managers the drudgery of poring over details. The details, of course, are not hidden from the managers. Managers interested in the basis for specific evaluations or recommendations can use their terminals to draw the detailed reports—tabulations, graphs, or whatever—prepared by the SQE and available in the data and information system data base.

Surrogate

Concerned above all else with the quality of software, the SQE shares the customer's greatest concern. Unlike the customer, the SQE is never more than minutes away from those developing the software and knows exactly what steps are being taken to ensure satisfaction of the customer's expectations. For software developed under contract, this enables the SQE to take the role of point contact for the customer on matters having to do with quality. For software for the general marketplace, the SQE can help the customer support people in analyzing problems having to do with product quality.

Nowhere do we see the need for a surrogate more clearly than in qualification. For custom software, the customer will likely (and properly) want to be directly involved with qualification, particularly during planning. When it comes to the actual qualification exercise (which may continue for days or weeks), the customer may not want to be in continual attendance. However, knowing an SQE is on hand and evaluating test results, perhaps even personally running the tests, will often satisfy the customer's concern for objectivity during qualification.

For software developed for the mass of anonymous customers, giving SQEs primary responsibility for qualification should provide management with the assurance that an objective evaluation has been made of the product's fitness for release. As the users' surrogate, the SQE will see performance from the users' point of view, not that of the developer who may be satisfied by a product that works as it was designed to do.

Collector

Section 9.1 noted that most of the raw input to the data and information system should come from terminals on-line to the data base and from tools. That is, data originate with process owners: analysts, programmers, testers, and customer support staff. When activity is particularly intense, as during testing, it is all too easy for the process owner to forget to enter information into the data base. Even data generated by tools do not necessarily get logged under recognizable names. How many desktop computer users sometimes forget to save files or give them names (or extensions) violating the users' personal conventions?

We don't want to lose data, but we shall inevitably unless someone sufficiently detached from the origin of data looks over the data base periodically to see that all the expected data are present and accounted for. Some data surely will be missing, but if the data are of recent origin, the input can be captured and entered. For that someone, we nominate an SQE.

Peacekeeper

In the early days of SQA, management often took the position that SQA acted as "the cop on the beat," looking after all discrepancies between the actual performance of technical staff and that called for by the combination of project plans and published standards. We consider the term "cop on the beat" confrontational, and not at all consonant with TQM. We don't choose to believe that technical staff are potentially destructive people who adhere to approved procedures only when they think someone is looking over their shoulders. We do, however, believe that in the course of developing software people can unwittingly drift from the course set by plans and standards, not to mention letting action items slip between the chairs. Acting much like an auditor, an SQE can support the project by notifying staff of deviations from plans and standards, especially a pattern of such deviations, so that mid–course corrections can be made to put the project back on track.

One reason to deviate from plans and standards is that they may be impractical. For example, if a representative of Customer Service is required to sign every approved change, even during development of Release 0.0, and if Customer Service plans to assign someone to the project only during beta test, it is bureaucratically impossible to make changes until beta release. Plainly, this is an unacceptable situation, and changes will be made, anyhow. The question is how. If one finds that changes are going through the controlled change process, despite no participation by Customer Service, it's a small matter to simply modify the appropriate plans to make them workable. If, however, the controlled change process is completely abandoned because of the administrivia, substantive correction action must be taken before too much damage has been done. Frequent audits limit the amount of damage from impractical plans and standards by surfacing their shortcomings early in their use.

Most deviations from standards and plans are not the result of their impracticality. Typical reasons include the following:

- Staff misunderstands the plans or standards.
- Staff does not understand purpose behind specific requirements, and tacitly rejects the need for compliance.
- Content of plans and standards is not disseminated to staff.
- Staff is under too much schedule pressure.

Whatever the reasons, corrective action can be taken for all but the last item once a pattern of discrepancies is found. The last is unlikely to happen if the other TQM precepts are followed. If, despite all, it does happen, at least disclosure of the problem may force a needed replanning exercise.

With regard to action items—faults, further analyses, provisional waivers, and the like—affecting the product, an SQE can maintain vigilance over the log of open items, advising assigned personnel of overdue responses. By tracking actions all the way to their closing, The SQE can also take the responsibility for seeing that corrections, once made, are verified. This type of bookkeeping is not the sort of thing that either developers or their managers are likely to find much time for. Nor is it a task that one can assign a clerk, since the keeper of the book often needs to understand the sense of the action called for. The task is an obvious one to assign to an SQE.

Planner

We think that an SQE can help in the preparation of all project plans by making certain that they contain appropriate quality provisions. For example, a configuration management plan should comply with documented standards or policies. In reviewing the plan, the SQE will check to see that the plan complies with, say, the provision that emergency fixes to released products are permitted only when initiated by Customer Service.

Just as projects need development, test, and configuration management plans (often, customer support plans, as well) as roadmaps for staff to follow, they need quality plans. The quality plan need not be a separate document. One can incorporate explicit quality provisions into the other plans, or, better yet, weave quality provisions into the very fabric of the plans. For example, a section of the plan for development testing can address analysis of test results. However documented, quality plans need to be written. Another job for an SQE.

We are often asked the cost of maintaining an SQA function. Costs vary greatly, depending upon the tasks given to SQA and the degree of tooling, but they mostly range between three percent and eight percent of the cost of technical staff. We feel that in a TQM environment, a range of three percent to five percent is achievable without sacrificing any of the value of an independent software quality function. Perhaps the most important point to remember is that the more technical staff is responsible for the quality of their process, the lower the cost of SQA.

9.8   Cost of Quality

"Cost of quality" could mean something like the butcher's, "Look, you gotta expect to pay more for sirloin than for chuck." We have something else in mind, the costs that attach to quality both good and bad. Indeed, the greatest quality cost is the cost of poor quality. We classify quality costs as follows:

1. *Correction*—the costs of correcting product faults. We further divide this into two separate costs.
   - Correction of faults before delivery to customers.
   - Correction of faults in fielded software.
2. *Prevention*—the costs, specific to quality, of preventing faults.
3. *Appraisal*—the costs of finding faults and deviations from plans and standards.

Correction of faults found before delivery include costs of rework, whether of requirements models, designs, or code. As we noted much earlier, these get increasingly expensive the longer they are permitted to remain in the system. If prevention eliminates the cost of a correction, early appraisal reduces the cost.

Correction of faults found after delivery plainly costs more than correction of faults found before delivery. To the cost of rework we have to add the cost of validating the fix through some form of qualification. Such qualification may be restricted in terms of the fix itself, but except for fixes to user documentation it will still entail extensive regression testing of the entire system. Also, the cost of distributing the fix may be considerable. Finally, we may have to account for liability costs as part of the cost of correcting faults in fielded products.

Prevention costs include education and training, the purchase of development cost of tools specific to product quality, the training and temporary inefficiency that attaches to the introduction of new methods and tools, configuration management, all data collection and analysis pertinent to measuring the quality of processes, quality planning costs, improvements in customer support, and the sum of all labor involved in improving the quality of processes. In short, all costs beyond those theoretically possible to develop and ship software—whatever its quality, development time, and management headaches.

Appraisal costs are those of all fault detection processes, alpha and beta testing, qualification, audits, and the costs associated with collecting and analyzing data for measurements of product quality.

To actually quantify one's quality costs requires an unusually fine-grained cost accumulation system. For example, programmers would have to account for the time spent in planned design activity separately from the design of fixes. At that, inefficiency due to new techniques has to be estimated. Still, it is worthwhile to know the costs of quality. They are a vital part of management by fact.

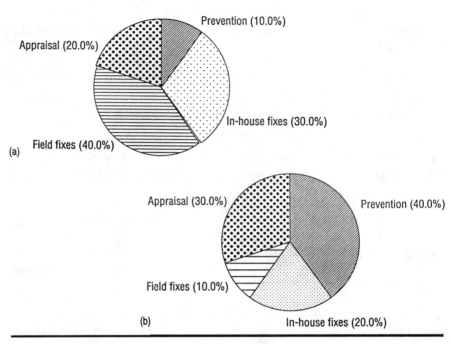

Figure 9.20 (a) Quality costs with immature quality system. (b) Quality costs with mature quality system.

We can view the cost of quality as a measure of success in establishing a mature TQM system. Figure 9.20a depicts the apportionment of quality costs we might expect to find in the early stages of establishing TQM, while Fig. 9.20b represents the result two or three years later. Note the relative sizes of the "before" and "after" pies. Maybe Crosby is right after all: quality can be free. But understand that TQM does not shrink the pizza overnight. Also, as we noted earlier, one should not attempt to make too many process changes at one time. The total amount of change one might have to plan and implement is, of course, a matter of one's current status. We'll leave that for the next chapter.

9.9 Summary

1. A mature quality system for software requires that four objectives be attained: customer/user satisfaction, project control, reduction of the cost of quality, and a process for continuous improvement.

2. "Management by fact" requires a data and information system having four primary elements: data collection, data storage, data analysis, and the dissemination of data and analysis results.

3. A data and information system for software should include project, product, and process data.

4. Motivated staff can make valuable contributions to the quality of software processes. Empowered staff can make valuable contributions to the quality of software products.

5. Control of development and maintenance projects is supported by defined task exit criteria and a variety of trend data.

6. Project control mechanisms must be flexible enough to accommodate regression of some design activities to an earlier stage.

7. Task completions and fault detection processes give rise to a number of investigative or corrective action items applying to both product and processes. These need to be tracked to ensure they are closed.

8. The fact that businesses have little reason or need to buy from many software suppliers makes it easier to develop partnering relations with those suppliers of the highest quality.

9. Constant improvement of the quality process requires recurring observation and evaluation of the constituents of the process and subprocesses.

10. Analysis of the improvement process entails knowing which improvements arose from the process, their effect both internally and on customers, and their effect on the quality position relative to competitors and benchmarks.

11. The primary software risks are delivery of unsatisfactory software, low estimates of the cost and time for development, inability to stay within cost and time budgets, undertaking infeasible projects, building short-lived products, and staff instability. All these risks are reduced by the application of TQM principles.

12. The implementation of process improvements is helped by committed management, staff participation in the improvement process, and caution in avoiding too much change at one time.

13. Software quality organizations can perform valuable support in analyzing measurements and processes, overseeing the collection of data, providing direct customer support during development and qualification, intelligently handling such bookkeeping chores as the tracking of action items, analyzing deviations from plans and standards, and making certain that quality provisions enter into all project plans.

14. Quality costs include correction of product problems found before delivery and by the customer, steps taken specifically to prevent problems, and the cost of detecting faults and evaluating performance.

15. TQM changes the distribution of quality costs, reducing the percentage consumed by correction and increasing the percentage taken by prevention, for a net reduction of the total cost.

References

1. Ishikawa, K. *What Is Total Quality Control? The Japanese Way,* Translated by D. Lu, Prentice Hall, Englewood Cliffs, NJ, 1985, pp. 63-64.
2. Dyer, Michael. *The Cleanroom Approach to Quality Software Development,* John Wiley & Sons, New York, NY, 1992.
3. Albrecht, A. J. "Measuring Application Development Productivity," *Proc. Joint SHARE/GUIDE Application Development Symposium*, October 1979, pp. 34-43.
4. Jones, T. C. *Programming Productivity,* McGraw-Hill, New York, NY, 1986.
5. Low, Graham and Jeffery, D. Ross. "Function Points in the Estimation and Evaluation of the Software Process," *IEEE Trans. Software Engrg.*, SE-16, No. 1, January 1990, pp. 64-71.
6. Siegel, Stan. "Why We Need Checks and Balances to Assure Quality," *IEEE Software*, January 1992, pp. 102-103.
7. Dunn, Robert. *Software Quality: Concepts and Plans,* Prentice-Hall, Englewood Cliffs, NJ, 1990, pp. 159-173.

Implementation

10

Assessment and Planning

Part Four deals with implementation of a quality process. *Implementation* implies setting near term goals, learning where one stands, determining a strategy to get there, and doing it. That's what this chapter is about. Whatever the goal, whatever the extent to which it was reached, one tacitly defines a quality process. Tacit is not good enough. Quality processes need to be made explicit so that everyone concerned can understand them, and they need to be instantiated for specific projects. We leave that for the next chapter.

Chapter 9 started with the goal of a mature software process and ended with the cautionary note not to attempt to change too much at any one time. Were we into redundancy, we might have said that maturity takes time. Recall the four objectives outlined by Chap. 9 for attaining a mature software process: satisfaction of customer and users, project control, reduced cost of quality, and a process for continuous improvement. For practical implementation, one needs to set short-range goals for each of these. To know what short-range goals are practicable, one needs to know where one currently stands. In short, implementation starts with self-assessment.

Comparison with competitors and benchmarks, discussed in Sec. 9.6, is one way to assess current status. In a sense, though, it's a bottom-line assessment in that one compares results of processes, not the elements of the processes. We might learn that our defect density of five faults per KNCSS compares unfavorably with the chief competitor's 1.5 faults per KNCSS, but we don't know why. We start this chapter and Part 4 with another way of determining status, self-assessment.

Self-assessment is not something one does once. With a process for continuous quality improvement in place, status keeps changing. Comparisons with competitors and benchmarks continue to provide bot-tom-line assessments, while self-assessments continue to provide insight for setting process objectives. In order to track the moving target of process status, self-assessments should be conducted annually.

10.1 Self-Assessment

Self-assessment requires a methodology. A traditional, if unspoken, way of assessing one's process has been in casual conversations with new hires several weeks into their employment. Managers generally make it a point to "run into" new hires, partly to let the person know that the interview was not the last contact the two will ever have, and partly to check on the supervisor's report that the new hire has fit in well with the rest of the team. When the employee has had previous professional employment, the course of conversation almost invariably gets around to the question, "What do you think of the way we do things around here?" The new hire responds with likes, muted dislikes (muted to avoid queering career prospects in the first month), and *surprising differences.* "I thought all companies required weekly reports," or "The Kaze CASE is really easy to learn, but I wish it did what my old system did—automatically save my work every 15 minutes. I forget to do so, and with the frequency of system crashes around here...." Such conversations cannot help but stimulate thinking about one's own processes.

Similarly, we learn something about our position in the state of the practice in the corridors outside seminar and conference rooms. "You people really require correctness proof evidence before releasing a module for integration? Gee, I didn't think anyone actually did that." Finally, we find anecdotal clues to our relative status from books, magazines, and professional journals. (Don't just look at the pictures, though. Read the text. Much of what is written has been tried out only on small projects.)

None of the casual approaches to learning one's status can compare with a deliberate methodology. We describe two popular methods. The first was developed specifically for software by the Software Engineering Institute (SEI) at Carnegie Mellon University. We base the second on the criteria for the Malcolm Baldrige National Quality Award.

The SEI capability maturity model

In a 1989 interview,[1] Watts Humphrey, then the director of the SEI's Software Process Program, said that the SEI's maturity framework was based on the concept of statistical repeatability established by W. Edwards Deming and J. M. Juran. Humphrey said that he was also influenced by Crosby's five-level maturity framework, although he had some difficulty in relating the framework specifically to software issues.

Coincidentally, at the time the SEI initiated the Software Process Assessment project that eventually led to the Capability Maturity Model (CMM), the SEI also started its Software Capability Evaluation (SCE) project in response to a request from the Air Force. Displeased with the results of its price- and delivery-oriented process for source selection, "...the Air Force sought a technically sound and consistent method that it could use to identify the most capable software contractors."[2] Once in operation, SCE auditors assessed contractor capabilities based on products of the process assessment project, most particularly a questionnaire, which has led many in industry to see the CMM simply as a means of supporting SCE. However, apart from any use in evaluating contractors, the CMM serves as a framework for self-assessment.

The five levels of the CMM are given in Table 10.1.

As we noted, the SEI publishes a questionnaire designed to permit a company (or SCE auditors) to determine which maturity level best describes its software process status. The initial issue of the questionnaire* contained 101 questions. Based on the 101 questions of 27 sites independently assessed through April 1991, 22 were at level 1, three at level 2, and two at level 3. None were at the highest two levels.[3] The assessments, however, were based largely on a numerical score yielded by the questionnaire answers. If one didn't score high enough on the 40 questions that determined a process at level 2 rather than level 1, the rest of the questions were immaterial. Accordingly, these assessments are arguable.

Apart from grades, the CMM can provide real insight into process maturity. For each maturity level, the CMM defines key process areas and key practices that constitute the process areas. The relation among these is depicted in Fig. 10.1, adapted from an illustration in an SEI publication.[4,p.25] The key process areas and practices are cumulative. Thus,

TABLE 10.1 The Five CMM Process Maturity Levels

Maturity level	Name	Chief process characteristic
1	Initial	Chaotic
2	Repeatable	Disciplined
3	Defined	Standard, consistent
4	Managed	Predictable
5	Optimizing	Continuously improving

*The SEI will update the questionnaire from time to time.

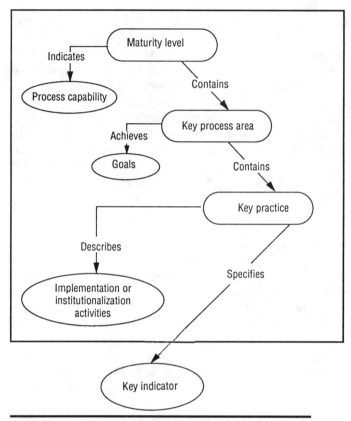

Figure 10.1   CMM schema.

an area and its practices identified for level 2 are a part, also, of levels 3, 4, and 5.

The key indicators are not part of the CMM itself, but are key practices or their parts used to determine the satisfaction of key process area goals. If identified as a key indicator, a key practice metamorphoses into a questionnaire entry. For example, software project planning is one of the level 2 key process areas, and a key practice within the area is the use of documented procedures for estimating the size of software products. If selected as a key indicator, this practice might give rise to the question, "Do you use a documented procedure to estimate software size (e.g., lines of code, function points, etc.)?"[4,p.34]

Table 10.2 identifies the process areas the CMM considers key for each maturity level. None, of course, apply to the default level. Recall that the process areas are cumulative; software configuration management applies to both level 2 and level 5.

TABLE 10.2 Key Process Areas for Each CMM Process Maturity Level

Level	Key process areas
1. Initial	None
2. Repeatable	Software configuration management Software quality assurance Software subcontract management Software project tracking and oversight Software project planning Requirements management
3. Defined	Peer reviews Intergroup coordination Software product engineering Integrated software management Training program Organization process definition Organization process focus
4. Managed	Quality management Process measurement and analysis
5. Optimizing	Process change management Technology innovation Defect prevention

To get to the practices the CMM finds applicable to each process area, one needs to refer to a document of approximately 380 pages.[5] We cannot hope to cover all of the practices, but we'll get to two of them to illustrate the use of the CMM in self-assessment. However, we need first to look at the goals outlined for each of the key process areas, since, before getting into the key practices tied to a goal, anyone using the CMM for self-assessment should decide the merit of adopting the goal. Some of the goals are fairly specific to directed DoD contractor relations, and are difficult to translate to other development and maintenance milieus. We need, also, to bear in mind that the DoD-contractor relationship is based on process standards published by the DoD that antedate the current acceptance of TQM.

Goals.   The goals for each of the key process areas (paraphrased from Ref. 6) are listed separately for each of the four real maturity levels in Tables 10.3 through 10.6.

Most of the goals are self-explanatory, particularly in light of Chaps. 5 through 9, but a few are worth looking at beyond the words. In the Software QA area of Table 10.3, the first goal addresses independent confirmation. Neither of the SEI documents[4,5] requires companies to adopt a specific organizational structure, but the material in Ref. 5 on SQA does speak of an SQA group with a reporting channel to senior

TABLE 10.3 Goals for the Repeatable Process Level

Key process area	Goals
Software CM	1 Controlled and stable baselines for planning, managing, and building the system 2 Integrity of system's configuration controlled over time 3 Known status and content of baselines
Software QA	1 Independent confirmation of compliance of product and process with standards, procedures, and product requirements 2 Management awareness of compliance problems 3 Senior management addresses noncompliance issues
Subcontractor management	1 Prime contractor selects only qualified subs. 2 Standards, procedures, and product requirements for the subcontract comply with prime contractor's commitments 3 Commitments between prime and sub are understood and agreed to by both parties 4 Prime tracks the sub's actual results and performance against commitments
Project tracking and oversight	1 Actual results and performance of project tracked against plans 2 Corrective actions taken when the actual results and performance deviate significantly from the plans 3 Changes to commitments understood and agreed to by all affected groups and individuals
Project planning	1 Plan developed that appropriately and realistically covers activities and commitments 2 All affected groups and individuals understand the software estimates and plans and commit to support them 3 Estimates and plans are documented for use in tracking activities and commitments
Requirements management	1 System requirements allocated to software provide a clearly stated, verifiable, and testable foundation for software engineering and software management 2 Allocated requirements define the scope of the software effort

management independent of software engineering* groups, project managers, and such support groups as software configuration management. The goal really means that the level 2 contractor has an SQA group to verify compliance. The second SQA goal addresses management awareness of *compliance problems.* This is what the SQA group's reporting channel to senior management is all about.

The last goal for subcontractor management at level 2 implies periodic status reviews, technical reviews, and "formal" reviews with subcontractors ("subs." in the table). Also, the subcontractors are

---

*In DoD parlance, *software engineering* means *programming.*

TABLE 10.4 Goals for the Defined Process Level

Key process area	Goals
Peer reviews	1 Product defects identified and fixed early 2 Product improvements identified and implemented early in life cycle 3 More effective staff via better understanding of work products and preventable errors 4 Establish and use rigorous group process for reviewing and evaluating product quality
Intergroup coordination	1 Project's technical goals and objectives understood and agreed to by staff and managers 2 All groups know responsibilities assigned to each and the interfaces between the groups 3 Groups are involved in intergroup activities and in identifying, tracking, and addressing intergroup issues 4 Project groups work as a team
Software product engineering	1 Software engineering issues for product and process are properly addressed in system requirements and system design 2 Software engineering activities are well-defined, integrated, and used constantly 3 As appropriate, state-of-practice software engineering tools and methods are used 4 Systematic development of consistent and appropriate software engineering products
Integrated software management	1 Projects planned and managed according to organization's standard software process 2 Technical and management data from past and current projects are available and used to estimate, plan, track, replan current projects
Training program	1 Skilled, knowledgeable staff and managers 2 Staff and managers prepared for effective use of existing and planned work environment 3 Staff and managers have opportunities to improve their professional skills
Organization process definition	1 Standard process defined and maintained for stabilizing, analyzing, improving performance 2 Specifications of common processes and documented experience collected and available
Organization process focus	1 Strengths and weaknesses of process understood; plans laid to systematically address weaknesses 2 Establish a group with appropriate knowledge, skills, and resources to define a standard process 3 Organization provides resources and support to record and analyze use of standard process in order to maintain and improve process

TABLE 10.5 Goals for the Managed Process Level

Key process area		Goals
Quality management	1	Measurable goals and priorities for product quality are established and maintained for each software project through interaction with customer, end user, and project groups
	2	Measurable goals for process quality are established for all groups involved in process
	3	Software plans, designs, and process are adjusted to bring forecasted process and product quality in line with goals
	4	Process measurements are used to manage the software project quantitatively
Process management and analysis	1	Stable software process under statistical process control
	2	Relationship among product quality, productivity, and development cycle time is understood in quantitative terms
	3	Variations attributable to specific applications of the process and not inherent in the process are identified and controlled

required to develop a software development plan with reference to the contractor's plan. In sum, these mean that the relationship between the level 2 contractor and its subcontractors should be similar to that between the DoD agency and the contractor.

In Table 10.4, under software product engineering, goal 4 calls for the systematic development of consistent and appropriate software engineering products. The term *software engineering products* means plans, requirements models, designs, code, and test specifications. By

TABLE 10.6 Goals for the Optimizing Level

Key process area		Goals
Process change management	1	Staff and managers actively involved in setting quantitative, measurable improvement goals and in improving the software process
	2	Standard software process and the projects' defined processes continually improve
	3	Staff and managers able to properly and effectively use the evolving processes and their supporting tools and methods
Technology innovation	1	Organization has a process and technology capability to allow it to develop or capitalize on the best available technologies in industry
	2	Orderly and thorough selection and transfer of new technology into the organization
	3	Technology innovations are tied to quality and productivity improvements of the organization's standard process
Defect prevention	1	Identification and elimination of sources of product defects that are inherent or repeatedly occur in the software process

consistent, the SEI means that each product is verifiable with respect to (appropriate) products generated earlier in the project.

In the last key process area of Table 10.4, the second goal speaks of a group to define a standard process. Reference 5 recommends that the group comprise a core of full-time software technical professionals, possibly augmented by part-timers. Very large software organizations, such as are maintained by some of the aerospace companies, can afford such a group. One has to wonder, though, if smaller organizations don't profit by the responsibility assumed by quality teams in contributing to the definition and continuous redefinition of software processes.

The second key process area of Table 10.5 has a goal calling for *statistical process control* (SPC) of the software process. Mostly, the SEI is calling for the analysis and use of measurements to adjust processes. The only reference to SPC, as known to quality professionals, is some talk of the upper and lower limits for process metrics. Little software engineering is subject to both upper and lower limits. One might apply such limits to the percentage of comment lines in a code file, but it's hard to find many such examples. We even have few processes that call for automatic adjustment on the basis of double bounds. We might expect that integration testing will yield fault densities lying between two limits, but exceeding the limits calls for investigation, not adjustment.

In Table 10.6, we find that at the optimizing level, the one goal attached to defect prevention has to do with revising the process to eliminate recurring errors or errors inherent in the process. This differs from the usual view of the military with respect to defect prevention, wherein we find the root causes of faults largely ignored and prevention spoken of only within the context of executing a specific contract. The defect prevention goal, in fact, exemplifies the CMM's focus on the processes that affect not one, but many contracts.

Practices.   In *Key Practices of the Capability Maturity Model,*[5] each key process area is described in terms of:

- Commitment to perform.
- Ability to perform.
- Activities performed.
- Monitoring.
- Verification.

Recalling the military origin of the CMM, we should not be surprised to find language bent a bit. *Ability to perform* is, essentially, preparation for executing an instance of a process. *Activities performed* include both activities and modes of operation. We recognize that extraction of isolated sections of the CMM document suffers from the loss of context provided by the complete document of some 380 pages. Nevertheless, the two examples that follow should give the reader a flavor of what the SEI is looking for.

For the project planning process area of Table 10.3, the commitments follow (and again, we paraphrase in places):

- A project software manager has the responsibility for negotiating commitments and developing the project software development plan (SDP).
- The planning of a software project follows a written policy.

The abilities follow:

- A documented and approved software statement of work.
- System requirements allocated to software are documented and approved.
- Responsibilities for developing the SDP are assigned.
- Adequate resources and budget for planning the software project are provided.
- Software managers and engineers involved in software planning receive training in software estimating and planning procedures.

The project planning activities follow:

- The software engineering group is an active participant in the project proposal team.
- Software planning is initiated in the early stages of, and in parallel with, overall project planning.
- Throughout the project's life, the software engineering group actively participates in overall project planning.
- Senior management reviews and approves all commitments made to individuals and groups external to the organization.
- A software life-cycle model with predefined stages of manageable size is identified or defined.
- The SDP is developed according to documented procedures and maintained under configuration management.
- The SDP directly or by reference covers the plan for software activities.
- Software product and process specifications needed to establish and maintain the stability of software activities are explicitly identified for inclusion in controlled baselines. [It is unclear to us why process

specifications should be baselined in the same sense as product specifications.]

- Software size estimates, critical target computer resources, and resources and costs required for development are derived per documented procedures.
- The software schedule is derived using a documented procedure.
- Software technical, cost, resource, and schedule risks are identified, assessed, and documented.
- Plans for the project's software engineering facilities, environments, and support tools are prepared.
- Software planning data are recorded for use by the project.

There is but one item under the rubric "Monitoring Implementation." It calls for the use of measurements to determine the cost and schedule status of the software planning activities.

"Verifying Implementation" has two entries. The first calls for the software project manager to conduct regular status and coordination reviews with the system's project manager during all planning activities. The second says that the SQA group reviews and audits the activities and products for software planning, reporting results as appropriate.

Each of these many items is extensively amplified. Indeed, the key process area, project planning, which we have just outlined, runs through 18 pages of (fairly large) print.[5,pp.L2-11-L2-28] Going through the 18 pages, the self-assessor can reasonably determine whether the company's process for project planning is a repeatable one as defined by the SEI. This, after all, is the sense of using the CMM for assessing one's status. We believe that use of the questionnaire, alone, is less likely to yield the insight sought after.

We take our other example, quality management, from maturity level 4. There is but one commitment; namely that the organization follow a written policy for managing quality on software projects.

The key process area has three abilities to perform:

1. Appropriate resources and funding for quality management are provided.
2. The staff implementing and supporting quality management receives training in the performance of quality management activities.
3. Staff and managers involved in the software process receive required training on software quality management (SQM).

For quality management, the activities follow:

- The project develops strategies to satisfy the quality needs of the organization, customer, and end users [operational military units].
- The project's activities for SQM are based on a documented and approved software quality plan for the project.
- Throughout the software life cycle, quantitative product quality goals are defined and revised.
- Quantitative process quality goals are established for the project.
- Software product quality goals flow down to subcontractors.
- Quantitative quality goals for software requirements, software design, code, and formal software tests are established and tracked.
- Alternative designs are considered to meet software product quality goals and software requirements.
- The groups involved in the software process review agree to and work to meet the project's quality goals for its process and products.
- Process data are monitored to identify actions needed to satisfy the process quality goals.
- The quality of the products are regularly compared with the quality goals.
- When quality measurements indicate process or product problems, corrective actions are taken.

As in the earlier example, this process area has but one monitoring entry; namely that the process for quality management be quantified and evaluated through measurements. Verification entails:

- Senior management review of process quality goals against the organization's quality policies.
- Quality management activities are regularly reviewed with senior management.
- Activities for managing quality are regularly reviewed with the project manager.
- The SQA group reviews and audits the activities and products for managing quality, reporting results as appropriate.

The last verification item would seem to lend itself to speculation about empire-building, possibly even to the suggestion that SQA has the role of checking to make certain that senior management is fulfilling its review responsibilities. The explanation, however, is fairly tame, citing only:

1. Reviews and audits of the preparation of a software quality plan

2. The process for establishing and tracking quality goals

3. The process for implementing corrective actions

The two SEI documents may provide a carefully drawn schema for assessing one's process status (making allowances for DoD-oriented goals, as we remarked earlier), but it is anything but a mechanism for quick looks. Before starting to write their report, teams of trained SCE assessors spend three to five days on site, most of which time is spent interviewing contractor personnel.[6]

The two SEI reports[4,5] may be ordered as the CMM Notebook directly from the SEI, ATT: Publications Requests, Carnegie Mellon University, Pittsburgh, PA 15213-3890. An Internet address—cmm-info@sei.cmu.edu—is also available for ordering. At publication (August 1991) the price was $75.

The Malcolm Baldrige National Quality Award

Since the 1988 announcement of the first Malcolm Baldrige National Quality Award winners, the influence of the Baldrige Award on the nation's perception of TQM has grown at an astounding pace. Articles about the award appear nearly every month in magazines devoted to quality, frequently in business magazines, and a cottage industry has flourished comprised of consultants who specialize in helping companies apply for the award. The award is given not to individuals, but to companies. Separate awards are made in each of three categories of business: manufacturing, service, and small business. The major part of a company's application is its 75-page response (50 pages for small businesses) to published award criteria. A company whose application gets a high score from a team of examiners will receive a site visit. A panel of judges makes the final award decisions.

Although the number of companies applying for the award is considerable (76 in 1993), the several hundred thousand copies of the Award Criteria that have been requested dwarfs the number sent to companies who submitted applications. While some requests are made by people who simply want to know what all the fuss is about, a great many copies are sent to companies who intend to use the criteria for assessing their progress toward TQM. Well they might: the criteria, 28 items divided among seven categories, represent a concise blueprint for TQM. We admit we are prejudiced. R. Ullman has been a Baldrige Award examiner, and R. Dunn has for several years been an examiner for the Connecticut Quality Improvement Award (based entirely on the Award Criteria), and under the auspices of the Connecticut Award, conducts workshops in the use of the criteria as a TQM roadmap. Moreover, Ullman is a Vice-President of ITT Defense and Electronics Corporation, which uses the Baldrige Award criteria to objectively measure the corporation's quality level. We may be biased, but few will deny that the 28 items, presented in only 17 pages,[7 pp.16-32] capture all aspects of TQM in succinct and appraisable terms.

Table 10.7 lists the seven Baldrige categories and the items constituting each. The 28 items, themselves, have several parts, called areas to address. All told, the 1993 criteria include 92 such areas. Let's take an example, Item 2.1, "Scope and Management of Quality and Performance Data and Information," which has three areas to address.

The first area under 2.1 speaks to the criteria for selecting data (for brevity, we'll use "data" to mean both data and information) that enter into the improvement of quality and operational performance. The

TABLE 10.7 The Seven Baldrige Award Categories

1 Leadership
   1.1 Senior Executive Leadership
   1.2 Management for Quality
   1.3 Public Responsibility and Corporate Citizenship*
2 Information and Analysis
   2.1 Scope and Management of Quality and Performance Data and Information
   2.2 Competitive Comparisons and Benchmarking
   2.3 Analysis and Uses of Company-Level Data
3 Strategic Quality Planning
   3.1 Strategic Quality and Company Performance Planning Process
   3.2 Quality and Performance Plans
4 Human Resources Development and Management
   4.1 Human Resource Planning and Management
   4.2 Employee Involvement
   4.3 Employee Education and Training
   4.4 Employee Performance and Recognition
   4.5 Employee Well-Being and Satisfaction
5 Management of Process Quality
   5.1 Design and Introduction of Quality Products and Services
   5.2 Process Management:Product and Service Production and Delivery Processes
   5.3 Process Management: Business Processes and Support Services
   5.4 Supplier Quality
   5.5 Quality Assessment
6 Quality and Operational Results
   6.1 Product and Service Quality Results
   6.2 Company Operational Results
   6.3 Business Process and Support Service Results
   6.4 Supplier Quality Results
7 Customer Focus and Satisfaction
   7.1 Customer Expectations: Current and Future
   7.2 Customer Relationship Management
   7.3 Commitment to Customers
   7.4 Customer Satisfaction Determination
   7.5 Customer Satisfaction Results
   7.6 Customer Satisfaction Comparison

*This element does not apply directly to software development and maintenance.

applicant is asked to list the key types of data used and to note the role played by each type in improving quality and operational performance.

The second area wants to know how the company assures the reliability, consistency, and rapid access to data across all parts of the company.

The third area asks the applicant to list the key methods and indicators by which the company evaluates and improves the scope and management of data. In this area, the applicant is expected to address the review and update of data, explain how the interval between data collection and access is shortened, and describe how access to data is broadened. The applicant also needs to discuss the way data enter into process improvement.

Collectively, the three areas of Item 2.1 permit companies to demonstrate the breadth and depth of their quality-related data. Used for self-assessment, the item forces companies to think about the system they have for collecting and disseminating data and the connection between the data in the system and their quality objectives. Moreover, companies are channeled into evaluating the approach and deployment (i.e., the breadth) of their data system. *Approach* and *deployment* enter into most of the award items (the Award Criteria says which). A third dimension of the criteria, *results* (that is, the outcome of the quality system) enters into 11 of the 28 items.

Each of the items has a value (points) assigned to it. Examiners score each item on a scale of 0 percent to 100 percent, where 50 percent represents a sound, prevention-based, well-deployed, system that shows generally good results and trends. The examiners multiply the percentages (as decimal fractions) by the values to arrive at a total score. The Award Criteria offer some guidance to the assignment of percentage scores, but reasonably reliable scoring requires examiner training or the equivalent offered by various consultants. In any case, the company using the Baldrige criteria can calculate a total score for itself if it cares to quantify the status of its quality system. We think it more important to go through the criteria with great care, documenting the many insights the self-assessors will gain. It is difficult to examine oneself against the Baldrige criteria and not see where one needs to improve. And that is what self-assessment is all about.

The Baldrige criteria change a bit each year as the Awards Office at NIST, in collaboration with many others, improves the quality of its own product. Since the beginning, two things have remained constant: the seven categories and the three dimensions of approach, deployment, and results. Curt Reimann, director of the Awards Office, speaking of the framework established at the beginning of the award, said:

...we defined everything necessary and sufficient to create and sustain a quality effort. What is the minimum number of components required to define and sustain a quality culture? [He then named the seven categories.] Anything else we had seen in the field of quality could be subsumed under these. Moving one element would be like kicking the third leg of a stool. It would fall down. Nor would anything be gained by subsuming one element under another; it would be muted. We were trying to send seven clear messages to the community.*

Plainly, the criteria for the Baldrige Award are not specific to software. One can quite easily relate certain items to software development and engineering, but others require some deeper thinking. Element 2.1, discussed earlier, is a simple case. Simply restrict the scope of the element to the types and use of data such as those discussed in Secs. 9.1, 9.3, and 9.6 of the last chapter. Element 5.2 (Process Management: Product and Service Production and Delivery Processes) can easily be translated into the processes associated with software development and testing (the substance of Chaps. 5 through 8 and some of the analyses discussed in Chap. 9). On the other hand, when assessing themselves with respect to Element 1.1 (Senior Executive Leadership), companies other than software publishers have to consider how policies of the top rung of management have influenced their software quality system and how the members of that rung have personally involved themselves in the software end of the business.

Alternatively, management of a software organization within a larger one can think of their organization as a separate company. (Fantasies are cheap. Go ahead. Be a CEO.) This doesn't change the interpretation of the criteria very much. "Senior Executive Leadership" becomes the management of the software department or division. "Strategic Quality Planning" reduces to the planning for future software activities and the integration of key software quality requirements into the business needs of the company. All other categories and the items within them are simply restricted to software matters, including software support for customers or users. Deployment is limited to functions involved with software requirements modeling, analysis, design, construction, testing, qualification, configuration control, and customer support. Figure 10.2, a slight modification of a figure in the *Awards Criteria*,[7, p.5] depicts the relations among the seven categories when restricted to self-assessment of a software organization within a company or a division of one.

Management, the concern of Category 1.0, drives the entire improvement process, and through feedback provides continuous redi-

---

*In a May 1990 interview with R. Dunn.

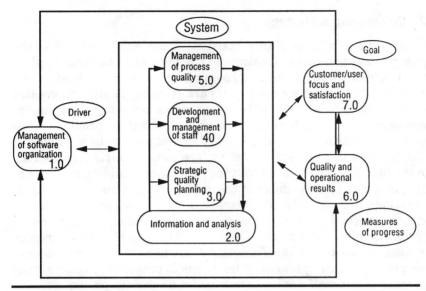

Figure 10.2   Baldridge Award schema.

rection. The actual system for improvement is treated by Categories 2.0 through 5.0, wherein Category 2.0, Information and Analysis, has the special position of serving as the foundation for the others. Category 6.0 deals with the direct measurable results of improvements. Feedback from Category 6.0 is critical to the success of the process. The goal of the entire process is the topic of Category 7.0, and the diagram highlights feedback from the measurable results of that Category. The essential difference between the results of Categories 6.0 and 7.0 is that the results of the former tell us if we are getting the progress we planned, while the results of the latter tell us if we planned the correct progress.

A free copy of *Awards Criteria* is available from:

Malcolm Baldrige National Quality Award
National Institute of Standards and Technology
Route 270 and Quince Orchard Road
Gaithersburg, MD 20899

$24.95 plus $3.75 postage and handling (1993 prices), fetches a packet of 10 copies from:

American Society for Quality Control
Customer Service Department
P.O. Box 3066
Milwaukee, WI 53201-3066

10.2 Developing a Strategy

Strategies start with business matters. Some short scenarios: the company is not increasing its share of the market at the rate implied in the business plan. Sales are booming, more so than that of the competition, but customer complaints are booming at an even greater rate. The company's main software products are—to use a euphemism—mature, and attempts to produce innovative products have made little headway in development. The main software product has the lion's share of the market, but each release is tougher to produce than the last, raising doubts about the capability of adding features at a rate sufficient to stay ahead of the competition. A marked swing in the marketplace to Unix platforms requires revamping the entire product line, which, unless the workforce is expanded, will slow down the rate of adding new product features. The size of staff is greater than needed to sustain the diminished business of military systems development, arousing fear of losing the best people through resignations when other staff are let go in a major downsizing move.

Plotting the course

Whatever the problems, and in the rapidly changing world of software there are always problems, they have to be prioritized. Business strategies dictate strategies for improving software quality systems. We know where our quality system stands—we have just undergone another iteration of our self-assessment process. Using the analyses of Chap. 9, we know how to address our weaknesses. Now we have to plan the next round of TQM upgrading.

Start by popping the top problem off the priority stack. With reference to Fig. 9.1, determine which of the four objectives—customer/user satisfaction, project control, reduction of COQ, process for continuous improvement—are affected. Next, using the latest assessment results, identify the primary rib of the objective that needs to be addressed. If self-assessment was based on the Baldrige model, one might look especially hard at self-assessments made with respect to the Baldrige criteria listed in Table 10.8. As the main business problem let's hypothesize a workforce inadequate to support both the programming of new features and the maintenance required for changeover to a new software platform. One solution might be to increase productivity without a loss of quality, or alternatively, decrease the cost of quality to permit expansion of the workforce. Figure 9.1 suggests that the cost of quality objective is a good candidate for scrutiny. Table 10.8 lists four Baldrige categories particularly pertinent to the objective. Looking at the last self-assessment, one recalls that the company was wanting in

TABLE 10.8 Baldrige Criteria for the Four Primary Software TQM Objectives

Objective	Most pertinent Baldrige Award criteria
Customer/user satisfaction	All of Category 5 Items 6.1, 6.2, and 6.4 All of Category 7
Project control	All of Category 5
Reduction of COQ	Item 3.2 Items 4.1, 4.2, and 4.3 Items 5.1 and 5.2 Items 6.1 and 6.2
Process for continuous improvement	All of Category 2 All of Category 3

Items 4.1, 4.2, and 4.3. This should prompt an analysis of the "caliber of staff" rib of Figure 9.4, which in turn will lead to a plan for upgrading staff or increasing their involvement in quality matters.

We do not mean to suggest that strategies necessarily arise out of cut-and-dried procedures such as the above. But what most needs doing is usually driven by business factors, and one can devise a strategy to remedy matters by taking into account the weaknesses identified in self-assessment and the candidates for analysis implied by Figs. 9.1 through 9.5.

In analyzing the possible courses of action to handle the business problem of greatest priority, one should not hesitate to peek at the ones just below it. Perhaps a twist here or there of the developing strategy will ease them as well.

Measurements

We have made much of measurements throughout the book. We return to the subject because, apart from business matters, measurements may have to be among the first strategic considerations. Companies that do not have more than a rudimentary software data and information system suffer a major handicap in trying to develop effective strategies.

A company at the TQM entry level (level 1 of the CMM or a composite score of less than 20 or 30 percent using the Baldrige criteria) desperately needs data. Regardless of specific business problems, work must begin on fashioning a data and information system. The business problems, however, will help to define where data are most needed. If new releases are getting more difficult to produce, we need to know why: we need to measure the product component by component, know more about the kinds of defects, know the percentage attributable to configuration ambiguities. If we need to increase productivity to shift over to Unix, we need to know the percentage of time spent by our labor force on each development and maintenance activity. Now, it is possible that anecdotal evidence is sufficient to explain the problem. For the new products that run into so much difficulty they are abandoned, we may know marketing specifications have been changing at so rapid a rate that software managers have been unable to stabilize development. But we may not know how far down in the development process changes have been propagating, with the result that we cannot come up with a process improvement that can meet Marketing half way.

To establish or improve a measurements system—where the word *system* means more than just an arbitrary set of collected data and the reports generated from them—one starts by listing the data, analyses, and reports that relate to the problem at hand. Next, one looks at the data currently gathered, the current analyses, the current reports (and the people who get them). Match the two, and see what is missing or what is not needed. Than start building the system, bottom-up.

Emerging technology

Chapters 5 through 8 contained a number of references to state-of-the-practice technology. Nowhere does technology seem to change so rapidly as in any field closely related to computers. Examples include publishing, medical instrumentation, air navigation instruments, telephony, telemarketing, financial services, and software development and maintenance—the field that makes it all possible. Publishing shops that stay competitive spend a lot of time looking over new systems for desktop publishing, press control, graphics generation, and the like. Software shops that stay competitive spend a lot of time looking over new programming paradigms, test methods, tool systems, and hardware/software/network platforms.

Self-assessment and analyses inherent in the quality process may reveal the need to upgrade technology, but to what? To know what technology one should aspire to, one needs to know what technology is available. Understanding this, software professionals spend considerable time attending paid seminars, attending seminars sponsored by hardware and software suppliers, and reading professional magazines. While these activities inform the professional of products and methods in current use, they provide only marginal help in identifying all the technology that may help support goals just a few years down the road.

Most of the technology we are now familiar with arose first in university or industrial software laboratories. (Most often, a software laboratory is a project or a collection of projects established to develop a specific new technology or determine the feasibility of its application in routine use.) To factor the technology of five years from now in one's planning, one has to keep track of what is going on in software laboratories. The journals and magazines of the professional societies are the best place for this, although from time to time backlogs of refereed articles may grow to two years. Each year brings new book titles dedicated to specific technological fields. The scope of such books often includes work still in the laboratory.

Whether a technology is currently at industrial strength or still in the laboratory, it enters into both short-term and long-term goals. Many companies have developed the practice of using small pilot projects to try out technology that appears interesting. Even if the technology does not immediately get used in important projects, may never get used, experience with it adds to the company knowledge base. A high-quality, competitive, company keeps itself technically sharp by giving its people hands-on experience in emerging technologies. Even in software development, the interval between laboratory and wide industrial application is seldom a matter of just a couple of years. Smalltalk, which would eventually popularize O-O in the United States, was developed at XEROX PARC in the 1970s, although most software practitioners knew little of it until the August 1981 number of *Byte* magazine. C++ entered general use in the mid-1980s, further widening the potential for application of O-O. Not until the early 1990s, however, did O-O become universally recognized as a standard software technology. One had time to think about the usefulness of O-O in the late 1970s and early 1980s, play with it in the mid and late 1980s and factor it into one's strategic plans, and by 1990 be fully equipped to use it on a major project—possibly ahead of the competition.

Help from the staff

We have already discussed the advantages of participative management in the several forms it can take within a quality system. At the risk of repetition, we note that strategic planning should involve quality teams, including cross-functional quality teams, to the extent possible. The advantages are several: practitioners are often the people who know best what needs improving, what works, what doesn't work. They generally know no less about emerging technology than their managers, and since no one knows everything, are likely to make unique contributions to the company's knowledge base of technology. Nonsupervisory staff are more likely to be recent hires, able to bring practices of other companies to the table. Finally, the very fact of helping to chart the company's future gives team members a proprietary interest in quality.

Benchmarking redux

We have spoken of benchmarking as a way of comparing the status of one's quality system and its results with the best in the business. Apart from using business factors to drive strategic planning, anyone who benchmarks specific attributes of quality—cycle time, fault density, and the like—is bound to aspire to the achievements of the benchmarked companies. Benchmarking affects planning in yet another way: knowing that another company has achieved some goal confirms the suspicion that the goal is reachable. Of course, this does not confirm that the course plotted to get there is feasible. Benchmarking can only show one that the right thing is being done, not that it is being done right.

10.3   Standard Processes

TQM depends on standard processes. You cannot get "from here to there" without a "here." Absent a standard process, measurements mean nothing. We can buy off-the-rack suits only because size designations imply a set of proportions. More basic than measurements, project control vanishes without concrete expectations of the results of effort. Standard processes are fundamental to quality systems. Moreover, processes cannot really be standard unless they are defined.

Process definition

Elsewhere we have written that standards can be defined explicitly in documentation or implicitly by the use of tools. The latter, of course, is the better, since it makes compliance with standards inescapable. Standards usually take the form of text, supplemented by graphic depiction of processes. With the document specifying the use of tools, all bases are covered.

The strategy for the CMM level 1 programming shop must include early definition of its process. At the very least, the definition should identify the discrete tasks followed for development and the functions responsible for their execution. The approach taken at General Electric Aerospace (now part of Martin-Marietta Corp.) requires that a process definition answer six questions:

1. What tasks comprise the process?
2. Who performs them?
3. When do they take place?
4. How are they implemented?

5. Does the definition stand up to a formal audit?

6. Does the definition support continuous process improvement?[8]

In answering the first question, care should be taken to go beyond the bare essentials of the task and include specification of ancillary work. For example, the description of the task that covers coding should include code reviews. We note, also, that in answering this question, one necessarily asks the corollary question, "how useful is the task as presently performed?" If the answer to the second question involves several discrete functions, as it certainly will in all but the smallest companies, it makes sense to define the process not monolithically, but in a set of sub-process definitions, tied together by a superordinate process definition. The answer to the third question can include task entrance criteria. For example, one does not start system tests until some specified person has attested to the satisfactory completion of integration tests, the configuration manager confirms all is well with the library, and so on. The answer to the fourth question is the one that constitutes the greatest part of a process definition. This is where technology most enters into the process. Paradigms, languages, tools and their use, methods, library control procedures—all must be specified so that people know exactly what to do and what is expected of them. The process definition should also include task exit criteria.

Whether one will have a formal audit, as conducted as part of a SCE for example, the fifth question implies that the authors of the process definition should stand back from their work and assess its quality. An independent, objective, assessment will be even more valuable. We do not mean to suggest that SQA perform the assessment. If there is an SQA group, its members should have participated in the definition of the process, leaving only the illusion of their objectivity. The last question is the one that we have touched upon a number of times: you cannot get from here to there if you don't know where here is. Moreover, to support continuous improvement, the process definition must specify the measurements that will be made, analysis of them, and their use.

Planning for change

Process definitions are engraved on computer disks, not stone. They will be changed, and frequently at that, as part of the process of continuous improvement. To accommodate change, process definitions should be under configuration control. But planning for change means more than a mechanism for document stability. Change comes from constant review and improvement, the substance of Sec. 10.2, and also the effect of external influences.

Contractual or marketplace obligations may require changes to the process definitions. Military contractors, for example, will be bound to make some changes when DOD-STD-2168A is eventually updated or superseded. Telecommunications suppliers need to change their processes to comply with the latest software requirements implied by certain of Bellcore's technical reports. To the extent possible, companies should attempt to learn of changes in external direction before they are published. Several avenues are available to get such information. For example, military contractors have learned much from software conferences sponsored by the NSIA Quality and Reliability Assurance Group, and telecommunications suppliers have had the opportunity to join Bellcore staffers in meetings on forthcoming requirements.

Another type of external influence is that of technology. For example, the company that plans GUIs for its next generation of products will have to find a way to interpret its use of function points for GUI, rather than transactional, input; or, alternatively, settle on an entirely different estimating procedure. The company planning to offer versions of its products for a new software platform will have to incorporate new system calls in its standard implementation techniques. (Yes. Standards are required even at that low a level.) The company proposing to provide modem-to-modem downloading of new releases will have to change its documented customer support procedures. And all of these technology influences are beyond those that attach to the use of new development technology.

Companies seldom get around to defining processes until they decide to do something about the process itself, upgrading methods, technology, and controls. For the company that has no documented process, the first cut may seem impossible simply because the process is changing even as attempts are made to capture it. But even for the company with a more mature software process, process definition continues to be an iterative procedure. Two ways to plan for inevitable (and desired) change are to:

1. appoint someone custodian of the process definition or of each of several sub-process definitions, and

2. establish one or more quality teams with responsibility for revising the definition(s).

Generality

Consider the company with three divisions generating software: OP, which develops and maintains operating systems, ENV for programming environments and stand-alone compilers, and APPL for applications programs. OP uses O-O for new systems, but most of the maintenance is on old systems of conventional procedural architectures. OP's new systems are programmed in C++, while most of the old systems are programmed in C with some assembly language thrown in. ENV uses conventional programming methods, but is heavy in GUIs. ENV uses C almost exclusively for new software, except that the LISP environment product is a combination of LISP and C. APPL uses a proprietary 4GL for all new products, but maintains old ones in a variety of languages.

All three divisions use independent test departments, independent configuration management groups, and beta testing, but only OP and ENV have SQA functions. APPL has software quality engineers, but they are integrated into programming teams. There are other differences, too, but the point should be clear at this point: it won't be easy to establish standard processes to cover the entire company. What is not clear is whether such standardization is something one would want to do.

Customer satisfaction is one reason for standardization. Customers should feel they are dealing with a company, not with a division that may get reorganized, as divisions often do, out of existence. Moreover, customers of products produced by more than one division prefer a single face for their supplier. The more products look and feel alike, the more they are supported in similar manner, the happier the customers. So, to the extent possible, standards on interfaces, user documentation, and customer support should be established. Oh yes. Also a policy having to do with customer satisfaction.

Company-wide standards also serve the purposes of senior management. Senior management needs to know that processes affecting configuration management in each division assure the integrity of the company's investment and potential for future business. This implies a commonality at one level or another. Perhaps the best that can be done is a policy statement such as "Configuration management policies and procedures shall be in place to..." We expect that companies can usually standardize configuration management processes at a lower level of abstraction than the policy statement. We see no need to have audit practices, archiving practices, reporting channels for configuration control managers, and the like differ from one division to another.

Similarly, one can find other processes that lend themselves to some level of standardization. Some obvious examples include employee training and education, recruitment practices, formation and empowerment of quality teams, beta test site selection and administration, the process of determining customer perceptions, product edition labeling, and certain measurements. Standardization of these aspects of software development and maintenance not only simplifies management but also smooths the transfer of staff from one division to another, permitting an efficient means of balancing the workload. The framework for process improvement can also be fairly common throughout a company. One way to handle diverse divisions, hinted at by the policy statement on configuration management, is to set company-wide policies that identify the processes requiring division definition and the minimum content of the definition standards.

Of course not every company is so large or diversified that it has an OP, ENV, and APPL division handling disparate product lines. (Some have a more complex situation. Look at IBM, with systems software for various hardware platforms, applications software of all kinds, a division to handle government contracts, and research labs.) The more common the three immediate aspects of process definition—task definition, the when and how of task performance, and task organizational responsibilities—the better. And there is always a level of abstraction at which one can find commonality.

Before concluding this discussion, let's look at its opposite number: commonality of standards among projects. It is hard to find an excuse for having two projects in the same product line working to different standards. This is a very visible symptom of process immaturity. It may be hard to find an excuse for different standards, but we can think of two. One valid reason for different standards of user interface and documentation arises when these standards must conform to those of diverse customers, a likely condition for an engineering or custom software firm. The other good reason for differences in standards among projects is that the methods or technology of one project are a departure from the defined norm. Section 10.2 addressed the problems of phasing in new processes and the use of them on pilot projects. However, even when a project deviates from the defined processes, it should do so under provisional standards; provisional, because the first use is always something of a revelation.

10.4 Summary

1. Companies need to perform self-assessments of their processes to ensure that quality remains the focus.

2. The Capability Maturity Model of the SEI provides a self-assessment methodology specific to software. Its use by other than military contractors requires some interpretation.

3. The Malcolm Baldrige National Quality Award provides a framework for self-assessment, but requires some interpretation when applied only to software organizations within companies not devoted to software products or services.

4. Business factors drive planned process changes, but strategies for change arise from self-assessments and analyses such as those discussed in the opening pages of Chap. 9.

5. Strategies often require early improvement of the system for software measurements.

6. Emerging technology exerts a major influence on planning strategies.

7. All staff should be brought into the planning process.

8. Benchmarking can often confirm the feasibility of goals.

9. Software processes definitions, which encompass task identification and delineation and group responsibilities, should be fashioned so that they can support continuous process improvement.

10. The frequent updating of process definitions recommends establishment of definition custodians supported by standing quality teams.

11. Uniform software processes cannot always be defined across the company, but there exists a level of abstraction at which every element needs to be and can be standardized.

References

1. Gruman, Galen. "Behind the SEI Process-Maturity Assessment," *IEEE Software*, September 1989, pp. 92-93.
2. Humphrey, Watts and Curtis, Bill. "Comments on 'A Critical Look'," *IEEE Software*, July 1991, pp. 42-46.
3. Baumert, John. "New SEI Maturity Model Targets Key Practices," *IEEE Software*, November 1991, pp.78-79.
4. Paulk, Curtis, Chrissis, *et al. Capability Maturity Model for Software, CMU/SEI-91-TR-24,* Software Engineering Institute/Carnegie Mellon University, Pittsburgh, August 1991.
5. Weber *et al. Key Practices of the Capability Maturity Model, CMU/SEI-91-TR-25,* Software Engineering Institute/Carnegie Mellon University, Pittsburgh, August 1991.
6. Bollinger, Terry and McGowan, Clement. "A Critical Look at Software Capability Evaluations," *IEEE Software*, July 1991, pp. 25-41.
7. *1992 Award Criteria*, National Institute of Standards and Technology, Gaithersburg, MD, 1993.
8. Henry, Joel and Blasewitz, Bob. "Process Definition: Theory and Reality," *IEEE Software*, November 1992, pp. 103-105.

11

Policies, Standards, and Quality Plans

We have stated that plans for software projects should include plans to ensure quality. As an historical aside, we note that in the proverbial fashion of putting carts before horses, software project quality plans were the earliest tangible artifacts of software quality processes. As we shall see, software quality requirements and plans for specific projects continue to command considerable attention in industry and government. Chapter 11 deals with the documentation of software quality processes as they are applied to individual projects.

Perhaps the most important tenet of this book is that software quality processes must be intertwined with development and maintenance processes. With the great diversity in the types of software developed and maintained and equal diversity in the technological and managerial approaches used, there can be no single set of development and maintenance standards or policies of managerial purpose. Accordingly, there can be no single standard for software quality plans. Nevertheless, even as Chap. 10 found a sufficiently abstract level to address the contents of standards for documenting development and maintenance processes, we can generically define the contents of software quality plans and the documents from which they derive, among which is a policy statement.

11.1 A Software Quality Policy

Ideally, a software quality policy should derive directly from the documentation of Senior Management's commitment to quality. Even in the absence of such documentation, however, we can identify the salient points of a software quality policy. The policy should:

1. Define software quality within the context of the organization's business or operations

2. Define the standards that govern software development, maintenance, and support

3. Stipulate responsibilities for quality—not just those of an SQA function, but everyone's

4. Identify the required set of project plans and stipulate, in general, the contents of quality plans

5. Specify the requirement for a formal process to ensure that software is qualified for release

6. Stipulate the need for a process of continuous evaluation and improvement of software quality

With the exception of the fourth item, we have discussed all of these points in preceding chapters. Let's see how GoodFolks Instruments Corp. incorporates the six items in a single policy statement:

> The quality of the software embedded in our products is paramount to the success of our company. In addition to satisfying specific technical requirements, our software must be reliable, maintainable, and constructed to minimize user hazard. [These are the aspects of quality most important to GoodFolks.] To this end, the Software Laboratory will maintain a set of documented standard practices to cover all work tasks that the laboratory is charged with. These standards will define all methods, tools, and responsibilities used in the development and maintenance of software. The standards are subject to review by the Office of the President or its delegate [do you think they might have had an SQA function in mind?] to ensure that quality informs all activities involved in the development and maintenance of software. The standards will include interfaces with the Customer Support Department, the Project Office (for configuration management), and the Quality Assurance Department. The standards will also include templates for individual project plans for new products or feature releases: software development plans, software configuration management plans, software test plans, and software quality plans.
>
> Consonant with the quality goals outlined above, Software Laboratory staff and their managers are responsible for establishing specific quality objectives for each project and ensuring that the objectives are met. The objectives for each project will be documented in its software quality plan. The plan will also cite the methods used to ensure adherence to all plans and to validate the achievement of stipulated quality objectives. In specific, software quality plans will identify:

- Measurements taken and responsibilities for their analysis and evaluation [larger projects than those of GoodFolks merit a separate measurements plan]
- Uses of trend analysis for maintaining control of projects
- Means of certifying or calibrating new software tools peculiar to the project
- In-process reviews
- All planned passive and active fault detection methods
- Means taken to ensure that tests are controlled as specified in the test plan
- Means taken to identify deviations from procedures specified in the configuration management plan
- The method of certifying that tasks are completed as planned and the means by which such certification can be used to provide management with visibility of project status
- Means by which the quality of the products and processes of software vendors will be assessed
- Means to ensure prompt analysis of problems reported by customers [GoodFolks doesn't absolve the project team of responsibility for the product once it is shipped]
- Means of ensuring that software vendors deliver products or services in compliance with contract stipulations
- Methods for ensuring that customer problems, product faults and discrepancies in adhering to the defined process are tracked and corrected, or otherwise closed
- Quality records required to be retained at the conclusion of the project—both for subsequent maintenance projects and for improving software processes
- Quality objectives for the project and criteria derived from them that must be met before the software is released
- Techniques used to ensure the qualification of the software for application in GoodFolks products, control of the product during the qualification process, and the approval steps taken to confirm qualification.
- Means for ensuring the attainment of objectives for the quality of customer support

All processes involved in the development and maintenance of software will be continuously reviewed by the departments responsible for the processes to the purpose of improving quality levels. As part of their review process, the departments will compare quality levels with those of selected competitors and appropriate benchmarks. Annually, as part of their business plans, the directors of each department will present to the Office of the President the results of their comparisons, a discussion of the process analyses undertaken during the year, the results of improvement projects undertaken during the year, and their plans for the coming year.

The GoodFolks people could have gotten more specific, but policies are the good, grey, documents that do not change from year to year. Policies articulate the long course that one follows. One might tack back and forth any number of times to make the course good, and each tack will have headings different from the last, but the course remains the same. Accordingly, GoodFolks leaves it to the standards—including project plan templates—to fill in the specifics. As we noted in Sec. 10.3, we expect standards to change with technology, contractual or marketplace obligations, and the results of the improvement process. But the long term-goal—a mature quality system—remains constant. In any case, we do not have to worry that the GoodFolks' software standards will fail to support the company's quality policy: the GoodFolks policy said that the Office of the President (or its delegate) could be counted on to review all standards.

Although GoodFolks is not involved in supplying products for which the marketplace establishes software standards, they stay abreast of published industry-wide standards, as well as the standards published by a professional society. Any ideas they can glean from these standards may be useful for their own purposes. We turn to such standards now.

11.2   Published Standards

The standards we summarize have been published by the DoD, Bellcore, the International Organization for Standardization (which we know as ISO), and the IEEE. The first, obviously, applies to military software, the second to telecommunications software, and the third and fourth are intended for any software. Table 11.1 lists the documents.

We should note that DOD-STD-2168[1] is a companion to DOD-STD-2167A,[2] which sets forth standards for development. That is, DOD-STD-2168 tracks the activities stipulated in the development standard.* In the sense that any software quality process should be specific to the development processes in place, a software quality plan gains by being specific to a software development plan. IEEE-Std 730.1[3] tracks not one, but a raft of IEEE standards governing software

---

*Absent DOD-STD-2167A, the military still reserves the right to impose DOD-STD-2168 on a contact.

TABLE 11.1 References from Four Sources

Software quality program or system requirements	Software Quality project plans	Software measurements
DOD-STD-2168 Military Standard: Software Quality Program	DI-QCIC-80572 Data Item Description: Software Quality Program Plan	
Bellcore TR-TSY-000179 Software Quality Program Generic Requirements (SQPR)		Bellcore TR-TSY-000929 Reliability and Quality Measurements for Telecommunications Systems (RQMS)
ISO 9000-3 Guidelines for the application of ISO 9001 to the development, supply, and maintenance of software		
	IEEE-Std 730.1-1989 Standard for Software Quality Plans	IEEE-Std 982.1-1988 Standard Dictionary of Measures to Produce Reliable Software IEEE-Std 982.2-1988 Guide for using above

development, most notably the standard on software verification and validation plans, IEEE-Std 1012.[4]

In the second column of Table 11.1, the data item description[5] ("DID" in DoD-speak) simply specifies the manner of documenting a software quality plan fashioned after DOD-STD-2168.

ISO 9000-3,[6] which at this writing has been released only as a draft, derives from ISO 9001, Quality System-Model for quality assurance in design/development, production, installation, and servicing.

Bellcore's SQPR[7] is the only one not closely tied to other documents. Bellcore does publish other documents that address software quality (e.g., one on software reliability and acceptance[8]), and all such documents are cross-referenced. However, SQPR presents all of Bellcore's views on software quality programs and their planning.

Quality planning

It is informative to compare the thrusts of the software quality programs and the plans referenced by Table 11.1. If we take Bellcore's TR-TSY-000179, the pair of DI-QCIC-80572 and DOD-STD-2168, ISO 9000-3, and IEEE-Std 730.1 and place them side by side, we have Table 11.2.

TABLE 11.2 Comparison of Software Quality Programs

Quality program or plan requirements	Bellcore SQPR	DOD-STD-2168 and DID	ISO 9000-3	IEEE-Std 730.1
Commitment to quality	strong		some	
Management review of quality program		strong	strong	strong
Process definition and documentation of standards	strong	strong[1]	strong	strong
Project planning	strong	strong[2]	strong	some
Reviews and audits	moderate	strong	strong	strong/some[4]
Evaluation of external specifications	some	strong	implied	strong[5]
Design evaluation	some	strong	moderate	strong[5]
Code evaluation	some	strong	moderate	strong[5]
Test	strong	strong	strong	moderate
Qualification	strong	strong	strong	some
Library control or evaluations of	strong	strong	strong	some
Change process or evaluations of process	strong	moderate	strong	some
Problem reporting	strong	during development	implied	some
Corrective action tracking	strong	strong	strong	strong
Delivery verification, inspection, or certification	strong	strong	some	moderate
On-site service	strong		strong	
Adequate programming environment	moderate	control of		some, indirectly
Risk management				some
Storage and handling	moderate	moderate	strong	strong
Product measurements	some		strong	strong on test metrics[6]
Measurements or evaluations of programming process	some	moderate	stong	post-mortem review
Analysis of measurements	strong		implied	
Management visibility/control	some	some, indirectly	some	some

Quality program or plan requirements	Bellcore SQPR	DOD-STD-2168 and DID	ISO 9000-3	IEEE-Std 730.1
Supplier selection and control of new software	some	strong on control	strong	strong
Control of off-the-shelf or reused software		strong		
Staff training			moderate	
Customer support	strong	moderate[3]	strong	manuals
Quality records	some	some	moderate	some

[1]Quality program, only.

[2]Quality program, only. However, companion DOD-2167A strong on other plans.

[3]To the extent of evaluation of deliverable elements of programming and test environments.

[4]*Strong* on formal reviews, *some* on in-process audits.

[5]By indirection. Standard calls for a report of verification and validation activities.

[6]Metrics such as branch coverage and requirements demonstration.

In Table 11.2 we have subjectively "scored" the requirement coverages as *strong, moderate,* and *some.* (In some cases, we have provided a narrower estimation.) Blanks mean that the requirement did not enter into the document or document pair. The judgments refer more to the relative emphasis of the requirement within the document(s) than an absolute sense of how thoroughly the requirements were satisfied. Also, scores less than *strong* do not necessarily mean that the authors of the documents thought the matter unimportant. For example, the DoD documents have little to say about on-site service or direct customer support, but such support is usually contracted for apart from system development. On the other hand, Bellcore's client-owners, the regional holding companies (RHCs) formed at the time of the 1984 AT&T divestiture, buy release after release of software updates for their major pieces of telecommunications equipment. Accordingly, they are much concerned with the standing relations between suppliers and customers.

As another example, the DoD largely views quality standards as applicable solely to the contracts at hand. New software releases (other than fixes) are likely to come about only as modifications of old software for the next generation of procurements. Accordingly, its requirements documents have little to say about the improvement of software processes in its quality standards.* Bellcore, however, expects suppliers to provide new telecommunications features (selective call rejection is a

---

*This is not to say that the DoD has no interest in the improvement of the software processes used by industry, as witnessed by the Software Engineering Institute and other DoD initiatives to support process improvement.

recent one) for installed equipment at regular intervals. Bellcore appears to take the position of having a vested interest in continuous quality improvement; hence the strong positions of SQPR on measurements and the programming process.

ISO 9000-3 is also directed to software developed under contract. Nevertheless, like SQPR, it takes a longer view of the improvement of software processes than does DOD-STD-2168. In the entire ISO 9000 series of documents, we find an underlying premise that mature quality systems are essential to smooth contractual relations. Interestingly, though focused on the producer, ISO 9000-3 cites certain responsibilities for the consumer, as in the preparation of a requirement's specification.

The original IEEE standard on software quality plans reflected in large measure an earlier generation of quality standards—the DoD's MIL-S-52779A and its look-alikes, the FAA's FAA-STD-018 and NATO's AQAP-13. Control and oversight then were seen as the primary functions that software quality programs could satisfy. The current version, IEEE Std 730.1, shows the influence of more recent DoD standards, especially DOD-STD-2167A and DOD-STD-2168. The emphasis on control and oversight of a documentation-driven programming process remains, but some attention is paid also to the underlying process and risk management (mentioned by 2167A, if not by 2168).

The most interesting conclusion that one can draw from Table 11.2 is in the number of requirements to which the diverse standards are, to one extent or another, congruent.* This, despite the great diversity of styles exhibited by the documents. These common requirements constitute the most general view of the topics that software quality programs need to address. None of the standards, by the bye, requires a separate software quality assurance organization, although all four state that software quality plans should identify who is responsible for fulfilling the various requirements of the plans. Note also that each of the standards, to one extent or another, addresses most of the elements of project quality plans cited in the GoodFolks policy statement.

Measurements

Of the documents having to do with quality planning, Bellcore's has the most to say about measurements. Yet, Bellcore also publishes TR-TSY-000929[9] (RQMS), which sets forth requirements for product measurements, most of which are made after product delivery. The

---

*Of course, we must recognize that the committee that drew up each of the standards did so after a review of all such standards published to date.

measurements reflect difficulties experienced by Bellcore's client-own- ers. RQMS covers more than the software embedded in telecommuni- cations systems. However, software enters into most of the document's measurements, and many are specific to software. Of those possibly involving or specific to software, a partial list includes:

System outages—number and duration per month

Installation problems—by month, percentage of systems that expe- rienced an abort during updating

Patches (a patch is any interim fix delivered between releases):

- Cumulative number of patches plotted against cumulative opera- tional time
- Percentage of defective patches per month
- By month, number of developed patches not deployed to all sites within two weeks

By severity level, cumulative problem reports plotted against cumu- lative operational time

Cumulative number of faults and unfixed faults found between the start of system test and final release

By severity level, cumulative problem reports plotted against cumu- lative operational time

Statistics on the time to respond to customer problems

By severity level, statistics on the time to develop and distribute fixes

All of these measurements require data segregated for each software release, and some of the measurements also require composite data. Although in many cases the form of presenting the measurements permits immediate insight, the RQMS document also requires suppli- ers to perform certain analyses of the measurements. Among these are root cause analysis, identification of frequently changed compo- nents/modules, identification of fault-prone components/modules (sev- eral criteria are suggested), and for critical elements, failure mode and effects analysis.

Bellcore has also published a provisional document on in-process quality metrics, IPQM.[10] After refinement, this document may even- tually be released as a firm set of requirements. A partial (and simpli- fied) list of the metrics that Bellcore may one day require includes:

- Estimates of software size made at several stages of development and at release.

- Code complexity by module and feature.
- Per feature, planned and actual labor hours each week.
- Planned and actual dates for the start and completion of features.
- Planned and actual completion weeks for development milestones.
- A stability metric based on the number of changes to development artifacts.
- A "churning" metric based on patch activity during the several stages of testing.
- By feature, percentage of test cases planned, executed, and passed.
- By feature, percentage of coverage attained by executed test cases and by passed test cases.
- Defect density per feature.
- Defects reported and detected during each stage of development. Also, a measure similar to the effectiveness of fault detection introduced in Sec. 7.2.
- Number and percentage of artifacts reviewed for each development stage.
- Per development stage, actual number of audits performed and the objective for the stage.

As we had warned, we have greatly simplified our presentation of the proposed Bellcore in-process metrics. For example, many require the reporting not only of actuals but of objectives, and some have equations for computing variances. But even as presented, it is evident that Bellcore is concerned that telecommunications suppliers get their arms around their software processes.

Table 11.1 listed measurement standards published by the IEEE, a dictionary of measures,[11] and a guide for their use.[12] These are not "requirements" documents, but an attempt to formulate measurements in a common language and use. Measurements in the documents apply to product or process or, in some cases, both. The measurements fall into 39 categories, most of which have been encountered in preceding pages of this book. For each category, the dictionary defines an application, the primitives that enter into the calculations, and the calculation (called *implementation*) itself. As an example, we take the measurement of *manhours per major defect detected*:

The dictionary says that the measurement applies to design and code inspections. The primitives for the measurement are:

T_1, the time spent by the inspection team in preparing for the inspection meeting.

T_2, the time spent by the inspection team during the meeting.

S_i, the number of major (i.e., nontrivial) defects detected during the ith inspection.

I, the total number of inspections to date.

The calculation is given as

$$M = \frac{\sum_{i}^{I} (T_1 + T_2)_i}{\sum_{i}^{I} S_i}$$

along with the advice that it should be used after approximately 8000 lines of detailed design or code have been inspected.

For our example, we selected a metric obvious to anyone who cares about the cost effectiveness of inspections. We did so to give the flavor of the IEEE standard without getting into the nitty-gritty of the measurement itself. Many of the measurements, however, offer heartier fare than our example and are well worth looking at.

11.3   Software Quality Project Plans

The GoodFolks policy on software quality (Sec. 11.1) stated the items that must be addressed by project plans for software quality. What's good enough for GoodFolks is good enough for us. Recursively, Good-Folks amplifies the list of items by telling its staff to find references for the items in the sections, up to 11.3, of this book. Accordingly, in Sec. 11.3 we discuss the preparation of project plans, rather than their content.

The GoodFolks company not only states requirements for the contents of project-specific quality plans, they have published an internal standard for the format of such plans. Before allowing its authors to get into responding to the specific quality plan requirements of the policy, the standard requires introductory paragraphs to identify:

- The project.
- The author(s) of record.
- The manager who approved the plan and the date of its release.
- The scope of the project (e.g., software Release 3.0 of the RICERCAR product, to support features Fugue and Canon).
- Other project plans by name and number with which the plan intersects. This is necessary because of differences of kind among GoodFolks projects. For example, a new release of an existing

product may reference the configuration management plan drawn for the initial release if that plan is still in effect, something we would not expect for the software of a new product.

- Specific quality objectives for the project.

The balance of the project quality plan addresses the items specified in the policy, each under a separate rubric (e.g., measurements, trend analyses, etc.). Before addressing these, let's look at the last of the introductory items.

Specific quality objectives derive from both the overall objectives of GoodFolks (recall: reliability, maintainability, safety) and the peculiarities of the project itself. Assume that the project—software release 3.0 for an existing product—will provide two new features: a graphic user interface and an interface to a new family of medical instruments. We might expect that the objectives would include such items as the following:

1. *Regression testing.* Test series SR00, SR10, and SR20 developed for earlier releases will be repeated with no change in archived results.

2. *Reliability of new features.* Ignoring aberrant output of no real consequence, new features will produce expected output over the full range of functions and input conditions with a failure intensity of no more than .001 failure/CPU hour. [The project quality plan will state the criteria for demonstrating or calculating that the objective has been achieved.]

3. *Safety of operation when coupled to Medproc instruments.* Prior to its release, demonstrations shall confirm the capability of the software to provide appropriate alarms and assume a fail-safe state for any of the failure modes of the Medproc instruments shown in Table QP1.

4. *User interface.* The user interface will use the same protocols and conventions as those of Megasoft Fenster 4.1. [Fenster 4.1 is the graphics operating system under which the product runs, although preceding releases of the product did not really have a graphics user interface of their own.] The resolution of any conflicting input will result in a fail-safe state. [Though these appear to be functional requirements, they are too vague to design to. They are really objectives.]

5. *General safety objectives.* The safety provisions of Release 2.0—operation with momentary power failure, operational modes in event of instrumentation failure, and calibration objectives—apply without change to release 3.0.

6. *Complexity.* The complexity of individual modules and inter-module coupling shall not exceed the lower bound of Table 5 of Standard Practice M101.4. Data tables shall not exceed 3 dimensions.

7. *General maintainability.* The provisions of release 2.0 regarding structure, documentation, and quality records apply also to release 3.0.

Finally, we get to the items that the policy statement requires quality plans to include. To simplify the preparation of the plan, as well as ensuring that all the items are accounted for, the information is entered into the computer using a context-sensitive editor as a template. The editor allows the preparer to jump arbitrarily from rubric to rubric. On selecting a new rubric from the master menu, the preparer is greeted by a sub-menu specific to the item. Typical of the sub-menu options are a laundry list of measurements, places to insert the name of the person(s) responsible, time limits (where promptness is relevant), and the like. At any time, the preparer can ask for a summary report of items left undone. Needless to say, the summary report will be used also by the manager approving the plan.

The editor also prompts the preparer on procedures. In responding to the query "Procedures to be followed," the user can write a new procedure, refer to a Software Quality Operating Procedure (found in the Software Quality Assurance Standards), or, using what amounts to a macro capability, request the canned procedure to be inserted in-line in the plan. Although insertion of canned procedures sounds like the most effective way of using them—self-sufficiency of documents is a virtue—a simple reference to a lengthy (and familiar) procedure helps to keep the length of the plan from growing to an intimidating size. Project quality plans, even those on disk, need to be of reasonable length if they are going to be used on a daily basis.

11.4 Reference Quality Documentation

The canned procedures referred to or incorporated as macros by a software quality assurance plan can constitute the most tangible embodiment of a company's software quality standards. Reused from project to project, such procedures require interpretation only to tailor them to project specifics—using such project terminology as component names and the like. Let's return once again to Sec. 11.1 and the elements of software quality plans found in the GoodFolks policy on quality, and see what standard procedures can apply to each of the elements. In doing so, we'll extend the meaning of *procedure* to include more narrative material, such as found in quality training courses. Accordingly, we'll refer to *quality training material* (QTM) and *standard operating procedures* (SOPs).

The first item cited in the policy relates to measurements, analysis, and evaluation. This is best handled by QTM. We should expect the author of the quality plan to import the material into the plan editor (or, at worst, word processor) and edit out anything not applicable to the subject project.

Specific trend analyses are also handled best by QTM. One can prepare SOPs, but only to the counter-productive purpose of regimenting management use of data.

The certification and calibration of software tools should follow a consistent pattern; hence, an SOP. The SOP should call for demonstration of "advertised" operational features, demonstration of the tool's capability to defend against user errors, recourse to help screens and user manuals, and compatibility with other tools. Certification and calibration should include both specific tests and a period of use by project programmers. The SOP should specify the types of tests and exercises, the preparation of a detailed memo (not unlike a supplementary user's manual), and the publication of a list of the programmers who had a hand in the testing and presumably can serve as an in-house resource in the use of the tool.

In-process reviews call for separate SOPs for each kind of review. Each SOP should list the generic artifacts reviewed, define the preparation necessary for the review, define the generic dramatis personae for the review, provide a checklist, and define the contents of the report (or minutes) of the review. The quality plan will state when the review is to take place, but the SOP says what the review comprises.

The list of passive and active fault detection methods can be drawn from that in a QTM. The QTM, in turn, has to provide specificity. For example, beyond simply listing functional testing as a method, the QTM should state how test cases are designed (including tool use), how one traces results back to external specifications, and the like. The quality plan states where functional testing will be used (e.g., unit test, thread integration after communication has been established, system test), but the QTM says what functional testing means in the language of the organization.

The control of tests is a matter for SOPs, one for each type of test employed by the company. Each SOP should refer to library control practices, authorization for on-the-spot changes, test reports, and similar matters. Even for unit tests under the control of the programmer who wrote the code, it may be necessary to remind the programmer of the form of the test report. If test audits are included in the process, the SOPs should also specify the circumstances for conducting an audit, the material audited, the responsibility for the audit, and the form of audit reports.

Deviation from planned configuration management procedures lends itself to an SOP specifying audits of library journals, configuration management records, build lists, and the like.

Certification of task completion also can be handled by one or more SOPs, perhaps a generic one with a subordinate section for each type of task. The minimum content would include a checklist for each type of task citing logged artifacts, reviews, tooled analyses, or whatever, and the responsibility for signing the completed checklist. Beyond the minimum, the SOP can specify the people to whom the completed checklist is distributed. Some companies have called for audits of the artifacts of development tasks as further evidence of their completion. If this is believed necessary (though scarcely in the spirit of TQM), the SOPs need to specify the particulars of the audits.

An SOP to cover software vendors is less useful than QTM outlining prudent measures to ensure that suppliers have their own quality process in place. Recall the discussion in Sec. 9.5 of partnering with suppliers. Developing a profitable relationship entails much more than simply applying contractual commitments. One can write SOPs on the preparation of procurement specifications and acceptance testing, but, given the diversity of acquired software, it will necessarily be thin on substance. Again, we call for QTM outlining the preparation of procurement specifications, responsibilities, types of testing, use of user manuals during tests, and assurance that the supplier can maintain and reproduce the product.

Ensuring the prompt analysis of customer problems is another matter for QTM, but an SOP can specify periodic publication of the status of open problems. Both the content of the report and its distribution should be outlined. The training material should include an operational flow of the handling of problems.

The tracking of corrections lends itself to an SOP calling for the entry of items into the log (as Sec. 9.1 pointed out, much of this can be automatic, but it does no harm to list the sources), periodic publication of the log, analysis of open items, reports on overdue closures, and other matters discussed in Chap. 9. All that remains for the quality plan is identification of the applicable sources and the people responsible for tracking.

An SOP for record and code retention, covering the period of and means of retention, should not be overlooked. At a certain level, one should be able to determine the type of records that can be retrieved for any past project executed by the organization. The quality plan need simply identify the records and code libraries that apply.

The development of quality criteria from quality objectives is too complex an issue for an SOP. However, QTM on the subject can be accompanied by an SOP calling for the responsibilities for sign-off (and possibly review) of the criteria. We would expect QTM not only to cite the potential sources for quality criteria (contract, technical specification, etc.), but also the methods for relating the likely content of such sources to specific measurable criteria. For example, for a given product line, QTM can establish fault count density, complexity, and code annotation criteria for given levels of maintainability—all, of course, based on the company's experience. Thus, a product with an expected life of 10 feature releases will be allowed no more than 0.2 known faults per KLOC, no more than...

Some of product qualification can be covered by SOP—signature authority, audits that need to be completed, control responsibility, and other administrative issues. However, more recondite matters—selection of a suitable regression test set, customer involvement, selection of beta test sites, and the like—can be intelligently handled only by QTM. Moreover, despite the guidance provided by QTM, the quality plan will have to be explicit on most of these matters.

An SOP can certainly specify the steps taken to ensure periodic backup of libraries, audits to check on security provisions, the backup of documentation, and the storage of material on all media at more than one site. It remains for the quality plan to specify who is responsible.

Finally, we have the means for ensuring that customer support quality objectives will be met. Considering the diversity of customers, one might expect that this can only be addressed by reference to QTM. However, a given company, or given department, has a limited scope of customers. It is quite possible to document SOPs to cover the analysis of customer data, evaluate statistics on the time it to takes to respond to customer calls for assistance, and similar responsive forms of customer support. Similarly, SOPs can establish checklists for precautions for the installation of new releases at customer sites, the dispatch of customer training kits, and other proactive forms of support. A quality plan need only specify which SOPs apply (often just a matter of looking at the contract) and assigning responsibility for execution and evaluation. Customer support is often given short shrift. Too bad. Long after the developers have done their thing, the customer is still looking for support, and ultimate customer satisfaction may be more a measure of quality support than quality product.

11.5   Summary

1. Software quality standards should derive from a high-level policy on software quality.

2. For a given project, software quality standards are given specificity by a software quality plan.

3. At the project level, useful views of software quality requirements, including the requirements for quality plans, have been published by the DoD, ISO, IEEE, and Bell Communications Research (Bellcore). These views have much in common.

4. Bellcore has also published requirements for measurements programs, and the IEEE has published a detailed reference covering many measurements.

5. Using common company standards as a reference, and helped by a context-sensitive editor, the drafting of software quality plans need not be a costly process.

6. Much of the content of software quality plans can be drawn from quality training material and standard operating procedures.

References

1. DOD-STD-2168, *Military Standard: Defense System Software Quality Program,* Department of Defense, Washington, DC, February 29, 1988.
2. DOD-STD-2167A, *Military Standard: Defense System Software Development,* Department of Defense, Washington, DC, February 29, 1988.
3. *IEEE Standard for Software Quality Plans,* IEEE Std 730.1-1989.
4. *IEEE Standard for Software Verification and Validation Plans,* ANSI/IEEE Std 1012-1986.
5. DI-QCIC-80572, *Software Quality Program Plan,* Department of Defense, Washington, DC, April 29, 1988.
6. *International Standard ISO 9000-3: Guidelines for the Application of ISO 9001 to the Development, Supply and Maintenance of Software,* ISO 9000- 3:1991(E), June 1991, available in the United States from the American National Standards Institute (ANSI).
7. *Software Quality Program Generic Requirements (SQPR),* Technical Reference TR-TSY-000179, Bellcore, Piscataway, NJ, July 1989.
8. *Software Reliability and Quality Acceptance Criteria (SRQAC),* Technical Reference TR-TSY-000282, Bellcore, Piscataway, NJ, December 1986.
9. *Reliability and Quality Measurements for Telecommunications Systems (RQMS),* Technical Reference TR-TSY-000929, Bellcore, Piscataway, NJ, June 1990.
10. *In-Process Quality Metrics (IPQM) Framework Generic Requirements,* Framework Technical Advisory FA-NWT-001315, Bellcore, Piscataway, NJ, September 1992.
11. *IEEE Standard Dictionary of Measures to Produce Reliable Software,* IEEE Std 982.1-1989.
12. *IEEE Guide to the Use of Standard Measures to Produce Reliable Software,* IEEE Std 982.2-1989.

Measures of Goodness

Part

5

Measures of Goodness

12

Predicting and Estimating Reliability

No attribute of software quality has commanded as much attention as has the degree to which it can perform its intended function. We label this attribute *reliability*. Until a new operating system is fixed so that it no longer causes disk read-write heads to crash against the mechanical stops, its users think of the software as being unreliable. The airplane pilot who discovers that the recently installed (and software-driven) anti-collision system flashes so many false alarms that he ignores true warnings will regard the system as unreliable. While we can argue that some cases of unreliable performance arise from the use of software in a manner different from that intended—as when ignoring the specifications for the anti-collision system that warn it should be disabled during gross maneuvers—nearly all cases of unreliability can be traced to faults embedded in the software. For the purposes of this chapter, an instance of unreliability (read *failure*) is the direct result of one or more faults.

As with most things, we know more about the reliability of software when we can put numbers to it. There is nothing wrong with speaking of a product's reliability as being "good," "adequate," "poor," or "disastrous." But there is much right in being able to say that it has a calculated reliability of .0000314 failures per hour. Or that we shall have to test for another 130 hours before we can achieve a goal of .0000314 failures per hour. Or that we have 80 percent confidence that the reliability is no worse than .0000314 failures per hour. The later sections of this chapter deal with the techniques of assigning such numbers to computer programs while in test and after release. Before that, however, we deal with the prediction of reliability—or at least fault density—of software not yet in test. Such prediction serves two purposes: it provides early warning of potential problems, and it helps to estimate the extent to which testing will be slowed by debugging.

12.1   Modeling with Knowledge of the Code

Several techniques have been used to draw upon the properties of code to predict its failure incidence. In general, these predictive techniques offer less confidence than the estimations that derive from actual execution. However, the techniques are all that are available before testing can start. We begin by describing two measurement models without regard to their use in predicting faults or failure incidence.

Cyclomatic complexity model

Section 5.4 introduced the McCabe Cyclomatic Complexity Model, arguably the most popular of several models that attempt to quantify complexity. It will serve as an example of the prediction by complexity. First, a brief description of the model.

The Cyclomatic model couches the concept of complexity entirely within the decision structure of a program. With its roots in classical graph theory, the model has considerable intuitive appeal. Moreover, results seem to correlate well with anecdotal experience. The model that represents complexity is expressed by the simple equation

$$V(G) = e - n + 2p$$

where $V(G)$ = the cyclomatic number of classical graph theory, and, as used here, is the measure of complexity

e = the number of edges—that is, directed paths between nodes—in the program

n = the number of vertices, or processing nodes

p = the number of connected components

To illustrate the model, consider Fig. 12.1,[1] the directed graph of a program of only 36 statements. (The numbers on the drawing refer to the nodes between branch points.) With 9 vertices, 14 edges, and 1 component, its $V(G) = 14 - 9 + 2 = 7$.

Assume that a program about to be tested comprises m procedures, or connected components. To form the gross complexity measure, we simply sum each of the m $V(G)$ as calculated. Alternatively, we drop the 2p term of the calculation for each and form the gross complexity from:

$$V(G) = \Sigma_{i=1}^{m} V_i(G) + 2m$$

$$V_i(G) = e_i - n_i$$

The two methods are equivalent. As Chap. 8 noted, various tools automate the measurement.

Halstead's Software Science

In his *Software Science*,[2] Maurice Halstead proposed measures of software size that he postulated had more significance than the common LOC or NCSS. The core of the family of these programming yardsticks is based on four variables:

1. n_1 = number of unique operators in a program
2. n_2 = number of unique operands in a program

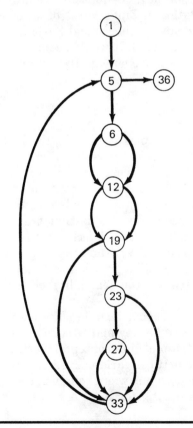

Figure 12.1   Directed graph of a small program.

3. N_1 = total count of the use of all operators

4. N_2 = total count of the occurrences of all operands

From these, the *vocabulary* of the program is defined to be

$$n = n_1 + n_2$$

The *length* is defined as $N = N_1 + N_2$. The *volume* is defined as $V = N \log_2 n$

Halstead also goes on to derive other measures, but they are based on the squishy ground of language levels and the rate at which programmers can make mental discriminations. To the critical observer, they seem to be as much the product of divination as of technical causality. The length and volume, however, have at least intuitive appeal as size measures. Halstead also gives an alternative formula for estimating length: $N = n_1\log_2 n_1 + n_2\log_2 n_2$.

Although Halstead offers no derivation of this equation, Laemmel and Shooman[3] show that their translation of Zipf's laws* of natural language into computer programs provides a theoretical basis from which this alternative form of N can be derived. It would seem, then, that the basic Halstead measures have a more substantive meaning than intuition alone can provide.

Estimating faults from structure

The cyclomatic complexity model, other complexity models, the Halstead measures (equated by some with complexity, rather than size) and other structural properties have all been the subject of regression studies to attempt to predict either the number of faults or the number of failures that will be found in testing. The results have been inconsistent at best. We expect the chief reason for this is that studies connecting structural properties and their effect on defects or failures have an inherent bias, reflecting the type of software and the programming environment. Nevertheless, one can use regression techniques applicable to local conditions to determine the feasibility of such prediction. More on this, shortly.

Two early examples of the use of regression techniques received much interest and comment. The study of Motley and Brooks[4] found that software size alone was a good predictor of fault content. In a study at about the same time using nine structural variables, Lipow and Thayer found that the number of branches alone was a reliable predictor of the faults that would be found during testing.[5] A number of

---

*Laws having to do with the statistical occurrences of words in natural languages.

studies based on multiple regression have resulted in more conflicting conclusions. Some of these have gone beyond looking at structural properties to look at development history. One study funded by the Air Force proposed a regression model including pages of design documentation, labor-months spent in preliminary design, and the like. A 1989 study published in an IEEE journal concluded that one could predict the number of faults using only three variables: programmer skill (measured in years of experience), the volume of design documentation, and the number of pages of problem reports written against design specifications. Such regression models have value for identifying areas of software engineering requiring close attention, but this is a far cry from using the models to make management decisions affecting the intensity or duration of testing.

As a practical matter, we suggest one look through the history of at least 10 past projects, using several measures in turn, and attempt to correlate the measures with either fault rates or initial failure rates. Try a complexity measure, Halstead volume, NCSS, and the total number of branches. Use linear regression analysis to form an equation $F(x) = ax + b$, where x is the measure and $F(x)$ the observed fault count or initial failure rate. Plot the regression line, as in Fig. 12.2. If there are no outliers, one has a predictor useful in one's own programming environment. If not, at least something has been learned.

The likelihood is that NCSS or another measure of size will turn out as good a predictor as any other. Still, if the suggested experiment indicates that a different measurement proves more reliable as a predictor, it is worth using.

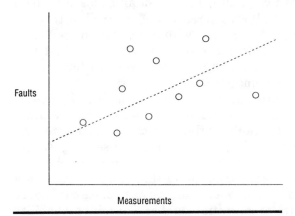

Figure 12.2 Faults as a function of a structural measurement.

12.2 Modeling with Seeded Faults

Section 7.4 suggested the use of *seeding* to determine test sufficiency. The section also suggested a technique to test the presumption of seed randomness. If the distribution of seeds does, indeed, appear random, we can go a step further and attempt to quantify the probability that a given percentage of the faults has been detected and removed.

Quantification, however, raises another problem with seeding. For obvious reasons, seeds represent simple faults, not the full range of faults that one is likely to find. Typical seeds reverse the sense of a relational (e.g., change <to>) or arithmetic operation (e.g., change + to −), change the value of an indexing constant (e.g., change 2 to 3), change a postfix operator to a prefix (e.g., in C code change n++ to ++n), and similar simple alterations affecting but one line of code. Such faults surely are among those unwittingly implanted in code, but the range of true faults also includes those ranging over several lines of code, recursive calls with an improper number of arguments, failure to correctly handle end-of-file flags, and other comparatively subtle defects. We also have code extending over several pages that reflects incorrect design decisions. And then we have error traps neither designed nor coded. The problem of matching seed complexity to that of true faults has been a major deterrent to the use of fault seeding. Many software engineers have said that seeding simply does not work, never has, and never will. Our own experience is more promising.

Short of embedding seeds of varying complexity, a solution not only time-consuming but likely to result in new bugs inserted in the process of correcting seeded faults, one has to temper faith in the results of seeding models with the sanity test proposed in Sec. 7.4. Recalling the test, after many bugs have been found, for each batch of detected faults we calculate a ratio R involving both the sum of all exposed faults b and those identified as seeds. If we can reasonably pass a line through the scatter diagram of (R_i, b_i) pairs, say with a correlation coefficient of .95 or higher, we dismiss randomness as a concern. Similarly, if with less conviction, if we find the ratios consistent we can temper our concern about the effects of unmatched bug complexity.

Let's assume that the scatter diagram proves a success. We should like now to place numbers on the confidence that we have an accurate estimate of the number of true faults in the program at the time testing started. Expanding on Harlan Mills' original work in seeding, Duran and Wiorkowski[6] published a metric to provide that confidence.

Assuming that the number of true faults that were detected is a subset of the starting number, the metric allows us to place confidence limits on the maximum size of the initial number. The joint probability of finding exactly a of A seeds and n of N true bugs is found from

$$q(a, n, A, N) = \frac{\binom{A}{a}\binom{N}{n}}{\binom{A+N}{a+n}}$$

Using the conventional reliability symbol, we define α as the risk of rejecting a true hypothesis, and compute the largest N such that

$$\sum_{k=0}^{n} q(a, k, A, N) > \alpha$$

If we think of this N as N_{max}, the procedure yields a confidence of $100(1-\alpha)$ that the true value of N falls somewhere within the inclusive limits of n and N_{max}. For example, if we establish an α of .05 and find that the corresponding N_{max} is 894, we can say that we are 95 percent confident that there were no more than 894 faults *ab initio*.

Of course, we remain at the mercy of seeding randomness and equivalence in the complexity of seeds and true faults. If successive batches of captured faults do not provide the necessary confidence that our seeds will be fruitful, we can forget the whole thing.

We might note that the metric of Duran and Wiorkowski is an example of *maximum likelihood estimation* or MLE. The use of MLE is a common practice of reliability engineering, and since we shall see more use of it in Sec. 12.3, we need to define it. For the purpose of definition, we consider the case of estimation of a single parameter. Given a random sample $x_1 \ldots x_n$ from a population whose probability distribution function (abbreviated "pdf") is $f(x,\theta)$, you seek an estimator Θ for the parameter θ. The *likelihood function of the sample*, defined as

$$L(x_1 \ldots x_n; \theta) = f(x_1; \theta) \ldots f(x_n; \theta)$$

is the *a priori* probability of obtaining the x_i that constitute the observed sample. MLE then resolves to the determination of that θ that maximizes L.

12.3 Modeling the Reliability of the Software Black Box

We use the term *black box* to reinforce the sense that the models in question are based solely on the performance of the program; that is, without reference to its structure. The models we describe—actually reliability growth models—assume that the expectation that the complex stochastic process from which failures arise can be described with a (necessarily) limited set of descriptors derived from performance alone. The models look at macroscopic failure parameters (e.g., number of test failures in a given day of testing), with each model founded on a set of premises purported to predicate the failure history. Common to all the models is the one premise that software failures can be described by a probability distribution. We have, then, models of a number of distinct types, each model representing diverse assumptions of fault modality, fault distribution, and the test and debug environment.

As an example of the distinctions among the various models, many assume a one-to-one correspondence between software faults and software failures. Others are more realistic. Experience has shown that from time to time a given fault can cause two quite different failures in the same run. Experience has also shown that some failures result from the concerted mischief of two independent faults. As another example of model differences, some require that the fault(s) causing a failure be removed before further testing takes place. Other models, while recognizing that few failures prevent further testing until a fix is in place, allow for the more common regimen in which testing continues to the extent possible while other programmers work on fixing past problems.

Many of the reliability growth models assume that software failures are Poisson distributed. Like the more widely known normal distribution, the Poisson is an approximation, given a large number of trials, to the canonical binomial probability distribution—the one used to determine the probability of rolling craps given 20 throws of the dice. If the probability of a specific outcome for a single trial is low and the number of trials is large, the Poisson closely approximates the binomial distribution. Poisson processes show up in many places. The loading of telephone trunk lines is Poisson distributed in time, as is the incidence of BMWs passing through a given toll booth.

Time enters into the input of all reliability growth models. Time can be execution time, calendar time, either, or both. Nevertheless, since only execution time reflects actual exposure to the hazard presented by software faults, we cannot expect useful results if execution time is not used. Linked to time, failures can be individual (a failure occurred at 3:17 on April 21, or a failure occurred 2.1 hours after the previous failure on April 21) or grouped (11 failures were experienced during 4 hours of execution on April 21). It all depends on the model. Other input may take the form of *ab initio* estimates (perhaps derived as in Sec. 12.1) of the initial number of faults in the program, debugging times, estimated rate of generating new faults, or other aspects of the testing-debugging or operational environment. Possible outputs are also diverse: the initial number of faults, the pdf for failures, failure rates, amount of time required to decrease the fault count to some arbitrary number, mean-time-to-failure (MTTF), and the like.

That an abstraction of the failure process of a program in a given test milieu can produce numeric results is not quite the same as proving the statistical validity of the results. Reliability models have been used for many years in the material world where there are random physical or biological processes (molecular migration, the feeding habits of termites, etc.) that in the aggregate govern observed failure phenomena. There are also systems of so great a number of independent parts, each subject to failure from latent defects or stress, that they too fail in accordance with well-behaved statistical patterns. The great number of factors that influence the introduction of software faults suggest that software, also, can be modeled similar to the way we model the material world. However, software failure results not from the influences on software faults but from the faults themselves. At the time we are most interested in the results of software reliability models—when we are ready to think about shipping product or estimating its performance in the hands of users—we should have a greatly reduced fault population. We suggest that care be taken in using any model results if they appear inconsistent between batches of failures.

We are also concerned about using mean-time-to-failure (MTTF). Statistical frequency distributions are one thing, single point statistics another. It is a common practice to predict the reliability of a piece of equipment on the basis of the MTTFs of the thousands of components plugged into it. Although we have never seen it done, perhaps the reliability of a large software system can be predicted from the MTTFs of the many individual programs that it comprises. In any case, beware attaching too much significance to calculations of a single software MTTF.

With these caveats, we are ready to look at representative models. To give the flavor of modeling, we shall start with models of historical significance, without regard to the amount of their use then or now.

Jelinski-Moranda model

This model, which the authors called the de-eutrophication model[7] because it estimates reliability during the period in which software is cleansed (of bugs, presumably, rather than of algae and water lilies) requires that each bug be removed as soon as it is detected. In common with most models of the early 1970s, the model assumes that the failure rate $\lambda(t)$—also called *hazard rate* $z(t)$—is proportional to the remaining number of defects, and that all bugs in the program are equally likely to cause a failure in the testing environment. The model also assumes that no new bugs are introduced during the debugging period.

For this, as well as other models, we need to define some terms derived from probability theory:

- Reliability, $R(t) = P$ (no failures in interval 0 to t)
- Cumulative distribution function of failures (cdf), $F(t) = 1 - R(t)$
- Frequency, or probability density function (pdf),

$$f(t) = \frac{dF(t)}{dt}$$

And more rigorously, we define the failure rate λ (t) to be the probability density function of time to failure, given the fact that failure did not occur prior to t. The condition on prior failure distinguishes λ (t) from $f(t)$.

From these,

$$\lambda\ (t) = \frac{f\ (t)}{R\ (t)} = -\frac{1}{R\ (t)} \frac{dR(t)}{dt}$$

The Jelinski-Moranda model defines the failure rate, constant between the $(i - 1)$st and ith failures as λ $(t) = \phi\ [N - (i - 1)]$, where N is the initial number of faults and ϕ is a proportionality constant. Both N and ϕ must be calculated (estimated).

The reliability function follows as:

$$R(t_i) = \exp\ [-\phi\ (N - n)t_i]$$

where t_i = elapsed time between $(i - 1)$st and ith failures
n = number of defects removed by $(i - 1)$st interval.

Recasting the reliability function in terms of the classic $R(t) = e^{-at}$, wherein MTTF is defined as $1/a$, we derive

$$MTTF = \frac{1}{\varphi\ (N - n)}$$

The historical significance of the model can be appreciated when we observe that its basic premises underlie many of the models since developed. Similarly, the contemporaneous Shooman Exponential Model,[8,9] which differs more in expression than in the postulation of software reliability growth, has given rise to a family of other models.

Returning to the basic Jelinski-Moranda model, N and ϕ can be estimated by MLE, using the following equations:

$$\sum_{i=1}^{n} \frac{1}{\hat{N} - (i-1)} = \frac{n}{\hat{N} - \frac{1}{T} \sum_{i=1}^{n} (i-1) X_i}$$

$$\varphi = \frac{n}{\hat{N}T - \sum_{i=1}^{n} (i-1) x_i}$$

where x_i are the elapsed times between successive failures and T = the sum of all the x_i through the nth interval.

It seems reasonable to assume that the first batches of bugs found in testing tend to be located in the more frequently traversed processing paths, thereby having greater vulnerability to exposure. For those who quarrel with the assumption that faults found late in testing have as great a likelihood of detection as those found early, the geometric de-eutrophication model[10] may be more intuitively satisfying. Figure 12.3 shows the difference between the basic model and the geometric model. To reflect the geometric progression, the failure rate for the ith interval is defined as $\lambda(t) = Dk^{i-1}$. D and k, the initial failure rate and failure rate step ratio, are calculated using MLE.

Goel-Okumoto nonhomogeneous Poisson process model (NHPP)

If the characteristics of the probability distributions that comprise a process are stationary, the process is considered *homogenous*. If they vary in time, it is *nonhomogenous*. Most of the models published in recent years have described nonhomogeneous Poisson processes, but the first to which the word *nonhomogeneous* was (later) applied was that published by Goel and Okumoto.[11,12]

The time before the ith failure is assumed dependent on the time to the $(i - 1)$st fault. The number of failures in nonoverlapped testing intervals are assumed independent of each other. That is, given the intervals $t_1 \dots t_n$, the failure counts $N(t_1)$, $[N(t_2) - N(t_1)]$,... $[N(t_n) - N(t_{n-1})]$ are statistically independent, where $N(t_i)$ is the cumulative number of failures to time t_i. Defining $m(t)$ as the cumulative number of failures (the mean value of the NHPP) and a as its limit (the mean of the distribution of $N(t)$ as $t \to \infty$), the model posits the intensity function

$$\lambda(t) = abe^{-bt}$$

where b is a proportionality constant.

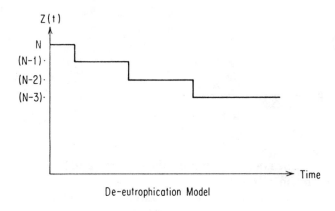

De-eutrophication Model

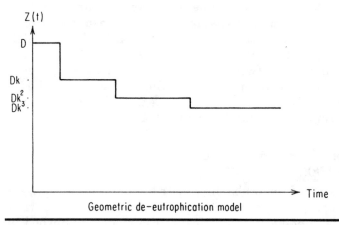

Geometric de-eutrophication model

Figure 12.3 De-eutrophication model (upper part of figure); geometric de-eutrophication model (lower part of figure).

Short of the limit, the mean value function is found from

$$m(t) = a[1 - \exp(-bt)]$$

For $t \geq 0$, $N(t)$ is Poisson distributed with the statistically expected value of $E\{N(t)\} = m(t)$, and, in general,

$$P[N(t) = n] = \frac{[m(t)]^n}{n!} e^{-m(t)} \quad n = 0, 1, 2, \dots$$

If n defects have been found by t, the model yields, as the conditional distribution of $N'(t)$ (the number of faults remaining in the system at time t) and its expectation,

$$P[N'\ (t)\ =\ x \mid N\ (t) = n]\ =\ \frac{a^{x+n}}{(x+n)\ !}$$

$$E[N'\ (t) \mid N\ (t) = n] = a - n$$

We also have the distribution of $N(\infty)$:

$$P[N(\infty) \to n]\ =\ \frac{a^n e^{-a}}{n!}$$

which recalls the earlier definition of a as the mean of the distribution of $N(t)$ as $t \to \infty$.

Finally, the conditional reliability for the next failure occurring at t, given that the last was detected at time s,

$$R\ (t) \mid s) = \exp\ [-a\ (e^{-bs} - e^{-b(s\ +\ t)})]$$

Note that the reliability is not an express function of the number of bugs found (although that number enters into the estimation of a and b). This should find favor with those who may find it difficult to accept the notion that the number of discovered or remaining faults is the direct determinant of the reliability of software.

Littlewood model

Bev Littlewood has authored or co-authored several software reliability models. The early Littlewood-Verrall model[13] permitted the failure rate to decrease between failures, reinforcing the intuitive feeling that the longer a program performs successfully, the more trustworthy it is. This characteristic is exhibited also by the model known variously as the Differential Debugging Model, [14] the Stochastic Reliability Growth Model,[15] and simply as the Littlewood Model. The Goel-Okumoto NHPP model also exhibited continuous improvement, but the Littlewood Model differs from the NHPP in a fundamental way: the former is a Bayesian model—that is, it assumes the parameters of the model to be random variables whose estimation will improve with each new round of input data. We briefly discuss it as an example of Bayesian models.

The model accepts the premise that each fault presents its own hazard without assuming any specific relation between a fault's failure rate and the time, relative to the start of testing, the fault caused a failure. Each fault has its own failure rate ϕ_j. Given that there were N initial faults of which i have been removed, the composite failure rate of the program is

$$\lambda = \phi_1 + \phi_2 + \ldots + \phi_{N\ -\ i}$$

The unknown ϕ_j are treated as a set of random variables Φ_j, each member having its own pdf. That λ is a function of the remaining defects recalls a fundamental premise of the Jelinski-Moranda model. Indeed, the Littlewood model may be viewed as a generalization of the Jelinski-Moranda.

The occurrence rates are given by a Gamma distribution (common to most Bayesian models). The pdf of failure at arbitrary time t is modeled as a function of the cumulative execution time during which faults have thus far been eliminated, and also of N, α, and β, the last two being parameters that shape the gamma distribution. N, α, and β are estimated from the historical data. Although the model has received much comment, arguably because of the elegance of its concept, the breadth of its application has suffered from the difficulty of solving for the parameters. The dotted line of Fig. 12.4 represents the failure rate of the model. As we noted earlier, with uneventful performance the hazard rate between failures continuously drops as intuition dictates. We note, however, that an alternative intuition might demand that when a failure occurs one loses the faith, as indicated by the solid line.

A hatful of other models

Thus far, we have seen only exponential decreases in failure rate. Models have been proposed, and used, that exhibit other shapes, such as:

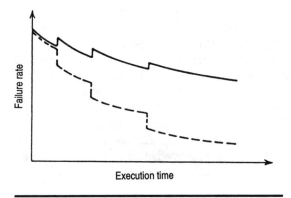

Figure 12.4

- The characteristic Rayleigh distribution of the Schick-Wolverton model.[16]

- The S shape of the Gompertz Distribution[17] (named after the nineteenth-century actuary concerned with predicting the survival rates of males of a given age).

- The serpentine shapes of hyper-geometric distributions as proposed by Mills (based on seed recapture) in an unpublished work later summarized by Schick and Wolverton,[16] and more recently (without regard to seeding) by staff of Tokyo Institute of Technology.[18]

Assumptions about faults and the testing environment have given rise to many variations, some of historic interest only, of the basic models. The rate of generating new faults and the rate of correcting faults both entered into the Shooman-Natajaran model.[19] The Goel-Okumoto Imperfect Debugging model[20] recognized that fixes do not always work. The Compound-Poisson Software Reliability Model[21] accounts for the clustering of software failures.

Every year sees another batch of models published, all attempting to come closer to the actual phenomena of software failure during testing. No model seems to have received as much attention as the Musa and Musa-Okumoto models originally published in 1984 and in book form in 1987.[22] An outgrowth of the early—and much remarked—Musa Execution Time Model,[23] the models account for both execution time and calendar time. Unlike most of the reliability growth models, the M and M-O models (as we shall call them for the sake of brevity) have been exposed to several independent validation exercises, especially the former. But the primary reason for the models' relative popularity may be that within the context of both calendar time and execution time they incorporate features of both the Jelinski-Moranda and Goel-Okumoto models—two of the more highly regarded historical models—without getting overly complex. Indeed, like the McCabe Cyclomatic Complexity Model, one of the models' most attractive features is their simplicity. Measured by use and independent validation, the M and M-O models are the most successful to date of the reliability growth models, and we go into them to a greater level of detail than other models.

12.4   The Musa and Musa-Okumoto Models

When taken as a pair, the two models are also referred to as the basic model and the logarithmic Poisson model. The difference between the two is shown in Fig. 12.5 where the Musa (basic) Model is represented by a solid line and the Musa-Okumoto (logarithmic Poisson) model by a dashed line. Each of the models has both an execution time compo-

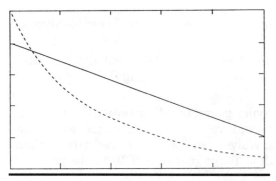

Figure 12.5 Musa basic and Musa-Okumoto logarithmic Poisson models.

nent and a calendar time component. Since programs only fail when they are executed, the units of time that elapse when programs are executed are the units of time during which faults are a hazard. Hence, changes in hazard rate should be couched in execution time. Calendar time, however, is a function of the allocation of people and (in some testing environments) machines. These resources are a function of calendar time, which in the M and M-O models is related to execution time. We start with the execution time component.

Execution time component

The failure intensity for the basic model is defined as

$$\lambda'(\mu) \; = \; \lambda_0[1 - \frac{\mu}{\nu_0}]$$

λ_0 is the failure intensity that had existed at the start of execution, while μ is the average (expected) number of failures up to a given point in time. Given infinite time, ν_0 failures would occur.

For the logarithmic Poisson model, the failure intensity is defined as

$$\lambda\,(\mu) = \lambda_0 \exp\,(-\theta\mu)$$

where θ, the relative change of failure intensity with failure experience, is referred to as *the failure intensity decay parameter.*

The use of either model entails estimating the model's parameters; λ_0 and ν_0 for the basic model, and λ_0 and θ for the logarithmic Poisson model. If an initial set of parameters can be arrived at, MLE can subsequently be used to update them with actual test experience. For the basic model, one can reckon the initial set either by predicting the fault content (as in Sec. 12.1), backtracking from seeding experience (Sec. 12.2), or simply looking at the fault history of previous projects for similar software—often the last release of the same product. Given a reckoned number of faults, and with the use of a factor to account for ratio of faults to failures, Musa *et al.*[24] provide a method for determining λ_0 and v_0. These are later refined by MLE. For the logarithmic Poisson model, no predictive technique for assigning θ had been devised as of this writing, leaving θ to be estimated by MLE applied to test data.

Given estimates of the parameters, the expected number of failures experienced at some time τ in the future is given by

$$\mu\,(\tau) = v_0 \left[1 - \exp\left(-\frac{\lambda_0}{\mu_0}\,\tau \right) \right] \qquad \text{for the basic model}$$

$$\mu\,(\tau) \;=\; \frac{1}{\theta}\ln\,(\lambda_0\theta\,\tau + 1) \qquad \text{for the logarithmic Poisson model}$$

Calendar time component

The calendar time component converts execution time to calendar time, taking into account resources needed for test activities, resources available, and the extent to which available resources can be utilized (i.e., not subject to bottlenecks). We define*

C_r as the usage rate of resources per hour of CPU time

F_r as the usage rate of resources per failure

Q_r as the quantity of each resource available

U_r as the utilization factor of the rth resource

The resources in question are those of test staff, debugging (correction) staff, and computer time. A premise of the model is that the amount of a resource actually consumed, χ_r, is linearly proportional to execution time τ and mean failures μ experienced:

$$\chi_r = C_r\tau + F_r\mu$$

---

*The following symbols, selected for mnemonic purposes, differ from those used by Musa et al. in Refs. 23 and 24.

Recalling that failure rate is the rate of change of μ, we can differentiate the equation to form

$$\frac{d\chi_r}{d\tau} = C_r + F_r\lambda$$

As we would expect, since λ decreases with testing, we see the rate at which resources are consumed per hour of execution time asymptotically approach the usage rate of the resource per CPU hour. For either model, the connection between instantaneous calendar time t and execution time τ for any of the limiting resources is given by

$$Time\ ratio = \frac{dt}{d\tau} = \frac{C_r + F_r\lambda}{Q_r U_r}$$

and is applied individually for each of the limiting resources.

At any one time, the maximum of the three time ratios (one each for test staff, debug staff, and computer time) determines the calendar time expenditure rate.

Estimating the parameters for the calendar time component requires project planning input, historical data, and a good understanding of one's own test and debug process, all of which are covered in Ref. 24.

As an example of how one might use both components, let's assume that we have been testing for many weeks and arrived at a fairly respectable failure rate, but one still in excess of our qualification criterion. From the execution time component (either model) we learn the additional execution time required to remove enough faults to achieve the failure intensity we have stipulated for product qualification. At this point, with the failure rate fairly low, the only resource limitation is machine time. We compute the time-ratio for the CPU resource, multiply it by the additional execution time, and learn that we can expect to ship product by the scheduled Christmas shutdown.

12.5   A Bit of Perspective

Let's not kid ourselves. A reliability growth model may tell us that we should be ready to ship in mid-July, but we're not going to schedule our summer vacation on that basis alone. Models are aids to making management decisions; they do not predicate decisions. Certainly, the longer one uses a model with success the more one trusts it. (Does that sound familiar? Recall the discussion of the Littlewood model.) And the more we can quantify expectations of the software process, the better will be our decisions. Still, many factors enter into decisions that affect customer/user satisfaction, and reliability growth models should not be used as a deus ex machina for relieving managers of responsibility.

We need to take special care not to rely entirely on models for achieving systems of extremely high reliability. As the failure rate asymptotically approaches the objective (as in Fig. 12.6) the time for the next failure gets longer and longer. For a system of extraordinary reliability, the asymptote is close to zero. Let us assume that we require a failure rate better than 10^{-11} per hour. Taking the basic Musa model, without regard for calendar time limitations, we have

$$\lambda(\tau) = \lambda_0 \exp\left[-\frac{\lambda_0}{\nu_0}\tau\right] \qquad \mu(\tau) = \nu_0 \left[1 - \exp\left(-\frac{\lambda_0}{\nu_0}\tau\right)\right]$$

Let's assume we have estimated λ_0 and ν_0 at 5 and 1000, respectively. At 1000 hours, the failure rate works out to .0337 failures/hr and we have removed 993 faults. We estimate that at 2000 hours, we shall have removed 999.95 faults—i.e., all of them—but the failure rate will be 2.27×10^{-4}, far from 10^{-11}. In fact, our calculation shows that λ doesn't reach 10^{-11} until τ equals 5388 hours. We're smart enough to know that model or no model, we shall not have removed all the faults at 2000 hours. We must continue testing. But do we have to continue testing for another 3388 hours? All of this, of course, is playing games with statistics, but it does indicate a limitation of statistical models. Using NASA data, Butler and Finelli[25] postulated that based on a log-linear reliability growth model it would take 42 years of testing to improve one system's failure probability per test input from 7.66×10^{-4} to 1.11×10^{-11}.

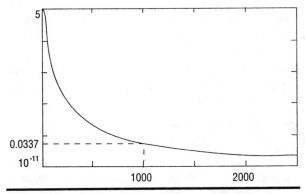

Figure 12.6 Modeling extraordinary reliability: the impossible dream.

We should also caution against attempting to use even a conceptually simple reliability model without programming the model. Attempting to continually update the model by hand will only lead to its abandonment in the face of more pressing matters. In an appendix, Musa *et al.*[24] provide specifications for programs to support the M and M-O models.

Finally, we note that some of the more enthusiastic users of models have told us that they use a composite of models. Perhaps the Jelinski-Moranda early in testing, the M-O in the middle phases, and the Goel-Okumoto when few faults are being found; perhaps the same models in different sequence; perhaps some other combination of models—in any case something that has worked for them. Also, successful users have found that one needs frequently to recalibrate the model in use. For the M-O calendar time component, for example, assumptions about resource limitations may have to be revisited more than once during the course of testing.

Despite the problems inherent in estimating future performance, the manager who puts a priority on customer satisfaction would do well to be equipped with whatever insights reliability growth models can furnish.

12.6 Summary

1. Faults, the source of failures, can be predicted before testing begins on the basis of complexity, size, measurements related to size, or other structural properties of the code.

2. Linear regression analysis permits one to attempt to develop a predictive model based on a structural property. The success of the attempt can be judged from the position of the regression line on the scatter plot of faults versus measurements.

3. Fault seeding succeeds only with random seed distribution and limited disparity between the complexity of seeded faults and true faults.

4. Inferences from seed recapture can bound the likelihood that the number of faults initially in the system exceeded some arbitrary number.

5. Reliability growth models use test data to estimate future failure incidence. These models attempt to formulate a statistical failure process.

6. A common premise of reliability growth models, one easily apparent in the early Jelinski-Moranda model, is that failure rates are proportional to the number of faults remaining in the system.

7. Most of models that have been developed assume that failure rate exponentially decreases with time. However other failure rate shapes have also been modeled.

8. The most widely accepted models seem to be the Musa and Musa-Okumoto models. In each, one component models failure incidence in terms of CPU test time, while a second component converts this to calendar time, based on constraints on certain test resources.

9. Reliability growth models provide data to aid managers in making decisions about test sufficiency. The models cannot be relied on as the primary decision factor.

10. Successful users of reliability growth models have in some cases used several models, switching from one model to another at different phases of test, and recalibrating the model as necessary.

References

1. Dunn, Robert. *Software Defect Removal,* McGraw-Hill, New York, NY, 1984, p. 183.
2. Halstead, Maurice. *Elements of Software Science,* Elsevier-North Holland, New York, NY, 1977.
3. Laemmel, A. and Shooman, M. *Software Modeling Studies: Statistical (Natural) Language Theory and Computer Program Complexity,* Polytechnic Institute of New York, issued by Rome Air Development Center as Report RADC-TR-784, April 1978.
4. Motley, R. W. and Brooks, W. D. *Statistical Prediction of Programming Errors,* RADC-TR-77-175, Rome Air Development Center, Griffiss Air Force Base, New York, NY, 1977.
5. Lipow, M. and Thayer, T. A. "Prediction of Software Failures," *Proceedings 1977 Annual Reliability and Maintainability Symposium,* IEEE Cat. No. 77CH1161-9RQC, pp. 489-494.
6. Duran, J. and Wiorkowski, J. "Capture-Recapture Sampling for Estimating Software Error Content," *IEEE Trans. Software Eng.,* Vol. SE-7, January 1981, pp. 147-48.
7. Zelinski, Z. and Moranda, P. B. "Application of a Probability-Based Model to a Code Reading Experiment," *1973 IEEE Symposium on Computer Software Reliability,* IEEE Cat. No. 73CH0741-9CSR, pp. 78-80.
8. Shooman, Martin "Operational Testing and Software Reliability Estimation During Program Development," *1973 IEEE Symposium on Computer Software Reliability,* IEEE Cat. No. 73CH0741-9CSR, pp. 51-57.
9. Shooman, Martin. *Software Engineering,* McGraw-Hill, New York, NY, 1983, pp. 296-402.
10. Moranda, P. B. "Prediction of Software Reliability During Debugging," *Proceedings 1975 Annual Reliability and Maintainability Symposium,* IEEE Cat. No. 75CH0918-3RQC, pp. 327-332.
11. Goel, Amrit and Okumoto, Kazuhira. "Time Dependent Error-Detection Rate Model for Software Reliability and Other Performance Measures," *IEEE Trans. Reliability,* Vol. R-28, No. 3, August 1979, pp. 206-211.
12. Goel, Amrit. "Software Reliability Models: Assumptions, Limitations, and Applicability," *IEEE Trans. Software Engineering,* Vol. SE-11, No. 12, December 1985, pp. 1411–1423.
13. Littlewood, B. and Verrall, J. L. "A Bayesian Reliability Growth Model for Computer Software," *1973 IEEE Symposium on Computer Software Reliability,* IEEE Cat. No. 73CH0741-9CSR, pp. 70-77.

14. Littlewood, B. "A Bayesian Differential Debugging Model for Software Reliability," *Workshop on Quantitative Software Models,* IEEE Cat. No. TH0067-9, October 1979, pp. 170-181.

15. Littlewood, B. "Stochastic Reliability Growh: A Model for Fault-Removal in Computer Programs and Hardware Designs," *IEEE Trans. Reliability,* Vol. R-30, October 1981, pp. 313–320.

16. Schick, G. and Wolverton, R. "An Analysis of Competing Software Reliability Models," *IEEE Trans. Software Engineering,* Vol. SE-4, No. 2, March 1978, pp. 104-119.

17. Nathan, Irwin. "A Deterministic Model to Predict 'Error-Free' Status of Complex Software Development," *Workshop on Quantitative Software Models,* IEEE Cat. No. TH0067-9, October 1979, pp. 159-169.

18. Tohma, Y. *et al.* "Structural Approach to the Estimation of the Number of Residual Software Faults Based on the Hyper-Geometric Distribution," *IEEE Trans. Software Engineering,* Vol. SE-15, No. 3, March 1989, pp. 345-355.

19. Shooman, M. and Natarajan, S. *Effect of Manpower Development and Bug Generation on Software Error Models,* Technical Report RADC-TR-76-400, Rome Air Development Center, Griffiss Air Force Base, New York, NY, January 1977.

20. Goel, A. and Okumoto, K. *Bayesian Software Prediction Models,* (5 Vols.) Final Technical Report RADC-TR-78-155, Rome Air Development Center, Griffiss Air Force Base, New York, NY, July 1978.

21. Sahinoglu, M. "Compound-Poisson Software Reliability Model," *IEEE Trans. Software Engineering,* Vol. SE-18, No. 7, July 1992, pp. 624-630.

22. Musa, J. D., Iannino, A. and Okumoto, K. *Software Reliability: Measurement, Prediction, Application,* McGrawHill, New York, NY, 1987.

23. Musa, J. D. "A Theory of Software Reliability and Its Application," *IEEE Trans. Software Engineering,* Vol. SE-1, No. 3, September 1975, pp. 312-327.

24. Musa, J. D., Iannino, A. and Okumoto, K. *Software Reliability,* McGraw-Hill, New York, NY, 1990.

25. Butler, R. and Finelli, G. "The Infeasibility of Experimental Quantification of Life-Critical Software Reliability," *Proceedings ACM SIGSOFT '91 Conference on Software for Critical Systems,* ACM Press, December 1991, pp. 66-76.

Index

A

Action items, *See* Correction log
Ada, 29, 39, 59, 140, 141, 143
    Ada Joint Program Office, 237
    APSE CAIS, 215, 237
ALGOL, 28, 29
American Society for Quality Control
    (ASQC), 6, 303
Analysis:
    coverage, 179-180, 197, 221-222
    data flow, 179-180
    failure mode and effects, 277
    root cause, 262-267
    static, 185-186
APL, 29, 31, 106, 143
Apple Computer, Inc.
    MacIntosh computer, 42, 102, 217, 219
Application generator, 35, 218
    See also language generations, fourth
Application languages 34
Applied Business Technology Corp. Pro-
    ject Workbench, 231
APS, 35
APT, 34
Ask/Ingres Division, Ingres, 35
ASQC, *See* American Society for Quality
    Control
Assembler code, 23-24
Association for Computing Machinery
    (ACM), 82
Atherton Technologies, Software Back-
    plane, 216, 234
ATLAS, 34
AT&T Laboratories, 5
Audit, 279-280
    configuration management, 158-159
    tools, 231-232

B

Baldrige Award, *See* Malcolm Baldrige
    National Quality Award
Baseline, 154-157
    allocated, 155, 165
    design, 156-157, 165
    functional, 155, 165
    operational, 165
    product, 155, 165
BASIC (programming language), 29, 31,
    140, 145
Bauer, Frederich, 82
Bell Communications Research, *See* Bell-
    core
Bell Laboratories, *See* AT&T Laborato-
    ries
Bellcore, 105, 160, 310
    IPQM, 323-324
    RQMS, 319, 322-323
    SQPR, 319-321
Benchmarking, 271, 308
Binary code, 22-23, 27
Boehm, Barry, 54, 209
Böhm, C., 139
Borland International
    dBase, 35, 37
Britcher, Robert, 191
Brooks, Frederick P., Jr., 115
Brooks, W.D., 338
Brown, Alan, 235, 236
Butler, R., 353
Byte Magazine, 307

C

C (programming language), 26, 29, 102,
    140, 145, 220
C++, 39, 102, 142-143, 215, 238

Cadre Technologies, Teamwork, 215,
    216, 223
Caine, Farber, and Gordon, Inc., PDL, 32
California, University of, 107
Call graph, 42
Carnegie Mellon University, 299
    PIE, 225
    See also Software Engineering Institute
CASE (Computer-Aided Software Engi-
    neering), 137, 185
    See also Software development envi-
        ronment; tools
Chen, P., 112
CMS-2, 29
COBOL, 28, 35, 37, 140, 143, 218, 233,
    272
COCOMO, 116
Coincidental correctness, 180
Comparisons with competitors, 263, 271,
    287, 318
Compiler code, 26-34
Complexity, 117-122
    cyclomatic measure, 117, 185, 336-
        337, 339, 349
Computer Science Corp., 107
Computer architectures, 21-22
Computer:
    definition of, 19-22
    desktop, 22
    mainframe, 22
    minicomputer, 22
    workstation, 22
Computer-aided design (CAD), 35
Concurrent processes, 131
    See also embedded software; program-
        ming, real-time
Configuration management, 153-171
    build control, 160-161
    catalog, 164-166
    change board, 164, 166-167
    edition identification, 95, 161-162
    lack of control, 94-95
    tools, 159-161, 231
    See also Library, control; Plans, con-
        figuration management
Connecticut Quality Improvement
    Award, 299
Constantine, Larry, 129
Continuous improvement:
    analysis, 262-270
    process, 262-276
    process change, 274-276

Control Data Corp.
    Automated Testing System, 223
Correction log, 232, 257-260
Correctness:
    coincidental, 180
    proof of 181n, 192-194
Cost of quality (COQ), 242, 280-282
Critical path analysis, 227-230
Crosby, Philip B., 6-7, 282, 288
Customer satisfaction, 241-243, 246-247,
    262, 311
Customer service, offices and staff, 279
Customer support, 246-248, 253, 262,
    268-269, 310-311, 330

D

Dart, Susan, 215
Data abstraction, 120-121
    abstract data types, 121, 127-128
    data typing, *See* programming lan-
        guage
Data and information systems
    analysis, 248-250, 277
    data collection, 245-248, 278
    dissemination, 250-251
    storage, 248
    See also Measurements
Data base management system (DBMS),
    35, 37, 59, 144, 158, 218, 226, 231
    relational, 217, 248
Data dictionary, 111-112, 133, 134
Data Processing Management Associa-
    tion (DPMA), 82
DBMS, *See* Data base management sys-
    tem
Debugging, 68-74
    source-level, 219-220
    aids, 213
Decomposition, 62-65, 128-130
    functional, 130
    stepwise design refinement 101n,
    See also process model, top-down
    See also top-down development, struc-
        tured design
Defects, *See* Faults
DeMarco, Tom, 111
Deming, W. Edwards, 6, 99, 288
Department of Defense, 29, 291-292
    Data Item Descriptions, 319
    DOD-STD-2167A, 133, 155, 216, 318
    DOD-STD-2168, 318
    MIL-S-52779A, 322

Department of Defense *(Continued)*
    See also Software Engineering Insti-
        tute; Process standards)
Design, 31-34, 61-68, 117-133
    detailed, 65-67
    preliminary, 50, 52, 133
    robust, 130-133
    top-level, *See* Preliminary
    See also Top-down development, struc-
        tured design
Diagram:
    bubble chart, *See* diagram, data flow
    call graph, 137
    cause-effect (fishbone), 241-244, 266-267
    data flow (DFD), 110-111, 133, 218
    decision tree, 134, 136
    entity-relationship, 112-113
    hierarchical chart, 62-64, 134
    state, 109-110, 133
    structure chart, 67, 137
    system verification diagram (SVD),
        107-108, 133
    tree structure, 134-135
    See also Flow chart
Digital Equipment Corp. (DEC):
    CMS, 159
    DEC/Test Manager, 223
    FUSE, 216, 238
    MMS, 160
    VAX, 220
    VMS, 219
Dijkstra, Edsger, 101, 139
Documentation:
    design, 133-138
    process, 308-309
    requirements, 55-57
    user, 165, 167, 254
    See also Pseudocode; Diagrams; Flow
        chart
Duran, J., 340-341

E

Elspas, Bernard, 193
Embedded software, 11-12, 220
Erickson, Robert, 160
Estimating, cost and staff, 114-117
    See also Plans
Exit criteria, *See* Project control

F

FAA-STD-018, 322
Fagan, Michael, 187

Fault detection effectiveness, 183-184
Fault seeding, 204-206, 340-341, 349
    See also Testing, mutation
Fault tolerance, 130-133
Faults, 87-89
    prediction, 204-206, 335-339
    tracking, 226, 232
Feigenbaum, Armand, 6
Finelli, G., 353
Firmware, 162-163
Flavors, *See* Lisp
Flow chart, 32, 137-138
Floyd, R.W., 102, 192
Focus (4GL language), 34-35, 143, 272
Forth (3GL language), 140
FORTRAN, 29, 30, 35, 140, 145, 220
Function points, 272
Functional configuration audit, 207

G

Gantt chart, 228
Gelperin, David, 178
General Electric Aerospace, 308
General Research Corp., RXVP80, 179
Gerhart, Susan, 180
Goel, Amrit, 345, 347, 349
Goodenough, John, 180
Gompertz distribution, 349
GPSS, 34

H

Halstead, Maurice, *Software Science,*
    337-339
Hetzel, Bill, 178
Hewlett-Packard, SoftBench, 216, 237,
    238
Hoare, C.A.R., 192
Humphrey, Watts, 288
Hyper-geometric distribution, 349
Hypertext, 238

I

IBM 191, 210, 312
    Cleanroom, 191, 194, 271
    MVS, 219, 225
    OS/2, 219, 238
IEEE:
    Computer Society, 82
    IEEE Software, 215
    software standards, 133
    standard P1175/D11 on tool integra-
        tion, 237

IEEE *(Continued)*
    Standard Glossary of Software Engi-
        neering Terms, 175-176
    See also process standards
Index Technologies, Excelerator, 214,
    215, 216, 218
Information Builders, Inc., *See* Focus
Information hiding, 121, 141-142
Information Systems (IS), 30, 59
In-process review, *See* Review
Inspection, *See* Review
Installation, 76-77
Integration:
    hardware-software, 199
    of tools, 214, 216, 233-239
    See also Testing, integration
Interactive Development Environments,
    Software Through Pictures, 215,
    216-217, 237-238
Interactive Software Engineering Inc.,
    Eiffel, 142-143
Interlisp, 215
International Organization for Stand-
    ardization Standard 9000-3, 319-320
    Standard 9001, 319
Interpreter code, 27, 29, 31
Intersolv, 35
Ishikawa, Kaoru, 6
    cause-effect (fishbone) diagram, 241-242
ISO, *See* International Organization for
    Standardization
ITT Corporation, 6, 299

J

Jackson Structured Development, 54,
    128
Jackson System Design, 54, 217
Jacopini, P., 139
Japan, industrial practices, 6, 113
Jelinski, Z., 343-344
Job Control Language (JCL), 127
Jones, Capers, 272
JOVIAL, 29
Juran, J.M., 6, 7, 249, 288

K

Kaiser, Gail, 215
KnowledgeWare, Inc., 35, 218, 238
    Inspector, 233

L

Laemmel, A., 338

Language generations
    fourth, 34-37, 53, 106
    second, *See* Assembler code
    third, 26-34
LDRA Test Bed, 179
Levels of abstraction, 101
Library:
    audit, 158-159
    contents, 157-158
    control, 157-162
Life cycle major activities:
    code, debug, test, 68-76
    concept and analysis, 49-50
    design, 61-68
    installation and evaluation, 76-77
    operation and maintenance, 77-81
    requirements definition, 55-61
Link editor, 40
Lipow, Myron, 338
Lisp, 29, 31, 37, 42, 52, 102, 140, 145
    Flavors, 39, 107, 142-143
    Littlewood, Bev, 347-348
Liverpool Data Research Associates, Ltd.,
Loader, 40
London, Ralph, 193

M

Maintainability, 90-92
Maintenance, 78-81, 122-125
Malcolm Baldrige National Quality
    Award, 81
    criteria, 7, 8, 272
    used for self-assessment, 299-303
Management by Walking Around
    (MBWA), 252-253
Mark 4 Systems:
    ObjectMaker, 218
Martin-Marietta Corp., 308
Maryland, University of, 192-193
MathSoft:
    MathCad, 35-36, 128
Maximum Likelihood Estimation (MLE),
    341, 344, 350-351
McCabe, Thomas, 117
McDermid, John, 235, 236
Measurements, 232-233, 305-306
    See also Data and information sys-
        tems; Project control
Meridian Software Systems, Promod,
    160, 216
Microsoft, 31
    MS-DOS, 219

Microtec Research, Xray/DX, 220
Mills, Harlan, 192, 271, 340, 349
MLE, *See* Maximum likelihood estimation
Modularity, 122-125
  module cohesion, 129-130
  module coupling, 129-130
  ripple effect, 141
  See also Information hiding
Mohanty, S.N., 176-177
Moranda, P.B., 343-344
Motley, R.W., 338
Musa, John, 349-352, 354
Myers, Glenford, 130

N

NASA, 210, 214, 353
  NASA-Johnson Space Center, 116n
Natajaran, S., 349
National Institute of Standards and
  Technology (NIST), 301, 303
National Research Council, Aeronautics
  and Space Engineering Board, 210
National Security Industrial Association
  (NSIA), 310
NATO, 82
  AQAP-13, 322
Natural (4GL language), 35
Nejmeh, Brian, 235
Network, 225
  client-server, 41
New York University, 59, 180
Novell, FConsole, 225

O

O-O, *See* Objected-oriented technology
Object-oriented programming, *See* Object-oriented technology
Object-oriented technology, 37-40, 67-68,
  101-102, 111n, 121, 128, 142-143,
  218, 307
  data base management system, 107
  for rapid prototyping, 106-107
  object management system (OBS),
    231
  object-oriented design (OOD), 128
  process model, 53
Obsolescence, 92-94
Okumoto, Kazuhira, 345, 347, 349
OOP, *See* Object-oriented technology
Operating systems, 40-41
  multitasking, 41

See also User interface
Oracle Corp., Oracle, 35
OSF/Motif, 238

P

PAISLey, 102, 103, 126
Pareto, Vilfredo, 249n
  Pareto analysis, 249
Parnas, David, 121
Participative management, 307
  See also Quality team
Pascal, 29, 102, 140-141, 220
  object Pascal, 102, 143
Patch, 160, 169
Perry, Dewayne, 215
PERT, *See* Critical path analysis
PL/1, 29, 30, 140, 143, 272
Plans, 60-61
  configuration management, 60-61,
    163-169
  development, 60
  quality, 61, 325-327
    preparation of, 280
  staffing, 114-117
  test, 177
  tools for, 226-231
Poisson distribution, 342, 348, 349
  See also Reliability growth models
Policy on quality, 315-318
Portable Common Tool Environment
  (PCTE), 237
Problem log, *See* Correction log
Process model, 50-55
  bottom-up, 52-53
  evolutionary, 53-54
  object-oriented, 53
  spiral, 54
  top-down, 50-52
  waterfall, 48
Process standards, 308-312
  Bellcore, 318-324
  commonality within a company 310-
    312
  DoD, 318-322
  IEEE, 318-322, 324-325
  ISO, 318-322
    upgrading, 274-276, 309-310
Program management:
  project accounting, 226-227
  work breakdown structure, 227
  See also Plans
Programmer productivity, 270

Programmers, 81-83
  education, 81
  involvement in quality, 252-253, 275
  See also Training
Programming:
  definition of, 20
  N-version, 133
  real-time, 131
  See also Embedded software
Programming design language, *See*
  Pseudocode
Programming environment, *See* Soft-
  ware development environment
Programming Environments, Inc.:
  T, 223
  T++, 223
Programming language:
  data typing, 140-141
  expressiveness, 143-144
  support for recursion, 145-146
  See also Language generations
Programming paradigm:
  definition of, 53n, 102
  taxonomy of, 102-103
Project control:
  task exit criteria, 254-255
  trend analysis, 256-257
  See also Program management; Meas-
  urements
PROM, *See* Firmware
  pseudocode, 32-33, 134-138

Q

Qualification, 329-330. *See also* Testing,
  qualification
Quality circle, *See* Quality team
Quality index, 251
Quality factor, 251
Quality function deployment (QDF), 113
Quality management evolution, 4-7
Quality team, 252-253, 275
Quantitative Software Management,
  116n
  SLIM, 116
Query-by-example, 34

R

Rapid prototyping, 57-59, 106-107, 272
Rayleigh distribution, 348
Real-time software, *See* Embedded soft-
  ware; Programming, real-time
Record retention, 329

Reifer Consultants, Inc., 116n
  SoftCost, 116
Reimann, Curt, 301-302
Reliability, 264
  estimation, *See* Reliability growth
    models
  failure rate, 343
  hazard rate, 343
  MTTF, 342-343, 344
  prediction, 335-339
Reliability growth models, 341-354
  Compound-Poisson, 349
  Goel-Okumoto Imperfect Debugging,
    349
  Goel-Okumoto NHPP, 345-347, 354
  Gompertz, 349
  hyper-geometric, 349
  Jelinski-Moranda, 343-345, 347, 349,
    354
  limitations, 352-354
  Littlewood, 347-348
  Musa execution time, 349-352, 353
  Musa-Okumoto, 349-352
  Schick-Wolverton, 348
  Shooman-Natajaran, 349
Repository, 217, 231-232, 237-238
Requirements definition, 55-60, 104-113
Requirements model, *See* Requirements
  definition
Reuse of software, *See* Software reusability
Review, 254-255, 317
  checklists, 189-191
  of code, 186-191
  of design, 186-188
  of requirements model, 174-177
  procedures, 328
Risk reduction, 271-274
ROM, *See* Firmware

S

Safety, 113, 177, 192, 194, 204, 210, 316, 326
Sage Software, PolyMake, 160
Sammett, Jean, 29
Schedule tracking, 226, 256-257
Schick, G., 348, 349
Seeding, *See* Fault seeding
SEI, *See* Software Engineering Institute
Self-assessment, 288-303
SETL, 59, 106
Shewart, Walter, 5
Shooman, Martin, 338
  Shooman Exponential Model, 344

Siegel, Stan, 276
Simplicity, *See* complexity
Simula-67, 39
Smalltalk, 39, 42, 107, 143, 215, 219, 307
SofTool, CCC, 159
Software development (definition), 47-48
Software development environment, 41, 215-216, 233-239
Software engineering, 82
Software Engineering Institute (SEI), 321*n*
  Capability Maturity Model, 288-299
Software Productivity Research, Inc, 116*n*
  SPQR, 116
Software quality (definition), 9
Software quality assurance, 7, 8, 10-11, 278-280, 291
  cost, 280
  organizations, 276-280, 291
  See also software quality engineers
Software quality engineering, 223
Software quality engineers, 10, 259*n*
  tasks for, 277-280
  See also Software quality assurance
Software quality processes and programs, 9-12, 241-284
Software Research, Inc.:
  TCAT, 179
  SMARTS, 223
Software reusability 38, 126-128
Specification documents, *See* Documentation
SQL, 35, 233, 251
Standard operating procedures, 217-330
Stanford University Specification Analyzer, 174
Statistical process control, 295
Structured programming, 139-140
Supplier quality
  partnering, 261-262
  vendor selection, 260-261
Swanson, E.B., 78

T

Technology, evaluation of for process improvement, 306-307
Testability, 88, 174-177
Testing, 125-126
  acceptance, 76
  alpha, 76, 208
  beta, 77, 208-209, 272

black box, 181-183
  vs. glass box, 178-181
bottom-up, 72
boundary, 202-203
documentation, 328
dynamic vs. passive, 174
glass box, 179-181
  vs. black box, 178-181
integration, 71-74, 197-200
module, 69-71, 125-126, 194-197
mutation, 197
purposes, 173-174
qualification, 75-76, 206-209
regression, 182, 209
  tools for, 222-223
sufficiency, 74-75, 204
system, 200-204
test case design or selection, 180-182
test case generator, 223-224
top-down 72-74
unit, *See* Testing, module
Thayer, T.A., 338
Thomas, Ian, 235
Tokyo Institute of Technology, 349
Tools, 219-240
  back-end, 218-226
  build, 220-221
  certification, 328
  cost of, 214
  coverage-based test beds 221-222
  estimating, 116-117
  for management, 226-233
  front-end, 216-218
  measurement, 224-226, 232-233
  See also Software development environment; Integration; Testing
Top-down development, 101
  structured analysis, 111, 217
  structured design, 128-130
  See also Process model, top-down
TQM, definition of 6
Traceability, 107-108
Training:
  programmer, 274, 321
  quality, 327-330
Truth table, 137
TRW, 54

U

Unit development folder, 232
UNIX, 40, 219
  make, 161, 220

UNIX *(Continued)*
  Programmer's Workbench, 214, 215,
    234
  SCCS, 159
U.S. Air Force, 289
U.S. Navy, 5
  MIL-STD-1679A
  Naval Air Systems Command, 6
Usability, 88-90
User interface:
  for tool integration, 235-239
  Graphical User Interface (GUI), 41-
    43, 217, 219
User satisfaction, *See Customer* satisfac-
    tion
User support, *See* Customer support

V

Validation, 147-148, 209. *See also* Verifi-
    cation
Verification, 147-148, 209, 264
  independent verification and valida-
    tion (IV&V), 209-210
  See also Validation

Verilog USA, Logiscope, 179, 186, 232
Vienna Development Method (VDM), 54-
    55, 102

W

Warnier-Orr development, 54
waterfall, *See* Process model, top-down
Western Electric, 5
Windows, 40-41, 217, 219
Wiorkowski, J., 340-341
Wirth, Niklaus, 101n
Wolverton, Raymond, 348, 349
Work breakdown structure (WBS), *See*
    Program management
Workstation, 23

XYZ

Xerox PARC, 39, 307
YACC, 35n
Yourdon, Edward, 129
  Cradle, 216
Zelkowitz, Marvin, 192
Zero defects, 271
Zultner, Richard, 99, 113